IP LOCATION

Martin Dawson
James Winterbottom
Martin Thomson

New York   Chicago   San Francisco   Lisbon   London   Madrid
Mexico City   Milan   New Delhi   San Juan   Seoul
Singapore   Sydney   Toronto

The McGraw·Hill Companies

McGraw-Hill books are available at special quantity discounts to use as premiums and sales promotions, or for use in corporate training programs. For more information, please write to the Director of Special Sales, Professional Publishing, McGraw-Hill, Two Penn Plaza, New York, NY 10121-2298. Or contact your local bookstore.

IP Location

1234567890 DOC DOC 019876

ISBN-13:   978-0-07-226377-0
ISBN-10:   0-07-226377-6

Sponsoring Editor
Jane Brownlow

Editorial Supervisor
Jody McKenzie

Project Manager
Vasundhara Sawhney

Acquisitions Coordinator
Jennifer Housh

Technical Editor
Greg Burdett

Copy Editor
Mike McGee

Proofreader
Karen Vaucrosson

Indexer
Steve Ingle

Production Supervisor
George Anderson

Composition
International Typesetting
and Composition

Illustration
International Typesetting
and Composition

Art Director, Cover
Brian Boucher

Cover Designer
12E Design

Martin Dawson—*To the Lyons-Dawson gang: Kate, Andrew, and Elena.*

James Winterbottom—*To my wife, Loraine; my children, Vanessa, Michael, and Emma; and to my parents, David and Elizabeth.*

Martin Thomson—*To Jamie, with thanks for the unquestioning support.*

About the Authors

Martin Dawson (BEng-elec, MEngSc) is the chief product architect of the Andrew Geometrix Mobile Location Center development team based in Wollongong, Australia. Martin Dawson's engineering career has spanned 29 years, from work in real-time embedded microprocessor control systems (the early days of local area network deployments) to paying his dues in a university network admin role. The past 19 years have been spent in networking and telecommunications. This includes a period of time with British Telecom Research Laboratories in the UK developing Service Creation Environments for Intelligent Networks (IN), and with Telstra, where he also developed IN services. Prior to joining Andrew Corporation, he worked for Nortel for 11 years developing a wide range of solutions with a focus on wireless IN services and the development of cellular location systems for emergency and commercial services.

He is currently active in forums for cellular and IP location technologies, and acts as consultant to industry, government, regulatory authorities, and emergency agencies. He is a member of the North American National Emergency Number Association (NENA) and has contributed to the working group focused on the development of solutions for VoIP emergency services.

James Winterbottom has over 20 years of experience in the Telecom industry and is currently a Senior Product Architect with Andrew Corporation's Geometrix Mobile Location Center. In recent years, James has worked in the cellular location industry, but throughout his career he has developed an expertise in CDMA provisioning and management systems, as well as intelligent network services. Currently, James is active in standards forums for IP location technologies, and acts as a consultant to industry, government, and regulatory authorities. He is a member of the North American National Emergency Number Association (NENA) and is active in NENA working groups concerned with determining and using location to support VoIP emergency services. He is also an active participant in the IETF, developing solutions to address the problems of determining, acquiring, and conveying location in IP networks. James is the official liaison from the ESIF Next Generation Emergency Services (NGES) working group to the IETF Geopriv and ECRIT working groups.

Martin Thomson is an engineer with Andrew Corporation. He has spent five years developing cellular wireless products for Nortel and Andrew Corporation, in particular the Mobile Location Center (MLC). Since 2004, Martin has been working in research for IP location and has produced a number of specifications, including several IETF Internet drafts. Martin has also been involved in the development of prototype systems for location in IP networks.

About the Technical Editor

Greg Burdett has 18 years of telecom experience and has worked in numerous senior management leadership positions for telecom companies. Greg also has multiple patents in the field of telecommunications (two awarded; two pending). Since 2001, he has focused his energy in the area of location, for both the cellular as well as IP location contexts. He was the Business Lead for the Mobile Location Center (MLC) business at Nortel until 2005, and led the activity to divest the MLC business to Andrew Corporation, which completed in August 2005. In October 2005, Greg launched his own consulting company, Jagged Networks (www.Jaggednetworks.com), where he provides consulting/advisory services to broadband service providers and location solution vendors in order to assist them with their VoIP 911/IP location product strategies.

Contents

Foreword

Resilience, redundancy, reliability, security, interoperability, and efficiency. These are all ingredients for a great book on emergency location information and exchange. It has been a pleasure to meet the authors of this book, both at conferences internationally and in the UK. I had the pleasure of meeting with Martin Dawson when he was our guest at the NICC in the UK and whilst visiting one of our BT 999 call centers. The challenges discussed in this book, as well as their solutions, have been discussed in parallel with the authors on the other side of the world by myself, my colleagues, and members of the NICC and BT. When I met Martin in the U.S.A. at ATIS, he was like a breath of fresh air, and I discovered I was not the only one shouting "VoIP emergency access is international and this must not be forgotten!" The presence of the authors at these bodies shows not only commitment, but also a determination to ensure that this flow of IP information can function globally. The fundamentals of the solutions in this book are, in 2007, being followed and are currently under consideration for implementation in Australia, the U.S.A., Canada, and Europe. Voice over IP (VoIP) or Multimedia Voice over IP (MVoIP) is a rapidly growing market. The growth is evident in both the replacement of traditional fixed line networks and the uptake of soft phones. The range of access technologies is ever increasing and the mainstream is based on IP.

Many calls to the emergency services are silent calls. They are calls from people in distress who are unable to talk due to the prevailing situation, or they are from injured or sick people who may have dialed 911, 112, 999, 000, or one of the other national variants of emergency access numbers, but dropped the phone. These callers' locations not only need to be identified but also passed, accurately, around the appropriate services. In today's world of commerce, mobility, and users that are nomadic in nature, we can no longer rely on the home address details of callers being their actual location. Indeed, many corporate networks and VoIP-outsourced networks have single points of break-out from their networks onto the PSTN (such that the caller's location within the corporate network is concealed). There is a need for communication providers to take heed of the contents of this book. It is a must-read, not only for efficient planning and network implementation, but also to help save lives.

Ian Hopkins
BT 999 Product Manager VoIP,
United Kingdom,
25th July 2006

Acknowledgments

Martin Dawson

Firstly, I have to thank my co-authors; they never cease to amaze me with their output, ingenuity, skills, and downright cleverness. Most of all, to my beloved Rosemontatorium crew: Thank you for your forbearance and support despite my apparent state of perpetual distraction.

James Winterbottom

I would like to thank my co-authors, the two Martins, for the effort they have put into making sure that this book covers all its topics as thoroughly as possible. Thanks also to Hannes Tschofenig for pointing me toward various specifications that I may have otherwise missed.

Martin Thomson

I would like to thank my co-authors for the opportunities I have been given while working with them. There are also a number of people at the IETF who have vigorously opposed some of the concepts that are documented in this book, which has ultimately forced me to refine my thinking, and for which I am grateful.

And from All of Us

Thanks to the team at Andrew Network Solutions in Wollongong, Australia and Ashburn, VA, U.S.A. for giving us the latitude to focus beyond the world of cellular location. Thanks also to the many wonderful people and personalities in the industry who contributed to bringing the ideas in this book to life, including Barbara Stark, Nadine Abbott, Anand Akundi, Tom Breen, Brian Rosen, Patti McCalmont, Greg Burdett, Guy Caron, Ed Shrum, Tom Anschutz, Perry Prozeniuk, Carl Reed, and Bill Barnes. Our apologies to those many others that we have neglected to mention.

Introduction

Defining Location

Location is a quantity which is so fundamental that it forms part of the gestalt of every human being. Everyone has an instinctive sense of what is meant by *location,* and yet if you were to ask for a definition of the term you might be surprised by the varied responses it would elicit. Ask somebody "Where are you now?" and you will get responses ranging from "I'm at home," "I'm in the car," "I'm at 27 Homebay Drive, Watsonia,"—or going to the extreme of subjectivity: "I'm in a state of confusion." In very rare circumstances, somebody may actually reply "I'm 32 degrees south latitude and 150 degrees east longitude...." All of the preceding are potentially correct and are expected responses, depending completely on the context within which the questions were asked. But in discussing location in this book, at least some refinement of the term is needed.

As a starting point, *location* in this book refers to "geographical location." That is, it is concerned with a spatial location associated with a physical point or region relative to the surface of the earth. It does not refer to other types of location such as a logical network location. For example, an IP device will certainly have a physical spatial location, but the IP address does not represent that location. The IP address represents a logical network location; it identifies the network and host-ID associated with the device and tells internetworking elements how to route the packets so they arrive at the correct network location. There is no direct correspondence between this location and the geographical location. They are not equivalent, as shown in Figure 1, and the process of going from an arbitrary IP address to a location is much more involved than a simple static translation from one to the other.

It is evident that context is a major consideration when even spatial location is being discussed. If someone says they are "in the car," then that may be all that is important in terms of the application of the dialog which is occurring with them. It may not be important what the geospatial coordinates of the car are, or the coordinates may be quite implicitly associated with the car. This version of location ("in the car") can be called application-specific. In other words, it is a version of the information which is relevant to

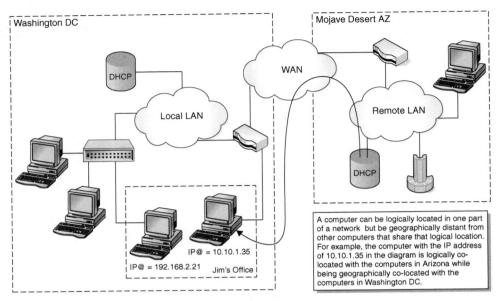

Figure 1   Logical network location versus geographic location.

the discussion at hand and which could mean something very different in another discussion—for instance, in another application. If location information is being sourced from a network element that is independent of the application using the location, then a more application-independent form of location information is desirable.

There is a form of location which is less open to interpretation, that is application-independent, and whose meaning tends to be immutable even over extensive periods of time. This is the geodetic form of location and it is generally expressed in degrees north or south of the equator, and east or west of the zeroth meridian. Given a well-defined shape for the Earth (a defined geoid; see Figure 2) and specific locations for zero coordinates, and allowing that it is the position relative to the surface of the Earth that is of interest despite the Earth's unceasing wandering against the backdrop of the greater universe, then the geodetic form provides a thoroughly objective and immutable form of location. The World Geodetic System of 1984 (WGS 84) specification (see Reference 1 at the end of the introduction) is an example of such an application-independent system for defining geographic location.

While geodetic form provides a definitive form of application-independent location specification, it is not a form which humans frequently use. One of the most common forms of location specification used by humans is the "civic address" form. This is commonly thought of in terms of the familiar street number, street name, municipality/city, state, and country form. There are a number of documented forms for such addresses (see References 2 and 3). Indeed, the variation in the civic address form across international jurisdictions is considerable. Street numbers do not exist in all jurisdictions, for

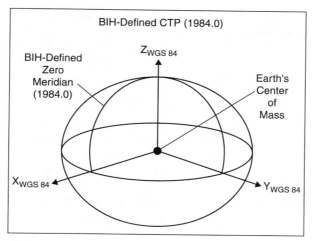

Figure 2   The standard Earth geoid, as defined in WGS 84.

example, and the naming of streets is also subject to considerable variation. Further, the scope of a given civic address form may vary depending on application. For instance, a room and building number may be definitive in the scope of a single business campus, but they do not provide a globally definitive location since they don't actually tell you where on earth that building is. Despite the scope for variation in the civic form of location, however, it is a familiar one which maintains a good degree of application-independence within a significant subset of all location-based applications.

In the rest of this text, when location is discussed, the meaning of the term *location* will refer to a spatial geographic location in either geodetic form or civic address form. Any other definition of the term will be identified where it is used in the text.

Why a Book on IP Location?

At this moment in history, it is not really possible to talk about IP location without discussing Internet telephony or voice over IP (VoIP) and the manner in which emergency services can be contacted using VoIP. This is described in more detail later but it stems from the fact that whether it's 911 in North America, 112 in Europe, 000 in Australia, or any of the many regional variants on the number, there is an almost global expectation and indeed critical need that emergency services be contactable via the most common publicly accessible voice[*] service. Up until now, that has been the public

---

[*] Yes—TTY, or teletype, is used in support of deaf callers and it could be argued that this isn't "voice". The distinction is noted with the observation that this alphanumeric character transmission function is also carried over traditional voice circuits using the telephone network. Hopefully the intent of the point above is not obscured by this specific subtlety.

switched telephone network. We have entered a period where the plain old telephony service (POTS), and the switched circuit network behind it, have gone into decline and are being replaced by broadband Internet access as the standard all-purpose communication network. It is similarly inevitable that ubiquitous and reliable mechanisms for contacting emergency services using Internet telephony* will be required, both for practical and legal reasons.

So what does geo-location have to do with IP telephony usurping POTS, and emergency services being a requirement for both? It is relevant for the simple fact that location information is fundamental to the delivery of a single-number emergency calling service. In many jurisdictions, it is necessary to route the call to a different emergency call center depending on the location of the caller. In almost all jurisdictions it is a requirement to automatically deliver the caller's location to the emergency call center operator, without relying on the caller to provide it verbally. For better or worse, and no matter what applications for location follow in its wake, emergency service for IP telephony establishes the fundamental requirement for an IP location component of Internet access.

The authors have worked for a number of years through the development of the cellular-location industry, in the development of requirements, architectures, protocols, and, ultimately, deployed technology to support location determination in mobile phone networks. What was the driver for this technology? Once more the imperative was established because of the need to provide location for emergency calls originating from arbitrary locations within those cellular networks.

When the Federal Communications Commission (FCC) in the United States issued a mandate in 1996 that cellular networks should support the enhanced-911 (E911) functionality including location-based routing and location delivery, there was a scramble by different players to come up with a magic solution to this imperative. Every other week another new company would announce some technology that "solved the cellular E911 challenge." In the end, though, there was no "magic" solution. Location services (or LCS as it is commonly, if puzzlingly, abbreviated) as a network function is complex. It's not just about how to measure where someone is—whether it's with GPS, or the triangulation of measured radio signals, or some other clever invention. This is just a small element and, often, it's not where the greatest industry investment ends up being spent. In order to provide consistent and reliable LCS, an entire network architecture must be developed. This must not only involve what's happening between the device and the radio access network, but the whole core network that is responsible for routing request messages telling the appropriate systems when a location needs to be determined. The location information has to have a standard and consistent way of being delivered through networks so that it reaches the application of interest—for example,

---

* Many assert that IP emergency "call" centers will be able to be contacted in many other forms—such as instant messaging and video. No disagreement; at time of writing, however, it is essentially a voice service and, it is certain, voice will continue to be a significant form of communication with emergency call centers into the future.

the emergency call center operator display. It has to be able to work for all manner of devices and not just those fitted with some specific vendor's technology.

In the end, for cellular, this meant the painstaking definition of an end-to-end network architecture with all the necessary protocols and parameter underpinnings. It touched everything from the application through the core network switches down through the radio controller elements, and the devices themselves. Without an end-to-end architecture based on open standards, there is no reliable, ubiquitous, and consistent location service.

With a history in the development of the LCS industry for cellular networks, the authors came to the emerging IP telephony and associated emerging emergency services imperative with a view that there could be no effective piecemeal solution to putting LCS in place for Internet services. In developments that, in many ways, reflected the same early days of cellular LCS, there were a number of concurrent, though somewhat uncoordinated, proposals. Examples include Reference 4 for DHCP and the LLDP-MED specification.

While the device's geo-location is not actually a piece of network configuration information, it is seductively tempting to just add it as another parameter that can be provided by DHCP. After all, that allows a device connecting to an IP network to utilize a standard mechanism, in order to "discover" its new location. The IETF specification, Reference 4, describes such an approach. However, the view of it is limited to the relationship between two single entities—the IP device and the DHCP server. There is no end-to-end network perspective on how this relationship fits into the larger picture of

Dynamic Host Configuration Protocol (DHCP) (see Reference 4)

DHCP delivers network configuration information to an IP device. The intent is to provide the device with all the information it needs to utilize the IP network it's connected to. This includes information such as the IP address allocated to the device, the address of the gateway through which the traffic destined beyond the LAN should be sent, and/or the identity of the Domain Name Service (DNS) that can be requested to translate the names of network hosts into their physical IP addresses in order to talk to them. RFC3825 describes an option on DHCP that allows the device to request and receive a specific form of location information.

Link Layer Discovery Protocol for Media End-Point Devices (LLDP-MED)

At much the same time that RFC3825 was working through draft stages in the IETF, the TIA was defining extensions to the link layer discovery protocol (LLDP) to support additional information elements applicable to media end-point devices. These were termed LLDP-MED (Link Layer Discovery Protocol for Media End-point Devices) and included the ability for those end-point devices to be informed of the location associated with—for example—the 802.3 Ethernet switch port to which they are currently attached.

access technologies, applications, and the entities which may, in practice, be responsible for determining and underwriting the location of an Internet user. It does not facilitate any interaction with the device in terms of determining location, nor does it deal with the many public Internet access service considerations, such as the fact that DHCP is not a protocol typically used to deliver configuration from a broadband access network to the subscriber's device. And it does not provide any way to securely fix location information as being from a recognized and/or answerable entity; this last part being quite important to the operators of emergency services.

As a generic LCS infrastructure solution, LLDP-MED is similarly constrained compared to DHCP. It has the advantage of supporting location provisioned to specific switch ports, but it is still highly specific to this family of access technologies—typically, enterprise deployments. It has no application, for example, to broadband Internet access via DSL. Neither does it address issues of location source security.

Despite their fairly narrow focus, both DHCP and LLDP, with their associated location information extensions, were actively proposed and discussed as solutions to the larger VoIP 911 challenge. The author's felt that both mechanisms—although valid for specific scenarios involving location acquisition—did not provide either the generality or the end-to-end integrity necessary to support a global and consistent LCS capability for Internet services and, in particular, did not support emergency services calls using Internet telephony.

Drawing on experiences from the development of the cellular LCS infrastructure for both emergency and commercial services, and by understanding requirements through participation in numerous forums such as the National Emergency Network Association (NENA), the IETF, and ETSI, as well as engaging in discussions with emergency network authorities and regulators globally, the authors developed what, in their view, is a complete architecture for LCS. It is based on end-to-end requirements, providing a logical model for LCS in IP networks and identifying the specific network elements, interfaces, protocols, and parameters necessary to support general LCS services.

Such an architectural perspective on LCS has a good deal of complexity associated with it. Understanding the individual parts is not adequate unless the overarching principles are also understood. Going from architecture to successful implementation in a particular IP access network type requires an application of those principles, lest the requirements get lost in the details. The relatively simple two-peer details of DHCP or LLDP can be understood from specifications without much elaboration. The authors recognize that understanding a complete IP location architecture demands more substantial support for someone new to the area. It is for this reason that we decided to write this book. It is our desire that it will give the reader a firm understanding of the architecture as well as guidelines on the best approach to successfully implementing it in their networks and using it with their applications. It is our earnest hope that this book will facilitate the deployment of location services for the Internet and provide the robust and consistent underpinnings to support important social functions such as reliable access to emergency services by those in need, and contribute to the general utility, power, and fun of the Internet in general.

References

1. US National Imagery and Mapping Agency, *"Department of Defense (DoD) World Geodetic System 1984 (WGS 84),"* 3d ed., NIMA, January 2000.

2. NENA 02-010, *"Standard Formats and Protocols for ALI Data Exchange, ALI Response and GIS Mapping,"* February 25, 2006.

3. Universal Postal Union (UPU), *"International Postal Address Components and Templates,"* July 2004.

4. Polk, J., Schnizlein, J., and M. Linsner, *"Dynamic Host Configuration Protocol Option for Coordinate-based Location Configuration Information,"* July 2004.

A Brief History of Location Services and Concepts

The history of applications for location information is as long as human history. Maps, street signs, and even the most basic of symbols scratched in stone to indicate the nearby presence of a waterhole are all examples of location-related information being brought to bear for the benefit of users. In more recent times, location-based applications have been commonly implemented on electronic communications networks. Even before cellular networks contained a specific infrastructure for providing location information directly to applications, such applications existed. For example, POTS-based 1-800 services would refer to a database relating the caller's number to their location so that the call would be routed to the nearest franchise associated with the dialed number. People have been assisted in contacting their nearest pizza restaurant in this way for many years—probably without giving that fact much thought. Taxi and courier companies have also, for many years, utilized GPS receivers located in vehicles coupled with a public or private wireless data connection to a home-base in order to track, schedule, and dispatch vehicles in an optimal fashion (see Figure 1.1).

Most recently, the media-rich capabilities of the Internet have created an enormous new scope for location-based services, and this is the key focus of this book. The vast quantity and range of content available over the Internet and World Wide Web can only be digested if there are mechanisms to sort the relevant from the irrelevant so that the information is customized to the needs of the user. This has been the motivation for the evolution of Internet search engines over the past decade. A significant parameter used in the refinement of Internet searches and content delivery is geographic location. For example, business directory services may be requested based on those servicing a particular city, or a list of movies showing in cinemas within a ten-kilometer radius may be asked for.

Mapping applications have become a commodity Internet service and it is common practice for travelers to obtain maps and driving directions from any of the many web-based services that provide this data based on the location information provided by the user.

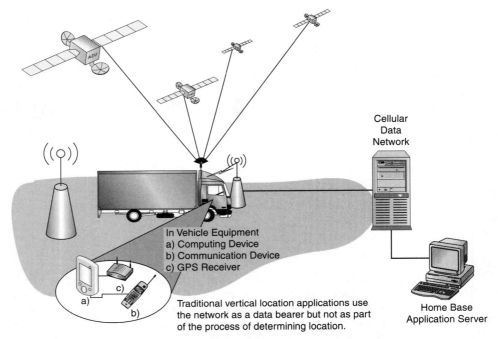

In Vehicle Equipment
a) Computing Device
b) Communication Device
c) GPS Receiver

Traditional vertical location applications use
the network as a data bearer but not as part
of the process of determining location.

Cellular
Data
Network

Home Base
Application Server

Figure 1.1   A vertical fleet application showing vehicle GPS, network, and application server.

Most recently, the popularity and attention given to applications such as Google Earth™ demonstrates the interest that the general population of Internet users have in accessing information about the physical and spatial world they inhabit.

A function that, with little exception, all of these applications benefit from is the ability to automatically identify the location of the user rather than have the user manually provide the location information when needed. That is, there is a need for a mechanism that can provide the "You are here" feature to location-based Internet services, as suggested in Figure 1.2. It has long been the case that users can reach services from more than just a single point of access to the Internet. That is, users are able to be nomadic and access the Internet from multiple and relatively arbitrary locations. For example, they may use a map service from home one day and then 24 hours later use the same service from a city on the other side of the country. Clearly the driving directions to a given destination will be quite different for the two points of origin. In this example, there are obvious benefits if the user does not have to manually provide the point of origin, not least because they may not even know the address associated with their new location.

In addition to the nomadicity associated with users of the Internet, there is a growing trend toward fully mobile access. The deployment of 3G cellular networks supporting always-on high-speed connections as well as newly introduced wireless broadband technologies such as WiMAX allows users to be in constant connection with Internet

(Image courtesy of Google—Google Brand Features are trademarks of or distinctive brand features of Google Inc.)

Figure 1.2 Adding the "You are here" to Internet applications.

services while they are in motion. The assumption of a static location associated with a user becomes increasingly invalid as this trend develops. By the same token, the frequent manual updating of location by users becomes increasingly impractical if they are continually moving. A mechanism by which an IP device can automatically obtain location information to provide to applications of the user's choosing becomes essential.

While no ubiquitous and consistent infrastructure exists for the automatic provision of location information in the Internet today, there is a precedent for this functionality in modern communications networks. The major standards for cellular telephony and 3G networks define a location services infrastructure. Driven largely by the imperative to support automatic location determination for the North American emergency (E911) service, these specifications have been almost universally implemented and the majority of modern cellular networks are now equipped with the ability to provide the automated location determination of cellular devices and the delivery of that location information to applications.

Emergency Services: A Case Study of an Important Location-Based Service

Before examining the manner in which a location services infrastructure may be introduced into Internet protocols, it is useful to look at the model and mechanisms implemented in a cellular network supporting E911 in North America. In order to support this service, functionality has to be provided with ubiquitous coverage and a consistent implementation that makes the service transparent regardless of the mobility of the users and their devices.

Cellular Network Architecture for North American Emergency Services

In 1996, the Federal Communications Commission in the United States issued an order that required cellular network operators to provide the mobile equivalent of the enhanced-911 (E911) service that had been available to wired telephony users for a number of years prior. The E911 service provides not just a common emergency service number but it also delivers the caller's phone number (automatic number identification—ANI) and their location (automatic location identification—ALI) to the emergency services call center operator.

For wireline telephone networks, of course, the ALI information was provided as a civic address and this was obtained by a database lookup using the ANI to obtain the subscriber address information associated with that number, as shown in Figure 1.3.

The challenge for cellular network operators was how to determine and deliver the ALI information when, being a mobile network, there was no strict association between the ANI and the device location. In addition, it was recognized at an early stage that it was not practical to deliver a definitive civic address form of location when any mechanism used to locate a mobile phone would have an uncertainty associated with it. For cellular networks, it would ultimately be necessary for the public safety answering points (PSAPs—where the call center operators work) to be upgraded so that they could display a geodetic form of location including the uncertainty associated with the

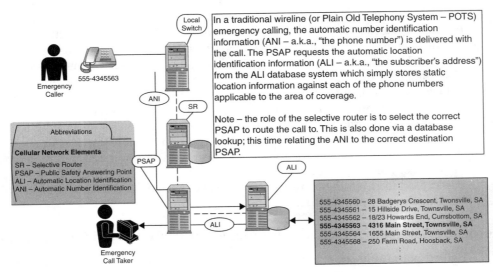

Figure 1.3 ANI-ALI in the emergency network—a wireline phone lookup.

location of callers. So, in recent years, PSAPs have been installing geographic information systems (GISs) which can overlay geodetic coordinates on maps of the emergency jurisdiction to provide the necessary information for emergency service dispatch. An example can be seen in the following illustration of a PSAP operator position where the graphical display for GIS information is part of the workstation equipment.

(*Photo courtesy of Holtam City Police Dept and Tarrant Co E911, TX*)

Reference may be made to Figure 1.4 which shows the typical functional elements of a GSM cellular network and the emergency services network that it delivers calls to. There are two critical aspects to this network architecture which would not be seen in a wireline network context. The first is the location services (LCS) infrastructure which exists in the cellular network side. This is primarily represented by the mobile location center (MLC) components; the serving MLC (SMLC) invokes network and/or handset measurements and performs calculations using those measurements to obtain a geodetic form of the location of the handset. The gateway MLC (GMLC) stores those measurements for presentation on request from the emergency network.

The second critical aspect is the automatic location identification (ALI) database which services the requests for location information from the PSAP, and which supports a real-time query interface to the GMLC operating in the cellular network. When the PSAP requests location information for the caller, it queries the ALI just as it would do for a wireline caller. The ALI then proxies this request to the GMLC in the cellular network, which has the caller's location stored. The GMLC responds with the caller's location. The ALI then proxies the response back to the PSAP together with appropriate indicators of the nature of the call, such as the fact that this is cellular and the

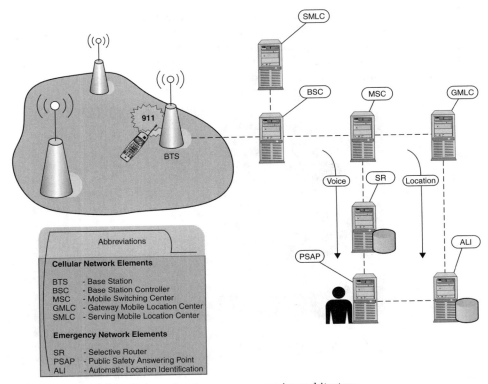

Figure 1.4 A typical GSM cellular network emergency service architecture.

provided location is in the geodetic form. Further, since the caller can be mobile, the PSAP can request updates on the location of the caller and the ALI will also proxy these subsequent requests to the GMLC. The GMLC will then initiate requests for updated locations through the cellular network to the SMLC. The paths of the voice and location information in the cellular example are also shown in Figure 1.4. Note that the location information follows a different path than the voice traffic.

Location Determination in Cellular Networks

There is a wide range of mechanisms through which location is determined in cellular networks, and some of these mechanisms are shown in Figure 1.5. The SMLC may simply obtain the identity of the serving cell in the network and, based on the location of the BTS associated with that cell, determine an approximate location of the handset. This location will typically be geodetic coordinates and a radius value representing the area of uncertainty associated with the location. The size of the uncertainty area will depend on the overall size of the cell serving the handset; the bigger the cell, the greater the overall uncertainty with respect to the location of the handset.

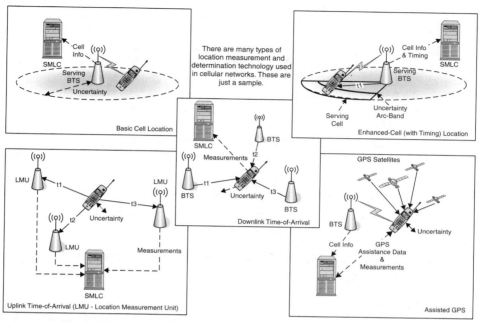

Figure 1.5 Location technologies in cellular networks.

The location calculation can be refined further with the aid of additional measurements taken by the SMLC. The measurements may be of signal timings, the strength of received signals, or the angle of arrival of signals at the base stations. In addition, the SMLC may request measurements from the handset. These may also be network measurements, including signal strengths and timing, or they may be of some external system such as the satellites in the global positioning system (GPS). Note that, with the exception of GPS, none of the measurements are a direct representation of location but, rather, something that can be used in conjunction with some other contextual information so that location can be calculated. Even in the case of GPS, the SMLC may ask for just the raw GPS measurements (the code phase offsets) from which ranges to the satellites can be determined and which may also be used in combination with other network measurements to improve the yield of GPS on its own. In order to calculate location, the SMLC has to have the necessary contextual information, such as the current location of the GPS satellites and base stations that the measurements relate to.

It can be seen that there are many "technologies" that can be applied to the process of location determination even in the specific field of cellular networks. However, all of these technologies can be characterized by the particular types of the parameters that are measured and the specific algorithms and necessary context information that permit a location to be calculated from those measurements. Regardless of the technology used to calculate it, the location information is rendered in a common form. In the cellular domain, this form is typically geodetic, with an associated area of uncertainty.

This form is then presented to the application layer, such as the emergency services network, so that the details of location calculation are transparent to the application. Indeed, the actual network technology need not be visible to the services. For example, the device may be situated in a GSM, TDMA, UMTS, or CDMA network, but the nature of the location information remains unchanged because the type of network is not necessarily significant to the service using the location.

At this point, it is worth pausing to highlight three key concepts:

- **Location measurement**   Obtaining the value of specific key and transient parameters associated with a target device which will be useful in determining location
- **Location determination**   Combining a set of measured parameters with contextual data and algorithms to calculate a location
- **Location acquisition**   Providing location information in an understood and consistent form to a recipient entity

In the simple example of an enhanced cell measurement in a cellular network, and with reference to Figure 1.6:

- The *measurements* include the value of the serving cell identifier and a timing measurement indicating how long signals take to go from the BTS to the handset.
- Location *determination* involves the use of the contextual information of the latitude and longitude of the BTS, the angular orientation and the number of

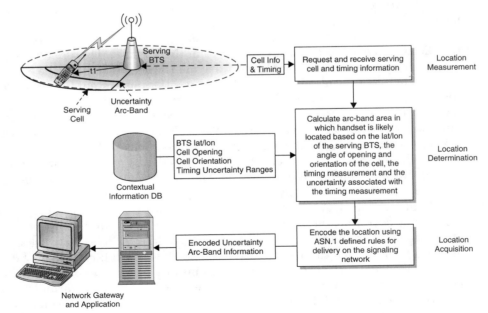

Figure 1.6   TA breakdown

degrees of opening of the serving cell. The algorithm calculates the distance from the BTS using the timing measurement and a corresponding margin of error and ultimately determines a specific arc-band within the serving cell sector that represents the area that the handset should be in to within a specific degree of confidence.

- The SMLC then takes that location information and encodes it in a standards-defined form for transmission through the network for *acquisition* by the using application. In the case of E911, this is via the GMLC, the ALI, and then on to the PSAP.

This separation between the process of collecting measurements, the process of calculating location, and the mechanism by which location information is acquired by users is a general model that is applicable beyond the specific domain of cellular network location. Indeed, it forms the basis for a generic architecture applicable to any sort of network, and in particular—from the perspective of this text—the various sorts of Internet protocol access networks.

Uncertainty and Confidence in Location Determination

Uncertainty and confidence are two important concepts associated with any measured location. The terms are in widespread use in both technical specifications and regulatory documents but they are often misunderstood.

It may be readily understood that any technique, however sophisticated, that's used to determine a location will be subject to some degree of error. While a geodetic location is most obviously thought of as a specific point on the surface of the geoid—that is, a latitude and longitude expressed to the necessary degree of precision to exactly identify the point—it should be noted that a measured location will actually cover an area on the surface of the geoid. In other words, the target of the location measurement is not known to be at a particular point but is only said to be somewhere within that area. This is known as an area of uncertainty. The shape of this area of uncertainty may vary. The method of location determination may represent its result as a simple circle centered on a specific point, or it may utilize strict bounding rules that allow it to represent the result as a polygon (see Figure 1.7).

In practice, it must be assumed that the target is equally likely to be at any location within that area of uncertainty—despite the tendency of many to presuppose that the center is the more likely location, especially if the uncertainty area is provided as a circle. In reality, there *may* be a greater or lesser likelihood that the target is at one point rather than another within that area of uncertainty, but the form of presentation, as a simple area, has no way to convey that information, so all points must be assumed to be of equal likelihood.

The question of "likelihood" is pertinent to how big an area of uncertainty is provided as part of a location. The answer depends not only on the accuracy of the measurement technology used to determine the location, but it also depends on what "confidence" should be associated with the result. Typically a location measurement technology will

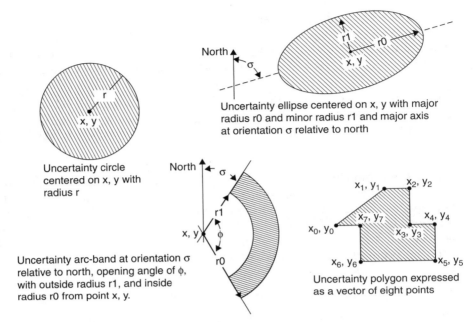

Figure 1.7   Uncertainty expressed as different shapes.

not provide hard edges associated with uncertainty. That is, it is not generally possible to say that the target is *definitely* within a particular area and *definitely not* outside that area of uncertainty. The likelihood of the target being within the area of uncertainty is known as the "confidence" of the result. In fact, confidence will usually vary in quite complex ways across the possible area within which the target may lie. Figure 1.8 shows the situation where confidence only approaches 100 percent asymptotically with distance from a determined point. So, for this situation, an area of uncertainty representing 100-percent confidence that the target is located within it would actually be a circle of infinite radius. This is hardly a useful representation of the location since it effectively says that the target is somewhere, but it could be anywhere.

Note that, in theory, the probability of a location point being the correct one can vary from one point to the next in a complex way that is governed by the environment, and the characteristics of the measurement technology brought to bear to determine the location. In other words, it is possible to define the location of a target as a locus of points in two- or three-dimensional space, with each point representing a possible location of the target and where each point has its own probability that this is the actual location. For most applications, and particularly where a human is the consumer of the location representation, this is not a practical form of representation. Thus, the form is usually simplified to a simple circle or other shape representing an area of uncertainty. The confidence that this area really does capture the correct location is the aggregate (or integral) of all the individual probability values for each of the points in that area.

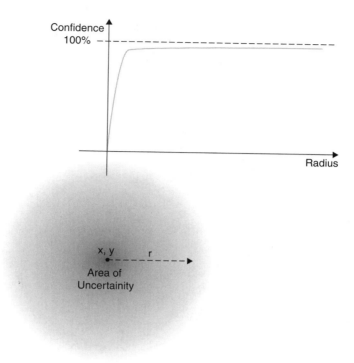

Figure 1.8   Non-linear location/confidence relationship.

This creates the situation where confidence information internal to the area is lost and all points should be assumed to be equally likely. To properly understand the significance of the area of uncertainty, the confidence level associated with that area should also be known. That is, if all points inside the area must be considered equally likely, it would be good to at least know what the likelihood is that the real location may be outside this area. Going back to the previous figure and noting that a circle of uncertainty with infinite radius isn't particularly useful, an arbitrary degree of confidence may be taken (see Figure 1.9).

For example, if we want to know the location of the user at the 67th percentile of confidence, the radius of the area of uncertainty can be expressed as the finite value of *r1* meters. In practice, this means that the application may assume that the target is within *r1* meters of the provided location but it will be correct only two times out of every three measurements. Thus, one in three times the actual location will be somewhere outside of the uncertainty, and will be more than *r1* meters away by an unknown amount.

If one in three times is too frequent for the application to have no information about the location of the target, then a higher level of confidence in the result is required. Going back to the figure, we can identify the uncertainty at which confidence is at 95 percent. This means that the area of uncertainty is now bigger at *r2* meters.

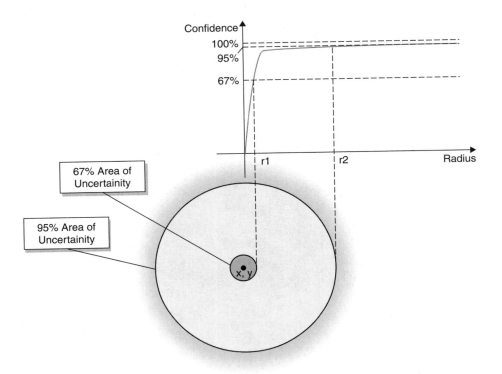

Figure 1.9 Obtaining an area of uncertainty at a specific confidence level.

While the area of uncertainty is now greater, the application can be confident that the location provided will be correct, in the sense that the target really is contained within the provided area of uncertainty, 19 times out of 20. This is a considerable improvement on two out of three. Of course, the optimal combination of uncertainty and confidence will be very application-specific. Many applications may not even care about uncertainty, let alone confidence, and will simply use the center of the uncertainty in all cases. The most sophisticated applications, however, will utilize not just the uncertainty information but will have the functionality to handle the boundary circumstance of the actual location being outside the area of uncertainty.

Returning again to emergency services, this is an example of an application that will care about both uncertainty and confidence. For a geodetic form of location, the uncertainty is generally represented as a circle around a point. This can be displayed on the operator's screen as that circle overlaid on the street map information. This can be used to provide guidance to the dispatched services in terms of where they should search for the subject of the call. Procedures must also exist, however, that acknowledge that the subject may even be outside of this area, since it is only provided at a specific level of confidence, and these contingency procedures are just as important a part of the application as directing services within the area of uncertainty. The exact nature of such contingency procedures will depend on the frequency with which the actual location

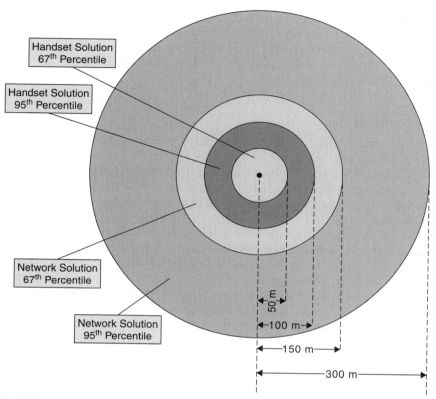

Figure 1.10 FCC-prescribed cellular uncertainty and confidence.

lies outside the area of uncertainty, and the frequency of these occurrences will depend on the confidence level where the area of uncertainty was generated.

In terms of U.S. emergency services, the FCC actually prescribed the specification for cellular location uncertainty to be two levels of confidence. For example, handset-based solutions such as GPS had to be accurate to within 50 meters, 67 percent of the time and to within 100 meters, 95 percent of the time. In the terms we have just been discussing, this can be represented by two concentric circles, one being an area of uncertainty with a radius of 50 meters and 67 percent confidence and the other being an area of uncertainty with a radius of 100 meters and a confidence of 95 percent, as shown in Figure 1.10. Network-based solutions, which would work with legacy handsets, were constrained to a looser accuracy requirement—150 meters at 67-percent confidence and 300 meters at 95-percent confidence.

The Rise of VoIP and the Creation of an IP Location Imperative

Before proceeding with the development of a location services architecture for IP, it is worth turning to the next page of the E911 story. This is because the next part of that story is about the development and mass uptake of telephony services on the Internet and other IP networks. This is commonly referred to as voice over IP (VoIP) and, just as cellular had done previously, it raised new challenges for the E911 services network. The examination of how this challenge was addressed by the industry is worthwhile because it highlights some additional requirements that an effective IP location services architecture should satisfy.

The Internet Services Model

For the many people who use the Internet today, the model by which services are accessed is very familiar. For example, there are e-mail services, web-based information services such as online banking, and instant-messaging type services, just to name a few. A common characteristic of these services is that it is generally expected that they can be accessed regardless of the manner in which the user connects to the Internet.

So, for example, if the user connects over their home network using a DSL connection, they can log onto their net-banking web site, enter their username and password information for authentication, and utilize the service. If they connect to the Internet at some other time using a wireless hotspot in a coffee shop, the expectation is that they will be able to access the net-banking service in exactly the same way. The net-banking service does not know or care how the user is connecting to the Internet.

That is, Internet services are generally made available to users in a fashion that is transparent with respect to the provider that the user is obtaining their network access from. This model applies equally to VoIP services. While there are certainly scenarios in which a broadband access provider may also provide a VoIP telephony service whose use is constrained to the single access that they provide, this is a special case and is in no way an essential characteristic of VoIP. Contrast this with wireline POTS (plain old telephone service) and it can be noted that it has been generally necessary to order the telephone network connection from the telephone service operator. If a third party was involved, it has been at a wholesale level with no visibility to the subscriber. This is because the definition of a "telephony service," in a POTS sense, includes everything from the physical network connectivity through to the call processing and call delivery functions. This can be characterized as being a "full services model" as opposed to an "Internet services model." IP telephony being obtained under an Internet services model primarily describes a call processing function that is accessible over any independently provided IP network and regardless of the physical connectivity type. This aspect of the Internet services model may be termed "access-provider service-provider decoupling" and has significant implications for location services in an Internet context.

Nomadicity and Mobility

One of the first visible impacts of VoIP to emergency service processing is that VoIP supports user nomadicity and mobility. Nomadicity refers to the characteristic wherein users may be accessing the telephony service from one location at a given time, even if they are tethered to a fixed point such as a wired home LAN on a broadband service, and somewhat later connect from a completely different location such as a hotel broadband service in another city. While this is not mobility in the sense of the user moving while concurrently using the voice service, it does mean that there can be no presumed association between the identity of the user and the location they occupy. For example, the phone number can no longer be used to determine a subscriber's home address with a presumption that this is their location when making a call.

Further, there is a category of Internet access technologies that supports full mobility of the user. For example, wide-area broadband wireless networks (such as WiMAX and Wibro) allow a user to connect to the Internet and access services even while traveling in a car at high speed.

From the perspective of emergency services, at least for getting the initial location of the caller and correctly routing the call, there is little difference between a nomadic or a mobile scenario. The main impact is that static, predefined, databases cannot be used for obtaining caller location based on, for example, their phone number. It becomes necessary to dynamically obtain the location information from one call to the next. This, of course, is the same challenge that was raised with the introduction of the cellular network, and the same fundamental architecture lends itself to addressing this issue. That is, it is necessary to provide network infrastructure to obtain the location information applicable at the time of the call for the purposes of routing and to provide a mechanism to deliver that information out of the IP network and into the emergency network for display to the call-taker at the PSAP.

In 2003, the National Emergency Number Association (NENA) in North America established a committee to look at the specifics of how to support emergency services (E911) access from mass market VoIP services. The solution was divided into three categories, each with a prefix of *i*, and were thus labeled i1, i2, and i3. The first of these dealt with basic 911. That is, it only concerned itself with defining some acceptable methods by which a call could be delivered to a PSAP at all, though not necessarily with any associated location information. The second, i2, looked at how to provide full E911 functionality with a common global routing infrastructure and a mechanism for delivering location that would work with minimum impact to the existing emergency network and its associated PSAP infrastructure. That is, it reused as much of the existing emergency network interface functionality as possible. The third, i3, looked at a time further down the track when an all-IP network would be established such that the caller has an end-to-end IP call in place with the PSAP. Working groups dedicated to both the i2 and i3 architecture definitions were established.

The i2 Architecture

In 2005, NENA published the technical document describing the solution defined by the i2 working group (See reference 1 at the end of this chapter). There is a great deal of detail in this document, and Figure 1.11 shows but a fraction of it. However, the salient points remain visible. In particular, note that the same voice and location information paths exist via the selective router and ALI network elements, respectively,

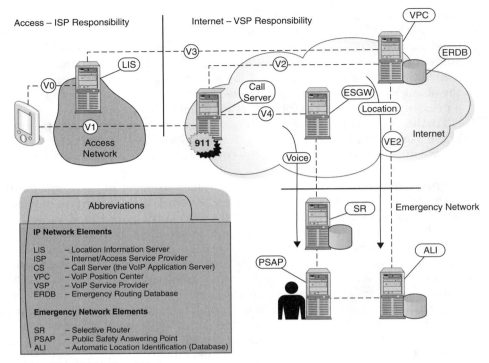

Figure 1.11 The NENA i2 architecture.

as were seen for the cellular architecture shown in Figure 1.5. Based on the mandate to minimize the impact on the existing emergency network elements, the i2 working group maintained and reused these mechanisms that had been defined for cellular emergency support.

The VoIP position center (VPC), shown in Figure 1.11, provides equivalent functionality to the GMLC displayed in Figure 1.5. The call-server queries the VPC to learn how the emergency call should be routed, and the VPC also caches the location information in anticipation of receiving a request for location from the ALI system. This is all largely the same as the manner in which cellular calls are treated and it addresses the mobility element of VoIP telephony by supporting the mechanism for obtaining location dynamically on a call-by-call basis.

A significant difference compared to the cellular architecture comes into play when consideration is given to the determination of location. The significance is driven not so much from the technical aspects as by the *organizational* aspects of VoIP. This stems from the access-provider service-provider decoupling that was defined earlier. There is no inherent need for the provider of the VoIP service processing the emergency call to have any direct knowledge of the form, nature, or ownership of the Internet access being used by the caller. While a cellular network operator can identify the radio cells of their network that is currently servicing the caller, the VoIP service provider has no such similar knowledge. While a cellular operator can direct signaling to the correct part of the network to invoke location determination, the VoIP service provider is reliant on some form of information being sent from the device from which the call is being made in order to begin the process of location determination.[*]

Literal Location vs. Location Reference

There are two obvious forms that the information provided by the device can take. It can either be the location information itself (the "literal" location) or it can be some form of reference information that tells the recipient where it can go to obtain the literal location information. The i2 architecture supports both concepts. Referring again to Figure 1.11, the IP device conveys the location information to the VoIP call server via the interface labeled V1. The call server passes the location information to the VPC over the interface labeled V2; it does this in part because of its need to be informed about how the call should be routed based on the provided location. The VPC is the entity that determines the correct routing information for the call server. If the literal location has been conveyed in these steps, the VPC already has what it needs to know to make a judgment on routing the call. However, if the location was conveyed as a reference, the VPC then goes to the system identified by that reference and retrieves the literal location. This occurs via the interface labeled V3. The ability for the VPC to request location directly via V3 is useful to obtain fresh updates of the caller's location throughout the call. Where the access network is a wireless WAN and, as in the case of cellular, the user may be mobile while making the call, PSAP/ALI is able to request periodic updates of the location. The VPC could not do this if it only had the initial literal location value rather than the reference, which permits a periodic re-query to the location information server (LIS).

A Question of Trust

A subtle but nonetheless very important issue arises where an access-provider service-provider decoupling exists. That is the question of the trustability of the location information that is provided to the application layer.

Recalling that the location information conveyance is started by the IP device itself, there could be a tacit assumption that information is correct. The correctness of the location information is clearly of importance to the VoIP service provider since they

---

[*] This statement is based on a presumption that, in an access-provider service-provider decoupled situation, the access provider need have no explicit knowledge about the application protocol (a VoIP protocol in this case) being used on the access that they provide. In the case of cellular networks, a caller may be roaming in another cellular provider's network. In the case of traditional switched-circuit cellular calls, it is actually the visited network that deals with the processing of the emergency calls. While this model could apply to IP telephony, it would actually require Internet access providers to support an entire emergency calling application that is potentially independent of the voice service and protocols that users would generally use for IP telephony. This would be a considerably more onerous obligation on Internet access providers than the general location information service that is described in this text.

will need it to correctly route the call, and it is of critical importance to the PSAP and the rest of the emergency service because the location information will be used as the destination to which to dispatch valuable resources such as police cars, ambulances, fire crews, and so on.

An assumption of trust with respect to the information provided by the device may be well and good in conjunction with an assumption that the user's intention is honest and the information has been determined to be in good faith and is a best-effort. However, what if the user is not honest? The emergency service is, by its nature, relatively anonymous. A phone number does not necessarily identify the actual user of the device should the subscriber possibly be somebody different. In addition, the PSAP has no basis for understanding the character or degree of answerability of any arbitrary individual subscriber at the given instant that their subscription is being used to make an emergency call. In a poll conducted amongst PSAP operators during the formulation of the i2 architecture, an overwhelming preference was expressed that some information about the source of origin of the location information be available. The reason is fairly obvious and it's that the ability to appear to be making a call from a specific location while actually being in any other arbitrary location in the world exposes the emergency network to acts of mischief or worse that could unnecessarily tie up valuable resources and deny their use in situations of genuine need. This has implications for personal safety and, also, for national security given that the emergency network is regarded as critical security infrastructure in most national jurisdictions.

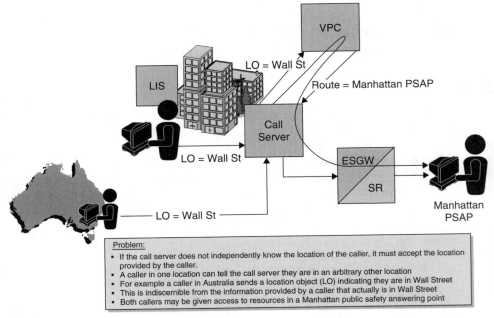

Figure 1.12 Spoofing a location in an emergency call.

In the cellular case, the location information is determined by the cellular network operator themselves. The emergency network operators, then, base their trust of the veracity of the location information on the recognizable identity of the provider of the location information—that is, the cellular operator. Further, if the location information is determined to be erroneous, the cellular operator is an entity that can be held answerable for this and steps can be taken to cooperatively ensure that the error does not reoccur.

So what can be done in the case of VoIP where the access-provider service-provider decoupling exists? The answer can be found in the functionality of the LIS, which is seen in Figure 1.11 as the network element at the end of the V3 interface and which is the entity that the IP device obtains the initial location information from over the interface labeled V0.

The LIS: A Location Server for Access Networks

There are lines in Figure 1.11 that identify some very important points of demarcation of responsibility in the context of the i2 architecture. The emergency network is responsible for dealing with the call and the dispatch of the correct first-responder resources. The VoIP provider is responsible for delivering the call to the correct PSAP based on the location of the caller and for ensuring that the location information is also delivered to the PSAP. In terms of the determination of the location information, however, the responsibility is shown as being with the access network provider.

In this architecture, a network entity called a location information server (LIS) is defined to exist within the access network. The primary function of the LIS is to provide location information to IP devices operating within the access network or to properly authorized applications requesting location through a reference mechanism. In terms of the question of trust previously discussed, the LIS should also support a mechanism that securely identifies the source of the location information. That is, the location information—if it is in a literal form—should be coded such that it securely identifies the source and time of applicability. Typically, this will be achieved by digital security techniques that provide a signature on the location information. The signature can be used by the recipient to determine the source of the information, the entity that signed the information, and to detect whether the information has been tampered with (for instance, changed since the signature was created).

As a case study, the emergency services application highlighted a number of requirements that an LIS should meet. It should be emphasized that an LIS and the location information it deals with are useful in far more ways than just emergency services and, similarly, the requirements are applicable to more applications than just emergency services. Let's list them.

- The LIS shall be able to determine the location of a client device based on its IP address.

- The LIS shall be able to deliver location information applicable to a device on request from that device.

- The device shall be able to ask for a literal location or for a unique reference that can be used by a third-party application and the LIS shall be able to respond accordingly.
- The LIS shall be able to ensure that it only delivers a device's literal location to authorized third-party applications.
- The LIS shall be able to provide location information in such a fashion that a third-party consumer of that location information can identify a responsible source of the location information.

At this stage, it should be pointed out that the preceding requirements do not in any way explain how an LIS actually operates or goes about meeting the requirements. Be patient, this information is on its way now that we are nearly finished establishing some context. Before getting into the nitty gritty of just how an LIS can work and how devices and applications talk to it, we shall revisit some of the lessons from the cellular network world once more and generalize them so that they are applicable regardless of the nature of the access network.

A Generic Architecture

The section on location determination in cellular networks earlier in this chapter described how an end-to-end network location service could be divided into three critical functions. While this functional decomposition was observed with respect to the cellular location services architecture, it can be equally applied to one dealing with the location of arbitrary IP devices. These functions are as follows.

- Location measurement
- Location determination
- Location acquisition

Before elaborating further, it should be noted from here on that "IP device" is used to refer to the IP network entity whose location is being determined. It is the subject of any location requests that are occurring and it can also be referred to as the "target" of the location request. An IP device may be any piece of network-connected equipment, such as a personal computer, a PDA, or a soft drink vending machine. The only requirement is that it be connected and have an IP address associated with it.

Figure 1.13 shows how the entities in a network-based location architecture participate in each of these functions. The LIS is shown as the element which collects measurements. These measurements may be obtained from

- Network fabric components (for example, switches, wireless access points, and circuit aggregators)
- Overlay network elements (for instance, location measurement units and network monitoring devices)

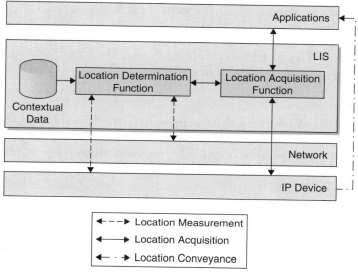

Figure 1.13   Location architecture functional layers.

- The IP device itself (such as a device taking GPS measurements, RFID beacon readings, or LLDP type measurements)

There is an additional function associated with the location services architecture, and that is the actual transporting of location information between one network entity and another. Note that this is distinct from "location delivery" because that term specifically refers to one network element providing an answer to an explicit request for location information. The transporting of location information occurs whenever one piece of application client or server code is communicating with another, and where one of the parameters of that communication is some piece of location information. For example, a VoIP device communicating with an SIP server may initiate a call by sending an INVITE message, and this message may include an optional parameter that would be interpreted as the location of the caller and may be used to route the call depending on what that location is—for example, to a pizza franchise which services the caller's location. Or, as another example, a web-based navigation application may require the desired destination to be provided as a specific XML form of location and be sent on HTTP.

This function is termed "location conveyance" in this text. An example of a location conveyance interface is also shown in Figure 1.13 where the IP device may send location information directly to an application using some application-specific protocol. The manner in which location conveyance is done is highly application-dependent. While there is good reason to identify a universally consistent method for performing location delivery in IP networks, location conveyance can be expected to take many forms depending on the nature of the applications, devices, and applicable protocols. This is the case whether the location information is delivered in a literal form or by reference.

The difference being that, in the case of the latter, a recipient network entity such as an application server may need to also be able to invoke the location delivery protocol toward the LIS.

Revisiting Figure 1.13, it can be seen that the LIS has two key functional protocols that it should support. These are as follows

- A *measurement* protocol for obtaining relevant measurement information
- An *acquisition* protocol for service requests for location information

From the perspective of the LIS, these protocols are applicable to the following interfaces

- Measurement—LIS to Network and LIS to IP device
- Acquisition—LIS to IP device and LIS to applications

There is one more important characteristic relevant to the process of "measurement" that needs to be discussed before we go on to look at the details of the measurement and delivery protocols. This has to do with the relationship that should be assumed between the LIS and the network, and the LIS and IP devices. The relationship with the network can be termed "static," and the relationship with the IP devices can be termed "dynamic." This is explained as follows.

A LIS is assumed to be strongly associated with a particular access network. For example, it may provide the LIS function for a switched Ethernet network servicing a range of subnets in a commercial office space. Alternatively, it may be associated with an ADSL network servicing subscribers in a particular market region. In any case, the LIS will have contextual information applicable to the access network that it can use to determine location. In the first of the previous examples, the LIS may have information about the building and room number that each Ethernet switch port terminates to. Or, in the case of the ADSL example, it may have information that relates a particular ATM circuit in the ADSL aggregation network to a specific DSLAM termination that in turn relates to a particular copper loop terminating at a specific subscriber residential address. These pieces of information are stored in the LIS and are known by it prior to any location requests occurring. By the same token, it is necessary for the LIS to be aware of the network measurements that are relevant to it and where it will obtain those measurements. This information is also kept by the LIS and, while it may be subject to modification over time, it is static in the sense that it applies regardless of when or where a particular location request may originate. The LIS is, therefore, in a position to establish a session with the important points in an access network, and to maintain those sessions over time, in anticipation of obtaining location measurements.

IP devices, on the other hand, will arbitrarily come and go within the access network without any foreknowledge on the part of the LIS. The first indication that an LIS may have of the presence of an IP device may be at the moment that the device presents a request for location acquisition to occur. In this sense, the relationship of the LIS with

IP devices is dynamic. Also, since IP devices attach themselves to the network for reasons outside the scope of influence of the LIS, there is no forward indication of what sort of measurements an IP device may be capable of providing—that's if it can provide any at all. Compared to the access network, where the LIS is preconditioned to understand what measurements it can obtain from the network, there has to be a more dynamic interchange to understand what measurements can be obtained from the IP device. There is also a dependency on the LIS to be able to cope with the types of measurement provided by the device or, alternatively, be able to "gracefully ignore" the measurements without compromising the quality of the location determination.

These qualitative differences in terms of whether the relationship is static or dynamic influence the specific details of the protocols associated with obtaining measurements from the network versus obtaining them from the IP device. This will be seen later in the text, and the description that follows explains why these differences will be seen.

Figure 1.14 recasts Figure 1.13 with the LIS as the hub of the architecture, simultaneously obtaining location measurements from the access network and servicing requests for location delivery from IP devices and applications. In terms of obtaining measurements from the access network, a new subentity is identified in the referenced figure. This is the access location entity (ALE). The role of the ALE is to make available the measurements that are required by the LIS. It is expected that a single instance of an LIS may service an arbitrarily large area of coverage by one or more access technology types. Further, it is assumed that this area of coverage may include an arbitrary number of IP networks of different routing domains. From this perspective, there needs to be some entity, whether

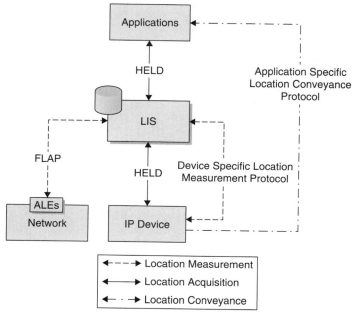

Figure 1.14 The LIS centralized architecture.

physical or logical, which is capable of collecting the localized network measurements and, as a signaling peer to the LIS for the measurement protocol, provide those measurements to the LIS. This signaling peer is identified as the ALE for that localized network.

The protocols that are defined in detail in the rest of this text are as follows.

- Network location measurement protocol—Flexible LIS-ALE Protocol (FLAP)
- IP Device and application location delivery protocol—HTTP Enabled Location Delivery (HELD)

These protocols have been defined to ensure that the LIS can fulfill the requirements listed earlier in this chapter. An LIS that supports HELD and the FLAP provided measurements applicable to the network it covers will be able to service location acquisition requests from any HELD-capable device or application. The one function that hasn't been described so far is how an IP device knows, or how it "discovers," the identity of the LIS servicing the network to which it has attached and that it should send location delivery requests to. This area of "LIS discovery" will also be described in detail further in the text.

Reference

1. NENA VoIP-Packet Technical Committee, "*Interim VoIP Architecture for Enhanced 9-1-1 Services (i2)*," NENA 08-001, Dec 2005.

2

Location, Presence, and Privacy

This chapter describes how location information is produced, transported, and consumed on the Internet. This includes the presence model and the GEOPRIV abstract model for location services and privacy.

Presence

A *presence service* provides a way of accessing information about an individual's status. This is possible because an individual publishes information about themselves to the service so others can acquire that information.

Presence evolved from instant messaging services, providing users with a way of finding where their friends were on the Internet. Presence information for instant messaging includes details on how to contact a user—that is, whether they are online and what their current network location is. Since this initial form, a range of presence applications have been defined and presence is now used to convey a wide range of user data.

The Presence Model

The presence model is defined in Reference 1 (at the end of the chapter) by three roles: a *presentity*, a *presence service*, and a *watcher*. Figure 2.1 shows this very simple model.

Abstract Models

The presence and GEOPRIV models are abstract concepts, which means that the ideas they define do not always directly relate to real-world concepts. Instead, they define a set of *roles* and the interactions between those roles. Each role is defined by a set of tasks that it performs. When an abstract model is applied to a real situation, each participant assumes one or more roles.

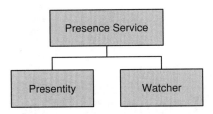

Figure 2.1   The presence model.

The *presence service* is a server that is the critical component in the system. It stores presence information and manages how that information is granted to users. The presence service is also responsible for protecting user privacy by limiting access to presence information.

The term *presentity* was coined to refer to the subject of a presence service; a presentity is the subject of presence information.

A presentity is identified by a presentity identifier, which is very much like an e-mail address—for example, alice@example.com. The presentity identifier is made globally unique by having the presence service allocate a name that includes the domain name of the presence service. Having the domain name of the presence service also means that if the name is known, the presence service can automatically be found.

A *watcher* is someone, or something, that is interested in the status of a presentity.

Example: Presence in Instant Messaging   When Alice starts her IM program, it publishes information about her presence to the presence service.

Bob wants to send his friend Alice an instant message (IM). Bob knows Alice by her name alice@example.com, so he uses that name to identify Alice to his instant messaging program. Bob's IM program then contacts the presence service at "example.com" to ask where it can contact alice@example.com. After ensuring that

Presence in IP Telephony

Internet telephony services now widely use presence so that users are able to contact each other.

In IP telephony, the presence service is often called a *Registrar*, which is a reference to the way that the presence service assigns names. The term *Location Server* is also used in some cases, where "location" refers to network location; however, the term Location Server can be misleading, particularly since it has a different meaning when it comes to physical location, hence this term is no longer widely used.

Bob is allowed to have this information, the presence service then tells Bob's IM program how to contact alice@example.com. Bob's IM program can then send the message to Alice's IM program.

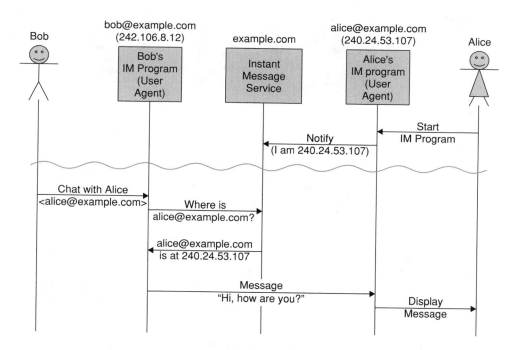

Subscriptions

Presence information may be acquired in a number of ways by a watcher. In the most simple use of presence, the watcher may fetch the information whenever it is required. If a watcher only fetches the information, this limits the possible applications of presence. Most instant messaging programs continually display the status of buddies, but if this information changes, the program is unaware of this until it requests the information.

A watcher can *subscribe* to the presence service for a particular presentity. The presence service then *notifies* the watcher if the presence information for that presentity changes for any reason.

A subscription enables immediate action when presence information changes. Typical actions include a notification to the user, as either a discrete message or a brief sound. This immediate action is why subscriptions are favored for presence applications.

Example: Subscriptions for Instant Messaging   A subscription means that Bob can be notified immediately when Alice becomes available.

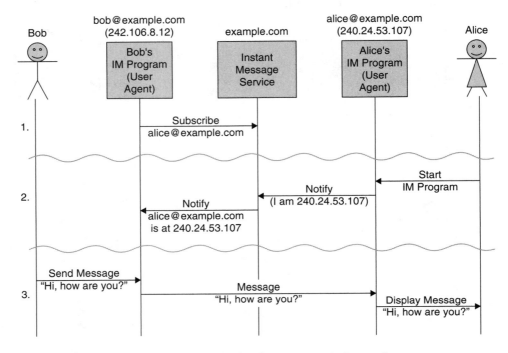

1. Bob's IM program subscribes to Alice's presence information.
2. Alice starts her IM program and becomes online. The IM program notifies the presence service. The presence service then sends a notification to Bob's IM program.
3. Bob can now see that Alice is online, so he sends her an instant message.

The Presence Document

The *Presence Information Data Format* (*PIDF*) is a document format defined by the IETF in Reference 2 for the representation of presence information. PIDF is a structured document that uses an XML format.

All presence documents contain a presentity identifier in the form of a Universal Resource Identifier (URI). Presence information, or status, is contained within one or more tuples. Each tuple can also include contact information and any other information relating to the given status, such as a time when the information was generated.

The following PIDF document indicates that alice@example.com is available (her status is "open") and that she may be contacted at the given Session Initiation Protocol (SIP) URI.

```
<?xml version="1.0"?>
<presence xmlns="urn:ietf:params:xml:ns:pidf"
          entity="pres:alice@example.com">
  <tuple id="e9e682a0">
    <status>
      <basic>open</basic>
    </status>
    <contact>sip:alice@240.24.53.107</contact>
  </tuple>
</presence>
```

Using Presence for Location Information

A physical location can be considered part of presence information in much the same way as a user's online status or any other type of presence information. However, providing physical location as a part of presence introduces some challenges.

Subscription, which is the most powerful feature of the presence model, is inherently suited to discrete-valued data. Location is a continuous datum, which can also change continuously. This could result in an enormous number of notifications from the presentity or presence service.

One method for limiting the number of notifications is to prevent subscription and thus force watchers to fetch location information. Watchers must then poll the presence service to receive updated location information.

Alternatively, the watcher can limit the conditions where the presence server sends notifications. This provides a limit to the notifications without removing some of the advantages of presence. The drawback to this approach is that the presence server must still be aware of changes in location.

Another aspect of this problem is that location information is sometimes quite costly to determine in regards to time, processing capacity, and other resources. In these situations, location should only be determined when it is necessary to avoid incurring these costs.

For instance, a typical autonomous Global Positioning System (GPS) unit can take 15 seconds to determine a location when it has current satellite data; when no such satellite data is available, location determination can take up to 45 seconds. In addition to this time, determining a GPS location is processing-intensive, which can drain the batteries of a mobile device. Assisted GPS mitigates these costs by providing satellite data and performing the calculation phase on dedicated servers.

Subscription-based services offer applications greater flexibility, and are the core of future location-based services. To reduce the costs associated with location determination, it is the responsibility of the location service to appropriately limit how often location is determined, or to use less costly alternative methods. In many situations, the precision that GPS provides might be unnecessary, so quicker and cheaper methods can be used.

The GEOPRIV Model

The Internet Engineering Task Force (IETF) identified a need for standards guidance in the location services. The IETF formed a working group that was tasked with protecting the privacy of the end user of location services. The Geographic/Location Privacy (or GEOPRIV for short) working group has defined an abstract model for location services that includes a strong emphasis on privacy. This abstract model is defined in Reference 3.

The GEOPRIV model begins where location information has already been determined by the *Location Generator*. Location determination is out of scope for this model simply because there are far too many different ways to determine location. (see Figure 2.2.)

The model then describes how this information is published to a *Location Server* and retrieved by a *Location Recipient*, who is the consumer of the location information.

GEOPRIV Roles

The *Target* is the subject of location information, just as the presentity is the target of presence information. Sometimes the Target is referred to as a *Presentity Target*. The Target is described in GEOPRIV documents as an abstract construct, which can be either man or machine. In practice the Target is often a person—Alice's location is more interesting than where her computer is—but the Target could equally be used to identify items for applications like fleet management, asset tracking, or networks of sensors.

Although the Target is usually a person, it is often the *Device* that is used when a location is determined. Most methods for location determination work for devices, not people, but usually the assumption is made that the person and their device are in close proximity. The location of the Target can be determined directly, but this is more of an atypical situation.

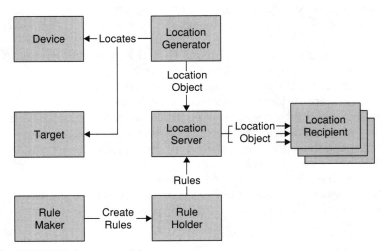

Figure 2.2 The GEOPRIV abstract model.

The *Location Generator* determines the location of the Device or Target. The GEOPRIV model doesn't describe how this is done, but thousands of options exist, some of which are described in this book.

The Location Generator sends location information to the *Location Server*, which is responsible for storing location and giving it to *Location Recipients*. The Location Recipient is the ultimate user of location information; this covers the whole range of location users, from an application that locates the nearest cinema, to the VPC in an emergency call scenario.

Privacy Roles   The Location Server is responsible for managing how, when, and to whom location information is given. This is the way in which the privacy of the Target is protected in the GEOPRIV model.

The Location Server follows a set of rules called an *authorization policy* when making decisions about whether or not it should give location information to a particular Location Recipient. The authorization policy applied by the Location Server is created by a *Rule Maker*. In most situations, the Rule Maker is also the Target—the person who is being located is considered the "owner" of the information, so it is reasonable to expect that they can control how that information is disseminated.

The simplest authorization policy is a list of people who are allowed to view location information, otherwise known as a "buddy list." More complex policies can specify other conditions, special actions that are triggered, and modify the location that a Location Recipient sees. Authorization policies are described in more detail later in this chapter.

Applying the GEOPRIV Model

The GEOPRIV abstract model describes a number of roles, which are only concepts used to facilitate discussion and allow analysis of a range of different configurations. To better understand how this model works, real examples should be studied to see how these roles interact.

A Human Example   The simplest realization of the GEOPRIV model doesn't require network protocols or sophisticated technology. Take the following telephone conversation as an example:

> Bob: *Hello, Bob speaking.*
> Alice: *Hi, it's Alice.*
> Bob: *Hi Alice, how are you?*
> Alice: *I'm well thanks. Bob, where are you?*
> Bob: *I'm at work.*
> ...

This example demonstrates how a single entity can assume more than one of the roles in the abstract model. In this conversation, Bob is the subject of the location information ("I'm at work"), therefore he is the Target. Presumably, Bob has also determined the location information and he is providing it, so he is both Location Generator and Server. While Bob may not have made a conscious decision, he has somehow decided that Alice is allowed to receive this information, so he has also assumed the role of Rule Maker. Alice is the Location Recipient; she is the user of the location information. There is no Device in this example because the Location Generator has directly determined the location of the Target.

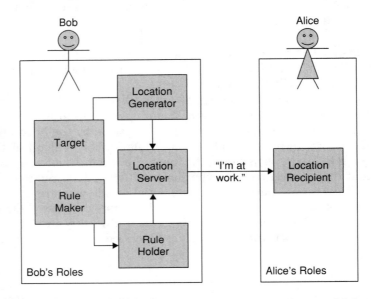

A GPS Application   Assume now that Bob has a mobile phone which contains a GPS unit. He uses an application on this phone that first determines his current location then sends this to a web site that displays a map showing the nearest cinema.

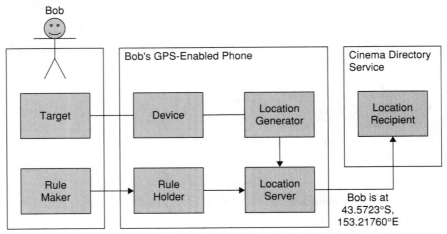

In this example, Bob is still the Target and Rule Maker, but his GPS-enabled mobile phone assumes a number of roles. The phone is the Device and, by virtue of its GPS unit, it is also the Location Generator. The phone sends the location to the cinema web site; therefore, it acts as the Location Server as well.

Fitting the GEOPRIV Model to i2

The i2 architecture described in Chapter 1 is a good example of a real application of location services. Applying the GEOPRIV model to the i2 architecture shows two possible arrangements of the GEOPRIV roles. These two variations are named based on how the Location Recipient first receives location information.

These configurations also apply to non-emergency scenarios and actually form the basis of two basic configurations that can be applied to a large proportion of location services.

Location By-Reference in i2   Location by-reference is named so because the location is not directly provided in the session establishment. Instead of location, a location key or location reference is included. The location key is allocated by the LIS and includes enough information for the VPC to contact the LIS and retrieve location information. In Figure 2.3, the path that the Location URI takes is shown dotted, since this is outside of the GEOPRIV model.

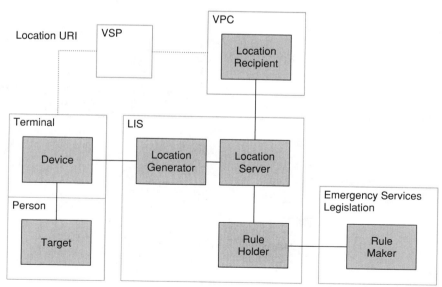

Figure 2.3   GEOPRIV roles in i2: location by-reference.

The location key is usually represented as a URI, which includes all the information that the Location Recipient needs to retrieve a PIDF-LO. For this reason, a location key is referred to as a *Location URI*.

Figure 2.3 shows a legislative authority as the Rule Maker—that is, the LIS is required to provide location information to the VPC.

Generalized Location By-Reference   For general location applications, the location by-reference system does not change substantially from the emergency i2 architecture. A range of location applications can use location information, which requires changes to the way that rules are created and managed. For general location usage, the user becomes the Rule Maker. Figure 2.4 also shows a separate Rule Holder; a separate service for rules enables easier management of the rules.

This generalized location by-reference configuration fits the presence model very closely. The Location URI is a presentity identifier, and by assigning it the LIS acts as a registrar; the presentity is the user or their phone; the presence information is a PIDF-LO; and the location application is a watcher.

Using the by-reference system has a number of advantages, particularly in mobile situations where location can change continuously. A Location URI gives the Location Recipient control over when location is determined; the location is determined when

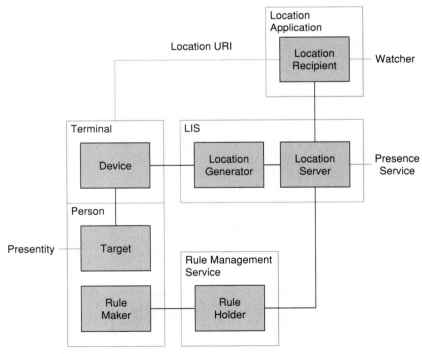

Figure 2.4   A generalized location by-reference configuration.

the Location Recipient requests it, which ensures that it is more current and, therefore, more likely to be accurate. A more detailed discussion of the advantages of this model can be found in Reference 4 at the end of the chapter.

Location By-Value in i2   In the location by-value configuration, location information is provided by-value as part of the session establishment (see Figure 2.5). A PIDF-LO is passed as part of call establishment to the VPC, which is the Location Recipient in this scenario.

Location by-value is very well suited to fixed Internet access. If location is not expected to change, it can be acquired prior to when it is used. This can provide a significant advantage in applications like emergency services, where time is critical.

A Unified Presence Model for Location

The model described in Figure 2.4 shows how a LIS can provide location information by-reference. Figure 2.6 displays a model that uses location by-reference to combine location information with other elements of presence.

The labeled interfaces in Figure 2.6 show the different stages involved in providing this presence service:

1. The configuration interface provides the Target (or Device) with the Location URI. The Target is given this information because the LIS does not have a preexisting relationship with the presence service. As part of the request for a Location URI, the Target includes a simple authorization policy that grants its presence service

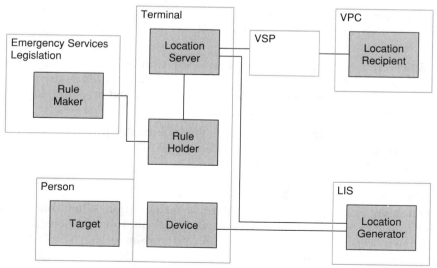

Figure 2.5   GEOPRIV roles in i2: location by-value.

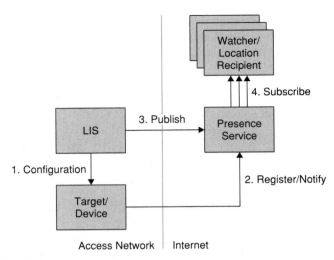

Figure 2.6 GEOPRIV roles in i2: location by-value.

access to location information. The HELD protocol, described in Chapter 3, provides all the necessary elements for this interface. HELD also provides request primitives that are useful for each of the interfaces in this model.

2. The Target provides the Location URI to the presence service. This occurs when the Target registers with the presence service and whenever the Location URI changes. The protocol used for this interface depends on the type of presence service. For the purposes of this book, this interface is assumed to be SIP, and the REGISTER and NOTIFY methods provide the Location URI to the presence service.

3. The presence service subscribes to location information from the LIS. The presence server then acts as a *compositor*, which combines the location information with other elements of presence to form a unified presence document for the user. Location then becomes part of the presence of the Target.

4. Watchers for this information subscribe to the presence service for the Target, which now includes location information. They can do this without prior knowledge of the Location URI or the LIS.

Combining location information with other presence information has the advantage of enabling existing presence tools for use with location. When this is enabled, Watchers don't need to be individually given location information or a Location URI, they can use a known presentity to request location information as they see fit. Changes in location information, and even the Location URI, are hidden from the Watcher; the presence service generates notifications as these values change.

Another advantage of this approach is that the LIS now needs to serve requests to a single entity: the presence server. This reduces the complexity of the LIS substantially—it no longer needs to serve large numbers of clients with the associated authentication for each.

This configuration does not preclude a direct request to the LIS. For emergency services, a direct request is still likely, since this reduces complexity and ensures that the emergency network can authenticate the source of the information directly, without the need for digital signatures on the location information.

Providing Subscriptions The presence service can provide a subscription service to each of the Watchers. However, as described earlier, the continuous nature of location information provides challenges for subscription-based systems. The extra step through the presence service to the LIS complicates this situation.

In order to address this, each Watcher provides a filter document to the presence service. The presence service then acts as a compositor for the filter documents, combining them into a single filter document. At this stage, the presence service can simplify the filter document by removing redundant filter rules. This filter document is then provided to the LIS.

In effect, each Watcher is then subscribing directly to the LIS for location information. The presence service optimizes this interaction by consolidating all the requests into a single subscription and combining the filter rules.

The PIDF-LO

In the GEOPRIV model, there is a difference between location information and its representation. Location information refers to only the data that describe a location, but a location object can contain far more information.

The PIDF Location Object (PIDF-LO) is the object defined in Reference 5 for the representation of location information. The PIDF-LO is simply a PIDF document with one tuple that includes location information. Because PIDF is designed to be very flexible, PIDF-LO can suffer from cardinality problems; location information can be included multiple times in different forms, which could confuse the location user. Care should be taken when constructing a PIDF-LO to ensure that the correct location information is used (see Reference 6).

The following example shows the most basic components of a PIDF-LO:

```
<?xml version="1.0"?>
<pidf:presence xmlns:pidf="urn:ietf:params:xml:ns:pidf"
    xmlns:gp="urn:ietf:params:xml:ns:pidf:geopriv10"
    xmlns:gml="http://www.opengis.net/gml"
    entity="pres:alice@example.com">
  <pidf:tuple id="e9e682a0">
    <pidf:status>
      <gp:geopriv>
        <gp:location-info>
```

```
            <gml:Point srsName="urn:ogc:def:crs:EPSG::4979">
              <gml:pos>-43.5723 153.21760 35</gml:pos>
            </gml:Point>
          </gp:location-info>
          <gp:usage-rules>
            <gp:retransmission-allowed>no</gp:retransmission-allowed>
            <gp:retention-expiry>
              2006-06-23T04:57:29Z
            </gp:retention-expiry>
          </gp:usage-rules>
        </gp:geopriv>
      </pidf:status>
      <pidf:contact>sip:alice@240.24.53.107</pidf:contact>
    </pidf:tuple>
</pidf:presence>
```

Location Information Types

The most important part of a PIDF-LO is the part that contains the location information. In XML, this is the location-info element. Location information is usually described in one of two forms: geodetic location information, which describes a location using coordinates, such as latitude and longitude; and civic addresses, which use features that are more readily recognized by people, such as countries, cities, streets, and house numbers.

Geodetic Location Information   Geodetic location information is based on coordinate systems, most commonly those that include latitude, longitude, and sometimes altitude. Geodetic location information is usually derived from technologies that locate wireless devices, although the location of fixed devices may occasionally be represented using geodetic coordinates.

Geodetic coordinates can represent virtually any location on, in, or near the planet. Geodetic coordinates are also easily understood by computer software because they only include a small amount of information and that information requires very little knowledge to understand—in other words, the user of geodetic coordinates only has to understand the Coordinate Reference System (CRS). For PIDF-LO, applications need only understand the two- and three-dimensional versions of the World Geodetic System (WGS) 1984 CRS, also known as WGS 84. WGS 84 is the CRS used by the GPS system and it is in wide use in existing cellular location systems.

The simplest geodetic location is a single point. The following PIDF-LO fragment shows the location 43.5723°S, 153.21760°E at an altitude of 35 meters:

```
    <gp:location-info>
      <gml:Point srsName="urn:ogc:def:crs:EPSG::4979">
        <gml:pos>-43.5723 153.21760 35</gml:pos>
      </gml:Point>
    </gml:location-info>
```

WGS 84

WGS 84 defines three Coordinate Reference Systems. The first is a Cartesian system that is centered on the Earth's core. This system is rarely used outside of calculations. The second and third CRSs use more familiar latitude and longitude, or latitude, longitude, and altitude values, and both are based on the WGS 84 ellipsoid.

Altitude in WGS 84 is measured in meters above the WGS 84 ellipsoid. The WGS 84 ellipsoid is a slightly squashed sphere that is chosen for its mathematical properties as well as being a reasonable approximation for the shape of the earth. Since the Earth isn't perfectly round, altitude above the WGS 84 ellipsoid can differ from the actual altitude above mean sea level by up to 100 meters (this occurs near Sri Lanka).

In a PIDF-LO document, geodetic location information is encoded using the Geography Markup Language (GML) version 3.1.1 (see Reference 7). GML is a rich and complex XML grammar for describing geographic features and it can be used to encode a wide range of information. The limited set of GML for use within PIDF-LO is described in References 7 and 8.

One advantage of geodetic location information is its ability to represent uncertainty. Uncertainty arises when a location determination method is imprecise. For instance, a simple and widely used method for determining the location of a wireless device uses the location of the radio transmitter. However, the device is rarely, if ever, right next to the actual transmitter. In fact, it could be anywhere up to several kilometers away. A geodetic location can include this information by describing an area instead of a point—for example, a circular area centered on the transmitter, as in the following:

```
<gp:location-info>
  <gs:Circle srsName="urn:ogc:def:crs:EPSG::4326">
    <gml:pos>-43.5723 153.21760</gml:pos>
    <gml:radius uom="urn:ogc:def:uom:EPSG::9102">
      4432
    </gml:radius>
  </gs:Circle>
</gml:location-info>
```

A small set of shapes suitable for representing uncertainty are defined for PIDF-LO in Reference 8. These shapes include both two dimensional areas and three dimensional volumes. The majority of these shapes are currently used in cellular networks to accommodate uncertainty in wireless location technologies. These shapes are shown in Figure 2.7.

Point   The point type represents a location with no uncertainty or a point where uncertainty is not applicable. A point can be specified in either two or three dimensions,

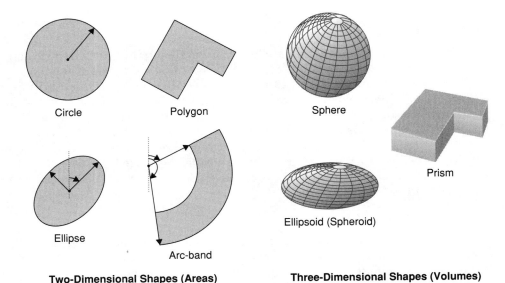

Circle Polygon Sphere

Prism

Ellipse

Arc-band

Ellipsoid (Spheroid)

Two-Dimensional Shapes (Areas)   **Three-Dimensional Shapes (Volumes)**

Figure 2.7 Shapes for the representation of uncertainty in PIDF-LO.

using a different Coordinate Reference System (CRS) code for each. In three dimensions, latitude, longitude, and altitude are specified, whereas in two dimensions the altitude is omitted:

```
<gp:location-info>
  <gml:Point srsName="urn:ogc:def:crs:EPSG::4326"
             xmlns:gml="http://www.opengis.net/gml">
        <gml:pos>-43.5723 153.21760</gml:pos>
  </gml:Point>
</gp:location-info>
```

The point is not really a shape, but is included because of its wide applicability.

Circle and Sphere Shapes   The circle and sphere shapes take a point and add an uncertainty radius. The circle is a two-dimensional version that does not include an altitude, implying that the uncertainty is unknown. A sphere, on the other hand, uses a three-dimensional point.

```
<gp:location-info>
  <gs:Sphere srsName="urn:ogc:def:crs:EPSG::4979">
        <gml:pos>42.5463 -73.2512 17</gml:pos>
        <gml:radius uom="urn:ogc:def:uom:EPSG::9001">
          850.24
        </gml:radius>
  </gs:Sphere>
</gp:location-info>
```

Circles and spheres are useful in cases where the target is known to be within a certain distance from a fixed point. This is particularly useful for wireless systems, where a transmitter location and maximum range is known.

Ellipse and Ellipsoid Shape   The ellipse and ellipsoid are more specialized versions of the circle and sphere that permit more accurate representation of an area of uncertainty.

The ellipse is represented as a center point, half the length of two axes (semi-major and semi-minor) and an angle of orientation. An ellipse is a two-dimensional shape, therefore it uses a two-dimensional point as a center point. Figure 2.8 shows these parameters and how they apply to the elliptical shape.

The following XML might be used to describe the ellipse shown in Figure 2.8:

```
<gp:location-info>
  <gs:Ellipse srsName="urn:ogc:def:crs:EPSG::4326">
    <gml:pos>42.5463 -73.2512</gml:pos>
    <gs:semiMajorAxis uom="urn:ogc:def:uom:EPSG::9001">
      12.75
    </gs:semiMajorAxis>
    <gs:semiMinorAxis uom="urn:ogc:def:uom:EPSG::9001">
      6.70
    </gs:semiMinorAxis>
    <gs:orientation uom="urn:ogc:def:uom:EPSG::9102">
      43.2
    </gs:orientation>
  </gs:Ellipse>
</gp:location-info>
```

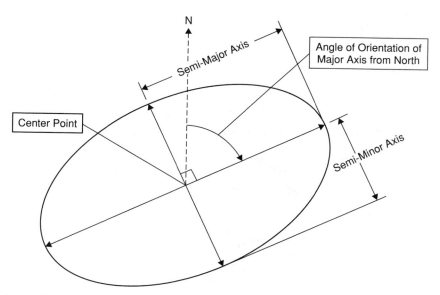

Figure 2.8 An ellipse is a two-dimensional conical section.

The ellipsoid is the three-dimensional version of the ellipse. The center point is specified with an altitude and a height value is added. The ellipsoid shown in Figure 2.9 shows how these parameters are used to describe a three-dimensional shape.

The XML for the ellipsoid is very similar to that for the ellipse:

```
<gp:location-info>
  <gs:Ellipsoid srsName="urn:ogc:def:crs:EPSG::4979">
    <gml:pos>42.3267 -73.0192 26.3</gml:pos>
    <gs:semiMajorAxis uom="urn:ogc:def:uom:EPSG::9001">
      7.7156
    </gs:semiMajorAxis>
    <gs:semiMinorAxis uom="urn:ogc:def:uom:EPSG::9001">
      3.31
    </gs:semiMinorAxis>
    <gs:verticalAxis uom="urn:ogc:def:uom:EPSG::9001">
      28.7
    </gs:verticalAxis>
    <gs:orientation uom="urn:ogc:def:uom:EPSG::9102">
      43.2
    </gs:orientation>
  </gs:Ellipse>
</gp:location-info>
```

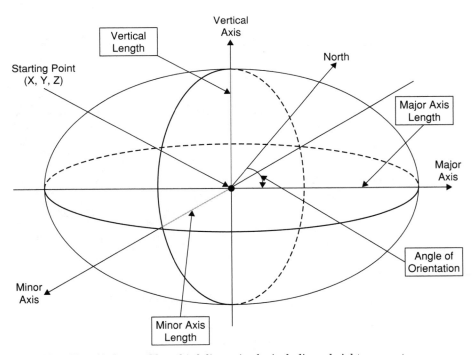

Figure 2.9 The ellipsoid shape adds a third dimension by including a height parameter.

Note that the orientation of the ellipsoid is limited to one value, which constrains the rotation to the horizontal plane. The major and minor axes always lie along the Earth's surface. Three angles would be necessary to provide full control over the orientation of the ellipse. This representation simplifies the specification of ellipsoids and improves interoperation with existing wireless standards, such as those used by 3GPP (see Reference 9) and OMA (see Reference 10).

An ellipse or ellipsoid shape is a common result of triangulation (or trilateration) and algorithms, so these shapes are useful for wireless and GPS location determination methods. An ellipse can also be used in place of a circle in wireless, when a directional antenna is used.

Polygon and Prism Shape   The polygon shape is described as a series of at least four points that define an enclosed area. The first and last points in this series must be the same.

Unlike most of the other two-dimensional shapes, polygons can be defined using either two- or three-dimensional points, but the three-dimensional points are usually reserved for when a polygon is used as the base of a prism.

```
<gp:location-info>
    <gml:Polygon srsName="urn:ogc:def:crs:EPSG::4326">
        <gml:exterior>
            <gml:LinearRing>
                <gml:posList>
                    42.556844  -73.248157
                    42.549631  -73.237283
                    42.539087  -73.240328
                    42.535756  -73.254242
                    42.556844  -73.248157
                </gml:posList>
            </gml:LinearRing>
        </gml:exterior>
    </gml:Polygon>
</gp:location-info>
```

Polygonal areas are very common in many applications, particularly those relating to civic structures like buildings and fenced allotments of land.

The prism type, shown in Figure 2.10, uses a polygon base and extends it to include a height value. A prism can be used to define a three-dimensional structure, which is very well suited to things like the floor of a building.

The XML for a prism encloses the polygon shape as follows:

```
<gp:location-info>
    <gs:Prism srsName="urn:ogc:def:crs:EPSG::4979">
        <gs:base>
            <gml:Polygon>
                <gml:exterior>
                    <gml:LinearRing>
                        <gml:posList>
```

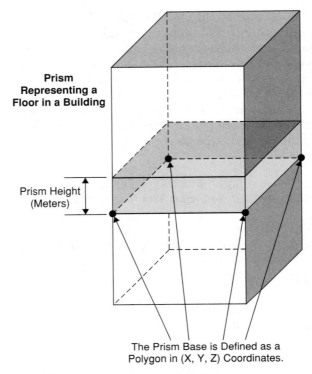

Figure 2.10   A prism is useful in representing a floor of a building.

```
          42.556844 -73.248157 36.6
          42.549631 -73.237283 36.6
          42.539087 -73.240328 36.6
          42.535756 -73.254242 36.6
          42.556844 -73.248157 36.6
        </gml:posList>
      </gml:LinearRing>
    </gml:exterior>
  </gml:Polygon>
</gs:base>
<gs:height uom="urn:ogc:def:uom:EPSG::9001">
  2.4
</gs:height>
</gs:Prism>
</gp:location-info>
```

The one catch with prisms is that the points of the polygon need to be specified in an anti-clockwise direction, otherwise the height is inverted. This is due to the way that the upwards direction is derived in three dimensions.

Arc-Band Shape   The arc-band shape is a shape type that is used in some wireless location determination methods where a target can be located a certain distance from a fixed point, usually a wireless transmitter. This shape results when a location can be determined to between two ranges and between two angles.

The arc band is a two-dimensional shape only, and is defined by a point, a minimum and maximum radius, a start angle, and an opening angle. Figure 2.11 shows how this shape is constructed.

The XML representation of an arc band might appear as follows:

```
<gp:location-info>
  <gs:ArcBand srsName="urn:ogc:def:crs:EPSG::4326">
    <gml:pos>
      42.5463 -73.2512
    </gml:pos>
    <gs:innerRadius uom="urn:ogc:def:uom:EPSG::9001">
      1661.55
    </gs:innerRadius>
    <gs:outerRadius uom="urn:ogc:def:uom:EPSG::9001">
      2215.4
    </gs:outerRadius>
    <gs:startAngle uom="urn:ogc:def:uom:EPSG::9102">
      266
```

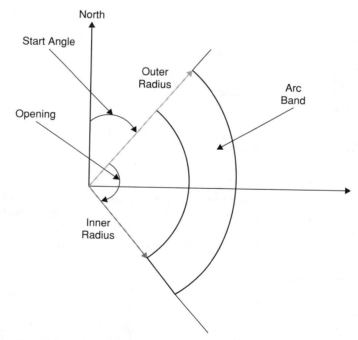

Figure 2.11   An arc-band shape and its defining parameters.

```
        </gs:startAngle>
        <gs:openingAngle uom="urn:ogc:def:uom:EPSG::9102">
          120
        </gs:openingAngle>
      </gs:ArcBand>
    </gp:location-info>
```

Civic Address Location Information   Civic addresses are locations that are suited for human use. A civic address includes countries, cities, suburbs, streets, house numbers and any information that might assist someone in finding a location. A civic address is not always helpful. Outside of towns and cities, geodetic coordinates are likely to be more precise. However, to a person, a civic address is almost always more useful than a set of coordinates.

The civic address format for PIDF-LO has been revised from its original form in Reference 5 to include a larger number of fields. The revised civic format is defined in (see Reference 11). The following example shows a few of the possible fields:

```
<gp:location-info>
  <ca:civicAddress xml:lang="en-AU"
     xmlns:ca="urn:ietf:params:xml:ns:pidf:geopriv10:civicAddr">
    <ca:country>AU</ca:country>
    <ca:A1>New South Wales</ca:A1>
    <ca:A3>Wollongong</ca:A3>
    <ca:A4>North Wollongong</ca:A4>
    <ca:RD>Flinders</ca:RD>
    <ca:STS>Street</ca:STS>
    <ca:RDBR>Campbell Street</ca:RDBR>
    <ca:LMK>Gilligan's Island</ca:LMK>
    <ca:LOC>Corner</ca:LOC>
    <ca:NAM>Video Rental Store</ca:NAM>
    <ca:PC>2500</ca:PC>
    <ca:ROOM>Westerns and Classics</ca:ROOM>
    <ca:PLC>store</ca:PLC>
  </ca:civicAddress>
</gp:location-info>
```

The exact form and content of civic addresses can vary greatly between countries, so the civic address format for PIDF-LO contains a large number of fields. A civic address always contains a country code, which is an ISO 3166 two-letter code, as is used for Internet domain names (for example, JP for Japan, AU for Australia, ES for Spain).

The country code is then followed by an ordered set of fields that have different meanings depending on the country. These fields start with A1, which is the largest national subdivision; A2 is a subdivision of A1; and likewise, A3 through to A6 are each subdivisions of the preceding division. These generic names allow for an interpretation that reflects the civic organization of an individual country. Table 2.1 shows several such country-specific interpretations, as specified in Reference 12.

TABLE 2.1   Ordered Civic Address Fields and Country-Specific Interpretations

Field	Canada (CA)	Japan (JP)	Korea (KO)	United States (US)
A1	province	metropolis (To, Fu) or prefecture (Ken, Do)	province (Do)	state
A2	county	city (Shi) or rural area (Gun)		county, parish, or borough
A3	city or town	ward (Ku) or village (Mura)	county (gun)	city or town
A4		town (Chou, Machi)	city or village (ri)	community place name
A5		city district (Choume)	urban district (gu)	
A6		block (Banchi, Ban)		

Beyond the A-elements, a civic address contains a large number of fields for the representation of streets, or thoroughfares. The thoroughfare fields are described in more detail in Reference 12.

The civic address format contains fields that can be used to specify a location quite precisely. Uncertainty does not apply to civic addresses in the same way that it does to geodetic locations. For a civic address, uncertainty is always implicit, and is expressed by excluding those fields that are not known.

The civic address format also includes fields that help a person find a particular location—for example, the LMK field can be used to describe a nearby landmark. A more complete list of acceptable fields can be found in Reference 13.

Because civic addresses are designed for people, they are often difficult for machines to interpret. A computer system that interprets a civic address needs to understand what each component of the address means for its application. This usually requires a database that includes information on towns, streets, and all of the civic address components. Take an application that displays a civic address on a map as an example: to determine where to plot the civic address, the application needs to convert it into coordinates, which requires an extensive database that includes data on every possible civic address. Applications that consume civic address information are either very limited in what they accept, in the region they cover or the allowed fields, or they have massive databases of information.

PIDF-LO Privacy Requests

PIDF-LO defines a number of fields that determine how a Location Recipient is expected to handle the data. In the PIDF-LO document, these requests are contained within the `usage-rules` element. These privacy-related fields include the following:

- **retransmission-allowed**   This field indicates whether the Location Recipient should or should not give the PIDF-LO to anyone else.

- **retention-expiry**   This time indicates a time beyond which the Location Recipient should not store the PIDF-LO.

- **ruleset-reference**   This URI refers to a document that describes a more complete set of rules which the Location Recipient is asked to respect.

- **note-well**   This note contains a request to a human viewer of the location information.

It is important to note that these fields are requests only; a dishonorable Location Recipient can easily disregard these requests if they so choose. This is why the rules that are provided to the Location Server are important—the Location Server can ensure that only trusted Location Recipients can receive a PIDF-LO document.

Controlling Access to Location Information

Up until the Location Server receives location information, it is within a controlled environment. It is reasonable to assume that most of this occurs within the access network and that appropriate measures are taken to ensure that the information can't be viewed by anyone. After the Location Server receives, or determines, location information, it is responsible for issuing PIDF-LO documents to Location Recipients.

An authorization policy records a user's prior consent. It is a document that states when, and how, information is provided. Most importantly, it includes who can receive location information. The Location Server decides which Location Recipients receive location information based on an authorization policy.

The GEOPRIV common-policy (see Reference 13) is an XML document format used for authorization policies. It is a typical authorization policy document, except that each rule includes a transformation. A transformation is essentially a special type of action that is used to modify information before it is sent to a particular recipient. Figure 2.12 shows how a common-policy document is structured.

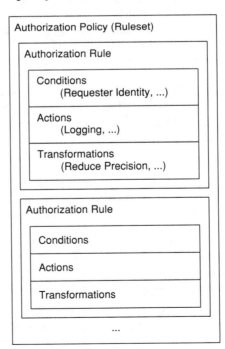

Figure 2.12 The structure of a common-policy document.

Authorization Policies

Authorization policies all share a common structure. An authorization policy is formed of a set of rules, each with a condition and an action, hence authorization policies are often called *rulesets*. The condition section outlines when the rule applies and the action is a list of instructions for the *policy enforcer*—the entity that is applying the rules.

The policy enforcer evaluates every rule in the authorization policy and provides an answer: either "allow" or "deny." If any rule contains conditions that can be met, the associated actions are performed and location information is sent. Conversely, if no rule contains conditions that can be met, a failure response is sent and the requester does not receive any information.

When it receives a request, the Location Server evaluates the common-policy document by performing the following procedure:

1. The conditions component of each rule in the document is evaluated. If the conditions for a rule pass, the rule is collected. At the end of this step, the Location Server will either have a set of rules that matched, or nothing. If no rules matched, then the request is denied.

2. The actions for all the rules that matched are combined into a single set of actions. The same is done for all the transformations. This helps prevent the same action or transformation from being performed twice because of redundant rules.

3. The Location Server performs all the resulting actions.

4. The Location Server takes the PIDF-LO and applies the transformations. Transformations alter the PIDF-LO for the Location Recipient, removing or obscuring different parts as the Rule Maker determines.

5. The PIDF-LO is provided to the Location Recipient.

The simplest and therefore, most common, form of authorization policy is a list of recipients that are allowed to receive location information. This is otherwise known as a *buddy list*, much like the lists maintained by instant message services. The following common-policy document includes a single rule that specifies a group of authorized recipients:

```xml
<?xml version="1.0"?>
<cp:ruleset xmlns:cp="urn:ietf:params:xml:ns:common-policy">
  <cp:rule id="ade146d0">
    <cp:conditions>
      <cp:identity>
        <cp:one id="sip:alice@example.com"/>
        <cp:one id="sip:bob@example.com"/>
```

```
            <cp:many domain="sample.net">
              <cp:except id="sip"carol@sample.net"/>
            </cp:many>
          </cp:identity>
        </cp:conditions>
        <cp:actions/>
        <cp:transformations/>
      </cp:rule>
    </cp:ruleset>
```

This authorization policy allows the SIP users, alice@example.com and bob@example.com, access to location information. It also allows everyone from sample.net, with the exception of carol@sample.net. The single rule in this authorization policy has no actions or transformations.

Common-policy is what is known as a policy framework. On its own, it specifies little more than conditions based on the identity of the recipient. Other specifications then define more conditions, actions, and transformations. The GEOPRIV-policy specification (see Reference 13) includes a range of conditions and transformations that are applicable to location information. Common-policy is also used as a basis for other specifications in other application areas.

Privacy for 3GPP Location Services

It is interesting to compare the model proposed by 3GPP in Reference 14 with the privacy model employed by GEOPRIV. The GEOPRIV model requires that the Location Server acquires the authorization policy and evaluates it. In contrast, 3GPP defines an enforcement node in their location architecture (see Reference 10), rather than a document. The architecture delegates the task of evaluating the policy to a separate node, called a Privacy Profile Register (PPR).

The PPR not only hosts a user's privacy policy, it also evaluates it. A network protocol, called the Privacy Checking Protocol (PCP) has been defined by the Open Mobile Alliance (OMA) in Reference 15 for querying the PPR. The GMLC gives the PPR sufficient information about the location request and then asks if the request should be permitted.

The most interesting feature of PCP is that it can be used before location information has been determined. In this situation, it can provide three answers: *allow*, *deny*, and *conditional*. A *conditional* response permits the location determination to continue, but it indicates that a second query to the PPR must occur after location information has been determined for a final evaluation. This feature avoids the cost of determining location in those situations when it isn't required. The PPR interaction is shown in Figure 2.13, with the conditional portion highlighted.

The 3GPP model does not preclude the use of an authorization policy, but the structure of this architecture removes the need for a standardized form.

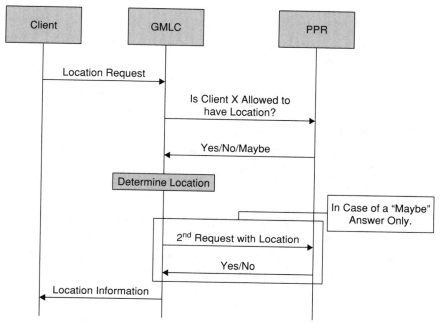

Figure 2.13 Delegating the evaluation of privacy rules in 3GPP.

Security for Privacy

Security is a very important part of protecting privacy. An authorization policy is only one aspect of ensuring privacy. Other aspects include authentication, data integrity and attribution, and encryption.

An authorization policy can require that Location Recipients are authenticated by the Location Server before they are given location information. In common-policy, this authentication is implicitly required, if an identity is specified, that identity must be verified by authentication. How that authentication is achieved is not specified, in order to permit the selection of the most appropriate method by the Location Server.

Data integrity and encryption are always employed by the Location Server for protocols that carry location information. Encryption ensures that the information can't be viewed by any but the intended recipient; data integrity ensures that it is not modified by an attacker for any reason. These measures are also employed in the access network before the location information reaches the Location Server for the same reasons.

The security aspects of this architecture in this area are many and varied. This section barely scratches the surface. It is not the intent of this book to cover security in detail. In the next chapter, the HELD protocol is described, with a little more detail on security, including the use of the Transport Layer Security (TLS) protocol, as well as a range of security controls.

References

1. Day, M., Rosenberg, J., and H. Sugano, *"A Model for Presence and Instant Messaging,"* RFC 2778, February 2000.

2. Sugano, H., Fujimoto, S., Klyne, G., Bateman, A., Carr, W., and J. Peterson, *"Presence Information Data Format (PIDF),"* RFC 3863, August 2004.

3. Cuellar, J., Morris, J., Mulligan, D., Peterson, J., and J. Polk, *"Geopriv Requirements,"* RFC 3693, February 2004.

4. Winterbottom, J., Peterson, J., and M. Thomson, *"Rationale for Location by Reference,"* (work in progress), January 2006.

5. Peterson, J., *"A Presence-based GEOPRIV Location Object Format,"* RFC 4119, December 2005.

6. Winterbottom, J., Tschofenig, H., and M. Thomson, *"GEOPRIV PIDF-LO Usage Clarification, Considerations and Recommendations,"* (work in progress), May 2006.

7. Cox, S., Daisey, P., Lake, R., Portele, C., and A. Whiteside, *"Geographic information—Geography Markup Language (GML),"* April 2004.

8. Thomson, M, *"Geodetic Shapes for the Representation of Uncertainty in PIDF-LO,"* (work in progress), May 2006.

9. 3GPP, *"Universal Geographical Area Description (GAD),"* January 2005.

10. OMA, *"Mobile Location Protocol (MLP) 3.2,"* MLS Enabler 1.0, November 2004.

11. Thomson, M. and J. Winterbottom, *"Revised Civic Location Format for PIDF-LO,"* (work in progress), April 2006.

12. Schulzrinne, H., *"Dynamic Host Configuration Protocol (DHCPv4 and DHCPv6) Option for Civic Addresses Configuration Information,"* (work in progress), January 2006.

13. Schulzrinne, H., *"A Document Format for Expressing Privacy Preferences,"* (work in progress), April 2006.

14. 3GPP, *"Functional stage 2 description of Location Services (LCS),"* January 2005.

15. OMA, *"Privacy Checking Protocol (PCP) 1.1,"* MLS Enabler 1.1 (work in progress), April 2006.

Location Determination and the Access Location Entity

This chapter describes how location is determined its, measurements, and their role in ascertaining location. A new network entity, the Access Location Entity (ALE), is defined to provide location measurements, and the Flexible LIS-ALE Protocol (FLAP) used for communication between the LIS and ALE is introduced.

This section provides background information necessary for the chapters that follow, which describe how location determination works within particular types of access networks.

Location Measurements

A location measurement is a datum that can be used to locate a device. A LIS uses measurements to determine location, and a location measurement can be used as a key into a location database, or as input to an algorithm.

A location measurement is a piece of data about a network that does not necessarily contain actual location information. Measurements of this sort hold no specific information about the network, thus the devices that provide location measurements do not need to know about location, only about the network characteristics that are important to their operation.

For instance, a wireless base station might report the strength of the radio signal it receives, or timing information—or a wired switch reports the port that traffic is routed to. Specific examples of measurements are shown in detail in Chapters 5, 6, and 7.

The Access Location Entity (ALE)

A centralized LIS provides a number of benefits, particularly for data management and client access, but its position in the network makes it unsuitable for acquiring network measurements. The Access Location Entity (ALE), by contrast, is located at the very edges of the network where it has access to the necessary information about network attachments.

The ALE is a generic label applied to a class of components that provide location measurements. The specific functions that an ALE provides depend on the type of access network, but they all have the common property of being responsible for providing location measurements. Figure 3.1 shows how ALEs from many different types of access networks can report to a single LIS. The LIS needs to understand each of these networks, but (as shown in Figure 3.1) the LIS hides this complexity by providing the same interface to its clients, irrespective of the type of access network.

The concept of a centralized LIS is important to the management of the location service. From an operational perspective, management of location data is the single most complex task involved in running a location service. Storing all location data in a central repository reduces the cost of operating the service. For this reason, the ALE should have as little configuration as possible so that it requires configuration changes less often.

The exact size and form of an ALE depends greatly on the access network. An ALE can be a standalone piece of overlay hardware that reads network packets to acquire measurements, or an ALE can simply be a small software component in a network device, like an Ethernet switch, that forwards preexisting data to the LIS.

Each ALE monitors a particular network sector at a particular network point. Multiple ALEs may be required at different points of the network to provide sufficient information to determine location. The LIS is responsible for collating information from multiple ALEs.

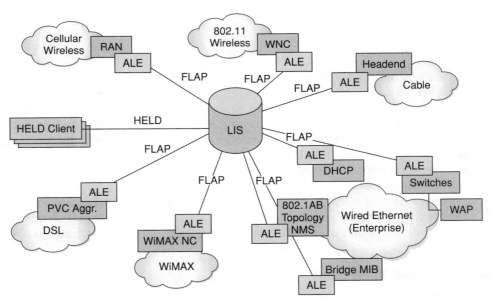

Figure 3.1 Different types of ALEs for different access networks.

Cost-effective ALEs will likely be overlay solutions in the short term. An overlay means that network operators can avoid the cost of purchasing or upgrading existing equipment by implementing custom-developed ALE functions that interwork with their existing equipment. However, future network equipment will need to contain an ALE function, where a small software or hardware addition provides the best engineering solution for purposes of size, performance, and functionality.

Evolution from Location in the Cellular RAN   The Radio Access Network (RAN) of a cellular network shares some of the properties of the IP access network. A server within this network performs functions similar to a LIS: a Serving Mobile Location Center (SMLC) for GSM, a Stand-Alone SMLC (SAS) for UMTS, or a Mobile Positioning Center (MPC + PDE) for IS-91/CDMA. Each of these network servers contains the necessary information and functionality to determine location information. Obviously, a cellular network uses different identifiers (MSISDN is common) to associate location information with a device rather than an IP network.

The ALE in the cellular network exists in a number of places, with the clearest analogue being the Location Measurement Unit (LMU). The LMU is analogous to an overlay ALE; additional ALE functions can also be found at other points of the network, including ALE functionality that's integrated into the BSC and BTS.

In order to determine the location of a device, the server relies on measurements from the RAN. This might be the identity of the cell site, or more detailed information about radio timing that is retrieved from the base stations within the network.

The division of responsibilities in location determination between the LIS and ALE in the IP location architecture are a clear formalization of the cellular model. The ALE is given a distinct role in this model, which further clarifies the distinction between location and other functions in the network. Figure 3.2 shows how the location determination function of a GSM SMLC talks to ALEs in the access network.

The LIS and ALE have clearly defined generic roles in the cellular architecture, which has lead to a few variations in the different network architectures. The LIS function is defined separately as a subtly different network node for each network type (SMLC, SAS, PDE).

Using Measurements

Location measurements can be thought of as a series of clues that can be matched to some specific data to form a chain. At the start of this chain is a device identifier (an IP address), and at the other end is a location. Location measurements form some of the links of this chain, while other links are in a database in the LIS, or are algorithms applied by the LIS. Figure 3.3 shows how this chain is formed for an Ethernet network, using one of the determination technologies discussed in Chapter 5. The IP address is linked to a MAC address by the DHCP lease query; MAC is matched to a switch and port by a Bridge MIB ALE; and the switch and port are linked to location by an entry in the LIS Database.

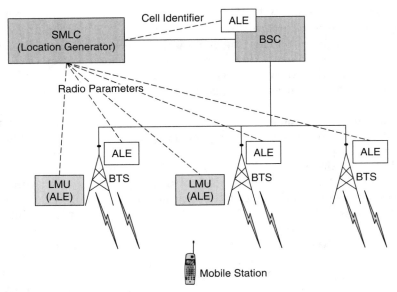

Figure 3.2   ALEs in the GSM access network (GERAN).

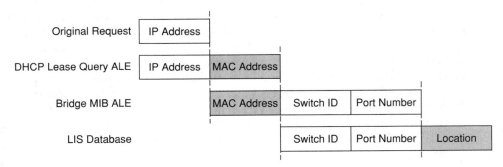

Figure 3.3   Location measurements are combined with a database to determine location.

Location measurements are usually pushed from the ALE to the LIS when a change is detected in the network. The LIS is then able to update location information dynamically in response to these changes. The subscription model discussed in Chapter 2 is enabled by dynamic updates.

The following example demonstrates how a location might be determined in a generic wired network. This example is simplified to demonstrate how location measurements are used; more thorough examples with real network architectures can be found in later chapters.

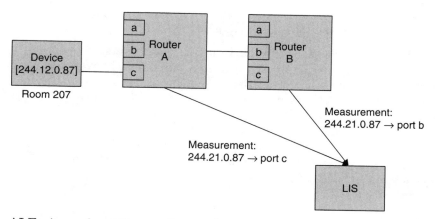

Measurement:
244.21.0.87 → port b

Measurement:
244.21.0.87 → port c

ALEs in each of the routing nodes provide the LIS with notifications when the network state changes. This information can be used together with information in a database to form a chain. The chain can be formed when location measurements are received from the ALEs; alternatively, the measurements can be stored and the chain formed on demand. In the following example, location measurements are stored and the location is generated when a request for the location of an IP address is submitted.

1. The LIS determines the starting point of the measurement process by finding a location measurement that includes the given IP address. A stored location measurement from *Router B* indicates that it can route messages for that IP address.

2. The LIS then uses the location measurement from Router B, which links the IP address to a port on the switch: *Router B, port b*.

3. The LIS database is then used to determine that "Router B, port b" leads to *Router A*.

4. A location measurement from Router A links the IP address to *Router A, port c*.

5. The LIS database determines that the cable plugged into port c on Router A leads to a network socket in *Room 207*.

The preceding example assumes dynamic updates from ALEs; however, the process could also use on-demand location measurements. If the LIS requests location measurements when it needs them, the process of location determination is very similar, except that the first step could require a search to determine where the chain begins. The FLAP protocol provides options for both dynamic and on-demand location measurements.

The Flexible LIS-ALE Protocol (FLAP)

The Flexible LIS-ALE Protocol (FLAP) was designed to provide a framework for reporting location measurements.

The Blocks Extensible Exchange Protocol

The BEEP protocol, despite its unfortunate name, represents years of protocol design. The stated goals for BEEP were to provide a framework for connection-oriented, asynchronous protocols that support the request and response-style exchanges. BEEP uses the "best" of the IETF standards offerings (TCP, TLS, SASL, and MIME) to achieve those goals.

Different uses of BEEP are separated into channels, each of which runs independently of the others, permitting multiple sessions within the one TCP connection. Each channel uses a single BEEP *profile*, which is a specific application usage. FLAP is defined as a BEEP profile.

It is useful to realize that at any point along the location determination chain, one piece of information is known and the other is required. FLAP names the known component *terminal* information—that is, the information identifies a particular terminal. The unknown part relates to how the terminal accesses the network. This is called *access* information. The ALE is responsible for providing access information when given terminal information.

For example, if an ALE in an Ethernet switch is queried, it can provide a link between a MAC address and/or IP address (terminal information) and a switch and port (access information).

The distinction between terminal and access information is a simplification that can be thought of as a key-value pair. The link between these values is provided by the ALE. FLAP provides a framework for reporting this link between terminal and access information.

FLAP is defined as a BEEP profile (see References 1 and 2). BEEP is a protocol framework that provides bidirectional, asynchronous communication between two entities—in this case, a LIS and ALE. BEEP is based on TCP, with support for Transport Layer Security (TLS) where additional security is required.

In the spirit of keeping all configuration data centralized, the LIS initiates the BEEP connection. The only configuration that may be required at the ALE is that which permits the authentication of the LIS. Using the Pre-Shared Key Ciphersuites for Transport Layer Security (TLS) (see Reference 3) means that all maintenance effort is kept at the LIS.

Extensions

FLAP uses XML-formatted messages so that it can be easily extended to accommodate different access network technologies. The base specification does not proscribe what specific terminal and access information will look like, except to provide start and end times for access information. Terminal and access elements provide a generic container that can be redefined depending on the access network technology. A technology extension defines what information is required for each of the terminal and access elements for that technology.

Vendor extensions are added on top of technology extensions and allow for enhancements to FLAP that are specific to particular ALEs or networks. Vendor extensions can be used for proprietary methods of improving the speed, accuracy, or security of location determination.

Both technology and vendor extensions are distinguished using *namespaces* for XML. Each extension is uniquely identified by a URN that is recognized by the LIS. The following message uses the Ethernet extension with additional vendor extension parameters:

```
<ntfy xsi:type="enet:ntfy"
      xmlns:vnd1="http://www.example.com/flap/terminal/hw"
      xmlns:vnd2="http://www.example.com/flap/access/skew">
  <enet:terminal
    <ip>192.168.0.1</ip>
    <enet:hwaddr>12:34:56:78:90:ab</enet:hwaddr>
    <vnd1:hw revision="1.2"/>
  </enet:terminal>
  <enet:access time="2005-04-14T10:51:23.000+10:00">
    <enet:switch><ip>192.168.0.1</ip></enet:switch>
    <enet:port>4</enet:port>
    <vnd2:skew>0.5127</vnd2:skew>
  </enet:access>
</ntfy>
```

The preceding example shows a notification from an Ethernet ALE. A terminal is identified by its IP and MAC address, along with a vendor extension that identifies a hardware revision. Measurement information includes a time, along with identification of the switch by IP address and the port of attachment. A second vendor extension, named "skew" carries the value 0.5127.

FLAP Messages

FLAP allows different ALE types to report location measurements as best suits them. The five FLAP message types can be used to convey location measurements both asynchronously and synchronously.

Notification   The recommended approach is to have an ALE report location measurements as network circumstances change. The Notification message can be generated by the ALE when it detects a terminal entering the network, a terminal moving within the network, or a terminal leaving the network. Figure 3.4 shows the standard usage for a Notification message.

Notification messages use the BEEP MSG/RPY exchange; such notifications are acknowledged with an empty RPY frame.

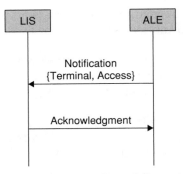

Figure 3.4   An ALE sends a Notification message to indicate a change in the network.

The following shows a BEEP frame that contains a simple request. This request comes from an ALE that provides measurements from a DHCP server:

```
MSG 1 0 . 406 395
Content-Type: application/xml

<ntfy xsi:type="dhcp:ntfy">
  <dhcp:terminal>
    <ip>192.168.2.10</ip>
    <dhcp:hwaddr>01020304050a</dhcp:hwaddr>
  </dhcp:terminal>
  <dhcp:access time="2005-04-15T14:02:25.160+10:00"
               expires="2005-04-15T16:02:25.160+10:00">
    <dhcp:relay>192.168.2.1</dhcp:relay>
    <dhcp:circuit-id>03</dhcp:circuit-id>
  </dhcp:access>
</ntfy>
END
```

The notification includes information about the terminal along with DHCP relay (see Reference 4) information that the LIS can use to locate the terminal. The LIS acknowledges this notification with the following empty BEEP frame:

```
RPY 1 0 . 63 0
END
```

Resynchronization   Network or system outages are inevitable in virtually any system, particularly one that is intended for continuous usage. Resynchronization enhances the robustness and reliability of LIS and ALE communications by providing the LIS with a means to quickly determine the current state of the ALE at startup time and after an outage.

Resynchronization uses the BEEP MSG/ANS exchange, which allows for multiple responses to a single request. A Resynchronization Request from a LIS can result in any number of Resynchronization Response messages being sent by the ALE. Each Resynchronization Response contains information about a single terminal and network attachment. Figure 3.5 shows the Resynchronization procedure.

A Resynchronization procedure can be used in two ways: a full Resynchronization is used at startup time, or after a long outage; and a partial Resynchronization can be used for short outages caused by a transitory fault, or a communications error.

When a LIS starts, it will probably not have any useful information about the state of the network. The full Resynchronization procedure provides the current state of all network attachments that the ALE can monitor.

After a short outage in either the LIS or the LIS to ALE link, the LIS can use the partial (or "since") Resynchronization procedure to request all notifications that it might have missed. The partial Resynchronization Request includes a start time, which triggers different behavior at the ALE.

The partial Resynchronization differs from a full Resynchronization because the LIS already has some information about the state of the network—the ALE only needs to provide the changes that have occurred since the indicated time. In effect, the ALE needs to send all the Notification messages it would have sent during the request period. This usage differs because responses to this sort of request include terminals leaving the network sector.

Partial Resynchronization is an optimization that reduces the impact of temporary outages. If this mode is not supported, the LIS can purge its current state and use the full Resynchronization.

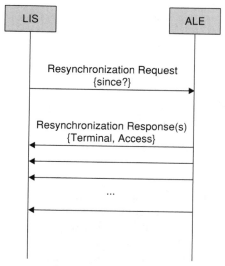

Figure 3.5   A Resynchronization Request triggers multiple Resynchronization Responses.

The following Resynchronization message is sent by the LIS. The `since` attribute indicates to the ALE that this is a partial Resynchronization starting at the given time.

```
MSG 1 0 . 0 108
Content-Type: application/xml

<sync since="2005-04-15T14:51:21.000+10:00"
      xsi:type="dhcp:sync"/>
END
```

The ALE responds to this request by providing a number of responses, each contained in a separate BEEP frame, followed by a NUL frame:

```
ANS 1 0 . 0 411
Content-Type: application/xml

<syncr result="200" xsi:type="dhcp:syncr">
  <dhcp:terminal>
    <ip>192.168.2.11</ip>
    <dhcp:hwaddr>01020304050b</dhcp:hwaddr>
  </dhcp:terminal>
  <dhcp:access time="2005-04-15T15:01:10.991+10:00"
               expires="2005-04-15T17:01:10.991+10:00">
    <dhcp:relay>192.168.2.1</dhcp:relay>
    <dhcp:circuit-id>02</dhcp:circuit-id>
  </dhcp:access>
</syncr>
END
ANS 1 0 . 411 253
Content-Type: application/xml

<syncr result="201" xsi:type="dhcp:syncr">
  <dhcp:terminal>
    <ip>192.168.2.12</ip>
    <dhcp:hwaddr>01020304050c</dhcp:hwaddr>
  </dhcp:terminal>
  <dhcp:access time="2005-04-15T15:17:57.521+10:00"/>
</syncr>
END
NUL 1 0 . 664 0
END
```

The absence of access information indicates that the terminal left the network, while the NUL frame indicates the end of the sequence of results.

These messages require that the ALE perform tasks beyond just reporting changes in the network. In order to support these messages, the ALE needs to maintain certain information. For the first usage, the full resynchronization, the ALE needs to maintain an image of the current state of the network sector.

The second usage, partial resynchronization, requires that the ALE also remember the most recent Notification messages it has sent, or might have sent. The ALE effectively buffers messages for the period of time that it intends to provide a partial resynchronization for; the number of messages, and the total time permitted, is limited by how much storage there is available for this feature. If an ALE is unable to provide sufficient history for a partial resynchronization, this is indicated to the LIS. The LIS then purges its existing state for that ALE and attempts a full resynchronization.

Lightweight ALE implementations can avoid storing any additional information, providing that they support the Access Query, which can be used by the LIS to build an image of state. However, this option increases the impact of an outage by requiring more messaging to recover state after the outage.

Access Query   The Access Query is a synchronous query that is provided to deal with limitations of ALE implementations. A direct request to the ALE can be used as a check, or to provide more recent information. A LIS can asynchronously probe for an ALE measurement at the moment it needs to do location determination.

The Access Query exchange is useful where the ALE doesn't support a reporting capability, or it only has a limited reporting capability. It is also useful where the access network is highly dynamic since location measurements in highly mobile networks can change too dynamically for notification methods to be practical. For example, radio signal strength can change constantly, even when the target is stationary. One consequence of Access Query is that in a network with multiple ALEs, without some form of notification, the LIS might have to query several ALEs before it can find the correct one.

The Access Query is sent by the LIS, and includes terminal information only. The ALE provides access information for that terminal in the response, as shown in Figure 3.6.

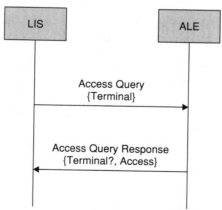

Figure 3.6   An Access Query is the synchronous method for retrieving ALE data.

The following Access Query includes information about a particular terminal:

```
MSG 1 0 . 63 176
Content-Type: application/xml

<aq xsi:type="dhcp:aq">
  <dhcp:terminal>
    <ip>192.168.2.10</ip>
    <dhcp:hwaddr>01020304050a</dhcp:hwaddr>
  </dhcp:terminal>
</aq>
END
```

The response to this message does not necessarily contain any terminal information:

```
RPY 1 0 . 801 294
Content-Type: application/xml

<aqr result="200" xsi:type="dhcp:aqr">
  <dhcp:access time="2005-04-15T14:02:25.160+10:00"
             expires="2005-04-15T16:02:25.160+10:00">
    <dhcp:relay>192.168.2.1</dhcp:relay>
    <dhcp:circuit-id>03</dhcp:circuit-id>
  </dhcp:access>
</aqr>
END
```

The Access Query procedure can be used in a number of ways to address the shortcomings of ALEs with limited functionality. Therefore, an Access Query can be used to check that a terminal is still attached to a network sector.

If an ALE does not generate Notification messages, an Access Query can be used to retrieve measurements. The LIS can poll for information from the ALE, or request information on demand. Using Access Query in this fashion can consume a large amount of network resources, therefore it isn't recommended.

LIS to ALE Notifications   In some cases, the LIS might detect that a particular terminal has moved out of the network sector monitored by an ALE before the ALE detects this change. This might be reported to the LIS by another ALE. For instance, DHCP is not particularly good at recognizing that a terminal has left the network. DHCP clients are not obliged to notify the server when they leave the network, so many do not.

In this case, a LIS-to-ALE, or downstream, Notification message can be sent to the ALE. This message is optional, and is provided as a courtesy to the ALE. The ALE can use this message as a trigger to release any resources it has committed in monitoring that terminal and to update any state it maintains. The downstream notification also prevents the ALE from erroneously reporting the presence of the terminal.

Acquiring Measurements from the Target/Device

The access network is one source of location measurements. However, the Target device can, in some circumstances, provide information that can assist in the determination of location. This is already seen in some cellular networks, where a cellular telephone provides measurement information to the network-based server.

The FLAP protocol is designed for network-based measurements and as such is not suited to carrying messages from the device. HELD, on the other hand, establishes a session between the Target and a LIS, which makes it a good candidate for carrying measurements from the device. HELD contains extension points that permit the inclusion of location measurements in a request message. The exact contents of any location measurements depend on the type of access network and the capabilities of the device.

At the time of writing, location measurements are not included in HELD messages, except in LIS-to-LIS interactions where one LIS acts on behalf of a device. However, there are a number of cases where a device could provide measurements.

Device-Assisted A-GNSS or A-GPS

Global Navigation Satellite System (GNSS) location determination methods can provide extremely good precision in location estimates, with results that are typically accurate to within meters of the actual location of the device. The United States Global Position System (GPS) is the predominant GNSS, which provides high precision location determination.

Device-assisted Assisted-GNSS (A-GNSS) is a prime example of a device providing location measurements to a server. Unlike autonomous GNSS, where the device calculates its own location, a device using device-assisted A-GNSS provides pseudorange measurements to the server. The server then uses knowledge about the position of GNSS satellites and a set of algorithms to determine the location of the device.

Other Device-Based Methods

In addition to GNSS measurements, a device can also report network-based measurements. For instance, a device can provide GSM radio information, such as the serving cell identifier, and the Timing Advance and Network Measurement Report values. The LIS takes these location measurements and combines them with data from a cell database and specialized algorithms to determine a location estimate.

Other options include the use of Radio Frequency Identifier (RFID) beacons, where the device sends the identity of nearby beacons to the server, which uses a database of known beacon locations to pinpoint the device. Device-based location determination and location measurements are explained in more detail in Chapter 9 of this book.

Hybrid Location Determination

Hybrid location determination methods are those that combine multiple sources of location measurements to estimate location. A hybrid method can address limitations that might exist where only one method is employed, increasing the probability that location information can be used. This is true for both network- and device-based location determination methods.

For instance, the trilateration used for GPS requires four satellite pseudoranges for an accurate estimate; a hybrid method can combine a smaller set of pseudoranges with other information to determine location.

References

1. Rose, M. *"The Blocks Extensible Exchange Protocol Core"* RFC 3080, March 2001 (TXT, HTML, XML).
2. Rose, M. *"Mapping the BEEP Core onto TCP"* RFC 3081, March 2001.
3. Eronen, P. and Tschofenig, H., *"Pre-Shared Key Ciphersuites for Transport Layer Security (TLS),"* RFC 4279, December 2005.
4. Patrick, M., *"D4CP Relay Agent Information Option,"* RFC 3046, January 2001.

The LIS, Location Acquisition, and the HELD Protocol

The previous chapter dealt with the aspects of taking and providing network measurements inside the access network. It described the abstraction of the ALE and its role in taking network measurements and passing them to the Location Information Server (LIS) using FLAP. In this chapter, we examine the LIS in more detail. We describe the various LIS interfaces, the different types of LIS, and we discuss in some detail the HELD protocol and how it accommodates the location acquisition needs of various types of users.

The Location Information Server

The Location Information Server (LIS) combines the functions of location determination and location distribution. The IETF GEOPRIV location architecture described in Reference 1, at the end of the chapter, describes two key functions, location determination performed by a location generator (LG), and location distribution performed by a location server (LS). These same two functions occur in the NENA-i2 and -i3 architectures but are combined into a single server called the LIS. Figure 4.1 shows how these two architectural views come together. For the remainder of this chapter, we shall restrict our terminology of this functionality to the term *LIS*.

The Location Information Server (LIS) is at the heart of the IP location architecture, and has the following key responsibilities:

- Determining the location of an IP device inside its domain
- Delivering location information to a Location Recipient
- Asserting that the location provided by an IP device inside its domain is reasonable
- Ensuring location dependability
- Protecting the privacy of the Target to which the location is attributed

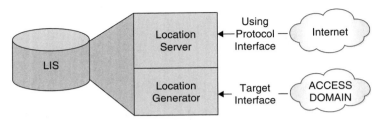

Figure 4.1   LIS to GEOPRIV mapping.

While a LIS may implement all of these functions, it is not required for it to do so. A LIS is categorized according to which of these functions it can perform (the various LIS types are described in later sections of this chapter).

The LIS determines the location of devices in the network through the use of network measurements that it obtains from ALEs distributed throughout the access network. ALEs were described in detail in Chapter 3. The ALE measurements and their use in location determination are access technology-specific.

The LIS provides a common access interface for obtaining location information that hides the access-specific aspects of the network, ensuring that location can be requested in the same manner regardless of the access medium. So the LIS looks and behaves like any other Internet-based service from a user's perspective.

The location of a device needs to be treated with a degree of confidentiality, and must not be handed out to just any requesting party. Location must only be made available to requesting parties that satisfy strict authentication and authorization policies. How authentication and authorization policies are enforced is a matter of application, and is strongly dependent on the network configuration and the intended use. Public access networks will likely demand very strong applications of these policies to protect against fraud and maintain the privacy of the network's users. Private networks have more flexibility as to the level of authentication and authorization they require before making location information available. The application of these policies is discussed in Chapter 10.

Location Distribution to the Target

One of the primary roles of the LIS is distributing location information to the Target. This can occur in one of two ways: as a literal location and/or as a location reference. A literal location is the actual location of the Target at the time of the request, and is distributed in the form of a PIDF-LO. This is also referred to as *location by-value* in the common vernacular. A location reference is, as the name suggests, a reference or pointer to a place from which a literal location can be retrieved. The differences were described briefly in Chapter 2, but will be reiterated and described in more detail here as they are important to the operation of a LIS and form key functionality provided by HELD.

Location By-Value   The location by-value model centers on the premise that the Target is also the owner and safe-keeper of its own location. The Target retrieves a literal location (PIDF-LO) from the LIS and decides when, and to whom, to provide it (see Figure 4.2).

Location By-Reference   Location by-reference requires the Target to employ a LIS to manage the dissemination of its location to authorized Location Recipients (see Figure 4.3). The Target requests a location reference from the LIS, which it subsequently makes available to would-be Location Recipients. Location Recipients wishing to know the location of the Target can use the location reference to retrieve the Target's location from the LIS. Unauthorized access to the Target's location is secured by the Target providing a set of access rules to the LIS, and the LIS requiring all querying nodes to satisfy these rules.

Justification for Location By-Reference   Reference 2 provides a range of comparisons and benefits for both the location by-reference and the location by-value model. The more salient points will be described here.

The use of a location reference permits location request decoupling between the Location Recipient, Target, and the LIS by permitting the Location Recipient to request the Target's location directly from the LIS as is required, and in the form that is required.

Figure 4.2   The location by-value model.

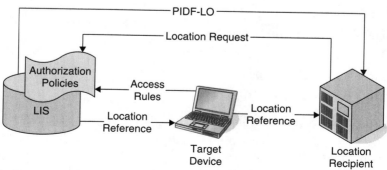

Figure 4.3   The location by-reference model.

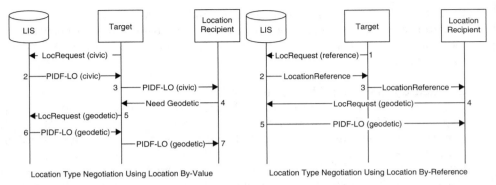

Figure 4.4 Location type negotiations.

There is no need to adapt each Target-to-Recipient protocol to support location request-response semantics.

Providing a literal location is often faster than providing a location reference since location by-value avoids the additional steps of first requesting and providing a reference. Where the recipient requires location in a form other than that was provided by the Target, and location format negotiations need to occur, a location reference can quickly become more optimal, as shown in Figure 4.4. Where location updates are frequently required by the Location Recipient, a location reference can reduce message overheads by 50 percent or more, making it a more suitable mechanism for providing the location of mobile devices.

The LIS Interfaces

The LIS has six basic interfaces. They are shown in the following list and depicted in Figure 4.5. These interfaces are described in more detail in the following subsections.

- The Measurement or ALE Interface
- The Target Interface
- The Third-Party Interface
- The Trusted-Party Query Interface
- The Call-back Interface
- The Provisioning Interface

The Measurement Interface   The Measurement Interface is used by the LIS to communicate with the ALEs residing in the access network. This interface is generally on a restricted access network similar to SNMP management traffic in large enterprise IP networks to ensure the integrity and authenticity of the measurements provided. The details of this interface were described in Chapter 3. Location determination techniques for specific types of access networks will be addressed in subsequent chapters.

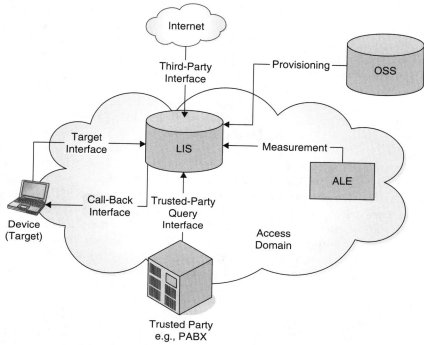

Figure 4.5   Basic LIS interfaces.

The Target Interface   The Target Interface is the interface used by client-devices inside the access domain to talk to the LIS. Using this interface, a Target may request its location or a reference to its location. Targets identify themselves to the LIS prior to, or as part of, making their requests for location. The Target Interface is designed to support a device requesting its own location. It is for this reason that device identity assertions to the LIS are implicit and included in routing information, such as IP and MAC addresses. As an "IP location" service, the IP address of the device is the key piece of identification information. Indeed, on the Target Interface, the LIS will only send responses back to that IP address. In the general query mode, this "return routability" assumption is used to ensure the confidentiality of the location information related to the device at that IP address.

In addition to providing support for Target location requests, the Target Interface supports the Target providing ancillary data about itself to the LIS. Such ancillary data include information like third-party authorization policies and call-back addresses. Third-party authorization policies dictate which third-parties may obtain the Target's location as described in the next section.

The Third-Party Interface   The Third-Party Interface allows nodes to request location information from the LIS for Targets other than themselves. The requesting nodes may be inside or outside the access domain of the LIS. Location requests are made using a location reference. The location reference is a unique identifier that is assigned by the LIS for a particular Target. This reference enables the LIS to identify and locate the Target. The location reference is provided by the LIS to the Target on request over the Target Interface, and the Target is free to distribute the reference to any third party whom they trust. The Third-Party Interface requires the LIS to authenticate requesting parties, and subsequently check authorization policies to ensure that information is only made available to nodes allowed to have it. Target authorization policies are provided to the LIS via the Target Interface.

The Trusted-Party Query Interface   The Trusted-Party Query Interface provides a means for trusted nodes within the access network to request location on behalf of a Target, without the Target explicitly providing the query node with a location reference, as is the case with the Third-Party Interface. Elements querying the LIS in this manner should be authenticated. The need for this interface arises in several situations which include, but are not limited to, support for legacy nonlocation-capable devices, and LIS-to-LIS communications that are necessary where location data are distributed across two or more LISes. These scenarios are described in detail in subsequent chapters.

The Call-Back Interface   The Call-Back Interface operates inside the access network between the LIS and the Target and provides a means for a Target to advertise its location determination and measurement capabilities to the LIS. The Call-Back Interface also provides a mechanism by which the LIS can contact the Target to make use of these capabilities. Details on how HELD supports this interface are discussed in Chapter 9.

The Provisioning Interface   The Provisioning Interface is used to provide network configuration and management data to the LIS so that it has a context in which ALE network measurements can be mapped to physical locations. As indicated in Chapter 3, this provisioning data may be used by computational algorithms or may provide direct associations between circuits and physical locations. The provisioning interface is specific to an individual LIS and access network; therefore, it is highly proprietary.

The HELD Protocol and Semantics

The HTTP Enabled Location Delivery (HELD) protocol (see Reference 3) is a location acquisition protocol designed specifically to meet the requirements for the LIS Target Interface, Third-Party Interface, Trusted-Party Query Interface, and Call-Back Interface. It is a web services protocol with the schema specification provided in Appendix B and protocol bindings provided in Appendix D. This section focuses on the HTTP binding as this is the recommended implementation for Devices.

When using the HTTP binding with the HELD protocol, connectivity between the Target and the LIS is done using secure HTTP (https). The LIS is identified by an

HTTP URL, which for now will be assumed to be known to the Device. The LIS must identify itself to a connecting Target using an X.509 server-side certificate asserted for the access domain in which the Target and LIS reside. The following sections explain the HELD protocol in detail. Subsequent chapters will look at how these fundamentals can be applied to real network deployments to provide access-independent location acquisition.

HELD is designed to provide basic location acquisition functionality but in a manner that is easily extensible. This extensibility is possible because of the way in which HELD messages have been structured to allow additional identifiers and data to be passed from the client to the LIS. Additional identifiers and parameters are used depending on applications and network configurations; references to several HELD extensions are made throughout the remainder of the book.

Target Location Acquisition

The HELD protocol supports first and foremost a Target requesting its own location from a LIS using the previously defined Target Interface. The HELD protocol makes the assumption that location is required and will be used in the form of a PIDF-LO. This means that an End-Point can use the location object returned to it from the LIS and need not craft a PIDF-LO object based on certain pieces of data, as is the case with DHCP and LLDP-MED acquisition methods.

Basic Location Request   The most basic location request supported by the HELD proto-col is the unqualified location request, where a Target is asking for any and all location information that the LIS may have on a Target's whereabouts (see Figure 4.6).

The HELD protocol XML for this request would be

```
<locationRequest xmlns="http://sitacs.uow.edu.au/ns/location/held"/>
```

The HTTP binding for the HELD protocol has been designed specifically so that it can perform this type of requesting using a simple HTTP GET to the provided LIS URL.

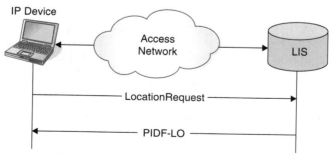

Figure 4.6   An unqualified location request.

The resulting PIDF-LO may contain one or more location elements depending on what physical location information the LIS is able to determine. The LIS must ensure that rules outlined in Reference 4 are adhered to in order to ensure that the location information can be correctly interpreted by subsequent users of this information.

Qualified Location Requests   The unqualified location request is certainly easy to implement, but it only provides what the LIS wants to give, which may not be specifically what the user is after. The HELD protocol supports the notion of a qualified location request, which allows the user to specify what type of location information they are interested in (see Figure 4.7).

There are five types of locations that a user can ask for: any, geodetic, civic, jurisdictionalCivic, and postalCivic. These types are described in detail in the following subsections. A HELD protocol request asking for geodetic location, a jurisdictionalCivic address, and a postalCivic address would look something like:

```
<locationRequest xmlns="http://sitacs.uow.edu.au/ns/location/held">
    <locationType>
        geodetic
        jurisdictionalCivic
        postalCivic
    </locationType>
</locationRequest>
```

It should be noted that a user can request a location in any one, or all, of the above formats at the same time and that the LIS should construct a PIDF-LO such that the location types are in the same order in which they were requested.

The any Location Type   any, as the name suggests, doesn't really provide any qualification at all. It simply says to the LIS that the Target is interested in any location

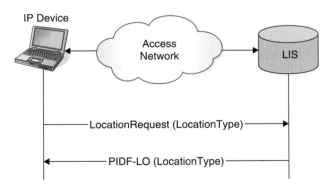

Figure 4.7   A qualified location request.

information that the LIS can provide on the Target's whereabouts. Locations returned by the LIS when the `any` qualifier is specified must include a location that is suitable for routing emergency calls in the area local to the end-point. Other locations may also be returned, but the emergency location is mandatory. Since a LIS covers the jurisdiction of interest, it may be assumed that the LIS can provide a location that is in the correct form for that jurisdiction.

The geodetic Location Type   `geodetic` is the way that the Target indicates to the LIS that it is interested in a location specified using latitude and longitude coordinates. The GeoShape specification (see Reference 5) leverages and extends the GML3.1.1 specification to describe the legal shapes that can be used to define the location of a Target in geodetic terms within a PIDF-LO. The HELD protocol mandates that any returned geodetic location must conform to the GeoShape specification. The shapes defined in the GeoShape specification are described in Chapter 2.

Different shape types generally have their origins in different determination techniques, so the type returned will likely be based on how the LIS determined the location of the Target. Choice of shape type should be made with care, in particular when being used for emergency services applications where all shape types may not be considered acceptable. For example, out of the eight shape types defined in GeoShape, only `Point`, `Circle`, and `Sphere` would be usable with the North American i2 specification (see Reference 6) [NENA-i2] due to restrictions imposed over the V-E2 interface defined in the specification. Extreme care needs to be taken if converting from one shape type to another so as not to introduce unnecessarily large errors in the resulting location.

The civic Location Type   The `civic` type is specified by the Target when they want a street address; they are not really interested in whether it is a postal or some sort of jurisdictional address. In response to this request, the LIS should provide the civic address (or addresses, if there are more than one) that it has for the Target.

The jurisdictionalCivic Location Type   A `jurisdictionalCivic` address is the address of the Target formed in such a way that it identifies not only the premises in which the Target is located, but also specifies the lowest level of governmental community in whose jurisdiction the Target is located. Often, this will be the normal street address, but in some situations it is not. Emergency service dispatch in the United States, for example, is done to a jurisdictional address, providing a standard postal street address instead may result in an emergency call not being routed correctly, or services being dispatched to the wrong location.

When civic address information is required for emergency services, the Target should request a `jurisdictionalCivic` location. If the Target requests the general `civic` location type and a `jurisdictionalCivic` type in the same request, then the LIS should ignore the request for the general `civic` type and only provide `jurisdictionalCivic` information.

When requesting a `jurisdictionalCivic` location type the default behavior of the LIS is to try and satisfy this request, but if it can't, it may just return the location in any form including `geodetic`.

The postalCivic Location Type   The `postalCivic` address is the address that one might use to send a letter or parcel to the Target. Often, this will be the same as the jurisdictional address, but as was described previously, this is not always the case. A postal address may not be appropriate for describing the physical location of a person; post office boxes are common for postal addresses. A LIS is not always able to provide this information.

If the user requests the general `civic` location type and a `postalCivic` type in the same request, then the LIS should ignore the request for the general `civic` type and only provide `postalCivic` information. If `postalCivic` and `jurisdictionalCivic` are requested in the same request, then the LIS should return both and construct the PIDF-LO to return the addresses in the same order in which they were requested.

When requesting a `postalCivic` location type, the default behavior of the LIS is to try and satisfy this request, but if it can't, it may just return a location in any form, including `geodetic`.

The exact Qualifier   When requesting a particular type of location by setting the value of the `locationType` parameter in the location request, the default behavior of the LIS is to try and satisfy this request, but if it can't, it may just return whatever information it has. Sometimes this is not good enough, and the user will need to know precisely if the information it has asked for has been returned. The HELD protocol supports this qualifier through the `exact` attribute contained in the `locationType` element. If the user wants to make sure that they only get what they ask for, then they can set this attribute to be `true`, and the LIS will return an error if any of the requested data cannot be provided. Inclusion of the `exact` attribute is optional, and when not provided it is assumed to have a value of `false`.

```
<locationRequest xmlns="http://sitacs.uow.edu.au/ns/location/held">
    <locationType exact="true">
        geodetic
    </locationType>
</locationRequest>
```

The signed Qualifier   There are three implicit expectations of any node providing location information:

- The information provided is current.
- The information is accurate at the time it is provided.
- The information is attributed to the specified target.

These same expectations are the basis for location dependability, which was described in Chapter 1. The degree of need for dependability of location information tends to increase when the cost of acting on misinformation is high. The signed attribute allows the user to request location information that has been digitally signed by the LIS, binding location and time to the Target.

```
<locationRequest xmlns="http://sitacs.uow.edu.au/ns/location/held"
                 signed="true">
   <locationType exact="true">
       jurisdictionalCivic
   </locationType>
</locationRequest>
```

A signed location may result in the whole PIDF-LO being signed using the techniques outlined in Reference 7. The drawback with this is that if the requestor was the Target, and he/she wishes to add things to the PIDF-LO, they can't do so without breaking the signature. A better way to sign the PIDF-LO is to use the XML transform provided in Appendix B. This transform excludes select parts of the PIDF-LO document, so a Target may modify those sections without impacting the dependability of the location information.

The responseTime Qualifier   If the requestor wants a response within a certain time, then he/she can set the `responseTime` qualifier to inform the LIS of this requirement. Sometimes an LIS will have more than one location determination option available, often with varying degrees of accuracy. The `responseTime` qualifier provides the LIS with criteria to choose a location determination mechanism. Where the LIS has a choice, it should always choose the location determination technique that will yield the most accurate result within the provided `responseTime`.

The responseTime can be specified as a number of seconds—2.2—or it can be specified as an XML period—PT2.2S. Either form is acceptable.

```
<locationRequest xmlns="http://sitacs.uow.edu.au/ns/location/held"
                 responseTime="PT2.2S">
   <locationType exact="true">
     jurisdictionalCivic
     geodetic
   </locationType>
</locationRequest>
<locationRequest xmlns="http://sitacs.uow.edu.au/ns/location/held"
                 responseTime="2.2">
   <locationType exact="true">
     jurisdictionalCivic
     geodetic
   </locationType>
</locationRequest>
```

The `responseTime` qualifier acts as a hint to the LIS. The LIS can use this time to select location determination methods that provide the best accuracy within this time. However, the requester must ultimately make a decision about whether or not to wait for a response, and whether the response is taking too long. Furthermore, the `responseTime` qualifier is optional, and if not provided, the LIS should always try to provide the most accurate location that satisfies the overall criteria of the location request.

Requesting a Location Reference

The HELD protocol supports location references in the form of a location URI, which can be requested by a Target instead of a literal location. The location reference model allows the Target to delegate its location distribution function to the LIS. To ensure that the LIS honors the Target's location authorization and privacy policies, the Target provides the LIS with a set of rules defining the policies applicable to the Target. The LIS needs to store these rules and ensure they are invoked whenever the location URI is accessed. Further, these rules and the location URI need to be linked to the Target and its location inside the LIS. The HELD protocol manages these data and their association through a context. A Target therefore requests a location URI by asking the LIS to create a context.

Location URIs in the HELD protocol must not contain any information that could be used to identify the device or Target. That is, they must not include things such as the IP or MAC address of the Target. The HELD protocol recommends that the location URI contains the public address of the LIS and a randomly generated sequence of characters that the LIS can use to uniquely identify the context-containing Target information.

Creating a Context   To create a context, the Target issues a `createContext` HELD message to the LIS, and includes rules that describe who may request the location of the Target. The rules may be provided directly from the Target to the LIS, in which case the rules are specified in accordance with Reference 8. For example, if the Target only wanted its VoIP call server to be able to request its location, it may create a context using the following message structure. Note that in addition to the rules, the Target must specify how long they wish the context to remain active on the LIS for. This is specified with the mandatory `lifetime` element.

```
<createContext xmlns="http://sitacs.uow.edu.au/ns/location/held">
   <lifetime>PT2H</lifetime>
   <rules>
      <ruleset xmlns="urn:ietf:params:xml:ns:common-policy">
         <rule id="f3g44r1">
            <conditions>
               <identity>
                  <one id="sip:mycallserver@goodcalls.com"/>
               </identity>
            </conditions>
         </rule>
      </ruleset>
   </rules>
</createContext>
```

Providing access rules to the LIS using common policy is fine but may become onerous if the set of rules is complex and large. An alternative is for the Target to provide the LIS with a URI indicating where the LIS can obtain the Target's rules from. This is done by providing a `rulesetURI`.

```
<createContext xmlns="http://sitacs.uow.edu.au/ns/location/held">
    <lifetime>PT2H</lifetime>
    <rules>
        <rulesetURI>
            https://www.example.com/~user/privacy/ruleset.xml
        </rulesetURI>
    </rules>
</createContext>
```

A Target may wish to keep much of its access policy hidden from a visited network, in which case it could adopt the location subscription approach described in Chapter 2. In this model, the core of the Target's policies reside in the home presence server, and only the presence server may request location from the LIS. This is easily accomplished using the first `createContext` example shown earlier.

When an LIS receives a set of rules from the Target, it will process them to make sure they make sense. If the LIS discovers a problem, it will send an error to the Target indicating that a problem was found. If the Target sent the LIS a `rulesetURI`, then the LIS will go off and fetch the ruleset, if the LIS is unable to fetch from the URI, or there is something wrong with the retrieved ruleset, then the LIS will inform the Target by way of an error message.

contextResponse: The Target's Handle to a Context   When a Target creates a context on the LIS using the `createContext` message, it needs a means of being able to identify the context on the LIS so that it can make changes to rules, and as we will see in subsequent sections, changes to other Target data in the context. The Target is provided a handle to the context via the HELD `contextResponse` message which is returned by the LIS after successfully processing a `createContext` message from the Target. The context handle returned to the Target by the LIS is a URI, and is referred to as a location URI.

As shown in Figure 4.8, the `contextResponse` message consists of an expiry time, a list of URIs, and a password. The expiry time indicates to the Target the time at which the context on the LIS will expire, this time may be shorter than, but never longer than, the context `lifeTime` requested by the Target.

The `contextResponse` includes a list of location URIs that the Target may hand out to would-be Location Recipients. Each URI in the list will be for a different URI schema, for example, sip, sips, or https. Each URI points to the same Target context on the LIS. The purpose of supporting multiple URI types is to allow flexibility in the range of applications that can access location information.

Finally, the `contextResponse` message contains a password which the Target will use when requesting the LIS to make changes to the data stored in the context.

```
<contextResponse xmlns="http://sitacs.uow.edu.au/ns/location/held"
                 code="200" message="OK">
  <context expires="2006-01-01T13:00:00">
     <locationURI>https://ls.example.com:9768/357yc6s64ceyoiuy5ax3o</locationURI>
     <locationURI>sips:357yc6s64ceyoiuy5ax3o@ls.example.com:9769</locationURI>
     <password>38cdj38mjcd-0-=54821kj28mp1qms.1</password>
  </context>
</contextResponse>
```

Context Data

In addition to the access rules and lifetime parameters provided by the Target when it creates a context on the LIS, the Target can provide other directives to the LIS including a profile, and call-back information. These additional fields are addressed in subsequent sections.

The profile Element   The `profile` element provides the Target with a way to instruct the LIS as to what information in addition to location should be included in any PIDF-LO generated in order to describe the whereabouts of the Target. The `profile` consists of four optional elements.

The PIDF-LO defined in Reference 9 was described in detail in Chapter 2. To recap, the PIDF-LO takes the base document for transporting presence information—the PIDF is defined in Reference 10 and adds a structure to contain location information and rules on how that location information may be stored, transported, and used. The `profile` element specifically allows the Target to dictate how the LIS should populate the `<retention-expires>`, `<retransmission-allowed>`, and `<external-ruleset>` fields in the `<usage-rules>` element of the PIDF-LO.

Asserting User Identity Using HELD   Knowing where a device is raises some concerns as to the privacy and associated rights extended to users of such devices, and while these concerns should not be discounted, the relevance of knowing the address of a temporary IP address or some other transitory network identifier should not be carried

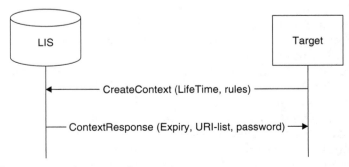

Figure 4.8   HELD context creation messaging.

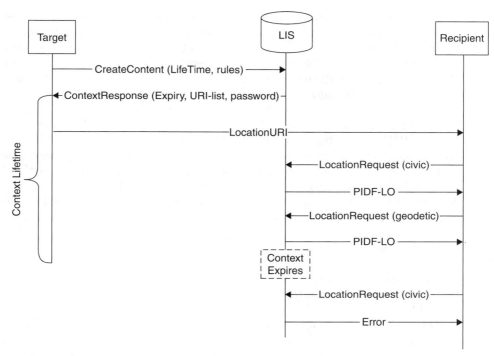

Figure 4.9 HELD context lifeTime and LocationURI usage.

to the extreme either. A strong legitimate concern regarding privacy arises when user identity and location information are explicitly bound together in such a way that it is easy to discern who is at a specific location at a specific point in time. And while there are privacy considerations that need to be taken into account when binding identity to location information, having this data bound together can provide strong assurances to service providers as to the integrity of the information and to whom it pertains.

The HELD protocol provides three mechanisms for a user to assert his/her identity to the LIS and are primarily designed to be used where a greater degree of trust by the Location Recipient is required. The first is for the user to simply provide the LIS with a URI that the LIS will use as the value of the presentity for all location objects created in order to describe the location of the end-point. The other two mechanisms make use of the SAML Assertion and EncryptedAssertion methods.

A HELD Target is able to tell the LIS what value to employ for the presentity element using the presentity field of the *profile* structure in a corresponding HELD message, with the intent being that the LIS will populate the presentity of any PIDF-LO documents generated with the value of the presentity provided by the Target. Where the Target does not have an SAML assertion with the provided presentity, the LIS does not need to accept the value provided. Where the LIS does provide a PIDF-LO with the proffered identity in the presentity field, the Target will need to ensure that their identity associated with any outbound messaging can be tied to the same value that is the presentity field of the PIDF-LO, for example, using SIP identity mechanisms. When used in this manner, fraud and false information can only be achieved easily if the Target and owner of the identity is directly involved, making him/her easily identifiable. For most applications where identity is required, this is adequate and is the recommended approach.

In some cases, a Target is able to provide information to the LIS that allows the LIS to make the association between the provided *presentity* value, and the actual device. HELD provides this functionality by supporting the SAML Assertion and EncryptedAssertion methods. Using these mechanisms, a Target can assert its true identity to the LIS, giving the LIS a means of determining if the assertion is true.

If the LIS is unable to validate the identity provided in the SAML assertion, then the LIS should return an error. HELD does not define how a client obtains a SAML assertion; it is assumed that best current practices are followed and a Target should only provide the LIS with a presentity representing its true identity when the Target explicitly trusts the LIS.

Setting <retention-expiry>   The <retention-expiry> field in the PIDF-LO is a date time field. It specifies the absolute date and time at which the holder of the PIDF-LO is no longer permitted to possess the location information. The profile element provides two ways in which the Target may instruct the LIS to populate the <retention-expiry> field.

The first is through the <retentionExpiry> field, which specifies an absolute date and time. Whenever the LIS creates a PIDF-LO describing the location of the Target, the <retention-expiry> element in the PIDF-LO will be set to the value that was provided in the <retentionExpiry> field.

```
<createContext xmlns="http://sitacs.uow.edu.au/ns/location/held">
    <lifetime>PT10M</lifetime>
    <profile>
        <retentionExpiry>2006-01-01T13:00:00</retentionExpiry>
    </profile>
    <rules>
        <rulesetURI>https://www.example.com/~user/privacy/ruleset.xml</rulesetURI>
    </rules>
</createContext>
```

The second way that the HELD protocol supports setting the <retention-expiry> value using the profile element is through the <retentionInterval> field. This field represents a duration, and is used to instruct the LIS to make holding a PIDF-LO valid for only a certain period of time after it is requested, for example, holding a PIDF-LO valid for only ten minutes. This is achieved by the LIS obtaining the time that a location request comes in, and adding the <retentionInterval> to this to obtain an absolute <retention-expiry> value for the PIDF-LO. The <retentionInterval> may be specified as an absolute in seconds (for example, 20.5) or in the XML duration format (for instance, PT10M).

```
<createContext xmlns="http://sitacs.uow.edu.au/ns/location/held">
   <lifetime>PT10M</lifetime>
   <profile>
      <!—sets the interval to 30 minutes (1800 seconds -->
      <retentionInterval>1800</retentionInterval>
   </profile>
   <rules>
      <rulesetURI>https://www.example.com/~user/privacy/ruleset.xml</rulesetURI>
   </rules>
</createContext>
```

Setting <retransmission-allowed>   The `<retransmission-allowed>` field in the PIDF-LO is a Boolean type. When set to "no," the PIDF-LO holder may not forward the document to any other node. When set to "yes," the holder may share the PIDF-LO with other parties. The HELD protocol allows the Target to indicate its preference for the setting of this value through the `<retransmission>` field in the `profile` element.

```
<createContext xmlns="http://sitacs.uow.edu.au/ns/location/held">
   <lifetime>PT10M</lifetime>
   <profile>
      <retransmission>true<retransmission>
   </profile>
   <rules>
      <rulesetURI>https://www.example.com/~user/privacy/ruleset.xml</rulesetURI>
   </rules>
</createContext>
```

Setting <external-ruleset>   In the PIDF-LO, the `<external-ruleset>` field contains a URI that references a complete set of rules and policies regarding the access and dissemination of the information in the PIDF-LO. The recommendation in Reference 9 is that this URI should use the HTTPS scheme and that the rule holder should authenticate the requesting node. The HELD protocol supports the Target, informing the LIS of the value to place in this field using the `<rulesetURI>` field in the `profile` element.

```
<createContext xmlns="http://sitacs.uow.edu.au/ns/location/held">
   <lifetime>PT10M</lifetime>
   <profile>
      <rulesetURI>https://www.privacy.com/~user/ruleset.xml</rulesetURI>
   </profile>
   <rules>
         <rule id="f3g44r1">
            <conditions>
               <identity>
                  <one id="sip:mycallserver@goodcalls.com"/>
               </identity>
            </conditions>
         </rule>
   </rules>
</createContext>
```

Updating a Context

The previous section explained how a Target can create a context on the LIS and what parameters the Target can include in the context to have the LIS customize the PIDF-LO with options that the Target would like. It stands to reason that a Target may wish to change certain aspects of their context over time—for example, who is authorized to request location information, or to extend the life-time of the context. The HELD protocol supports this functionality through the `updateContext` message.

In order to update a context, the Target must identify to the LIS which context is to be updated, and prove to the LIS that it is authorized to update the identifier context. The context identification and authorization mechanisms are provided to the Target when it first creates the context on the LIS. Context identification is achieved by the Target providing one of the location URIs that it received, and authorization is achieved by including the password received when the context was created.

```
<updateContext xmlns="http://sitacs.uow.edu.au/ns/location/held">
    <context>
        <locationURI>https://ls.example.com:9768/357yc6s64ceyoiuy5ax3o</locationURI>
        <password>38cdj38mjcd-0-=54821kj28mp1qms.1</password>
    </context>
    <lifetime>PT30M</lifetime>
</updateContext>
```

To understand why context identification and authorization are necessary beyond simply the Target's IP address, we need to look at an example. Let's take a residential broadband connection to a house. A typical deployment may consist of an ADSL home router that connects to the broadband network on one side, and the home network on the other with a network address translation (NAT) agent in between. The home router includes a DHCP server providing a private IP address range to hosts inside the house, and the NAT service to support routing traffic to the public Internet. To a LIS based at the ISP, all hosts inside the house appear to be at the same location since they are all identified by the same IP address: the IP address of the home router. Suppose that the house has a typical family in it: mom, dad, and their two teenage children, Bob and Alice, each with their own computer. If a literal location is being requested by each host, this is fine; they all get the same location. When a host requests a location reference, however, each will create its own context on the LIS. This means that the LIS requires some way other than simply an IP address to be able to identify which context to update. The reason for authentication is to make sure that an untrusted third party to whom Alice has given a location URI cannot simply change her access rules.

When a Target successfully updates its context, it will receive a `contextResponse` message from the LIS. This `contextResponse` message will contain the same set of location URIs; however, the LIS as a matter of policy may elect to provide the Target with a new password. This new password takes effect immediately and any attempts to use the old password will fail.

Anything that can be set using the `createContext` message can be changed using the `updateContext` message. There are two special cases that require specific explanation. The first is changes to access rules, and the second is changes to the `lifeTime` parameter.

Changing the Rules   When a Target wishes to change its access rules, it must pass the complete new ruleset to the LIS since there is no support in the HELD protocol for ruleset compositing. For example, suppose that a Target had a ruleset allowing Bob, Alice, Fred, and Mary access to its location, and that this had been sent to the LIS.

```
<createContext xmlns="http://sitacs.uow.edu.au/ns/location/held">
    <lifetime>PT2H</lifetime>
    <rules>
        <ruleset xmlns="urn:ietf:params:xml:ns:common-policy">
            <rule id="f3g44r1">
                <conditions>
                    <identity>
                        <one id="sip:Bob@example.com"/>
                        <one id="sip:Alice@example.com"/>
                        <one id="sip:Fred@example.com"/>
                        <one id="sip:Mary@example.com"/>
                    </identity>
                </conditions>
            </rule>
        </ruleset>
    </rules>
</createContext>
```

Suppose the Target decided that Bob was no longer its friend. The Target cannot simply say to the LIS, remove Bob from my access list; the Target must send a new access list to the LIS consisting of only Alice, Fred, and Mary.

```
<updateContext xmlns="http://sitacs.uow.edu.au/ns/location/held">
    <context>
        <locationURI>https://ls.example.com:9768/357yc6s64ceyoiuy5ax3o</locationURI>
        <password>38cdj38mjcd-0-=54821kj28mp1qms.1</password>
    </context>
    <rules>
        <ruleset xmlns="urn:ietf:params:xml:ns:common-policy">
            <rule id="f3g44r1">
                <conditions>
                    <identity>
                        <one id="sip:Alice@example.com"/>
                        <one id="sip:Fred@example.com"/>
                        <one id="sip:Mary@example.com"/>
                    </identity>
                </conditions>
            </rule>
        </ruleset>
    </rules>
</updateContext>
```

Similarly, if the Target wishes to add a new person to its buddy list, they must send the entire ruleset to the LIS, including the identity of the new buddy.

The Target needs to let the LIS know whenever it makes changes to the referenced rules; otherwise, the LIS will continue to apply out-of-date rules. This even applies when the Target has provided a ruleset URI, because the LIS doesn't know if the ruleset changes. The Target does this by sending the LIS a ruleset URI in an updateContext message.

This may be the same ruleset URI as was sent previously, but on receipt of a ruleset URI in an `updateContext` message, the LIS will retrieve and reapply the ruleset.

Updating lifeTime   The Target can extend the lifetime of their context by providing a new duration or absolute value for the `lifeTime` parameter in an `updateContext` message. The only way to terminate a context on the LIS is for the context to reach its expiry time. For a Target to terminate a context, it must therefore set the `lifeTime` parameter to zero or to a time in the past. This will result in the LIS terminating and purging data associated with the Target's context.

Location Assertion

Location assertion is the act of the Target proffering a location the LIS. A Target may do this for a number of reasons but the two main ones are the Target asking the LIS to provide some confirmation to the Target of where it is, and the Target wanting to get the LIS to provide some dependability signature so the Target can provide a signed location to a Location Recipient.

In the first scenario, a Target may know that it is in room 23 on the second floor of building 39, but it may not know the street address. Location assertion provides the Target with the ability to say to the LIS, "I am in room 23 on the second floor of building 39." In turn, the LIS may only be able to determine location down to a building number—in this case, building 39. The result of asserting location in this case would be the LIS being provided a populated civic location with all the necessary details to identify the location of the Target down to room 23 on the second floor of building 39. This same mechanism could be used to perform civic address validation, as is necessary for the NENA-i2 solution.

In the second scenario, suppose a Target is capable of determining location to a high degree of accuracy and precision using a differential GPS system, while the LIS is only able to determine the Target's location to a more coarse level using network-based radio timing techniques. What happens if the Location Recipient needs high accuracy location and a dependability signature? In this case, the Target can use GPS to determine its location, and then proffer this location to the LIS to validate it. If the proffered location falls within the area that the LIS would have assigned to the Target, then the assertion is successful and the LIS returns a signed PIDF-LO containing the GPS determined location. In this situation, the LIS has asserted that the location provided by the Target was as good, or better, than what the LIS could provide, and so the LIS signs the location as though it had determined it.

The HELD protocol supports location assertion through the `locationRequest` message. When a Target wishes to assert a location, it uses the `<assert>` element rather than the `<locationType>` element that was described earlier. The following subsection will describe the options available to a Target when asserting a location.

Asserting a Location   Support is provided for asserting a civic location, a geodetic location, or both a geodetic and civic location. As indicated, if the LIS is able to assert the proffered location, then the LIS will return the same location in the resulting PIDF-LO. If the assertion fails, then the default behavior of the LIS is to return the location that it does know for the Target. There is a provision on this behavior, however, and that is that the LIS must return a location in the same form that was asserted. That is, if the Target asserted a geodetic location, then the LIS must respond either with a geodetic location or an error. Similarly, if the Target asserts a civic location, then the LIS must respond with either a civic location or an error. If the Target asserts both a geodetic location and a civic location, then the LIS may respond with either location types, both, or an error if the LIS is unable to determine the location of the Target at all (see Figure 4.10). The LIS must never respond to a geodetic assertion with a civic address or civic assertion with a geodetic location. These rules are expressed in Table 4.1.

How location is determined is often important to a user of location information, and an LIS-provided location should always include an indication of how location was determined by populating the `<method>` parameter of the PIDF-LO. Yet when a Target asserts its location to the LIS, the LIS has no way of knowing how the Target determined this location. To assist the LIS, the `<assertion>` element of the `locationRequest` has a `method` attribute that should be set by the Target when the assertion is made. A civic assertion therefore might look similar to the one shown next. The full set of valid values for the `method` attribute is available from www.iana.org/assignments/method-tokens.

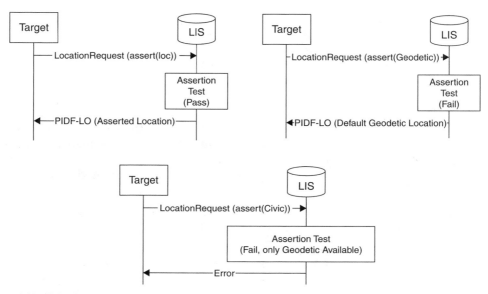

Figure 4.10   Location assertion using HELD.

TABLE 4.1   Location Assertion Truth Table

Target Assertion		LIS Response	
Geodetic	Civic	Geodetic	Civic
X		X	
	X		X
X	X	X	
X	X		X
X	X	X	X

```
<locationRequest xmlns="http://sitacs.uow.edu.au/ns/location/held">
    <assert method="Manual">
        <civicAddress xmlns="urn:ietf:params:xml:ns:pidf:geopriv10:civicAddr"
                      xml:lang="en-AU">
          <country>AU</country>
          <A1> NSW </A1>
          <A3>Wollongong</A3>
          <A4>North Wollongong</A4>
          <PRD>Corner</PRD>
          <RD>Flinders</RD>
          <STS>Street</STS>
          <RDBR>Campbell Street</RDBR>
          <LMK>Gilligan's Island</LMK>
          <NAM> Video Rental Store </NAM>
          <PC>2500</PC>
          <ROOM> Westerns and Classics </ROOM>
          <PLC>store</PLC>
          <POBOX>Private Box 15</POBOX>
        </civicAddress>
    </assert>
</locationRequest>
```

A Target asserting location should know when the location was determined, and when it will no longer be considered valid; thus, it should also tell the LIS this. The assert request supports the Target providing this information to the LIS through the timestamp and expires attributes. A geodetic assertion might therefore look similar to the following.

```
<locationRequest xmlns="http://sitacs.uow.edu.au/ns/location/held" signed="true">
    <assert method="Device-Based_A-GPS"
            timestamp="2006-01-01T13:00:00"
            expires="2006-01-01T13:05:00">
        <gs:Circle srsName="urn:ogc:def:crs:EPSG::4326"
            xmlns:gs="urn:ietf:params:xml:ns:pidf:geopriv10:geoShape"
            xmlns:gml="http://www.opengis.net/gml">
            <gml:pos>
               42.5463 -73.2512
            </gml:pos>
            <gml:radius uom="urn:ogc:def:uom:EPSG::9001">
```

```
                5.3
            </gml:radius>
        </gs:Circle>
    </assert>
</locationRequest>
```

Sometimes a Target will want the LIS to either accept the proffered location or to fail. Such a situation might occur if the Target wants the LIS to sign a location that the Target determined using GPS. The HELD protocol supports this by providing the optional `exact` attribute on the `assert` element. If the Target wants only what it has requested, it can set the `exact` attribute to yes, and the LIS will either return a PIDF-LO with the proffered location or an error message.

```
<locationRequest xmlns="http://sitacs.uow.edu.au/ns/location/held" signed="true">
    <assert method="Device-Based_A-GPS"
            timestamp="2006-01-01T13:00:00"
            expires="2006-01-01T13:05:00"
            exact="yes">
        <gs:Circle srsName="urn:ogc:def:crs:EPSG::4326"
            xmlns:gs="urn:ietf:params:xml:ns:pidf:geopriv10:geoShape"
            xmlns:gml="http://www.opengis.net/gml">
            <gml:pos>
                42.5463 -73.2512
            </gml:pos>
            <gml:radius uom="urn:ogc:def:uom:EPSG::9001">
                5.3
            </gml:radius>
        </gs:Circle>
    </assert>
</locationRequest>
```

Reporting Errors

There are three possible messages that may be sent by the LIS in response to a Target request, a PIDF-LO, an `error` message, or a `contextResponse` message. The `error` and `contextResponse` messages have specific result `code` and `message` attributes associated with them that provide guidance on how operations have completed on the LIS.

The `code` attribute indicates the actual outcome of the requested operation and follows a three-decimal form similar to that used in HTTP (see Reference 11) and SIP (see Reference 12). The `code` attribute is intended to be used more by the HELD-client software itself. The full list of defined codes is provided in the HELD protocol specification.

The `message` attribute contains a text-based reason describing what occurred on the LIS when the operation was processed. This attribute is intended to provide more information to a human operator.

```
<error xmlns="http://sitacs.uow.edu.au/ns/location/held"
       code="501" message="Location Unknown"/>
```

```
<contextResponse xmlns="http://sitacs.uow.edu.au/ns/location/held"
                 code="200" message="OK">
```

```
    <context expires="2006-01-01T13:00:00">
        <locationURI>https://ls.example.com:9768/357yc6s64ceyoiuy5ax3o</locationURI>
        <password>38cdj38mjcd-0-=54821kj28mp1qms.1</password>
    </context>
</contextResponse>
```

Third-Party Interface Authentication

The Third-Party Interface (described earlier) is the interface on which the LIS services location requests come in through a location URI. The LIS will only process `locationRequest` messages on this interface, and all hosts making location requests through this mechanism MUST be authenticated by the LIS. The LIS will not provide location information to any requesting host unless it first passes authentication and is subsequently authorized based on Target access policy and/or local rules and regulations to possess the location of the Target. If either authentication or authorization of the requesting host fails, then the LIS will return an error message with a code of 402.

```
<error xmlns="http://sitacs.uow.edu.au/ns/location/held"
        code="402" message="Authentication Error"/>
```

A requesting host may identify itself to the LIS in one of two ways, either using a client-side X.509 certificate signed by a certification authority acceptable to the LIS, or by using a Security Assertions Markup Language (SAML) identity assertion. The X.509 certificate method when combined with HELD using the HTTP binding provides an advantage over the SAML assertion mechanisms. This is because presentation of a client-side certificate is already an accepted practice in TLS session establishment, as is used for HTTPS. In contrast, the SAML assertion requires an extension to the location request message to include the SAML elements.

The requesting host may use any of the options described for the `locationRequest` message. A LIS will ignore any values contained in the `<profile>` element when the `locationRequest` message is received over the Third-Party Interface. It may also choose to ignore an asserted location value provided to it in a `locationRequest` message received over the Third-Party Interface.

The Trusted-Party Query Interface

The need for the Trusted-Party Query Interface is best described with examples, and specific examples will be provided in subsequent chapters where we look at location determination and acquisition in specific types of network deployments. As described earlier, the Trusted-Party Query Interface supports a node other than the Target requesting the Target's location. This support extends to the trusted node being able to request the location of the Target without the trusted node having been given a specific location URI by the Target. That is, the trusted node is able to identify the Target to the LIS in some manner. The HELD protocol supports this functionality through extensions which will be described in detail in subsequent chapters.

The LIS must authenticate all nodes attempting to request location through the Trusted-Party Query Interface. The mechanism chosen for authentication is left unspecified and will be dependent upon network configuration. X.509 client-side and server-side certificates are recommended, however.

LIS Discovery Using DNS

Service discovery in IP networks is always a thorny topic. Do I use DHCP, or SLP, or DNS, or do I devise something new? This section proposes a LIS discovery technique that can be achieved through DNS SRV records. The reason for this choice is that many IP networks, in particular residential broadband networks, do not have a common means of providing network configuration data. Some use DHCP, and some use PPP. What is nice about DNS is that all systems must support it, making it an obvious choice.

To use a DNS discovery mechanism for a local service, such as an LIS, you must know the domain in which you are operating, and this must be the actual name of the access domain. The domain name of the access provider in many circumstances is available directly from the home router via DHCP (Option 15) and in many cases this domain name is adopted for use with the home computers and networks. Knowing the domain name of the serving access network allows an IP device to query the local DNS server and perform service discovery for the LIS. The service discovery technique described here is based around DNS SRV records.

In some cases, the domain name of the access network is not known, for example, when a laptop is taken home from work, it often maintains the domain name of the company owning the laptop, such as andrew.com. In this situation, more complex access domain name discovery techniques are required, and ways of achieving this are described in the following subsections.

External IP Address Determination

Figure 4.11 shows the domain discovery problem as it relates to a typical residential broadband network. The home-router runs an internal DHCP server that provides IP addresses from a private address range. The home-router itself is provided an externally routable IP address from the ISP, and the home-router performs NAT between the internal and external networks. The externally routable IP address is associated with the domain name belonging to the ISP, my.isp.net, as shown in Figure 4.11. To discover the local access domain name, a client must first determine the external IP address of the home-router. Three mechanisms for discovering this IP address are described next.

STUN One way to determine the external IP address of the home-router is to use STUN. STUN is defined in Reference 13 and describes a mechanism for being able to determine the IP address on the public side of a NAT. STUN is a simple client-server based protocol and as such requires a STUN server. Due to the way in which STUN works, it is not necessary for the STUN server to reside in the same access network as the IP device, but it is necessary that the STUN server be reachable by the IP device.

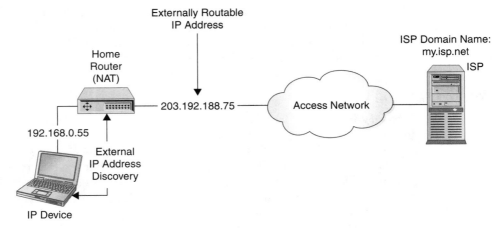

Figure 4.11   An external IP address discovery problem.

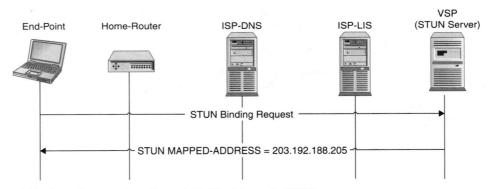

Figure 4.12   Learning an externally routable IP address via STUN.

It is likely that a voice service provider (VSP) will provide the STUN server to assist their customers in gaining access to a service from any access network. The rationale is that the User of the IP device must already have a trust relationship with the VSP, and so the various identity and integrity recommendations for STUN can be easily satisfied.

We will not go into a full working description of STUN, which is described in Reference 13. The expectation is that a STUN-client be associated with the HELD-client and that it issues a STUN binding request to the STUN-server. The STUN-server will respond with a MAPPED-ADDRESS message indicating the external IP address of the home-router gateway (see Figure 4.12).

Universal Plug and Play (UPnP)   The Universal Plug and Play (UPnP) mechanism makes use of the UPnP Internet Gateway Device (IGD) specification which is supported in many home-routers to allow PC applications to operate seamlessly through the router's

NAT function. The HELD-Client in this case acts as a UPnP Control Point (CP) and requests the external IP address of the router using the `GetExternalIPAddress` action defined in Reference 14.

This mechanism has the advantage that UPnP is a SOAP-based protocol running on top of HTTP, making it easy to implement as the HELD-Client is also built on top of HTTP.

WEB Report   To use the WEB report mechanism, a VSP or other known network entity establishes a web site, that when accessed returns the IP address of the requesting node. At the time of writing, a variety of web sites were available that support this functionality, for example, http://whatismyip.com/.

Domain Determination

Where the domain is not known, it must be determined. Once the device knows its external IP address, it can determine its access domain name by performing a reverse DNS lookup. This requires the ISP to populate `in-addr.arpa` records into its DNS for all IP addresses so that the resolution can occur. The generally accepted format for the resulting fully qualified domain name (FQDN) would be `ip-address.my.isp.net`.

DNS SRV Record LIS Discovery

The ISP must provide a DNS SRV record in the following form:

```
_locserv+https._tcp        SRV 1 0 <port> <Hostname of LIS>
```

In response to a query for the _locserv+https._tcp service, the DNS will return the FQDN and the port for the LIS service. The client will assume that all HELD requests are made against the root URI on the returned host.

For example, if the DNS were to return `held.lis.my.isp.net` with a port of `10001`, then the client may obtain location from that service with the following:
https://held.lis.my.isp.net:10001/.

Figure 4.13 shows the message flow between nodes when the DNS SRV LIS discovery mechanism is used. The figure shows STUN being used as an example for external IP discovery.

Types of LIS

An LIS is categorized based on the functions and services that it is able to provide. Three principle characteristics are used to classify an LIS, and an LIS that supports all of these is referred to as a Primary LIS. These characteristics include the following:

- The ability to determine location
- The ability to provide a location reference
- The ability to provide cryptographically dependable (signed) location.

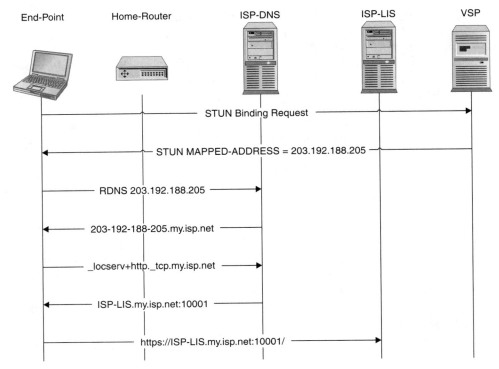

Figure 4.13   DNS SRV LIS discovery.

It should be noted that the ability to determine location includes the ability to support locations being asserted to the LIS.

The Gateway LIS   A Gateway LIS provides a point of contact for location requests without performing any actual location generation. The Gateway LIS does this by setting the location reference (location URI) from which the location of a target can be retrieved. The location URI indicates the address of the Gateway LIS, ensuring that Location Recipients request location from the Gateway instead of the Primary LIS.

A Gateway LIS on its own has no capacity for location generation; it typically exists closer to the public network than the LIS that provides location. The bulk of the location information must be served by another LIS—usually a Primary LIS.

In the configuration shown in Figure 4.14, the Gateway LIS appears to provide all LIS functions to both the IP device and the Location Recipient. Both the IP device and the Location Recipient are unaware of the existence of the Primary LIS. However, the Gateway forwards all requests to the Primary LIS for processing.

A Gateway LIS needs to maintain some state information relating to IP devices in its access domain. This is because it may receive a request for location information at any time, and this includes requests for update location information. If the Gateway

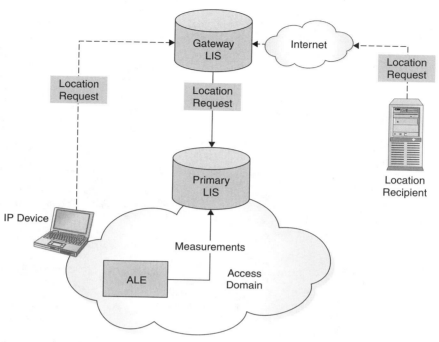

Figure 4.14   A Gateway LIS configuration.

LIS has a callback URI from the IP device, then it should use this mechanism to obtain the location of the device. If the Gateway LIS does not have a callback URI, then it must request location information directly from the primary LIS. An example of where a Gateway LIS may be deployed is in an ISP where physical access to a subscriber is provided by a local carrier. As a consequence of this type of access, the local carrier is able to provide location information and hence a primary LIS, but the ISP needs to be the external point of contact.

The Proxy LIS   A Proxy LIS provides a service to an access network that exists closer to the edge of a larger network. An LIS within the larger network provides the bulk of the location information service, but the Proxy LIS can provide a more precise location (see Figure 4.15).

The Proxy LIS can provide location information to the IP device, unless a signed location or a location URI is requested. The Primary LIS provides a signed location using a location asserted by the Proxy LIS, or a location URI if one is requested.

A Proxy LIS may be deployed by an organization to augment the LIS service provided by their network provider. Circumstances that may result in such a deployment include the Primary LIS being unable to identify locations within their geographic area with adequate precision, or regulatory requirements existing that cannot be met by the Primary LIS provider.

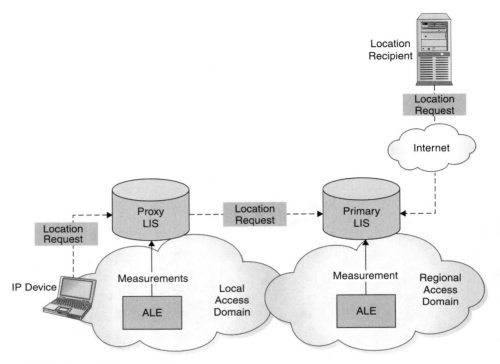

Figure 4.15   A Proxy LIS configuration.

The Proxy-Gateway LIS   The Proxy-Gateway LIS is, as the name suggests, a LIS that combines the functions of the Proxy LIS with those of the Gateway LIS (see Figure 4.16). The most common applications for this LIS type will be in enterprises and campus-based settings. A Proxy-Gateway LIS is able to determine location, provide location URIs, and defer to an upstream LIS where a signature is required for dependability reasons. We shall look at this LIS type in detail in Chapter 5 where we describe location determination and acquisition in enterprise environments.

Summary

HELD provides a query protocol interface for IP devices, invited applications, and authorized third parties making unsolicited requests for target device location. Requests include

- Location request by type
- Create, update, and delete contexts
- Location assertion and location signing

The LIS implements the HELD protocol. It combines context data with ALE measurement information to determine location and responds to HELD requests. Several

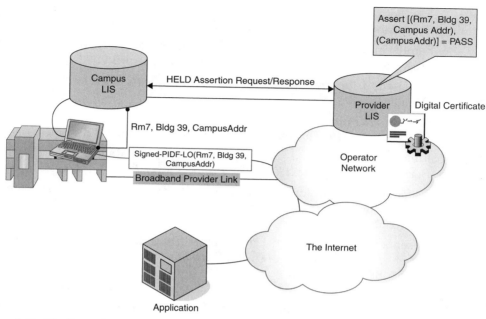

Figure 4.16 The Proxy-Gateway LIS.

types of LIS variants are possible depending on deployment scenarios. Examples of deployment scenarios are provided in the following chapters.

References

1. Cuellar, J., Morris, J., Mulligan, D., Peterson, J., and J. Polk, *"Geopriv Requirements,"* RFC 3693, February 2004.

2. Winterbottom, J., Peterson, J., and M. Thomson, *"Rationale for Location by Reference"*, draft-winterbottom-location-uri-01 (work in progress), January 2006.

3. Winterbottom, J., Thomson, M., and B. Stark, *"HTTP Enabled Location Delivery (HELD)"*, draft-winterbottom-http-location-delivery-03 (work in progress), May 2006.

4. Winterbottom, J., Tschofenig, H., and M. Thomson, *"GEOPRIV PIDF-LO Usage Clarification, Considerations, and Recommendations"*, draft-ietf-geopriv-pdif-lo-profile-04 (work in progress), May 2006.

5. Thomson, M. *"Geodetic Shapes for the Representation of Uncertainty in PIDF-LO"*, draft-thomson-geopriv-geo-shape-02 (work in progress), May 2006.

6. NENA VoIP-Packet Technical Committee, *Interim VoIP Architecture for Enhanced 9-1-1 Services (i2)*, NENA 08-001, December 2005.

7. Eastlake, D., Reagle, J., and D. Solo, *"(Extensible Markup Language) XML-Signature Syntax and Processing"*, RFC 3275, March 2002.

8. Schulzrinne, H. *"A Document Format for Expressing Privacy Preferences"*, (work in progress), draft-ietf-geopriv-common-policy-09, April 2006.

9. Peterson, J. *"A Presence-based GEOPRIV Location Object Format"*, RFC 4119, December 2005.

10. Sugano, H., Fujimoto, S., Klyne, G., Bateman, A., Carr, W., and J. Peterson, *"Presence Information Data Format (PIDF)"*, RFC 3863, August 2004.

11. Fielding, R., Gettys, J., Mogul, J., Frystyk, H., Masinter, L., Leach, P., and T. Berners-Lee, *"Hypertext Transfer Protocol – HTTP/1.1"*, RFC 2616, June 1999

12. Rosenberg, J., Schulzrinne, H., Camarillo, G., Johnston, A., Peterson, J., Sparks, R., Handley, M., and E. Schooler, *"SIP: Session Initiation Protocol"*, RFC 3261, June 2002.

13. Rosenberg, J., Weinberger, J., Huitema, C., and R. Mahy, *"STUN—Simple Traversal of User Datagram Protocol (UDP) Through Network Address Translators (NATs)"*, RFC 3489, March 2003.

14. UPnP Forum. *Internet Gateway Device (IGD) Standardized Device Control Protocol V 1.0: WANIPConnection:1 Service Template Version 1.01 For UPnP Version 1.0.* DCP 05-001, November 2001.

IP Location in Enterprise Networks

Chapter 4 described how an IP device might learn its location using the HELD protocol. In an enterprise network, the HELD protocol is not the only candidate for location acquisition; DHCP and LLDP-MED, described briefly in Chapter 1, also have a role to play. This chapter is broken into five parts: enterprise network access technology overview, location determination in enterprise networks, location acquisition in enterprise networks, enterprise location considerations, and enterprise location applications.

Enterprise Network Access Technologies

Enterprise networks are diverse. They can be large or small, flat or hierarchical, contiguous or disjointed, wireless or wired—the list goes on and on. There is no standard for what constitutes an enterprise network, consequently the technologies and mechanisms that are needed to determine location also vary from network to network. This section describes two enterprise access technologies and configurations.

Wired Ethernet Networks

Wired Ethernets are used extensively in Enterprise networks and can be configured and connected in a multitude of ways. Networks are constructed to keep interswitch and internetwork traffic to a minimum so as to optimize network performance. This is done by placing frequently communicating machines on the same switch or stack of switches. Where this is not possible, switches may be cascaded together and VLANs introduced to keep different LAN streams on the same switch separated.

IP addresses may be statically configured, or as is generally the case, provided dynamically using the Dynamic Host Configuration Protocol (DHCP) as described in Reference 1 at the end of the chapter, by a DHCP server. Increasingly, DHCP servers are becoming centralized functions requiring DHCP messages to transit several subnets. This requirement poses some problems to hosts needing dynamically allocated DHCP IP addresses since service discovery in DHCP is performed using IP broadcast messages that are blocked by IP routing functions to prevent network packet storms and worse.

This situation was addressed in the forerunner protocol to DHCP, BOOTP in Reference 2, through the use of *agents*, referred to in the common vernacular as *relay-agents*. A relay-agent generally resides in an IP gateway function (router) and intercepts DHCP broadcast traffic. The relay-agent directs the intercepted traffic to the DHCP server on behalf of the requesting node using unicast IP. In other words, the relay-agent knows the IP address of the DHCP server and is inherently trusted by it; a DHCP client has no visibility of the presence of the relay-agent. The functionality that a relay-agent can provide has grown over time, with the foundation for much of this functionality being defined in Reference 3, the DHCP Relay Information Option. The general purpose of many of the DHCP relay functions is to provide additional information to the DHCP server to aid it in making decisions about what network configuration values to provide to a host. It also happens that some of this information can aid in location determination, as will be seen later.

Traditionally, edge switches such as those shown in Figure 5.1 (switches A, B, C, D, and G) were relatively simple devices providing traffic separation through VLAN configurations. Edge Ethernet switches are becoming increasingly sophisticated with many offering advanced IP routing functionality such as Access Control Lists and DHCP relay functionality.

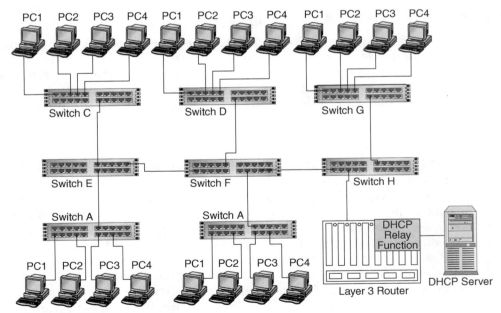

Figure 5.1 Wired Ethernet.

WiFi Networks

The 802.11 suite of protocols (a, b, g), collectively referred to as WiFi, provide wireless connectivity to a LAN. Speeds and QoS options vary from flavor to flavor, with 802.11g being commonly deployed and providing an access bandwidth of 54 Mbps. WiFi networks can be configured and rolled out in a number of ways. Such networks consist of standalone wireless access points (WAPs) and wireless network controller (WNC) configurations, discussed next.

The simplest form of WiFi network consists of one or more WAPs connected to a standard Ethernet switch, which in turn is connected to an intranet containing a DHCP server and other layer-3 routing infrastructures (see Figure 5.2). In this configuration, the switch is aware of the MAC addresses that it is serving down a specific port, and the IP address is delivered from a centralized DHCP server. If a device "roams" from one access point to an adjacent one, then its MAC address becomes associated with a new port in the switch and its packets are sent to the new serving WAP.

A more sophisticated approach to enabling WiFi networks introduces the notion of a wireless network controller (WNC), which manages a group of WAPs (see Figure 5.3). In this type of network, the WNC is able to control WAP handovers to improve the overall performance of the network.

Location determination techniques specific to WiFi networks are addressed in Chapter 7.

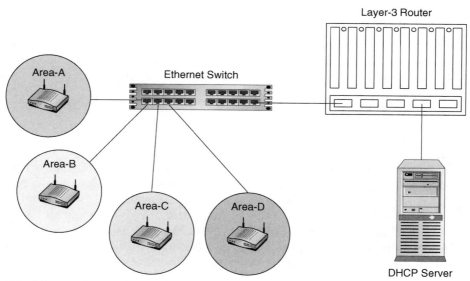

Figure 5.2 A basic WiFi network.

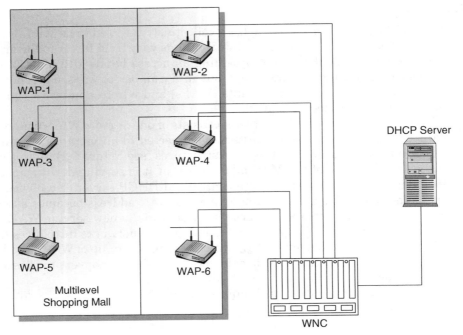

Figure 5.3   A wireless network controller network.

Location Determination in Enterprise Networks

The previous section described two common enterprise network access technologies and topologies. This section will look at ways in which data can be measured and used to determine the physical location of a device connected to an enterprise network.

Bridge MIB Interrogations

Most edge switches are referred to as "managed switches"—that is, they support an interface that allows the switch configuration to be set and the performance of the switch to be monitored remotely using the Simple Network Management Protocol (SNMP). One of the pieces of information that a managed switch keeps is a current list of all MAC addresses connected to each port on the switch. This information is generally accessible through what is referred to as the bridge Management Information Base (MIB), which is defined in Reference 4 (see Figure 5.4). By accessing the bridge MIB of a particular switch, it is possible for an ALE to see all client hardware (MAC) addresses connected to the switch and what physical interface (port) they are connected on. This MAC information can then be used by the LIS to determine where a particular device is. The LIS will do this by maintaining a "wire map" database that relates switch ports to location—typically, the office location that is at the other end of the UTP Ethernet

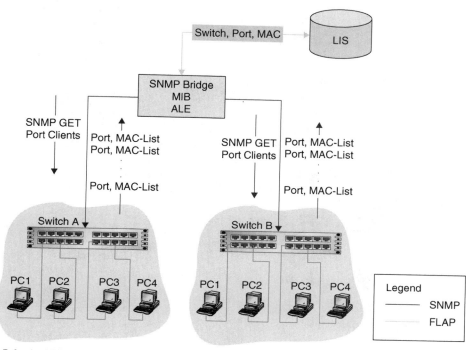

Figure 5.4 An SNMP bridge MIB ALE.

cable and that is plugged into a specific switch port. The location can be stored as a civic address and/or a geodetic lat/long.

In general, an ALE will be expected to poll the edge switches from time to time using SNMP GET messages. Often, a switch can be configured to provide an event in the form of an SNMP trap to indicate that an Ethernet link has gone up or down. Using this SNMP trap information, it may be possible to reduce the amount of polling required. It would be unwise to eliminate polling completely since SNMP uses UDP as a transport protocol and the arrival of messages is not guaranteed.

Static IP–to–MAC LIS Provisioning   The basic bridge MIB location determination mechanism allows the LIS to determine the location of a device based on a MAC address by tying it to a specific switch on a specific port. One problem with this approach occurs when a device tries to acquire its location, and the device is in a different IP subnet to the LIS, with potentially one or more layer-3 IP routers separating the device and the LIS. The problem is that the MAC address of the requesting device is not readily available to the LIS since it doesn't propagate through the layer-3 routers.

One way to overcome this is shown in Figure 5.5. Here, a static IP address is assigned to each device, and the IP-to-MAC address mapping is statically provisioned into the LIS.

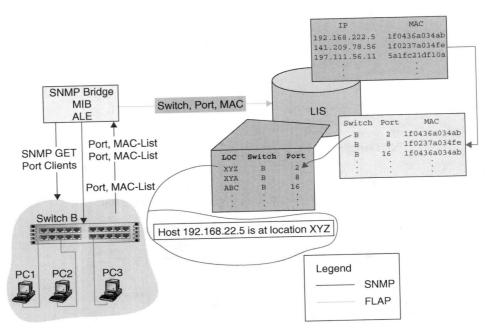

Figure 5.5 LIS static provisioning.

Static mappings for switch-port-to-location mappings are also provisioned into the LIS. The LIS now receives FLAP messages from the ALE periodically providing switch-port-MAC mappings that the LIS keeps in a dynamic table. As shown in Figure 5.5, this then allows the LIS to map IP address to location by following the chain of IP to MAC, MAC to switch and port, and then switch and port to location.

There are several downsides to this approach, the most significant being the need to do static IP address allocations when otherwise they would not be required. The other significant downside to this approach is what happens when the LIS doesn't have the MAC-to-switch and port mapping when a device requests its location. In this case, the LIS has to ask the ALE for the information, and in the basic form the ALE will only understand MAC addresses. If the network is small, then the ALE may just go out and poll all switches and ports for this information. If the network is large, this is impractical and mechanisms to speed up searches are required.

The search can be sped up by reducing the number of switches that need to be polled. One way is to not support dynamics in the network at all and simply hard-code MAC-to-location in the LIS. This does, however, make terminal movements awkward. Another way to do this is to have the ALE understand additional network configuration data such as which IP subnets are associated with which switches. In this situation, the LIS can pass down MAC and IP to the ALE when requesting network measurements, and the ALE can use the IP address to short-list the number of switches to poll. An alternative approach to providing additional configuration in the ALE is to include an ALE in each subnet and allow the LIS, based on IP address, to determine which ALE to query. Ultimately, the best approach is for the ALE to reside in the switch and for it to provide asynchronous notifications to the LIS. This results in the LIS only needing to search the network for the device's information when a notification has been missed or not received.

ARP Table—Assisted Bridge MIB Location Determination   In the configurations posed so far, the LIS has had to have static IP address-to-MAC address provisioning, something that is becoming less and less common in enterprise networks for general host connectivity. As was stated earlier, if the enterprise wants to use bridge MIB location determination methods and operate a LIS that is not in the same subnet as location requesting devices, then a mechanism to resolve the IP-to-MAC address mapping is required, or the requesting device cannot be readily identified by the LIS.

One device in a local subnet that always knows the IP address-to-MAC address mapping is the layer-3 router. A router keeps this information in its Address Resolution Protocol (ARP) table and this allows it to map IP address to MAC address for the purpose of routing messages (see Figure 5.6). In most cases, the ARP tables in a router are accessible through an SNMP MIB, so an ALE knowing the IP address of the requesting client can easily identify the router to query.

Location determination in this setup goes something like this:

1. A host requests its location from the LIS.

2. The LIS sends a measurement request to the ALE asking for measurements to do with IP address `192.168.222.5`.

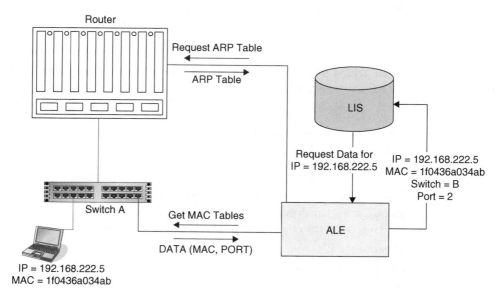

Figure 5.6   ARP table polling.

3. The ALE uses a subnet map to determine the correct layer-3 router, then requests its ARP table.

4. The ALE gets the ARP table, and determines the MAC address corresponding to the IP address `192.168.222.5`—in this case, `1f0436a034ab`.

5. From the router and client IP address information, the ALE knows which switch or switches to request MAC table information for.

6. The ALE queries various switches for the MAC and finds MAC address `1f0436a034ab` attached to port 2 or switch B.

7. The ALE sends back a FLAP message containing the IP address, MAC address, and switch and port information.

8. The LIS uses the switch and port information to look up the location.

It should be noted that in the preceding steps there are two distinct ALE functions, one to determine the IP address–to–MAC address mapping, and a second function to determine the switch and port on which the MAC address resides. These functions may be performed by two different ALEs, in which case the LIS would need to launch two separate FLAP requests. Alternatively, the LIS may receive FLAP notification messages for each of the events. In either case, the LIS needs to correlate the data to determine location.

This approach is impractical to perform in real time given the amount of data required to be processed. It is useful in situations where location requests from the LIS can be batched, so that hitting the ARP table yields many results, reducing the network load and search space, and the corresponding data can then be cached for near-term requests. This type of situation is not uncommon in enterprises where devices can move but do not move frequently, or moves can be tied closely to the time of the batched updates.

DHCP-Assisted Bridge MIB Location Determination   While a layer-3 router for a subnet must keep ARP tables for routing purposes, as was described in the previous section, sorting through them in real time in a network of any size will likely prove problematic. There is, however, another node that can usually provide IP address–to–MAC address mappings: the DHCP server. (see Figure 5.7.)

In this scenario, a DHCP ALE, or interface to an ALE, provides the IP-to-MAC address bindings that were provided previously by trawling through the router ARP tables in the earlier example. Where the ALE is not integrated into the DHCP server, the DHCP server may be interrogated using an external interface such as that proposed in Dynamic Host Configuration Protocol Leasequery (see Reference 5).

So the location determination steps become the following:

1. A host requests its location from the LIS.

2. The LIS sends a measurement request to the ALE asking for measurements to do with IP address `192.168.222.5`.

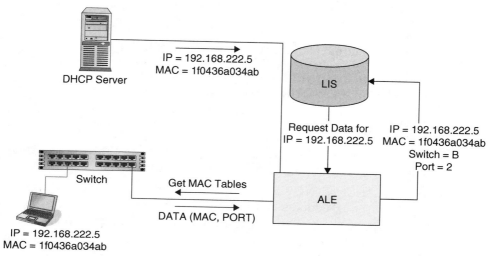

Figure 5.7   DHCP-assisted IP-to-MAC binding.

3. The ALE has the IP-to-MAC binding from the DHCP server; alternatively, the ALE may request this from the DHCP server.

4. From the client IP address information, the ALE knows which switch or switches to request MAC table information for.

5. The ALE queries various switches and finds MAC address `1f0436a034ab` attached to port 2 or switch B.

6. The ALE sends back a FLAP message containing the IP address, MAC address, and switch and port information.

7. The LIS uses the switch and port information to look up the location.

A DHCP Leasequery ALE   The previous section mentioned the existence of the DHCP lease query specification (see Reference 5). Here, we will describe how this protocol can be used to create an ALE. This section will assume that the LIS has identified the FLAP terminal/key as being the IP address, and therefore the returned access element will be the MAC address. That is, the DHCP lease query will include an IP address and needs a MAC address in the response.

The fields for the lease query message from the ALE to the DHCP server are described next:

1. Set the DHCP header with the following parameters:

op = 1
giaddr = IP address of the ALE
htype = 0

hlen = 0
chaddr = 0
ciaddr = Terminal IP address (the one we are looking for)

2. Include DHCP option 53 (message type) in the request with a value of 10, indicating a DHCPLEASEQUERY message.

The DHCP server will respond with one of three messages:

■ DHCPLEASEUNASSIGNED message, indicating that the DHCP server knows about the IP address but it is not currently allocated to a terminal.

■ DHCPLEASEUNKNOWN message, indicating that the DHCP server knows nothing about the IP address at all.

■ DHCPLEASEACTIVE message, indicating that the DHCP server has an active lease for the IP address. This message will also contain the corresponding MAC address.

The ALE will send various FLAP errors to the LIS in the event that either a DHCPLEASEUNASSIGNED or DHCPLEASEUNKNOWN message is received from the DHCP server. When a DHCPLEASEACTIVE message is received, the ALE will need to extract the MAC address from the `htype`, `hlen`, and `chaddr` header. For Ethernet, the `htype` and `hlen` fields will be 1 and 6, respectively, and the `chaddr` field will contain the actual MAC address in the first six octets.

The FLAP specification for the DHCP Lease query ALE support (see Figure 5.8) is provided in Appendix A. Sample message stanzas for the access query and access query response messages are provided next.

```
<aq xsi:type="dhcp-lq:aq">
  <dhcp-lq:terminal>
    <ip>192.168.222.5</ip>
  </dhcp-lq:terminal>
</aq>

<aqr result="200" xsi:type="dhcp-lq:aqr">
  <dhcp-lq:access time="2005-04-15T14:02:25.160+10:00"
                  expires="2005-04-15T16:02:25.160+10:00">
    <dhcp-lq:hwaddr>1f0436a034ab</dhcp-lq:hwaddr>
  </dhcp-lq:access>
</aqr>
```

DHCP Relay Location Determination

DHCP can be used to determine location through the use of a DHCP relay (option 82) defined in Reference 3. DHCP relay agents are deployed in networks where DHCP clients reside in different subnets to the DHCP server. They are required in these networks

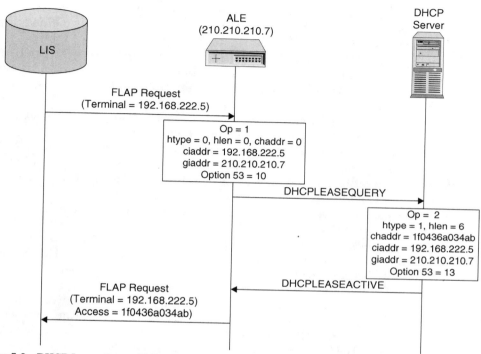

Figure 5.8   DHCP Lease Query ALE.

because DHCP requests are made using IP broadcasts and layer-3 routers will not pass broadcast traffic, so a means to deliver these messages to a DHCP server is required. Originally, DHCP relay-agent functions resided only in layer-3 routers and high-end switching nodes; however, it is a function that is becoming more and more prevalent in mid- to lower-end switching devices also.

A DHCP relay-agent intercepts DHCP broadcast messages and adds additional information before directly addressing the message to a known DHCP server as a unicast UDP packet. The DHCP relay-agent will look at the content of the intercepted message and, depending on the presence or absence of certain parameters, either add information or pass the message on to the DHCP server unmodified. Specifically, if the DHCP message does not have the `giaddr` header parameter set, the relay will set this parameter to be the IP address of the relay-agent (or IP address of the incoming interface if there is more than one). This functionality is defined in Reference 6.

NOTE: Reference 3 supports relay-agents adding location measurement data but not setting `giaddr` in trusted networks. However, many enterprise switches implementing DHCP relay set the `giaddr` field.

The relay-agent may also append data to more precisely specify the interface and port on which the request arrived. It is this information that is defined in Reference 3 and that is useful for location determination.

Reference 3 defines DHCP option 82, which is comprised of two sub-options: sub-option 1, the Agent Circuit ID; and sub-option 2, the Agent Remote ID. Sub-option 1, the Agent Circuit ID, is used to encode the identifier for the circuit on which the agent intercepted the client DHCP request. In the case of an enterprise-based Ethernet-managed switch, this would be the Ethernet port. Reference 3 provides a number of other examples to which the Agent Circuit ID may apply.

Sub-option 2, the Agent Remote ID, is designed to uniquely identify something at the other end of a permanent circuit that is terminated at the relay. Consequently, an Agent Remote ID must be globally unique. Examples of the Agent Remote ID are telephone number, MAC address, or a fully qualified user name (joe.blow@other.end.com). This reference also provides several other examples for Agent Remote ID.

One of the intended uses of the DHCP relay option data was to aid DHCP servers supporting a large number of geographically diverse hosts in making decisions about what configuration data to provide to which hosts. An unintended side effect of this functionality is that it can also aid network nodes that need to determine the physical locations of end hosts.

The precision of location determination using DHCP relay-agent data is dependent on how close to the edge network—for instance, the point of actual network attachment by a host—is to the DHCP relay-agent. As stated earlier, many older edge switches do not support DHCP relay functionality and defer it to larger switches and routers further into the core network (see Figure 5.9). Obviously, the further into the core, and the larger the area serviced, the less precise the yielded location will be since it must define a larger area to address all possibly connected hosts.

Conversely, enabling relays at the very edges of the network directly where hosts attach can yield relatively precise location information, providing that wiremap databases correlating switch and Circuit-ID information to locations are kept up-to-date (see Figure 5.10).

DHCP Relay Information Considerations   While DHCP relay-agent information may seem the perfect solution to location determination in the enterprise environment, it is not without its drawbacks. Some of these drawbacks are described in the subsequent sections.

Interpreting Relay-Agent Information   Reference 3 uses explicit language on how to interpret data transported in the Agent Circuit ID and Agent Remote ID fields, and this is an important note to anyone considering building or operating an LIS. These fields must be treated as literal strings—in other words, do not parse them in an attempt to extract specific tokens; data either match absolutely or they do not match at all.

DHCP Servers and Relay Information   Not all DHCP servers make use of DHCP relay data, and like all other DHCP options, if the server doesn't understand the data, the option is ignored. One of the most commonly used DHCP servers in enterprise

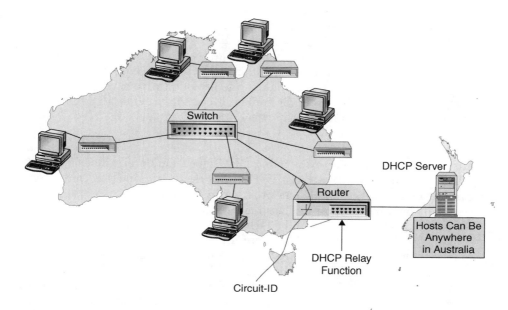

Figure 5.9 A DHCP relay in the core network.

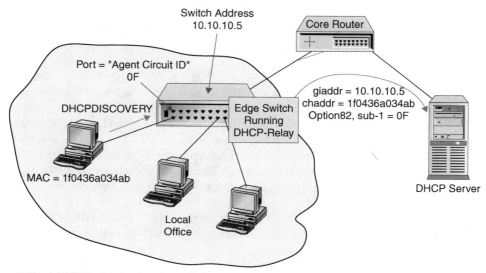

Figure 5.10 A DHCP relay in the edge switch.

environments today does not provide support for DHCP option 82. In addition to this, providing support for option 82 may be limited to configuration data assignment and may not extend to keeping the data in the lease database. Where the data is kept in the database, it can be retrieved using the DHCP lease query function described earlier. Some DHCP servers, such as the one provided with a Windows 2003 server, while not providing direct support for some options, do provide an extensive API, allowing adjunct functions to make use of this data.

Challenges or DHCP Methods in Wireless Networks   One other consideration that must be taken into account is using DHCP location determination in networks where a host may be mobile—a large WiFi network such as may be found on a university campus or in a large hotel. The problem in these situations is that DHCP relays are generally only in the communications loop at initial configuration time. Once a lease is established between a host and a DHCP server, messages are unicast—that is, they are exchanged directly between the client and the DHCP server. This makes it impossible to use relay information to keep tabs on a moving host.

The DHCP server identifier override sub-option describes a way in which a DHCP relay-agent can remain in the loop between the client and DHCP server for precisely the purpose of continuing to provide relay location measurements (see Reference 7). In this configuration, the client host must renew its lease or request a new configuration from the DHCP server in order for the relay-agent to provide the updated measurements. This may be a suitable compromise in many situations, particularly if the area of roaming can be encompassed by a single DHCP relay-agent. There are, however, still drawbacks with this approach, for example, if the host roams to an access point that is connected to a different switch/relay, then the measurements provided will be incorrect. These are not problems with the DHCP server identifier override sub-option or related concepts, so much as problems that may be encountered when trying to use it specifically to provide location determination measurements in certain network configurations.

The larger problems are more to do with the nature of mobile clients and DHCP client implementations. As stated, the DHCP server identifier override sub-option specification requires DHCP clients to do something—renew their lease or request configuration data—before the new location measurements are sent to the DHCP server. Lease times are generally, though not always, quite long, so relying on lease renewal is probably not a good approach for mobile devices. Assuming that the client can detect that it has changed access points, often it may not be able to; the client needs to do something like request network configuration data to ensure that network measurements are propagated to the DHCP server. A number of the more common DHCP client implementations, Windows XP among them, have a propensity to cache DHCP option configuration data. Requests for network data are responded to from cache, with actual requests to the network sent for options only when the cached data are deemed to be stale. This is actually consistent with the notion that network configuration data generally doesn't change too much, and highlights the problem of likening physical location information, which may change frequently, with network configuration information that does not.

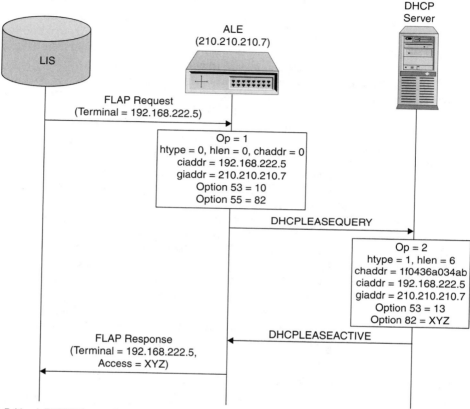

Figure 5.11   A DHCP Lease Query ALE extension.

A DHCP ALE   Thus far, we have described how information received by a DHCP server can aid in location determination. This section will describe how this information can be retrieved from a DHCP server and subsequently sent to a LIS using FLAP.

There are two basic approaches that will be discussed. The first approach is to incorporate the ALE functionality directly into the DHCP server. The second approach is to extend the DHCP Lease Query ALE described in the previous section titled "A DHCP Leasequery ALE."

On first impressions, a solution that requires modification to the DHCP server sounds complex and undesirable. However, certain environments, such as Windows XP, cater specifically for application developers that need to extend network server capabilities. In this environment, it is relatively easy to write a library that links to the DHCP server through the Windows-provided API, and extract the data required to send to the LIS. Indeed, for Windows, it is necessary since DHCP relay-agent data are not stored in the lease database, and the lease query functionality is not supported.

The second approach is to modify the DHCP lease query ALE to support returning the DHCP relay agent data associated with the DHCP lease. This mechanism is acceptable providing that the DHCP server supports the DHCP relay-agent option, stores relay-agent information in the lease database, and also supports the DHCP lease query protocol. Unfortunately, many DHCP servers do not support this.

The LIS-to-ALE queries and ALE-to-LIS notifications are the same regardless of which implementation is used. The key differences in the approaches lie in how the ALE extracts the data from the DHCP server. Where the ALE is coupled with the DHCP server directly, perhaps using an API, then the data extraction is internal and will not be discussed further. Where the ALE uses the lease query interface to extract relay data, Figure 5.8 changes to that shown in Figure 5.11.

The main difference here is that the ALE includes DHCP option 55 with a value of 82 in its request to the DHCP server, which indicates that the ALE is interested in DHCP relay-agent information. The DHCP server will include the DHCP relay-agent information in its response. However, DHCP option 82 sub-option 1, the Circuit-ID, must contain sufficient information to uniquely identify the switch and port within the access network, but it may not. This is because Reference 5 does not provide a way to obtain the address of the initial gateway that supplied the circuit information. This information was provided by the gateway in the `giaddr` field of the initial DHCP request, but this field cannot be used to communicate the gateway address in the lease query response because it is required to identify where the lease query response should be sent. Consequently, care must be taken when constructing an ALE in this manner to ensure that the preceding limitation is addressed.

Location Acquisition Alternatives and Comparisons to HELD

This section describes three location acquisition protocols, two of which are extensions of protocols that have their origins in enterprise networks, and the third being the HELD protocol. All three of the acquisition mechanisms are dependent on a central database to provide a mapping between physical location and a logical point of attachment (switch and port)—a.k.a., a *wiremap*. How and by which entities this information is accessed is discussed in the following sections.

Who Can Get Location?

Many people will answer this question by saying that only the end-point must be allowed to request its location. In reality, there is no right or wrong answer to the question of "who can get location?" since the acquisition of location very much depends on the application and circumstances. Existing free-phone services, such as those that allow you to dial to order a pizza, use location information attributed to your telephone number, yet this location isn't forwarded to the pizza shop even though the network needed to determine the phone's location. Requiring that location information only be made available to an end-point necessitates that all end-points in the network are location-capable. Being location-capable means that the end-point is able to request, acquire, and store location information. Furthermore, the end-point must recognize when location information is required by a service and make it available to the service or accept that the service will fail.

The majority of enterprises today do not have location-capable end-points, and the upfront cost to upgrade all end-points so that they are location-capable may be high. An example of exactly this kind of situation occurred around 2000 when cellular TDMA and GSM providers in North America were deciding what technology to endorse in order to meet the location requirement set by the FCC for Phase II emergency calls. If the phone helped in the location determination, using GPS, then it was a requirement that 95 percent of all phones would have to eventually be capable of GPS. This meant that the operator had to replace phones. Conversely, if the cellular operator used network-only determination, then the technology could service all existing and new phones. The estimated cost by some cellular operators to replace non-GPS-capable phones with GPS-capable phones to meet the 95-percent target was in the order of several billion dollars. Quite prohibitive! While most enterprises do not have millions of staff, many have thousands or even tens of thousands. Insisting on a wholesale swap-out or purchased upgrade of devices to make them location-capable is likely to be unpalatable in the short term.

The most commonly accepted alternative is to have a trusted network element request location on-behalf-of the end-point. This is referred to as an OBO request (see Figure 5.12). Take for example an IP-based PABX that terminates 5000 IP-phone extensions. If someone were to make an emergency call, the PABX could make a request

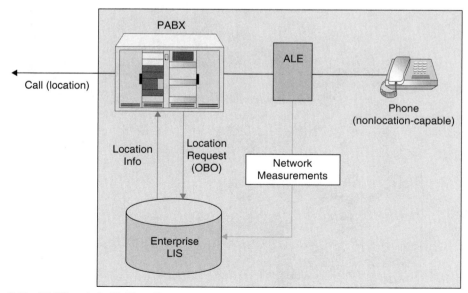

Figure 5.12   PABX on-behalf-of location request.

to the LIS for the location of the calling device. The PABX would identify the device for which the LIS is to provide the location by including the IP address of the calling device in the location request. The PABX can then either direct the call based on the location or provide the location to the necessary emergency authorities. This requires a software upgrade in the PABX to perform this OBO request without necessitating changes to the IP phones.

Link Layer Discovery Protocol Media Endpoint Discovery (LLDP-MED)

Link Layer Discovery Protocol Media Endpoint Discovery (LLDP-MED) is part of the IEEE 802.AB standard suite. The aim of LLDP-MED is to allow devices connecting to networks using the IEEE 802 suite of layer-2 protocols to advertise and discover capabilities of "logical" adjacent network nodes (see Figure 5.13). The technical recommendation in Reference 8 (TR-41.4) describes three Endpoint classes and the range of element capabilities for each class of Endpoint. We shall direct discussion to class III Endpoints, which are targeted towards end-user communication appliances, such as IP phones and the like, and specifically the ability to provide location information to these devices.

LLDP-MED requires location information to be published to an edge-device (switch) from a centrally managed database.

NOTE: While SNMP is not mandated by the LLDP-MED specification, it is used extensively in examples and will likely be the common deployment mechanism.

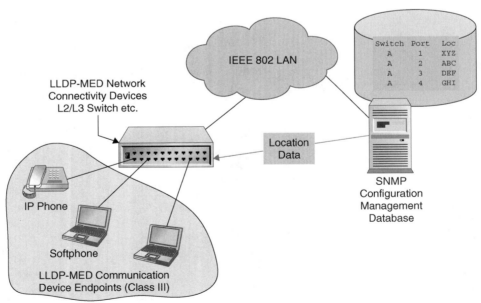

Figure 5.13   An LLDP-MED Class III device network.

Once published to the edge-device, the location information is stored in an SNMP MIB inside the switch. The switch will need to maintain location information for each discrete location that it serves. This may be a single location for an area with a cluster of office desks, or it may be a discrete location for each desk. Location information in LLDP-MED is delivered using the "Emergency Call Service Location Identifier Discovery Extension" and is targeted principally for emergency services usage. The amount of data that needs to be stored in the switch therefore is dependent upon local emergency regulations, the switch capability (capacity to store data), and the capability of the enterprise to accurately provide and maintain location data. Location formats available in LLDP-MED are aligned with those available over DHCP, namely the LCI geodetic form described in Reference 9 and the civic form described in Reference 10.

The intended use of LLDP-MED is that when a node attaches to the network it advertises its capabilities to its logically associated neighbors, and the neighbors reciprocate to the newly attached node. In this way, a node can learn, amongst other things, its location from the edge-switch to which it is connected. Location information is designed to be sent with an emergency call which requires the end-point to take the raw data received from LLDP and format it into a PIDF-LO. The end-point will need to have sufficient smarts and configuration data to allow this to occur so that the necessary mandatory fields are populated correctly. All this requires the node attaching to the network to be LLDP-MED-capable. So what happens if it isn't? The simple answer is that either the services are provided in a different way or they are unavailable.

As indicated earlier, while LLDP-MED does not stipulate SNMP must be used, employing it has the advantage that changes in network and switch configurations can be relayed back to a central NMS, allowing a network topology to be created. In this case, information about a specific device or hardware address connecting to the network is published to the NMS. If the end-device is not location-capable, then a LIS may use this information along with IP and MAC address bindings to determine the location of a device. This would allow support for things such as a PABX on-behalf-of location request to occur when location is not provided by the end-device, as illustrated in Figure 5.12.

DHCP Location Acquisition

DHCP location acquisition is described in Reference 9 and the DHCP civic draft described in Reference 10. Location data are treated the same as general network bootstrap data, and are provided to an end-point when the end-point first attaches to the network in the form of DHCP options. Location data can then be subsequently requested from the DHCP server either as part of a lease renewal, or network data refresh operation.

Reference 9 suggests that DHCP relay and Circuit-ID information is supplied to the DHCP server in the DHCP request, and that the DHCP server can use this information to determine the location of the end-point (see Figure 5.14). This mechanism for location determination was described in the earlier section titled "DHCP Relay Location Determination." Providing that end-points are not nomadic, then a static mapping from the end-point to the physical location can be used. The resulting key on which the

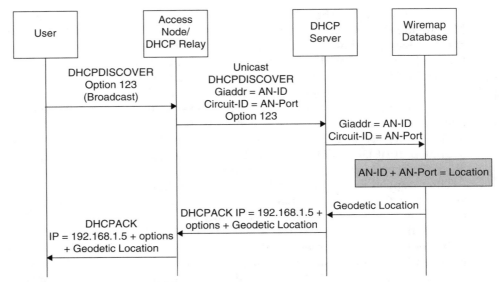

Figure 5.14 DHCP location acquisition.

mapping is performed may be a MAC address, IP address, or the "client identifier" defined in Reference 1. Where end-points may be nomadic and need to acquire a location at DHCP lease request time, the only viable option is to deploy a DHCP relay close to the point of network attachment since other mechanisms are likely to be too slow and result in DHCP client timeouts.

As with LLDP-MED, in order to use DHCP location acquisition, end-points need to be location-capable. DHCP is an end-point-to-server-based protocol, consequently DHCP location acquisition is not suitable for OBO-based location requests as is required for legacy devices. However, aspects of DHCP information, as described in the earlier section "Location Determination in Enterprise Networks," can be used to provide ALE measurements to a LIS. One advantage that DHCP location acquisition does provide in an enterprise environment is that almost all enterprises deploy DHCP as the primary means for providing host configuration data to end-points. This means that the updates required to end-points to support acquiring location data may be small. However, it is also true that, no matter how minor, modifications to end-devices are required for Reference 9 to be useful.

HELD Location Acquisition

The inner workings of the HELD protocol were described in Chapter 4. In summary, the HELD protocol is an application layer protocol designed specifically to allow devices to request location in the same way regardless of the type of access network. The basic HELD protocol, as defined in Reference 11, provides support for location-capable devices to request their own location, either in the form of a PIDF-LO or as a location URI. The general operation is simple. Upon connection to the enterprise network, the HELD client discovers the LIS and makes a subsequent request for location (see Figure 5.15). For an enterprise LIS, discovery may be a hard-coded address, or it may be based on the access domain name, as described in Chapter 4.

The preceding description works well for location-capable devices, but the HELD protocol also addresses the problems experienced by LLDP-MED and DHCP, when devices are not location-capable and location needs to be obtained on-behalf-of these devices. To support OBO requests, a requesting node needs to be able to provide an identifier for the Target in the location request to the LIS, and there is no means to do this in the basic HELD specification.

The HELD protocol was designed to be extensible, and it was understood that certain network configurations and applications may require an on-behalf-of location query mechanism. This LIS requirement was identified and described in Chapter 4 as the Trusted-Party Query Interface. To support this capability, the HELD protocol messages were specified to allow extensibility through the inclusion of additional XML namespaces. Appendix D provides an XML schema that defines a variety of identifiers that can be used by an OBO requesting node to identify a Target end-point to the LIS.

Taking the example of the IP-based PABX depicted in Figure 5.12, assuming the use of the HELD protocol and the identity extensions defined in Appendix D, the information flow would look similar to Figure 5.16.

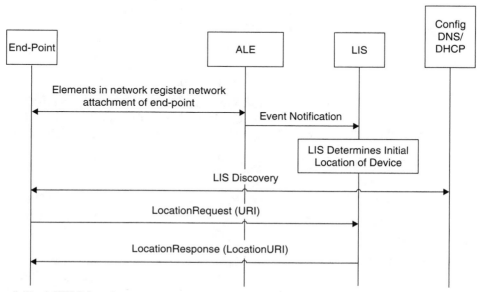

Figure 5.15   A HELD location request.

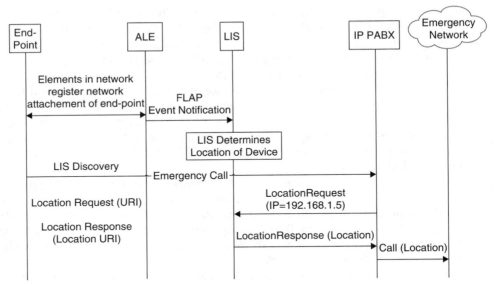

Figure 5.16 A HELD on-behalf-of location request.

The steps in Figure 5.16 are as follows:

1. End-point attaches to the network.

2. Network attachment is detected by an ALE, and the associated network measurements are passed to the LIS using FLAP.

3. The LIS uses the measurements contained in the FLAP message to determine the location of the end-point.

4. The end-point makes an emergency call.

5. The PABX determines that the call is an emergency call, and makes an OBO location request to the LIS using the IP address of the end-point as the Target identifier. The HELD protocol request would look something like the following:

```
<locationRequest xmlns="http://sitacs.uow.edu.au/ns/location/held">
    <locationType>any</locationType>
    <heldDevice
         xmlns="http://sitacs.uow.edu.au/ns/location/held:deviceIdentifiers">
        <ipV4>192.168.1.5</ipV4>
    </heldDevice>
</locationRequest>
```

6. The LIS trusts the PABX (this may be achieved through network provisioning or through the use of X.509 certificates) and uses the Target identifier contained in the location request, IP address 192.168.1.5, to retrieve the location of the end-point.

7. The LIS constructs a PIDF-LO and returns the location of the end-point to the PABX.

8. The PABX includes the PIDF-LO received from the LIS in the outbound emergency call.

The advantage of this configuration is that the number of devices and network elements that need to be location-capable is greatly reduced. It is in essence only the PABX. While the solution calls for a LIS, this function is also notionally required in both the LLDP-MED and DHCP location acquisitions since it provides the mapping between logical network identifiers and physical locations. The need for ALEs is very much dependent on the network configuration and how device attachments are detected and subsequently mapped to physical locations. In DHCP, the ALE is in essence a relay, while in LLDP-MED the ALE is an integral part of the switch and protocol design. Separating location acquisition from location determination enables OBO functionality to occur, and so reduces the cost of deploying location-aware and location-capable networks without the need to upgrade every end-point.

Enterprise Location Considerations

This section will look at issues that need to be taken into account when introducing a LIS into an enterprise. It will describe such things as Network Address Translation (NAT), VPNs, and data management.

NATs, Firewalls, and VPNs

Network Address Translations (NATs), firewalls, and Virtual Private Networks (VPNs) are generally problematic because they alter or disguise the identity of end-points connected to the network. NATs are designed to translate from localized private address spaces into more publicly routable IP addresses. Firewalls, which often employ NATs, are designed to restrict the flow of certain types of traffic. While VPNs are designed specifically to make hosts residing on remote networks appear as though they are residing on the local enterprise network. These problems are not insurmountable, providing thought is given as to where and how location determination and acquisition are to occur.

VPNs are most easily addressed by ensuring that the local access network determines and provides location to the end-point prior to the end-point establishing a VPN back to the enterprise. For this to work effectively, the end-point needs to be location-capable. While it is technically possible to support nomadic non-location-capable devices through VPNs, the complexities and practicalities make it infeasible, as extensive changes to VPN servers and other network nodes both in the enterprise and the public network would be required.

NATs are a little more problematic since many hosts with discrete IP addresses, that may also be geographically diverse, may reside behind a single IP address attributed to a Network Address Translation device. In many cases, the most practical thing to do is to add a LIS inside the domain controlled by the NAT. This is the same approach that is

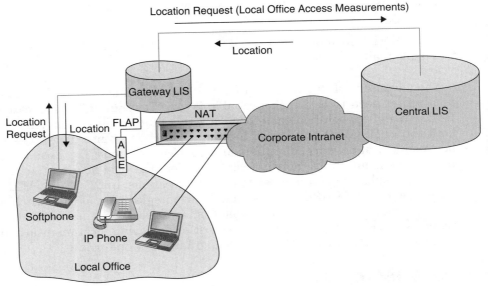

Figure 5.17 A Gateway LIS operating as a relay.

applied to many local services such as DHCP servers, web servers, and DNS servers within enterprises today. In other cases, where the geographically served area of the enterprise is small, it may be fine for all hosts behind the NAT to be attributed with the same location. Home offices and small shop fronts where Internet connectivity is achieved through DSL or cable modems are a good example of where a single location is suitable.

Where putting a full LIS behind the NAT doesn't make sense—where there is a centralized corporate infrastructure team—then a Gateway LIS can be employed to perform a relay function, and relay location requests to the central office LIS (see Figure 5.17).

The steps for location determination and acquisition in this model are:

1. Softphone connects to the local office network.

2. ALE measurements are passed to the local Gateway LIS if required.

3. Softphone requests location from the local Gateway LIS, and assumes a simple HELD protocol GET, which might look like:

```
<locationRequest xmlns="http://sitacs.uow.edu.au/ns/location/held"/>
```

4. The Gateway LIS forwards the request, plus any measurement data to the central LIS. This request would look something similar to:

```
<locationRequest xmlns="http://sitacs.uow.edu.au/ns/location/held"
                 responseTime="2" signed="true">
    <locationType>
```

```
         geodetic
      </locationType>
      <heldDevice
            xmlns="http://sitacs.uow.edu.au/ns/location/held:deviceIdentifiers">
         <dhcp>
            <giaddr>192.168.5.9</giaddr>
            <agentID>4E6574676561722D31</agentID>
            <circuitID>30312F3530</circuitID>
         </dhcp>
      </heldDevice>
   </locationRequest>
```

5. The central LIS determines the location and returns a PIDF-LO to the Gateway LIS.

```
<?xml version="1.0" encoding="UTF-8"?>
<presence xmlns="urn:ietf:params:xml:ns:pidf"
   xmlns:gp="urn:ietf:params:xml:ns:pidf:geopriv10"
   xmlns:gs="urn:ietf:params:xml:ns:pidf:geopriv10:geoShape"
   entity="pres:user76@remote.office.example.com">
   <tuple id="sg89ab">
      <status>
         <gp:geopriv>
            <gp:location-info>
               <gs:Circle srsName="urn:ogc:def:crs:EPSG::4326"
                  xmlns:gs="urn:ietf:params:xml:ns:pidf:geopriv10:geoShape"
                  xmlns:gml="http://www.opengis.net/gml">
                  <gml:pos>
                     42.5463 -73.2512
                  </gml:pos>
                  <gml:radius uom="urn:ogc:def:uom:EPSG::9001">
                     850.24
                  </gml:radius>
               </gs:Circle>
            </gp:location-info>
            <gp:usage-rules>
               <gp:retransmission-allowed>yes</gp:retransmission-allowed>
            </gp:usage-rules>
            <gp:method>dhcp</gp:method>
         </gp:geopriv>
      </status>
      <timestamp>2003-06-22T20:57:29Z</timestamp>
   </tuple>
</presence>
```

6. The Gateway LIS returns the location to the softphone.

There may be some benefits in including a default location that the local Gateway LIS can return to all clients in the event that the central LIS is unreachable. Such a precaution certainly guards against central LIS failure, but may be less useful where link failures to the central office occur, particularly if the local office is dependent on the central office for all outbound communication and, in any case, is a LIS implementation-specific detail.

Data Management

The key to determining and providing accurate location in any environment is ensuring that information relating to the configuration of the network is correct. Ensuring that this information is correct has been a major hurdle in the deployment of accurate location services for cellular operators the world over, and has resulted in significant changes in work practices to maintain data integrity across networks. This same problem will impact IT work practices for IP telephony devices, if legal obligations come into effect requiring accurate emergency call location within enterprises or, indeed, where accurate location becomes an important aspect of the enterprises applications.

Many IT departments have strict controls and integral knowledge of phone extension placements. This stems in part from the connection-oriented nature of phones, and the convenience of staff not needing to change extension numbers simply because they move desks. In some parts of the United States, legislation mandates that certain types of premises must report locations of no larger than a certain size (8000 sq. ft. in one instance) in the event of an emergency. Such policies have resulted in PABX manufacturers supporting the grouping of phone extensions that are in physical proximity to one another.

Often, the controls and data management associated with the placement of telephone extensions is not extended to recordkeeping practices for Ethernet and data ports in enterprise environments. As IP devices within the enterprise become telephony-enabled, this lack of accurate recordkeeping represents a gap in the knowledge required to determine and provide accurate location information. This is particularly true in environments that employ practices such as hot desking and require staff to use softphone applications tied to their laptop or PC. In these scenarios, a staff member may be anywhere within the building and an extension number is not tied to a physical location as it was with a more traditional phone system. To address these issues, accurate records of switch-port terminations and other data records will need to be maintained, and this data will need to be propagated into the LIS in a timely fashion. Ideally, applications will evolve that allow IT staff to enter this information directly into the LIS, and the LIS can serve as a record of data interconnection as well as an operating database for terminal location acquisition.

Enterprise Location Applications

The most commonly used example for location has been in emergency applications; however, it is also useful in a great many applications that have nothing to do with emergency services, such as asset tracking or staff location, for example. Both of these are useful applications in a variety of environments. In this section, we shall describe two main applications, staff location/asset tracking, and variants on the emergency application. In the latter case, specific emphasis is placed on voice-hosted services; a growing trend in campus enterprises to reduce the spiraling costs of telecommunications.

Staff-Locator/Asset Tracker Application

In large enterprise campuses that support mobility of staff and assets, it is often important that people and things can be located quickly. In these types of environments, the devices and people that are going to be located have consistent or unique names, but their logical network addresses may not be known. For example, Dr. Smith is known, but the fact that his PDA has a MAC address of 0xab12cd34ef56 is probably not known. Furthermore, what happens if Dr. Smith buys a new PDA? How is he identified so he can be located? This shows that people, and sometimes assets, have common names that generally don't change through the course of their lifetime, and it is useful to be able to identify and locate them using their common names. In this section, we shall describe two ways in which a staff-locator/asset tracker application can be built using the location determination and acquisition techniques we have described thus far. The first method will use a client-based application, and the second will be network-centric.

A Client-Based Locator Application   In this solution, a device will start a HELD client when it boots, the HELD client will discover the LIS, and will either periodically request refresh location information or it will obtain a location URI by creating a context on the LIS. Generally, a single HELD client will reside on the end-host and it will provide an API that will allow multiple applications to make use of its services.

In this case, a thin staff-locator client will request the location or location URI from the HELD client via the API and will publish the name of the person, the IP address of the device, and the location information to a server running the staff locator application (see Figure 5.18). Likewise, when the application is shut down, it will deregister its information with the application server.

The staff locator application server is able to provide location information about registered users to people needing access to this location information. Where the location is provided as a literal by the thin-client, the application server can provide an immediate response to the request. Where the location is provided as a reference by the thin-client, the application server will first need to retrieve the device's location from the LIS. The type of network and the type of device involved will govern whether a literal location or a location URI is the most appropriate form of location information.

A Network-Based Locator Application   In many cases, the device-based application described in the previous section will work fine, but in some instances, modifying the equipment to include a locator application, no matter how thin, may simply not be possible. In such circumstances, a network-based application may be more appropriate.

Most of us have used a PC at work at one time or another, and usually your PC will have a name. If so, you can create a public-read directory on your PC so that other people in your office can access data that you want to share. Thus, if you get your IP address dynamically allocated, for the previous solution to work the DHCP server needs to tell the DNS server that a particular host has been allocated a particular IP address (see Figure 5.19). The mechanisms to do this are described in Reference 12. When a host requests an IP address from a DHCP server, it specifies its name (using DHCP option 12 defined in Reference 13) to the DHCP server. Once the lease is established, the DHCP server can dynamically update the DNS server with the hostname and IP address.

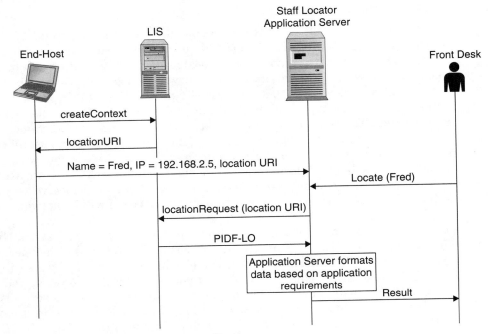

Figure 5.18   A client-based locator sequence diagram.

So, looking at our previous example of Dr. Smith, the DNS server knows the name and IP address of all hosts in the network, including Dr. Smith's. This is closer, for if I know the name of Dr. Smith's host, I can now ask the DNS server for his PDA's IP address and I can then ask the LIS to find the IP address. But what if I only know his name or phone extension? The answer is Lightweight Directory Access Protocol (LDAP).

LDAP is a directory service protocol that allows a directory client to query a directory server, and it is very commonly deployed in enterprises. Things that might be kept in an LDAP directory server are things such as Dr. Smith, his phone extension, his mobile number, his e-mail address, his login name, and also possibly the hostname of any host Dr. Smith is currently logged into, including his PDA. Providing that asset and staff data are maintained in the LDAP server, then the server can be queried and the data obtained as required.

At this point, we can use a LIS to determine the location of anything on our network that is active by using a unique identifier in the LDAP directory.

Through the use of a secure web application server, web applications that allow fast location of assets and staff are possible (see Figure 5.20). Client applications, such as those running on the Reception and Asset Monitor hosts, may be simple web browsers, allowing the complexity to reside solely in the server. Care must be taken with such

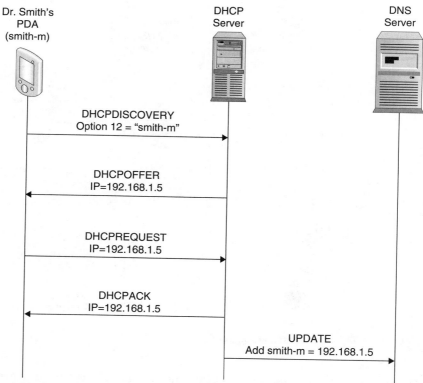

Figure 5.19   A DNS dynamic update.

systems to maintain security so that location information relating to personnel and staff is not available to people who are not authorized to obtain it. Authorization to this information within an enterprise will be subject to company policy and federal, state, and local government regulations.

An Emergency Application

One of the major imperatives for location in IP networks is to support the routing of emergency calls, since an IP address outside the context of a local network provides little or no indication as to the physical location of a Target. IP telephony requires location for emergency routing to ensure that the call is delivered to the PSAP in the correct geographical area to deal with the emergency. There are two options available, provide a literal location with the call, or provide a location reference with the call. A location reference may be provided explicitly in the form of a location URI, or implicitly as a SIP AOR

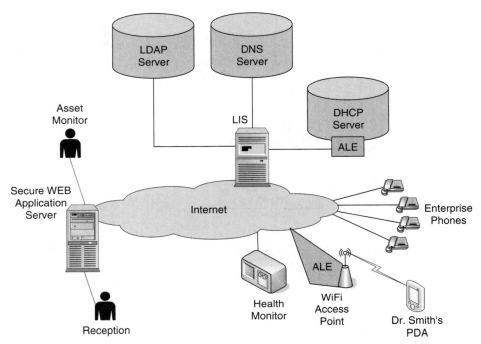

Figure 5.20 Asset and staff tracking configuration.

or the extension number of the caller encoded as tel-uri (tel-uri's are defined in detail in Reference 14). Where DHCP or LLDP-MED are used for location acquisition, the options are more limited, the end-point must provide a literal location object in the body of the call signaling. In a network where the HELD protocol is employed, a range of additional hosted services are available.

Hosted Voice Service with a Literal Location   In this situation, the enterprise outsource their call service to an Internet call service provider to reduce cost, and provide the IP call-server with a literal location when an emergency call is placed. Using the NENA-i2 architecture as a model, let's walk through a call example.

1. The phone on the right-hand side of Figure 5.21 makes an emergency call.

2. The PABX detects the emergency call and requests a PIDF-LO from the enterprise LIS for the phone making the call. The PABX uses the phone's IP address as an identifier to the enterprise LIS, as described earlier in this chapter.

3. The enterprise LIS determines the location of the phone.

   a. The enterprise LIS may simply return the PIDF-LO to the PABX.

   b. Or the enterprise LIS may request a signed PIDF-LO from the access provider before returning a PIDF-LO to the PABX. We will address this situation more in the next chapter.

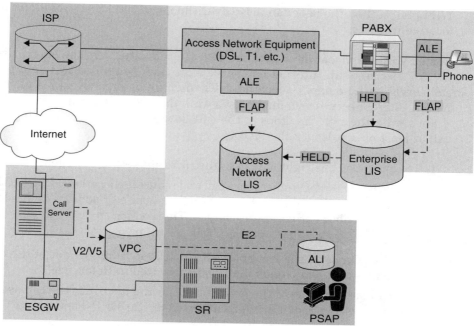

Figure 5.21   Emergency routing with a literal location.

4. The PABX inserts the PIDF-LO into the body of the outbound SIP invite message.

NOTE: The document cited in Reference 15 supports PIDF-LO conveyance in the body of a SIP invite message. The SIP specification does not support a proxy inserting items into the body of a SIP message, consequently the PABX is considered a Back-to-Back-UA (B2BUA) when used in this mode, not a proxy (see Reference 16).

5. The call-server receives the invite message and identifies the call as an emergency call, requesting routing information from the VoIP Positioning Center (VPC). This may be over the webservices-V2 interface, or through the SIP V5 interface. The call-server passes the PIDF-LO to the VPC in the routing information request.

6. The VPC determines the correct routing information based on the location provided in the PIDF-LO.

7. The VPC returns the routing information to the call-server and the call-server routes the call.

8. The PSAP may now request the location from the VPC. No location updates are possible.

In the provided example, the call is routed based on a literal location that is provided in-band with the call setup information. This same location is then made available to the PSAP. This is okay for a standard desk phone, but if the device was a dual-mode

WiFi phone, then the user can move over time, and the PSAP would not be able to get location updates.

Hosted Voice Services with a Location URI   In this situation, the enterprise outsources its call service to an Internet call service provider to reduce cost, and provide the IP call-server with an explicit location URI when an emergency call is placed. Using the NENA-i2 architecture as a model, let's walk through a call example.

Let's walk through the steps of the call flow assuming SIP signaling for the actual call at least once it leaves the PABX.

1. The phone on the right side of Figure 5.22 makes an emergency call.

2. The PABX detects the emergency call and requests a location URI from the LIS for the phone making the call. The PABX uses the phone's IP address as an identifier to the LIS as described earlier in this chapter. This creates an active context on the LIS.

3. The LIS responds with a location URI to the PABX.

4. The PABX inserts the location URI into the location header of the outbound SIP invite message. This functionality is supported in Reference 15.

5. The call-server receives the invite message and identifies the call as an emergency call, requesting routing information from the VoIP Positioning Center (VPC).

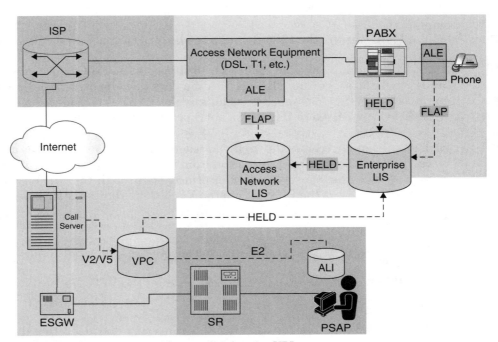

Figure 5.22   Emergency routing with an explicit location URI.

This may be over the webservices-V2 interface, or through the SIP V5 interface. The call-server passes the location URI to the VPC in the routing information request.

6. The VPC uses the location URI to request location information from the enterprise LIS.

   a. The enterprise LIS may simply return location information to the VPC.

   b. Or the enterprise LIS may have been requested to provide a signed PIDF-LO that it may, in turn, need to request from the access provider before returning a PIDF-LO to the VPC. We will address this situation more in the next chapter.

7. The VPC determines the correct routing information based on the location provided by the LIS.

8. The VPC returns the routing information to the call-server and the call-server routes the call.

9. The PSAP may now request the location from the VPC whenever it likes during the course of the call. In turn, the VPC can request location updates from the enterprise LIS.

10. At the completion of the call, the PABX terminates the active location context on the LIS.

The preceding call-flow, like the flow from the earlier example, is strictly NENA-i2–compliant. The advantage of this flow over the previous flow is that it allows the PSAP to request updates on the location of the caller, making it more suitable in situations where the caller may be moving around the enterprise campus.

The problem with this model is what while the call-server has a direct relationship with the enterprise, the VPC may not, since VPCs typically operate at the national level. Not having this direct relationship requires the VPC to establish a secure session with the enterprise LIS each time it needs to request a location. While this is not a long process, it does add some delay, so care must be taken to ensure that the LIS has sufficient bandwidth and accessibility to the Internet for VPC communication.

Hosted Voice Services with an Implicit Location Reference   In this situation, the enterprise outsources its call service to an Internet call service provider to reduce cost, but does not provide the IP call-server with a literal location or an explicit location URI when an emergency call is placed. Instead, the call-server must glean other information from the call-setup messaging to obtain location information. Using the NENA-i2–architecture as a model, let's walk through a call example.

Let's walk through the steps of the call flow assuming SIP signaling for the actual call once it leaves the PABX.

1. The phone on the right side of Figure 5.23 makes an emergency call.

2. The PABX addresses the outbound SIP message with a from header set to the directory number of the phone, say `tel:+1-201-555-0123`.

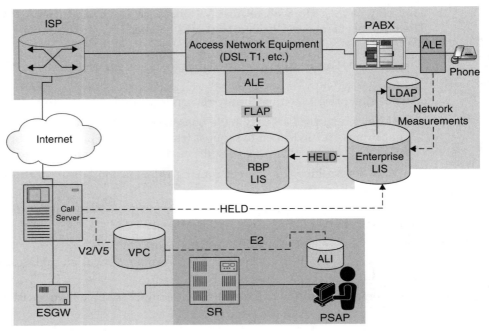

Figure 5.23 Emergency routing with an implicit location reference.

3. The call-server receives the invite message and identifies the call as an emergency call. The call-server extracts the "from header" from the SIP invite message and uses the tel-uri to determine which enterprise LIS to request the location from.

4. The call-server uses a nailed-up connection, or establishes a connection to the enterprise LIS and requests the location for `tel:+1-201-555-0123`.

NOTE: To make a location request in this fashion requires the HELD protocol device identifier extension specified in Appendix E.

5. The enterprise LIS uses an LDAP server to determine who the extension belongs to and their host name (see the section on Staff locator application earlier in this chapter). Once the hostname is known, DNS can be used to obtain the corresponding IP address. The LIS then uses the IP address to determine the location.

6. The LIS returns the location to the call-server.

7. The call-server sends the location to the VPC.

8. The VPC determines the correct routing information based on the location provided by the LIS.

9. The VPC returns the routing information to the call-server, and the call-server routes the call.

The solution described in this section does not strictly follow the NENA-i2 architecture. It does, however, result in the PABX not needing to be location-capable, which generates potentially lower infrastructure costs. This solution makes use of the fact that there is a preexisting relationship between the call-server and the enterprise network. Having the preexisting relationship reduces session establishment time between the call-server and the LIS, making the response faster. This also allows the enterprise LIS to remain shielded from the general Internet and thus less vulnerable to outside attack. Note that in this solution, location updates to the emergency network are not supported.

Enterprise Location Conclusions

Several options are available to an enterprise for both location determination and location acquisition. Option selection largely depends on existing deployment, the cost to upgrade, and the motivations to deploy location. The largest flexibility revolves around deployments that make a clear separation between location determination and location acquisition. The greatest flexibility in the use of location information comes where location information is available to entities other than just the end user. Such systems provide immediate support for legacy or location-incapable end-points. In addition, they allow network-enabled location applications to be created and made operational without the need to create and deploy specific applications to all end-points involved.

References

1. Droms, R., *"Dynamic Host Configuration Protocol,"* RFC 2131, March 1997.
2. Croft, B. and J. Gilmore, *"Bootstrap Protocol,"* RFC 0951, September 1985.
3. Patrick, M., *"DHCP Relay Agent Information Option,"* RFC 3046, January 2001.
4. Decker, E., Langille, P., Rijsinghani, A., and K. McCloghrie, *"Definitions of Managed Objects for Bridges,"* RFC 1493, July 1993.
5. Woundy, R. and K. Kinnear, *"Dynamic Host Configuration Protocol (DHCP) Leasequery,"* RFC 4388, February 2006.
6. Wimer, W., *"Clarifications and Extensions for the Bootstrap Protocol,"* RFC 1542, October 1993.
7. Johnson, R., *"DHCP Server Identifier Override Suboption,"* draft-ietf-dhc-server-override-03, (work in progress), October 2005.
8. TIA, *"Link Layer Discovery Protocol for Media Endpoint Devices (LLDP-MED),"* TR 41.4.
9. Polk, J., Schnizlein, J., and M. Linsner, *"Dynamic Host Configuration Protocol Option for Coordinate-based Location Configuration Information,"* RFC 3825, July 2004.

10. Schulzrinne, H., *"Dynamic Host Configuration Protocol (DHCPv4 and DHCPv6) Option for Civic Addresses Configuration Information,"* (work in progress), draft-ietf-geopriv-dhcp-civil-09, January 2006.

11. Winterbottom, J., Thomson, M., and B. Stark, *"HTTP Enabled Location Delivery (HELD),"* draft-winterbottom-http-location-delivery-03, (work in progress), May 2006.

12. Vixie, P., Thomson, S., Rekhter, Y., and J. Bound, *"Dynamic Updates in the Domain Name System (DNS UPDATE),"* RFC 2136, April 1997.

13. Alexander, S. and R. Droms, *"DHCP Options and BOOTP Vendor Extensions,"* RFC 2132, March 1997.

14. Schulzrinne, H., *"The tel URI for Telephone Numbers,"* RFC 3966, December 2004.

15. Polk, J. and B. Rosen, *"Session Initiation Protocol Location Conveyance,"* (work in progress), draft-ietf-sip-location-conveyance-02, March 2006.

16. Rosenberg, J., Schulzrinne, H., Camarillo, G., Johnston, A., Peterson, J., Sparks, R., Handley, M., and E. Schooler, *"SIP: Session Initiation Protocol,"* RFC 3489, June 2002.

6

IP Location in Wireline Public Carrier Networks

In the previous chapter, we examined location determination and acquisition techniques that can be applied to enterprise IP networks. In this chapter, we will look at location determination and acquisition techniques for residential broadband networks, and specifically focus on DSL and cable networks.

Digital Subscriber Line (DSL) Networks

DSL is the fastest growing technology, enabling the deployment of residential broadband networks globally. By the end of 2005, there were 139 million DSL subscribers worldwide and 48.2 million subscribers in Europe, while China, the Middle East, and Africa all had growth rates above 100 percent. This fantastic growth rate has largely been due to DSL's ability to work over existing copper telephone lines that run to most houses in urban areas throughout the world.

DSL uses special modems at each end of the phone line that make use of the bandwidth available in the wires that is not used for conventional voice traffic. This allows a residence to have high-speed Internet connectivity and a normal telephone service at the same time over the same copper pair. At the telephone exchange, the DSL signal is separated from the voice traffic and ultimately routed through the subscriber's ISP.

Incumbent telephone companies have a preference toward DSL broadband since it enables them to make use of existing copper cables to provide next-generation network access at a fraction of what it would cost to install new purpose-built cable plants (see Figure 6.1).

It should be noted that DSL networks are evolving, and that the responsibilities of nodes, and the interfaces between them, are changing. This section provides a cursory overview of the responsibilities and interfaces between nodes only. For intricate details

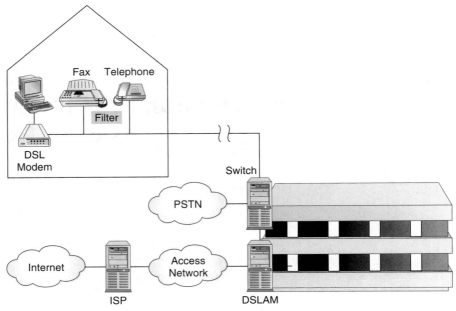

Figure 6.1 Basic DSL deployment.

about any specific issue concerning DSL networks, the reader should refer to the DSL forum web site at www.dslforum.org/index.shtml.

DSL Entities

DSL networks often require the cooperation of several organizations in order for a service to be delivered. This is because different aspects and functions may reside in the different organizations and all are required for any connection to be established and maintained. The DSL forum is the internationally recognized organization that is responsible for formulating architectures and recommendations for DSL networks. The main entities required to establish and maintain a DSL connection that have been identified by the DSL forum are shown in Figure 6.2, while the complete architecture is detailed in the DSL Forum's Technical Report (see Reference 1 at the end of the chapter). The entities shown in Figure 6.2 are described in detail next. The loop provider is responsible for:

- Providing a physical loop from the local network equipment to the customer's premises
- The integrity of the physical loop and its repair
- Granting the access network provider aggregated access to remotely deployed DSL equipment owned, operated, and maintained by the loop provider

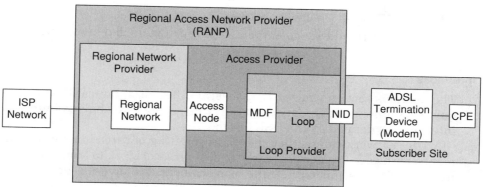

Figure 6.2 DSL access entities.

The access network provider is responsible for:

- Providing digital connectivity to the customer via the physical loop
- The performance and repair of the access transmission equipment

The regional network provider is responsible for:

- Providing connectivity between the access network and Internet service providers.
- Regional network performance and repair
- Possibly performing aggregation services to Internet service providers and/or providing any connectivity within the regional broadband network on behalf of the Internet service providers

The regional/access network provider (RANP) is responsible for:

- Aggregating subscriber traffic and/or routing and forwarding traffic throughout the network
- Aggregating subscriber traffic to ISPs for IP address allocation and network authentication

The Internet service provider (ISP) is responsible for:

- Overall service assurance
- Providing or specifying required CPE and software to support a given service
- Being the customer contact point for any and all customer-related problems concerning the provision of the service

■ Authenticating customers for access

■ Providing IP address to authenticated customers and managing IP address pools

DSL Interfaces

The previous section showed that several different organizational bodies may be required to provide DSL connectivity. In this section, we shall examine the main DSL interfaces as defined by the DSL forum.

A DSL network can be thought of as consisting of three main communications segments, with each segment running its own protocol stack to transport data around the network. These segments are the loop segment, the access segment, and the service provider segment, which are highlighted in Figure 6.3.

The segments shown in Figure 6.3 are deemed the U-interface, the V-interface, and the A10-interface, respectively, by the DSL forum in Technical Report (see Reference 2). The DSL forum defines an additional interface, the T-interface, which runs from the DSL modem to a host device inside the customer premises. Where the customer premises are large—say an enterprise campus—then the location solutions described in Chapter 5 should be applied. Where the customer's premises are small, like a residential house, unit, or apartment, then the T-interface is of little consequence with regards to location. This is because the same location can be applied to the modem and to all hosts directly connected to it. As a result, the T-interface is not described further in this document.

The U-Interface   The U-interface is associated with the loop segment, which provides the connectivity between the DSL modem and the Access Node (DSLAM). Seven protocol

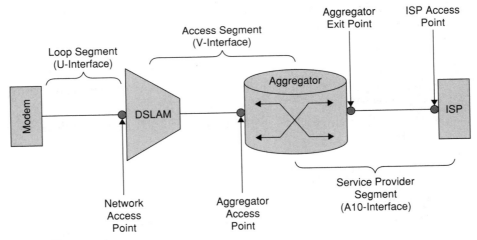

Figure 6.3 DSL segments.

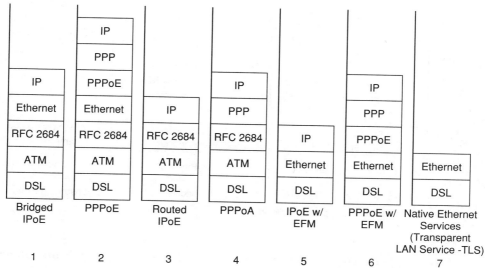

Figure 6.4 U-Interface protocol stacks.

stacks are defined in the DSL forum, and run over two transport variants, either ATM over DSL, or Ethernet over DSL. They are shown in Figure 6.4 and are described in detail in Reference 3 and Reference 4.

Most DSL residential broadband routers will run IP over Ethernet (IPoE), PPP over Ethernet (PPPoE), or PPP over ATM (PPPoA). These equate to stacks 1 and 5 for IPoE, stacks 2 and 6 for PPPoE, and stack 4 for PPPoA. Since these stacks represent the vast majority of residential broadband deployments, these stacks will be the ones used for examples in this chapter.

The V-Interface The V-interface is associated with the access segment which provides the connectivity between the Access Node (DSLAM) and Regional Aggregator. Generally, the V-interface uses an ATM or Ethernet transport. ATM is the more traditional means of providing connectivity from the DSLAM to the core network. This is achieved by having one Permanent Virtual Circuit (PVC) established from the DSLAM to the Aggregator for each DSL port on the DSLAM. Ethernet is becoming more common and is generally preferred in newer DSLAMs. In networks that use an Ethernet U-interface, traffic stream segregation is maintained through the use of VLANs. As will be shown in later sections, there are several ways that VLANs can be used to keep data streams orthogonal between the DSLAM, the Aggregator, and ultimately the ISP.

The A10-Interface The A10-interface is associated with the service provider segment which provides connectivity between the Aggregator and the ISP. The three protocol

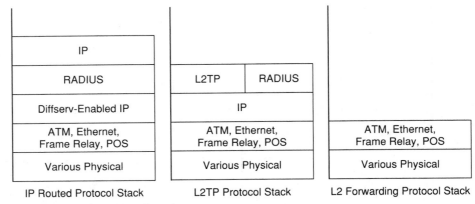

Figure 6.5   A10-interface protocol stacks.

stacks supported over the A10-interface are shown in Figure 6.5, and all are described in examples later in this chapter.

Protocol Background

Before we further explore DSL, it is very important to be grounded in some of the protocols used in the DSL protocol stack. Many of the public Internet providers have their roots in dial-up, and dial-up used serial point-to-point (PPP) connections. ISPs generally use a central database to manage user authentication and configuration profiles, user session establishment includes querying the profile database using RADIUS to authenticate the user and obtain configuration parameters to complete the connection. The growth of Ethernet and the shear volume of PPP and RADIUS deployments resulted in the need to encapsulate PPP packets into Ethernet frames. This is referred to as PPP over Ethernet (PPPoE).

This section is a quick tutorial/introduction to PPP, PPPoE, RADIUS, and RADIUS accounting. Understanding what these protocols are, how they evolved, and why they are pertinent today will help greatly with understanding the subsequent sections describing DSL location determination and acquisition. The introduction concludes with a cursory look at the Layer 2 Tunneling Protocol (L2TP), and the RADIUS and RADIUS accounting extensions required to support it.

Point-to-Point Protocol (PPP)   Point-to-Point Protocol (PPP) is not a single protocol but a suite of protocols consisting of literally dozens of specifications. We are not interested in all of them however, only a very few select ones. The base PPP specification is defined in Reference 5 and describes PPP as a protocol designed for transporting multiprotocol datagrams over point-to-point links. The base PPP specification describes PPP encapsulation and Link Control Protocol. Support for network-layer protocols is provided in

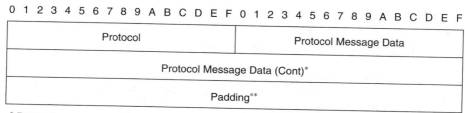

Figure 6.6   PPP data encapsulation.

PPP through network control protocols (NCPs) that are established across the link after the link has been configured and tested, and often after a peer has been authenticated.

The encapsulation mechanism in PPP is simple, and is designed for the peers to easily determine which protocol a specific packet is destined for. The general encapsulation model is shown in Figure 6.6.

PPP consists of a number of phases. The first phase is the link establishment phase. In order to establish communications over the link, it needs to be configured and tested, this is done using the Link Configuration Protocol (LCP).

One of the things that a peer can request during the link establishment phase is that authentication occur. This actually occurs after the establishment of the link using the PPP authentication protocols, of which the two most common are password authentication protocol (PAP) and challenge handshake authentication protocol (CHAP). PAP and CHAP are defined in Reference 6, with CHAP being later updated in Reference 7.

After the link has been established and peers have authenticated one another, the peers can request to start using other network-layer protocols such as IP. This is done through configuring a network control protocol (NCP). The NCP for the Internet Protocol is called Internet Protocol Control Protocol (IPCP) and is defined in Reference 8. IPCP follows a similar message sequence to LCP, and will not be described in detail here except to say that it supports assignment of an IP address and identification on DNS servers amongst other things. After the IPCP NCP is configured, then peers can start to exchange IP datagrams. IP datagrams are encapsulated as shown in the previous figure, by setting the protocol value to 0x0021, and placing the datagram itself into the protocol message data section of the PPP payload.

PPP over Ethernet (PPPoE)   PPP over Ethernet (PPPoE) is documented in Reference 9, and used extensively in ADSL deployments. PPPoE consists of two main parts, a peer discovery part, and a PPP establishment part. Discovery is required because PPP is a peer-to-peer protocol and it is necessary for an Ethernet host to first find a peer with which it can establish a relationship.

PPPoE Discovery   PPPoE functions follow a client/server model in the discovery stage, with the client being a host or DSL modem, searching for a server (access concentrator AC) and establishing a session with that server.

1. The client discovers the AC by sending out a broadcast message called a PPPoE Active Discovery Initiation (PADI) packet. A PADI packet can include data passed from the client to would-be ACs specifying options that the client needs, or certain characteristics of the client. These are specified in what are referred to as *Tags*. A PADI request providing information about the point of attachment of a client would look something like Figure 6.7.

2. Any ACs that see this message then respond with a PPPoE Active Discovery Offer (PADO) packet indicating that they can service the client. This response is unicast addressed to the client's Ethernet address.

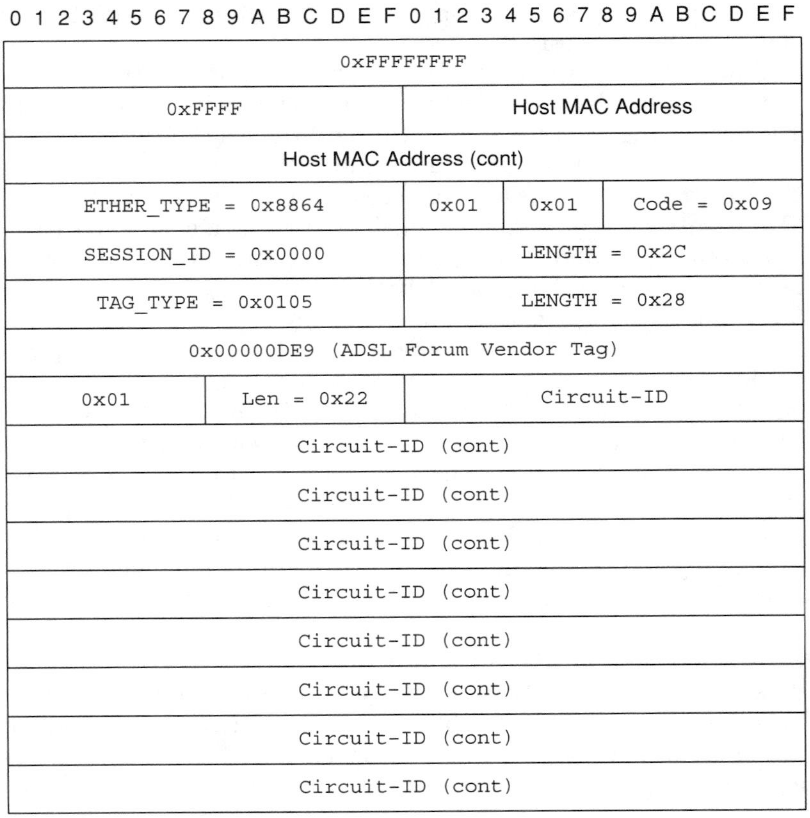

```
0 1 2 3 4 5 6 7 8 9 A B C D E F 0 1 2 3 4 5 6 7 8 9 A B C D E F
```

0xFFFFFFFF			
0xFFFF		Host MAC Address	
Host MAC Address (cont)			
ETHER_TYPE = 0x8864	0x01	0x01	Code = 0x09
SESSION_ID = 0x0000		LENGTH = 0x2C	
TAG_TYPE = 0x0105		LENGTH = 0x28	
0x00000DE9 (ADSL Forum Vendor Tag)			
0x01	Len = 0x22	Circuit-ID	
Circuit-ID (cont)			
Circuit-ID (cont)			
Circuit-ID (cont)			
Circuit-ID (cont)			
Circuit-ID (cont)			
Circuit-ID (cont)			
Circuit-ID (cont)			
Circuit-ID (cont)			

Figure 6.7   PPPoE PADI message with TAG.

3. The client will select one of the AC responses. The client will use the MAC address of the selected AC response to identify the AC as its peer.

4. The client determines the service-name to request from the AC, and along with other options places them in a PPPoE Active Discovery Request (PADR) packet. The client sends the PADR packet to the selected AC in hopes of establishing a session. This is a unicast Ethernet packet and is sent to the MAC address of the selected AC.

5. The AC receives the PADR packet and generates a unique SESSION_ID for the PPPoE session and returns this in a PPPoE Active Discovery Session (PADS) confirmation packet to the client. This packet is addressed to the client's MAC address. A SESSION_ID of 0 is returned if the AC cannot provide the requested service-name.

6. The two peers, the client and the AC, have each other's MAC addresses and share a common SESSION_ID. The PPP stage can begin at this point.

7. Either peer can terminate the session by sending a PPPoE Active Discovery Terminate (PADT) packet.

PPP Session Establishment   Once the PPPoE session is established, then PPP session negotiation can occur. PPP data are encapsulated into Ethernet packets that are addressed directly to the AC, and the SESSION_ID must be set to the value that was assigned in the PPPoE discovery stage. A typical Ethernet frame carrying a PPP payload therefore would be similar to Figure 6.8.

RADIUS   The Remote Authentication Dial In User Service (RADIUS) was designed to support network access servers (NASs) managing large numbers of PPP sessions for users connected over dial-up modem lines. This support allows the NAS to query

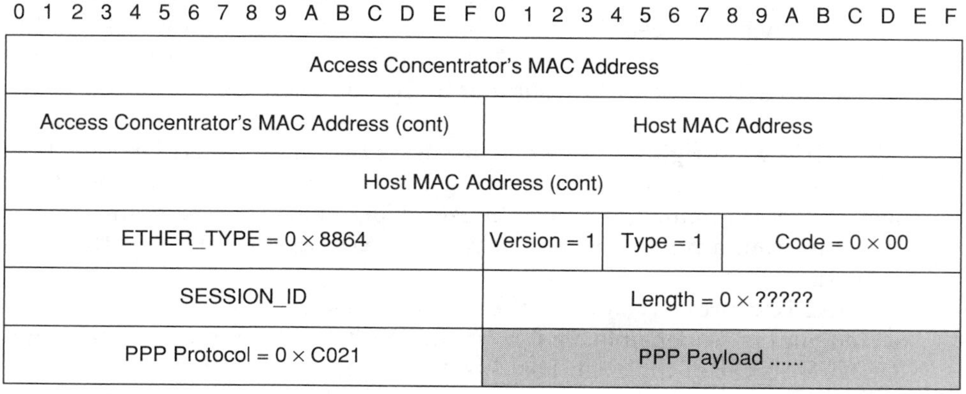

```
0 1 2 3 4 5 6 7 8 9 A B C D E F 0 1 2 3 4 5 6 7 8 9 A B C D E F
```

Access Concentrator's MAC Address			
Access Concentrator's MAC Address (cont)		Host MAC Address	
Host MAC Address (cont)			
ETHER_TYPE = 0 × 8864	Version = 1	Type = 1	Code = 0 × 00
SESSION_ID		Length = 0 × ?????	
PPP Protocol = 0 × C021		PPP Payload	

Figure 6.8   PPPoE data encapsulation.

a central database to authenticate users against a known profile and receive parameters necessary for connection establishment.

RADIUS is a client-server protocol and is defined in Reference 10, with extensions to RADIUS being defined in Reference 11. A RADIUS client (normally the NAS) must have a preexisting relationship with a RADIUS server, which is achieved through the use of a shared secret. RADIUS is based on UDP, consequently each packet exchanged between the client and server must be authenticated by the originator. The general steps in using RADIUS are as follows:

1. Client determines that user authentication is required and what services are needed. The client generates an Access-Request message which contains the set of attributes identifying what data are known and what data are required in order to establish a data connection. Some common attributes included in Access-Request messages are:

   ```
   User-Name
   User-Password
   NAS-IP-Address
   NAS-Identifier
   NAS-Port
   NAS-Port-Id
   NAS-Port-Type
   Framed-Protocol
   ```

2. The RADIUS server authenticates the NAS using a shared secret password. Assuming that the NAS is authenticated, the RADIUS consults a database of user information and proceeds to validate the user data and assimilate the requested configuration data. The RADIUS server may validate the user based on a number of criteria, such as a username and password, a challenge-response, or the physical port on which the user attaches to the NAS. If the user is not validated, then the RADIUS server sends an Access-Reject message and the NAS takes the necessary actions. If the user is validated, then the requested data is returned to the NAS in an Access-Accept message. One attribute that we will be depending on in later descriptions is the `Framed-IP-Address` attribute, which is the IP address that the RADIUS server is assigning to the end user.

RADIUS was originally designed for users to dial into a local modem bank and access a local service. The nomadic nature of Internet users however quickly introduced the need for access roaming—that is, a user being able to access their home account while dialed in from a remote service provider. RADIUS accomplishes this through the use of proxies.

A RADIUS proxy resides in the remote network to which a user is physically connected, and is responsible for forwarding NAS RADIUS requests through to the home RADIUS server of the user. For this, two things are needed: first, the RADIUS proxy server must be able to identify the home RADIUS server or the user; and second, the RADIUS proxy server must have a shared secret with the user's home RADIUS server.

The introduction of standard network access identifiers (NAIs) defined in Reference 12, resulted in an expectation that usernames would be provided with a realm leading a fully qualified username, such as bob@example.com, where example.com represents the realm. Using this notation, a proxy RADIUS server is now able to easily identify the home RADIUS server or the user. Negotiation of shared secrets between the two organizations is an operational issue and is not described here.

In addition to requesting authentication and configuration services from a server and supporting user roaming, RADIUS supports the generation and supply of accounting attributes. These will be covered in the next section.

RADIUS Accounting

One of the functions supported by the RADIUS protocol is the ability for the NAS to generate accounting records for a specific session that can be used for statistical and/or billing purposes. RADIUS accounting is defined in Reference 13, with extensions provided in Reference 11.

At the start of service delivery, the NAS generates an accounting start record which describes the user and the type of service being provided. This record is sent by the NAS to a RADIUS accounting server in the form of an Accounting-Request message. The RADIUS accounting server will acknowledge the accounting request message with an Accounting-Response message.

Looking at the Accounting-Request message in more detail, the NAS provides an indicator as to what kind of information is included in the accounting message, this will typically be a start, stop, or interim update, though status values exist for failures, L2TP, and tuning accounting on and off. This information is conveyed through the `Acct-Status-Type` RADIUS attribute. This value is set to 1 to start an accounting session, 2 to stop an accounting session, and 3 to provide interim updates.

The other attribute that is somewhat crucial to RADIUS accounting messages is the `Acct-Session-Id` attribute, which is allocated by the NAS to allow accounting records to be correlated. Any RADIUS attribute may be sent in a RADIUS accounting message with the exception of the password values. As will be seen in later sections, dependency will often be placed on the `User-Name`, `Framed-IP-Address`, `NAS-Identifier`, and `NAS-Port` attributes.

At the conclusion of service, the NAS will send an Accounting-Request message with an Acct-Status-Type of stop to the RADIUS accounting server to indicate that the session has concluded. The NAS may include additional parameters that can be used for statistical and accounting purposes.

The Layer 2 Tunneling Protocol (L2TP)   The Layer 2 Tunneling Protocol (L2TP) is defined in Reference 14, and while it is of some interest, the extension required to RADIUS and RADIUS accounting messages to support L2TP are of more interest since these contain the measurements that will be used to determine location in a later section. We shall briefly describe all three here.

L2TP was designed to support tunneling of PPP packets across a network in a manner transparent to end users and applications (see Figure 6.9). The system is comprised of an L2TP access concentrator (LAC) that resides in a local network, and an L2TP network server (LNS) residing in the home network. PPP sessions are initiated against the LAC, which tunnels the requests across to the LNS, where the PPP session is terminated and configuration values assigned.

A tunnel exists between an LAC and an LNS, and each assigns a tunnel identifier to the tunnel when the tunnel is created. The identifiers are different at each end, with the LAC sending messages to the identifier determined by the LNS, and vice versa. Sessions are created within the tunnels to facilitate data flows between two end-points. As with tunnels, session identifiers are assigned independently by the LAC and LNS, and are exchanged during session establishment. This means that the tunnels, and the sessions within the tunnels, can only be lined up between the two entities using internal state data. As we will see shortly, this makes it hard to get the information necessary to determine location.

To make L2TP work efficiently in existing network deployments, changes needed to be made to RADIUS, and subsequent RADIUS accounting messages. To support tunneling identifiers in RADIUS, new attributes were identified and these are documented in Reference 15. The attributes described in Reference 15 are for general tunneling applications; specific use of these attributes in L2TP is documented in Reference 16. To assist servers at either end of the tunnel to reconcile accounting records (see Reference 17), RADIUS accounting for L2TP, recommends that the `user-name`, `account-tunnel-connection`, `Tunnel-Client-Endpoint`, and `Tunnel-Server-Endpoint` attributes be included. As will be shown, these attributes provide us with the measurements necessary to determine location in DSL networks that deploy L2TP.

Location Determination and Acquisition in DSL Networks

This section will describe how the location of an end-point can be determined in DSL networks and how to subsequently make this location available to nodes that require it.

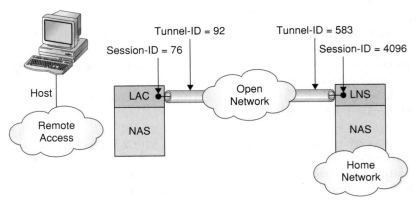

Figure 6.9   L2TP network architecture.

Much of the information presented in this section is based on work that has been done in the U.S. National Emergency Number Association (NENA). This work was conducted to address the location determination and acquisition problems confronting residential broadband providers in the United States and Canada. This work is not definitive, it's descriptive, and deliberately ignores aspects of DSL networks relating to QoS and traffic type separation based on service type. The intention of this work is to show that the network correlators necessary to determine an end-point's location are present in network measurements available today over a variety of possible DSL deployment configurations.

Figure 6.2 illustrates the general DSL connectivity architecture, showing a clear separation between the network (Internet) service provider (ISP) and the region access network provider (RANP). The RANP owns the physical access and is responsible for delivery messages from the router to the ISP. The ISP is responsible for authenticating users, allocating IP addresses, and generally routing user data throughout the Internet. All of these functions are required to provide the DSL IP service. The information from both the ISP and RANP is required in order to determine the physical location of an end-point and associate it with an IP address. Remember that the end-point is essentially unaware of the RANP, and subscribes to the ISP for Internet connectivity. The ISP is able to allocate an IP address, but will likely have little direct information that will allow it to tie the end-point to a physical location. This information resides in the RANP. To provide location services in this environment, two LISes are required, a gateway LIS at the ISP that can serve as a point of contact, and a primary LIS based

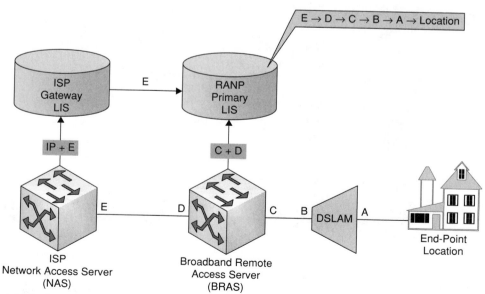

Figure 6.10   A generic DSL LIS configuration.

in the RANP that can provide location information. This is the general model that was derived within NENA and is shown in Figure 6.10. All of the configurations described in the subsequent sections are simply extensions of this model.

Figure 6.10 illustrates that the RANP LIS must be able to link all of the circuit information together in order to be able to determine the location of the end-point. In reality, the RANP LIS merely needs to be able to associate E with the location, and this may or may not require it to follow the circuit chain back to point A. Examples of how this chain is populated and followed will be shown in subsequent sections.

The connection between the ISP gateway LIS and the RANP primary LIS will likely be a nailed-up secure connection that is authenticated at connect time. The recommendation is that this connection be made on TLS, and the HELD protocol be used with a BEEP binding. The HELD protocol BEEP binding specification is provided in Appendix D.

IP Connectivity over the Service Provider Segment   In this configuration, the A10-interface uses the first protocol stack shown in Figure 6.5, and data are directed from the RANP Aggregator to the ISP NAS using IP routing. Figure 6.11 illustrates the setup and information flow for this configuration using ATM as a transport from the end-point to the ISP.

At first glance, Figure 6.11 appears complex. This is because there are several different data flows and operations represented in the diagram, and all are required in

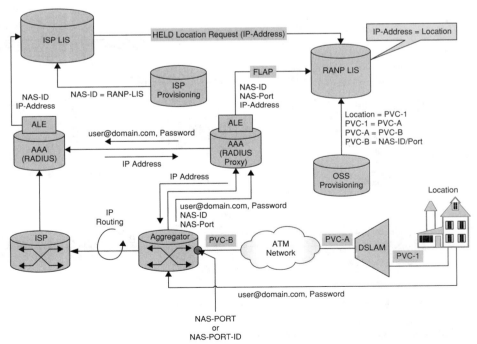

Figure 6.11   IP routing over the A10-Interface using ATM and RADIUS.

order to establish an IP connection from the host to the ISP so that the location of the host can be determined. To simplify things we will describe the system in parts, starting with provisioning.

Connectivity flows from the Location, on the lower right-hand side, to the Aggregator in the lower left-hand side of Figure 6.12. In this configuration, the connectivity is established over ATM using a series of Permanent Virtual Circuits (PVCs) between the various switching stages:

1. PVC-1 extends from the home router to the DSLAM.
2. PVC-A extends from the DSLAM to an ATM switching network.
3. PVC-B extends from the ATM switching networks to the Aggregator.

NOTE: Most DSL services use a default set of vpi/vci values for all modems connected to the DSLAM. Values commonly used are 0/35, 8/35, 0/38, and 0/32. Using common vpi/vci values on the DSLAM reduces the amount of per-port provisioning that is required by the DSLAM operator.

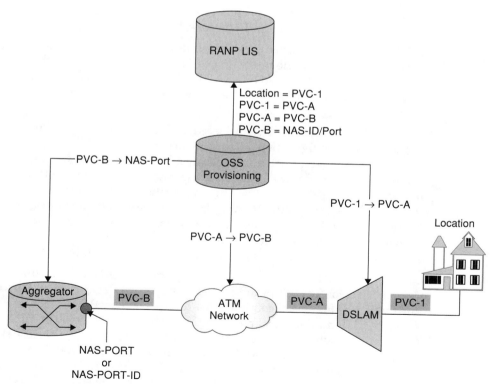

Figure 6.12   Switch and RANP-LIS provisioning.

These PVCs form a fixed chain that must be provisioned and established between the switching nodes in order to facilitate higher-layer protocol connectivity through the network. Since the PVCs are established through provisioning, an extension of this data can be used to populate the RANP-LIS using an OSS provisioning system. This allows the RANP-LIS to perform PVC-to–physical location associations.

Similarly, the ISP-LIS needs to know how to associate incoming circuit identifiers to a specific RANP-LIS. This is again done through provisioning.

Now, let's look at how the session is established from the end-point to the ISP, and how network measurements can be obtained to aid the LISes in determining the location of the end-point. This is depicted in Figure 6.13 with the session establishment being described in detail in the DSL Forum document (see Reference 18).

1. The end-point initiates a PPP session as defined in Reference 5 with authentication, as defined in Reference 6. For the example, let's assume Password Authentication Protocol (PAP), though CHAP can equally well be used. The end-point sends its fully qualified username, `user@domain.com`, and its password in the session establishment.

2. The Aggregator terminates the PPP session and forwards the session establishment messages, along with the Aggregator identifier (NAS-Identifier) and incoming port information (NAS-Port) to a proxy-RADIUS server running in the RANP's domain. RADIUS is defined in Reference 10.

3. The RANP's RADIUS server uses the domain component of the fully qualified username, `domain.com`, in the preceding example to determine which ISP RADIUS to proxy the request to. The RANP's RADIUS server forwards the PPP session establishment messages to the ISP RADIUS server for authentication and IP address assignment.

4. Assuming that the user is authenticated by the ISP RADIUS server, an IP address, along with other configuration data are returned to the RANP proxy-RADIUS server. The ISP RADIUS server will also generate a RADIUS accounting message (RADIUS Accounting is defined in Reference 13) that indicates, amongst other things, that a particular user has signed on, is using a specific IP address, and that their connection is coming via a specific BRAS. This information can be processed by an ALE, built to analyze RADIUS accounting messages, and forwarded to the ISP LIS. This provides the ISP LIS with the data necessary to identify the RANP-LIS that has the association between IP address and location for a given end-point.

5. The RANP proxy-RADIUS server will generate a RADIUS accounting record on receipt of the configuration data from the ISP RADIUS server. This accounting record will include the incoming NAS-Identifier (the BRAS), the incoming port, the allocated IP address, and possibly the outbound port from the BRAS to the ISP NAS. Similar to what occurred at the ISP, a RADIUS ALE can process the RADIUS accounting messages and send the data to the RANP-LIS. At this point, the RANP-LIS can associate an IP address with an incoming BRAS (NAS-Identifier) and port on the BRAS (NAS-Port). Earlier in this section, we showed that the NAS-Identifier

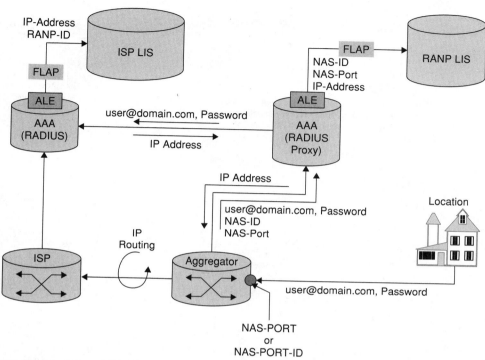

Figure 6.13   A session establishment and measurement collection.

and NAS-Port information needs to be provisioned into the BRAS and, furthermore, needs to be associated with a dedicated PVC. The RANP-LIS now has the linkages it requires to associate an IP address with a location.

Thus far, we have looked at how to establish a DSL session and how to obtain the parameters and correlators that will permit a LIS to determine the location of an endpoint. Now, it's time to look at a location request (see Figure 6.14).

Let's assume that the HELD client running on a host inside the home network has discovered the ISP LIS using the mechanism described in Chapter 4.

1. The HELD client then launches a location request to the ISP LIS. The NAT inside the home router changes the source IP address of the outbound message to have the IP address of the home router. This is good, since it's the IP address that the ISP-LIS knows about.

2. The ISP-LIS receives the location request and verifies that the source IP address of the message is indeed an IP address that has been allocated by the ISP for use. The ISP-LIS looks up the address of the RANP through which the location request message came. The ISP-LIS is then able to determine the RANP-LIS to query for the

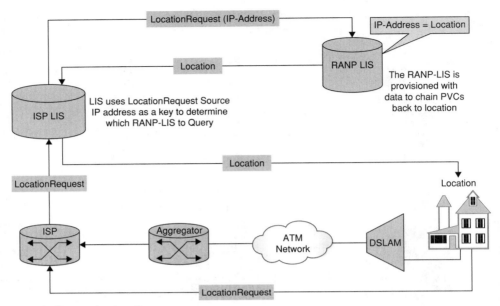

Figure 6.14   Requesting location.

location information. The ISP-LIS sends a location request to the RANP-LIS over the Trusted-Party Query Interface, and using the HELD identity extensions defined in Appendix E, it includes the IP address of the host that it wants the location of.

3. The RANP-LIS uses provisioned data and data that it obtained from the RADIUS-ALE to map the IP address through a chain of PVCs to a physical location. The RANP-LIS constructs a PIDF-LO and returns it to the ISP-LIS.

4. The ISP-LIS receives the PIDF-LO from the RANP-LIS and may cache it before sending it back to the requesting host.

The RADIUS ALE for IP Routing   In the previous subsections, we described how RADIUS accounting messages can be analyzed to provide circuit correlators that a LIS can then use to link an IP address to a circuit chain, and subsequently to a location. In this section, we look specifically at what RADIUS accounting attributes are required from the ISP RADIUS and from the RANP proxy-RADIUS to support this functionality.

Starting from the ISP, we need to know which RANP the end-point's traffic will be coming through. This may be done implicitly—in other words, knowing the identity of the proxy-RADIUS forwarding the PPP session messages. Alternatively, it can be done through the proxy-RADIUS forwarding the NAS-ID information relating to the BRAS that serviced the request. In the latter case, the RADIUS accounting message must contain a `NAS-IP-Address` attribute, and/or the `NAS-Identifier` attribute, as defined in Reference 10, and it must be sufficient to allow the ISP-LIS to identify the RANP network. This may be done by provisioning data into the ISP-LIS ahead of time, which is a reasonable approach given that business relationships between the ISP and RANP must exist for connectivity to occur in the first place.

When the ISP RADIUS allocates an IP address for the user, it will send a `Framed-IP-Address` attribute in the response message. This must also be echoed in a RADIUS accounting message. All the data may be available in the same RADIUS accounting message, or they may span several accounting messages that are linked with a common `Acct-Session-Id` attribute as described previously. Regardless of how this occurs, ultimately the data must contain:

```
NAS-IP-Address (BRAS identifier)
NAS-Identifier (BRAS identifier)
Framed-IP-Address
User-Name [optional]
```

The RANP-LIS needs sufficient details to allow it to link the incoming traffic stream into the provisioned circuit chain so that it can link the stream to a source location. The RANP RADIUS server receives information from the BRAS that provides much of this information, namely the `NAS-Identifier` and/or `NAS-IP-Address`, and `NAS-Port`. In some cases, a `NAS-Port-Id` (defined in Reference 11, RADIUS Extensions) will be provided in place of, or as well as, the `NAS-Port`. Either is fine, providing it identifies where the data stream enters the BRAS, with sufficient information to allow the RANP-LIS to follow a circuit chain to the location. The response from the ISP RADIUS will include the `Framed-IP-Address`, and the RANP RADIUS may include this information in a RADIUS accounting message along with the stream identification data.

```
NAS-Identifier (BRAS Identifier)
NAS-IP-Address (BRAS Identifier)
NAS-Port (BRAS Identifier)
NAS-Port-Id (BRAS Identifier)
Framed-IP-Address
```

This tuple of data will allow the RANP-LIS to directly link the IP address to a provisioned circuit chain and hence to the physical location of the end-point. It may be that the RANP-RADIUS does not include all of this information in a single accounting record. If this is the case, then the RANP RADIUS-ALE will collate the accounting records based on the session identifier and send the complete FLAP message to the RANP-LIS.

To ensure that a solution exists across all of these scenarios, the ISP-LIS should not make assumptions about what information the RANP-LIS may or may not receive from a RADIUS-ALE. Consequently, the recommendation is that the ISP-LIS provide a database tuple capable of holding the following:

```
User-Name
Framed-IP-Address
NAS-Identifier (BRAS Identifier)
NAS-IP-Address (BRAS identifier)
NAS-Port (BRAS Identifier)
NAS-Port-Id (BRAS Identifier)
```

When the ISP-LIS queries the RANP-LIS, it should provide as much of the following data as possible in the location request to ensure that the RANP-LIS is able to identify the circuit chain, and hence the location of the Target.

```
Framed-IP-Address
NAS-Identifier (BRAS Identifier)
NAS-IP-Address (BRAS Identifier)
NAS-Port (BRAS Identifier)
NAS-Port-Id (BRAS Identifier)
```

The HELD identity extensions schema is provided in Appendix E. A HELD location request from the ISP-LIS to the RANP-LIS containing the identity extensions previously shown would look similar to the following code fragment. Note that the Framed-IP-Address is the target identifier and is contained in the <ipv4> element. The NAS-IP-Address is self-explanatory. The NAS-Port-ID is broken up into its constituent parts—in this example, ATM is used with the NAS-Port-ID, being composed of Slot/Port VPI:VCI.

```
<locationRequest xmlns="http://sitacs.uow.edu.au/ns/location/held">
   <heldDevice
      xmlns="http://sitacs.uow.edu.au/ns/location/held:deviceIdentifiers">
      <ipV4>192.168.5.9</ipV4>
      <nas-ip-address>10.10.10.10</nas-ip-address>
      <atm>
         <slot>3</slot>
         <port>0</port>
         <vpi>100</vpi>
         <vci>33</vci>
      </atm>
   </heldDevice>
</locationRequest>
```

The RANP-LIS should maintain at a database tuple as follows and populate as much data as it can from network measurements that it receives from its RADIUS-ALE.

```
Framed-IP-Address
NAS-Identifier (BRAS Identifier)
NAS-IP-Address (BRAS Identifier)
NAS-Port (BRAS Identifier)
NAS-Port-Id (BRAS Identifier)
```

The full FLAP specification for a RADIUS ALE is provided in Appendix A. A FLAP notification from a RANP RADIUS ALE to the RANP-LIS would look similar to the following XML fragment.

```
<ntfy xsi:type="radius:ntfy">
   <radius:terminal>
      <radius:user-name>joe@mynet.example.com</radius:user-name>
      <radius:framed-ip-address>192.168.0.1</radius:framed-ip-address>
   </radius:terminal>
```

```
<radius:access time="2005-04-14T10:51:23.000+10:00">
    <radius:nas-ip-address>10.10.10.10</radius-nas-ip-address>
    <radius:nas-port-Id>atm 3/0:100.33</radius:nas-port-id>
</radius:access>
</ntfy>
```

ATM Layer 2 Over the Service Provider Segment   Figure 6.5 showed the A10-interface protocol stacks, and in the previous section we looked at the first stack which provided IP routing over the A10-interface between the RANP BRAS and the ISP. In this section, we will look at a pure layer-2 connection from the DSL modem at the customer premises, through the RANP BRAS, and on to the ISP. We shall also examine location determination and acquisition where this is performed using ATM. In subsequent sections, we will describe Ethernet-based solutions.

Breaking down Figure 6.15 in a similar fashion to how we broke down Figure 6.11, we can see that the provisioning components are quite comparable. An external provisioning system links ATM PVC identifiers from the end-point location, through the DSLAM, through the ATM network, through the Aggregator, and on to the ISP NAS. This same data are also provisioned into the RANP-LIS so that it can make associations between ATM virtual circuit identifiers and a physical location. The ISP-LIS provisioning in the ATM layer-2 configuration (shown in Figure 6.15) is different from that used in the IP routing configuration (shown in Figure 6.11) in that the ISP NAS-Port information is used this time to identify the RANP-LIS to contact, rather than the RANP BRAS identifier.

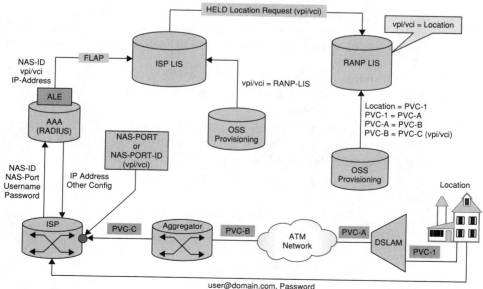

Figure 6.15   ATM layer 2 over the service provider segment.

The session establishment in this configuration is simpler than that of the IP routing configuration. Here, the end-point establishes a PPP connection directly with the ISP; the DSLAM, ATM, and aggregation networks pass the data transparently from the end-point to the ISP NAS.

The ISP NAS passes the NAS-IP-Address (or NAS-Identifier), NAS-Port (or NAS-Port-Id), User-Name, and User-Password to the ISP RADIUS for authentication. If authenticated, the end-point is provided with an IP address and other configuration data. The ISP RADIUS then generates a RADIUS accounting record consisting of:

```
NAS-IP-Address or NAS-Identifier
NAS-Port or NAS-Port-Id
Framed-IP-Address
User-Name
```

The value of the NAS-Port or NAS-Port-Id parameter will be that of the incoming ATM PVC, which consists of a virtual path indicator (vpi) and a virtual circuit indicator (vci). An ALE capable of analyzing the RADIUS accounting messages then passes this information on to the ISP-LIS. The ISP-LIS may use either the NAS indicator (NAS-Identifier or NAS-IP-Address) or the NAS port identifier (NAS-Port or NAS-Port-Id) value to determine which RANP-LIS to send any location requests to. Which indicator is used will depend on ISP-LIS provisioning and network configuration. The ISP-LIS uses the NAS-Port or NAS-Port-Id values as the Target identifier in any location requests made to the RANP-LIS.

As we did in the previous section, let's assume that the end-point has discovered the LIS using the DNS mechanism described in Chapter 4. Let's also assume that the RANP-LIS and switching elements have been suitably provisioned. The data flows for location determination and acquisition are therefore depicted in Figure 6.16, with the further assumption that the ALE resides in, or is tightly coupled with, the ISP RADIUS server.

Let's step through the flow in Figure 6.16 to be clear about what is going on.

1. The end-point attempts to establish a PPP session with the ISP NAS and includes authentication parameters—in this case, the PAP, User-Name, and User-Password parameters.

2. The ISP NAS sends the messages up to the ISP RADIUS server, including the NAS-Identifier and the NAS-Port. The NAS-Port parameter contains the vpi/vci of the incoming PVC for the end-point's data stream.

3. The ISP RADIUS server validates the end-point and assigns an IP address and other configuration data.

4. The ISP RADIUS server also generates a RADIUS accounting record containing:

```
User-Name
Framed-IP-Address
NAS-Identifier (or NAS-IP-Address)
NAS-Port/NAS-Port-Id (vpi/vci)
```

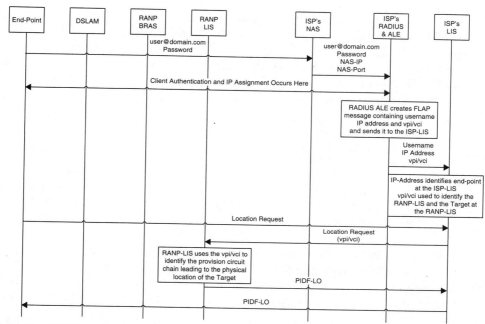

Figure 6.16 ATM layer-2 service provider segment location acquisition.

The RADIUS ALE tightly coupled with the RADIUS server creates a FLAP message containing the IP address, NAS-Identifier, and vpi/vci values, and sends this to the ISP-LIS.

5. The end-point makes a location request to the ISP-LIS.

6. The ISP-LIS uses the source IP address of the location request message to establish the identity of the Target. Using the IP address, the ISP-LIS is able to retrieve the corresponding vpi/vci associated with the Target's traffic stream, and the incoming NAS-Identifier. The ISP-LIS uses either the vpi/vci or the NAS identifier to determine the RANP-LIS to send the location request to. The ISP-LIS constructs a location request message to the RANP-LIS using the vpi/vci value for the RANP-LIS to use as the Target identifier.

7. The RANP-LIS uses the vpi/vci values to identify the provisioned circuit chain, and to determine the physical location of the end-point. The RANP-LIS constructs a PIDF-LO with the end-point's location and returns it to the ISP-LIS.

8. The ISP-LIS may cache the PIDF-LO before returning it to the end-point.

By carefully controlling the provisioning at the ISP-LIS and the RANP-LIS, it is possible to obtain measurements that allow an IP address to be associated with circuit identifiers and, hence, a physical location.

The RADIUS ALE for ATM Layer-2 Connectivity   In this configuration, only one RADIUS ALE type is required: the ISP RADIUS ALE. This ALE needs to be able to provide the LIS with an IP address to NAS-Identifier (if the ISP has more than one NAS), and a vpi/vci to identify the RANP-LIS, and then serve as a Target identifier for the RANP-LIS. A FLAP notification message for this ALE looks similar to the code fragment that follows.

```
<ntfy xsi:type="radius:ntfy">
    <radius:terminal>
        <radius:framed-ip-address>192.168.0.1</radius:framed-ip-address>
    </radius:terminal>
    <radius:access time="2005-04-14T10:51:23.000+10:00">
        <radius:nas-ip-address>10.10.10.10</radius-nas-ip-address>
        <radius:nas-port-id>atm 3/0:100.33</radius:nas-port-id>
    </radius:access>
</ntfy>
```

The ISP-LIS needs to include all of this information in any location requests made to the RANP-LIS so that the RANP-LIS is able to enter the circuit identifier chain. The full HELD identity extensions schema is provided in Appendix E. The following code fragment provides an indication of what the ISP-LIS location request to the RANP-LIS may look like.

```
<locationRequest xmlns="http://sitacs.uow.edu.au/ns/location/held">
    <heldDevice
        xmlns="http://sitacs.uow.edu.au/ns/location/held:deviceIdentifiers">
        <ipV4>192.168.5.9</ipV4>
        <nas-ip-address>10.10.10.10</nas-ip-address>
        <atm>
            <slot>3</slot>
            <port>0</port>
            <vpi>100</vpi>
            <vci>33</vci>
        </atm>
    </heldDevice>
</locationRequest>
```

Note that the `Framed-IP-Address` is the target identifier and is contained in the `<ipv4>` element. The `NAS-IP-Address` is self explanatory. The `NAS-Port` is broken up into its constituent parts. In this example, ATM is used with the `NAS-Port`, which is composed of Slot/Port VPI:VCI.

1:1 VLAN Layer-2 Forwarding over the Service Provider Segment   This configuration is similar to the ATM layer-2 forwarding solution described in the previous section. In this configuration, however, instead of data streams being kept orthogonal through discrete ATM PVCs, data are kept orthogonal by uniquely tagging them with VLAN tags. Let's look at the network configuration.

Figure 6.17 shows a network configuration where each customer premises has its data stream tagged with a unique VLAN identifier. There are several variants to this approach described in Reference 3, largely dealing with how the VLAN tags are determined. We shall describe only the most direct one here and assume that they are provisioned ahead of time.

A DSLAM will tag each incoming customer data stream with a VLAN tag that is unique within the scope of the DSLAM. This tag is referred to as the C-TAG. Data leaving the DSLAM, toward the core network, are tagged with a second VLAN tag, the S-TAG, which identifies the DSLAM within the broadband network. The combination of the S-TAG and C-TAG uniquely identifies a DSLAM and DSLAM port within the broadband network. The combination of S-TAG and C-TAG can be used to represent in excess of 16 million ports. In reality, a DSLAM may have more than one S-TAG assigned to it, and the selection of which S-TAG to use may be dependent on a number of criteria including the desired QoS, or the value of the C-TAG allocated. These are predominantly provisioning details not directly pertinent to our discussions. What is important is that RANP-LIS knows, or is able to learn, the S-TAG and C-TAG associations to a specific data stream.

As before, let's start with provisioning. The RANP has a provisioning system that provides tagging and routing information to the DSLAM, core network, and BRAS. It also provides a direct association between S-TAG, C-TAG, and the location in the RANP-LIS. The ISP-LIS must be provisioned with sufficient information to be able to identify which RANP-LIS to query for a location when a request comes in. This may be

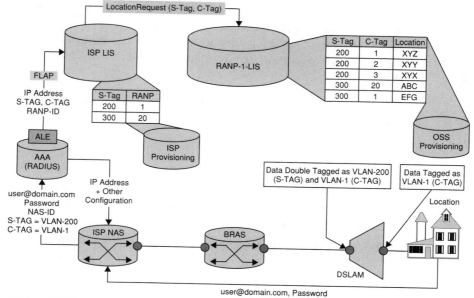

Figure 6.17   1:1 VLAN forwarding on service provider segment.

done based on the S-TAG value, the value of the NAS-Identifier/NAS-IP-Address, or some other means.

Going through connection establishment, the end-point initiates a PPP session with the ISP. The data enter the DSLAM and are tagged with a C-TAG of 1. The data leave the DSLAM and are tagged a second time with an S-TAG of 200. The data travel through the core network with two VLAN tags and arrive at the BRAS. The BRAS examines the combination of S-TAG and C-TAG and directs the data to the ISP-NAS.

As with the previous examples, the ISP-NAS sends a RADIUS message to the ISP RADIUS server containing an identifier for the NAS (either NAS-Identifier or NAS-IP-Address), the incoming port information (either NAS-Port or NAS-Port-Id), and the end-point's user credentials. The NAS-Port or NAS-Port-Id contain the S-TAG and C-TAG VLAN identifiers.

Assuming the end-point successfully validates, as with previous examples, an IP address and other configuration data are returned to the end-point and the ISP RADIUS server generates a RADIUS accounting record. The RADIUS accounting record is then analyzed by a RADIUS-ALE. The RADIUS accounting record would contain the following attributes:

```
User-Name
Framed-IP-Address
NAS-Identifier or NAS-IP-Address
NAS-Port or NAS-Port-Id (containing the S-TAG and C-TAG values)
```

The RADIUS-ALE sends the information to the ISP-LIS in a FLAP message. The ISP-LIS will cache this data for use when a location request is received.

Let's look at a location request in this configuration.

As with the previous examples, let's assume that the end-point has discovered the ISP-LIS using the LIS discovery mechanism described in Chapter 4 using Figure 6.18 as a reference.

1. The end-point attempts to establish a PPP session with the ISP NAS and includes authentication parameters—in this case, the PAP, User-Name, and User-Password parameters.

2. The ISP NAS sends the messages up to the ISP RADIUS server, including the NAS-Identifier and the NAS-Port. The NAS-Port parameter contains the S-TAG and C-TAG of the VLANs for the end-point's data stream.

3. The ISP RADIUS server validates the end-point and assigns an IP address and other configuration data.

4. The ISP RADIUS server also generates a RADIUS accounting record containing:

```
User-Name
Framed-IP-Address
NAS-Identifier (or NAS-IP-Address)
NAS-Port/NAS-Port-Id (S-TAG and C-TAG)
```

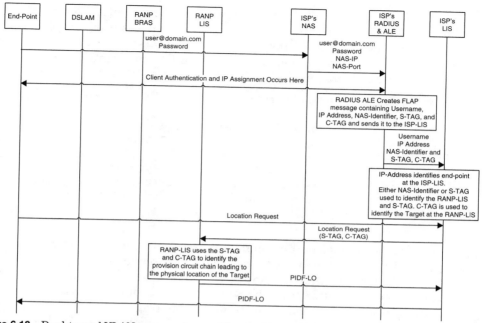

Figure 6.18 Dual-tagged VLAN on a service provider segment location acquisition.

The RADIUS ALE tightly coupled with the RADIUS server creates a FLAP message containing the IP address, `NAS-Identifier`, and S-TAG and C-TAG values, and then sends this to the ISP-LIS.

5. The end-point makes a location request to the ISP-LIS.

6. The ISP-LIS uses the source IP address of the location request message to establish the identity of the Target. Using the IP address, the ISP-LIS is able to retrieve the corresponding `NAS-Identifier`, S-TAG, and C-TAG values associated with the Target's traffic stream. The ISP-LIS uses either the `NAS-Identifier` or the S-TAG to identify the RANP-LIS to send the location request to. The ISP-LIS constructs a location request message to the RANP-LIS using the S-TAG and C-TAG values to identify the Target at the RANP-LIS.

7. The RANP-LIS uses the S-TAG and C-TAG values to identify the DSLAM and DSLAM port, allowing it to determine the physical location of the end-point. The RANP-LIS constructs a PIDF-LO with the end-point's location and returns it to the ISP-LIS.

8. The ISP-LIS may cache the PIDF-LO before returning it to the end-point.

1:1 VLAN Tag RADIUS-ALE   The RADIUS-ALE in the 1:1 VLAN tag configuration that has been described in this section is in essence the same as the RADIUS-ALE that was described for the ATM layer-2 forwarding configuration described in the previous section. The ALE must provide an IP address that has been assigned by the RADIUS server, username, an identifier for the NAS, and the NAS-Port on which the data arrived. A FLAP notify message for an ALE in this configuration would look similar to the following code fragment.

```
<ntfy xsi:type="radius:ntfy">
   <radius:terminal>
      <radius:user-name>joe@mynet.example.com</radius:user-name>
      <radius:framed-ip-address>192.168.0.1</radius:framed-ip-address>
   </radius:terminal>
   <radius:access time="2005-04-14T10:51:23.000+10:00">
      <radius:nas-ip-address>10.10.10.10</radius-nas-ip-address>
      <radius:nas-port-id>eth 3/0:43.76</radius:nas-port-id>
   </radius:access>
</ntfy>
```

The ISP-LIS caches the data and later uses NAS-Identifier or the S-TAG to map to a RANP-LIS identity in order to service location requests from end-points. The ISP-LIS needs to include the NAS-IP-Address and NAS-Port-id information when requesting location information from the RANP-LIS. Appendix E provides the detailed HELD identity extensions schema. The following code fragment provides an example of what the ISP-LIS location request to the RANP-LIS may look like for this configuration.

```
<locationRequest xmlns="http://sitacs.uow.edu.au/ns/location/held">
   <heldDevice
      xmlns="http://sitacs.uow.edu.au/ns/location/held:deviceIdentifiers">
      <ipV4>192.168.5.9</ipV4>
      <nas-ip-address>10.10.10.10</nas-ip-address>
      <vlan>
         <slot>3</slot>
         <port>0</port>
         <ctag>100</ctag>
         <stag>33</stag>
      </vlan>
   </heldDevice>
</locationRequest>
```

Note that the Framed-IP-Address is the target identifier and is contained in the <ipv4> element. The NAS-IP-Address is self-explanatory. The NAS-Port-id is broken up into its constituent parts. In this configuration, Ethernet is used with the NAS-Port-Is, which is composed of Slot/Port S-Tag:C-Tag.

N:1 VLAN Layer-2 Forwarding Using PPP   The previous sections described how layer-2 forwarding through the network can be done when there is a 1:1 ATM PVC or a 1:1 VLAN association for the data stream from the DSLAM, through the core network, to the ISP NAS. This section presents the N:1 VLAN configuration described in detail in Reference 3. In this configuration, multiple data streams share a common VLAN

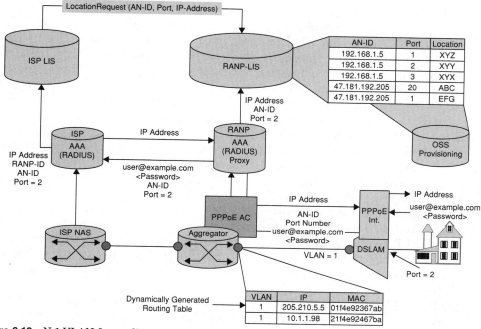

Figure 6.19 N:1 VLAN forwarding.

identifier out of the DSLAM, hence the term 1:N. Data are routed through the core using a combination of VLAN- and ARP-based routing tables at the BRAS as shown in Figure 6.19.

This mechanism poses some major advantages for core and edge network providers over the 1:1 path provisioning approaches because it simplifies routing and provisioning operations in the core. It is attractive from a location determination standpoint because it shortens the length of circuit chains that need to be provisioned in order to determine the location of the end-point. To understand these advantages, we need to look at the network configuration in detail.

The key difference in this configuration is that there is a PPPoE intermediary in the DSLAM itself. When the end-point tries to establish its PPPoE connection, the intermediary in the DSLAM inserts a vendor-specific tag, as described in the section detailing PPPoE. This tag is used to identify the DSLAM and the incoming circuit identifier. The DSLAM tags the data stream with a common VLAN tag (an S-TAG) and sends the PADI with the circuit-id TAG to the aggregator. The Aggregator terminates the PPP session and sends a query to the RAN-P proxy RADIUS. Here is where the difference comes into play. The aggregator puts the circuit-id information contained in the PPPoE tag from the intermediary in the NAS-Port-Id/NAS-Port field in the outbound RADIUS message, instead of the value of the actual aggregator NAS-Port on which the data stream was received. A RADIUS ALE at the RANP is now able to provide the

RANP-LIS with the end-point's actual point of ingress to the access network, reducing the level of circuit chaining that needs to be provisioned into the RANP-LIS.

The RANP proxy RADIUS forwards the data to the ISP RADIUS and receives configuration information for the end-point after the end-point has been successfully authenticated. This configuration information is subsequently provided to the end-point and the connection is established. The ISP RADIUS server generates an accounting message with the data, including the circuit information relating to the access node. This information is processed by a RADIUS ALE and passed to the ISP-LIS (see Figure 6.20).

Much of the message flow in Figure 6.20 is described in the preceding text. The location acquisition flow consists of the end-point having first discovered the identity of the ISP-LIS using the mechanism described in Chapter 4. The end-point sends a HELD location request to the ISP-LIS. The ISP-LIS identifies the end-point based on its IP address, and recovers the `NAS-Identifier: Access-Node-Id+Circuit-Id`. The ISP-LIS uses this information to determine the RANP-LIS to query. The ISP-LIS queries the RANP-LIS using the `Access-Node-Id+Circuit-Id` as the Target identifier in the HELD request. The RANP-LIS uses the Target identifier information to recover the location of the end-point, constructs a PIDF-LO and returns it to the ISP-LIS. The ISP may cache the location information before returning it to the end-point.

The RADIUS ALE for the N:1 VLAN Configuration To understand how to construct this ALE, we need to understand the format of the circuit tag provided by the PPPoE intermediary in the DSLAM, and the subsequent format of the NAS-Port and

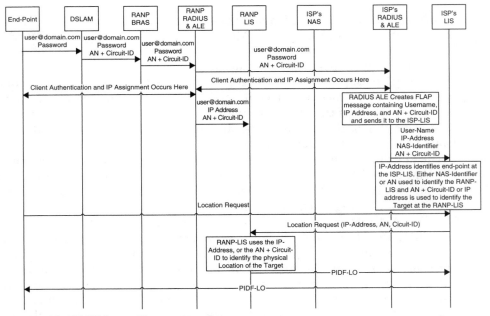

Figure 6.20 N:1 VLAN forwarding message flow.

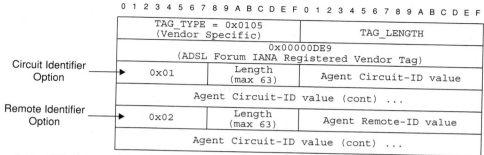

Figure 6.21 PPPoE intermediary circuit tag.

`NAS-Port-Id` RADIUS attributes. The format for this circuit tag is defined in Reference 3, but is repeated here for clarity (see Figure 6.21).

The Agent Circuit ID field is used by the intermediary to specify the access node (DSLAM) being used, and the port circuit on which the data stream is entering the access node. Reference 3 makes the following recommendation for the format of this field.

```
<Access-Name-Identifier> <L2-Type> <slot>/<port>:[circuit-id]
```

For ATM, where the data stream is coming from access node 7692, slot 3, port 0, vpi 100 vci 33, the Agent Circuit ID would be as follows:

```
AN-7692 atm 3/0:100.33
```

For an Ethernet connection, using access node 7692, slot 3, port 0, and vlan 43, the Agent Circuit ID would be encoded as follows:

```
AN-7692 eth 3/0:43
```

The agent remote id is used to uniquely identify a client connected to a specific port on the DSLAM. Reference 3 doesn't provide any specific guidance on how to format this field.

The format previously illustrated is the expected format of the `NAS-Port` or `NAS-Port-Id` fields where the N:1 VLAN configuration is used. This is the case for both the RANP RADIUS ALE and the ISP RADIUS ALE.

In addition to this data, the ISP RADIUS ALE must provide the `Framed-IP-Address` to identify the Target, and either `NAS-Identifier` or `NAS-IP-Address` to aid in determining the identity of the RANP-LIS to query. The full FLAP schema for the RADIUS ALE is included as part of Appendix A, the following xml stanza is indicative of what an ISP RADIUS ALE notify message looks like for this configuration (ATM as the transport is assumed).

```
<ntfy xsi:type="radius:ntfy">
   <radius:terminal>
      <radius:user-name>joe@mynet.example.com</radius:user-name>
      <radius:framed-ip-address>192.168.0.1</radius:framed-ip-address>
   </radius:terminal>
```

```
    <radius:access time="2005-04-14T10:51:23.000+10:00">
        <radius:nas-ip-address>10.10.10.10</radius-nas-ip-address>
        <radius:nas-port-id>AN-7692 atm 3/0:100.33</radius:nas-port-id>
    </radius:access>
</ntfy>
```

The subsequent location request from the ISP-LIS to the RANP-LIS must include the access node identifier and the access node circuit information. Using the preceding example, a HELD location request from the ISP-LIS to the RANP-LIS will look similar to the following code extract.

```
<locationRequest xmlns="http://sitacs.uow.edu.au/ns/location/held">
    <heldDevice
        xmlns="http://sitacs.uow.edu.au/ns/location/held:deviceIdentifiers">
        <access-node-id>AN-7692</access-node-id>
        <atm>
            <slot>3</slot>
            <port>0</port>
            <vpi>100</vpi>
            <vci>33</vci>
        </atm>
    </heldDevice>
</locationRequest>
```

N:1 VLAN Layer-2 Forwarding Using DHCP   Up to now, all the configurations described used PPP for session establishment. In part, this is a reflection of the fact that the majority of DSL services use PPP as a link session layer, largely (but exclusively) because of its tight coupling with RADIUS. As described previously, one of the advantages of RADIUS is that it allows roaming to be easily supported. This function also eases provisioning constraints for core network providers, particularly where IP routing or L2TP is used across the service provider segment. The reason for this is that the connection from the end-point to the service provider can be established dynamically at a connection based on the realm associated with the user-name, rather than requiring per-circuit provisioning end to end, as is required with ATM and dual-VLAN layer-2 pass-through configurations. Reducing provisioning reduces complexity, and therefore reduces the likelihood of errors occurring. Regardless of all this, DHCP is used in DSL deployments. In this section, we shall look at the N:1 VLAN configuration again, but this time using DHCP in place of PPP.

In Figure 6.22, a DHCP relay-agent, as described in Reference 19, resides in the DSLAM. The relay-agent appends circuit information associated with the end-point's point of attachment to the network. Unlike the DHCP relay-agent usage described in Chapter 5, the relay-agent in the DSLAM doesn't specify a return address by setting the giaddr fielding in the DHCP header, nor does it change the discovery message from broadcast to unicast. It simply attaches circuit information. As was pointed out in Chapter 5, the options described in Reference 19 do not provide a clear way for the relay-agent to identify itself to the DHCP server other than by setting giaddr. In a DSL environment, where the access network may be owned by a different provider than

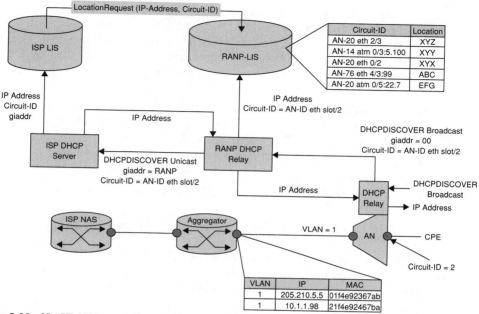

Figure 6.22   N:1 VLAN layer-2 forwarding using DHCP.

the ISP, the DSLAM may not be directly accessible from the ISP DHCP server. If it is not, then the DSLAM cannot set giaddr, since giaddr tells the DHCP server where to send response messages. To overcome this limitation, the circuit-id provided by the relay-agent in the DSLAM must also encode the identity of the relay-agent. Reference 3 provides guidance on how to do this. The format for the circuit-id mandated in Reference 3 is the same as that proposed in the previous section for the RADIUS NAS-Port and NAS-Port-Id attributes. Let's step through Figure 6.22, describing the steps for location determination and acquisition.

1. The end-point (usually a DSL modem) sends a DHCPDISCOVER broadcast message to the network.

2. The DHCP relay-agent in the DSLAM intercepts the DHCPDISOVER and appends the circuit-id information described previously. The DHCP relay-agent then rebroadcasts the DHCPDISCOVER message towards the core network using a common VLAN (N:1).

3. The Aggregator sends the DHCPDISCOVER message to a DHCP relay-agent in the RANP.

4. The RANP DHCP relay-agent sets the giaddr with its address, and based on the value of the circuit-id, sends the DHCPDISCOVER as a unicast message to the ISP DHCP server.

5. The ISP DHCP server then allocates an IP address and provides network configuration data back to the RANP DHCP relay-agent, and subsequently back to the requesting end-point. Using a DHCP ALE similar to those described in Chapter 5 for enterprise environments, information can either be pushed from the DHCP server to the ISP-LIS, or requested from the DHCP server using the DHCP lease query mechanism.

6. The end-point then makes a location quest to the ISP-LIS, which uses the `giaddr` field or `circuit-id` data to aid it in determining which RANP-LIS to query for location information. The ISP-LIS uses the `circuit-id` information as the Target identifier in the location request to the RANP-LIS.

7. The RANP-LIS uses the `circuit-id` as a key in its database to provide the physical location of the end-point, constructs a PIDF-LO, and returns this to the ISP-LIS.

8. The ISP-LIS may cache the location before returning it to the end-point.

The obvious question that comes to mind with this model is, "Why not simply return location to the end-point using Reference 20, or the civic format?" There are several reasons why not. First, providing a location in the DHCP response requires a real-time lookup of the RANP-LIS prior to a response being sent to the end-point. This may not be feasible. Second, it would require all DSL modems to support the DHCP options, something that they might not do. Third, it would necessitate that all hosts inside the home network also support the DHCP options, something that, again, they may not be able to do. All in all, the network and functional constraints imposed by DHCP acquisition as described in previous chapters make it generally unsuitable as a means of dependable location delivery.

L2TP over the Service Provider Segment   L2TP over the service provider segment is the last of the DSL configurations we shall consider, and in many ways it is the most complex—at least from a location determination perspective. The configuration involves PPP over ATM or Ethernet from the DSLAM to the BRAS. A query is made from the BRAS to the RADIUS server for routing information, and the RADIUS server responds with a layer-2 tunnel identifier. The BRAS will either create a new tunnel, or a new session in an existing tunnel. The BRAS then generates a RADIUS accounting message containing all the data, including the tunnel session identifier. Unlike the other DSL configurations described thus far, where the RANP RADIUS ALE is important to some degree, the RANP RADIUS ALE in this configuration is critical. This criticality arises because the tunnel and session identifiers provide the association back to the provisioned circuit chain, but these are dynamically determined as the session is established. They cannot be derived at the RANP-LIS based solely on information provided by the ISP-LIS. Figure 6.23 shows the configuration in more detail.

The first part of this configuration is much the same as the 1:1 VLAN tag, or IP routing over the service provider segment configurations. The RANP-LIS and core network switches need to be provisioned with circuit/switching information to allow a connection

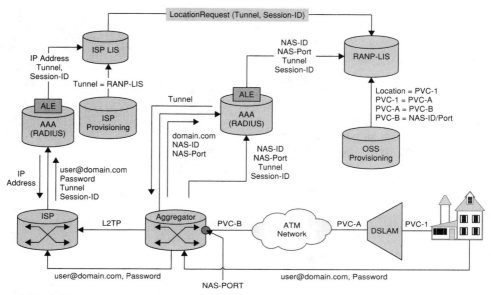

Figure 6.23 L2TP over the service provider segment.

from the home location, through the DSLAM, through the core network, and to a known port on the BRAS. PPP AC in the aggregator makes the request for authentication and routing information from the RANP RADIUS server. Based on the realm of the username, the RADIUS determines that the aggregator needs to route the data across a layer-2 tunnel to the ISP. As was described in the section on protocols, the RADIUS server may provide a tunnel identifier, or an IP address representing the remote end of the tunnel. On receiving this information from the RADIUS server, the aggregator will either create a session in an existing tunnel, or create a new tunnel with a new session. In either case, the aggregator will generate a RADIUS accounting message indicating the incoming NAS (`NAS-Identifier`), the `NAS-Port`, the tunnel, and the `session-id` for the session in the tunnel. In this mode, it is critical for a RANP RADIUS ALE to provide an `NAS-Identifier`, `NAS-Port`, tunnel, and `session-id` to the RANP-LIS. This allows the RANP-LIS to provide the association between the tunnel and `session-id`, the circuit across the service provider segment, and the `NAS-Identifier` and `NAS-Port`, which is the start to the provisioned circuit chain.

The ISP NAS needs to report the identity of the tunnel, the `session-id`, the username, and the password. An accounting record associating tunnel, `session-id`, and `Framed-IP-Address` needs to be provided to the RADIUS ALE for communication to the ISP-LIS.

The ISP-LIS will use the tunnel, consisting of source and destination IP addresses to identify the RANP-LIS to query, and employs the `tunnel` and `session-id` attributes to identify the Target to the RANP-LIS. The RANP-LIS uses the `tunnel` and `session-id` parameters to identify the provisioned circuit chain, and hence the

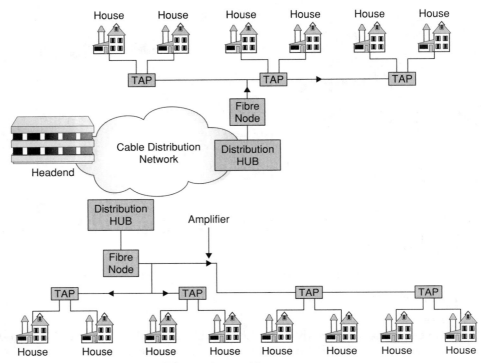

Figure 6.24 Data flow for L2TP over the service provider segment.

physical location of the Target. A PIDF-LO is constructed containing the resulting location and is returned to the ISP-LIS and ultimately to the end-point.

The data flow for the preceding description is provided in Figure 6.24.

L2TP RADIUS ALE   The L2TP RADIUS ALE needs to operate at both ends of the tunnel. According to Reference 17, RADIUS accounting records should contain the User-Name, Acct-Tunnel-Connection, Tunnel-Client-Endpoint and Tunnel-Server-Endpoint attributes. It further indicates that the L2TP Call-Serial-Number, a 32-bit number which is the same at both ends of the tunnel, should be populated into the Acct-Tunnel-Connection field. This provides the RADIUS ALE with the attributes necessary to identify the two ends of the tunnel, and the session in the tunnel. This information is combined with the incoming NAS-Identifier and NAS-Port information for the LAC NAS in order to provide the link to the provisioned circuit chain.

```
User-Name
Acct-Tunnel-Connection
Tunnel-Client-Endpoint
Tunnel-Server-Endpoint
NAS-Identifier
NAS-Port
```

At the ISP-LIS, the L2TP accounting information is combined with the `Framed-IP-Address` to provide the linkage from IP address to provisioned circuit chain.

```
User-Name
Acct-Tunnel-Connection
Tunnel-Client-Endpoint
Tunnel-Server-Endpoint
Framed-IP-Address
```

A L2TP ISP RADIUS ALE FLAP notify message will look similar to the XML stanza shown next. The XML schema for the RADIUS ALE is provided in Appendix A.

```
<ntfy xsi:type="radius:ntfy">
    <radius:terminal>
        <radius:user-name>joe@mynet.example.com</radius:user-name>
        <radius:framed-ip-address>192.168.0.1</radius:framed-ip-address>
    </radius:terminal>
    <radius:access time="2005-04-14T10:51:23.000+10:00">
        <radius:nas-ip-address>10.10.10.10</radius-nas-ip-address>
        <radius:nas-port-id>eth 3/0:100</radius:nas-port-id>
        <radius:l2tp>
            <radius:tunnel-client-endpoint>
                47.181.192.205
            </radius:tunnel-client-endpoint>
            <radius:tunnel-server-endpoint>
                47.181.195.222
            </radius:tunnel-server-endpoint>
            <radius:acct-session-id>15383</radius:acct-session-id>
        </radius:l2tp>
    </radius:access>
</ntfy>
```

The ISP-LIS uses the `Tunnel-Client-Endpoint` value to identify the RANP-LIS to query, and it uses the `Tunnel-Client-Endpoint`, `Tunnel-Server-Endpoint`, and `Acct-Tunnel-Connection` to identify the Target to the RANP-LIS. To do this, the ISP-LIS must use the HELD identity extensions schema provide in Appendix E. The following code fragment illustrates how the next example would translate into a HELD location request for this configuration.

```
<locationRequest xmlns="http://sitacs.uow.edu.au/ns/location/held">
    <heldDevice
        xmlns="http://sitacs.uow.edu.au/ns/location/held:deviceIdentifiers">
        <l2tp>
            <sourceIP>47.181.192.205</sourceIP>
            <destinationIP>47.181.195.222</destinationIP>
            <sessionID>15383</sessionID>
        </l2tp>
    </heldDevice>
</locationRequest>
```

DSL Network Summary

DSL networks provide broadband access to subscribers over existing twisted copper pair cables. In general, several operators need to cooperate in order to provide IP connectivity from the subscriber to an ISP. Data may be transported over a variety of different physical and link layers in order to reach their destination, and mechanisms are needed to provide measurements and mapping between these layers in order to ensure that the ultimate location of the end-point can be determined. LISes and ALEs are required in both the RANP and ISP networks to ensure that measurements and location information can be returned to the end-point when requested.

Cable Networks

Cable television dates back to the late 1940s and stems from the problem of some areas receiving only weak televisions signals. To counter this, communities established common antennas in good areas of reception and ran cables past households allowing them to obtain a strong clear signal. This scheme was called Community Antenna Television or CATV, a name that is still used today to describe cable television and data deployments. The North American cable industry formed an alliance in 1995 to develop specifications for data over cable networks called Data Over Cable Service Interface Specifications (DOCSIS), and it is these DOCSIS-based networks that are currently the heart of modern cable networks in North America. This section provides a brief overview of cable networks as they relate to DOCSIS-based deployments. The details of framing and network registration, as well as authentication, are not considered.

The Anatomy of Cable Networks

Cable networks have come a long way since the basic concept of a shared antenna. The general principle and architecture of cable networks is that first and foremost they are broadcast networks, with signals being sent from a single headend to a multitude of receivers in people's houses. Data signals in cable networks are carried in channels where each channel is allocated a band of spectrum within the cable's total available bandwidth. Channels in the United States generally have a bandwidth of 6MHz—the basic channel bandwidth adopted into the DOCSIS suite of specifications (see Figure 6.25).

Originally, all channels in a cable system were for downstream use only; however, the advent of demand for pay-per-view, voice, and data has resulted in cable networks migrating to become two-way systems providing both upward and downward links. In general, end users of data networks consume more data than they produce, consequently cable networks, like their DSL counterparts are asymmetric in nature—that is, far more bandwidth is allocated to the downward channels than the upward channels.

The evolution of cable networks has led to more intelligence being required in the cable headend controller. This is of particular importance for the management of cable modems where optimal use of uplink resources is crucial to overall network performance. The device in the headend is responsible for cable modem management in the Cable Modem Termination System (CMTS). A CMTS supports multiple low bit-rate

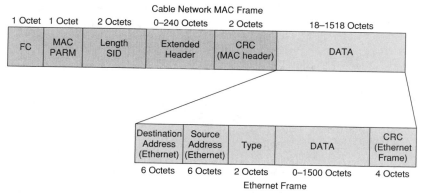

Figure 6.25   A modern cable network configuration.

uplink data channels and a single high-speed downlink data channel. All cable modems listen to the same downlink, and each cable modem is told specifically which uplink channel it may use and when it may use it. Uplink channels are slotted to gain maximum efficiency and sharing of the bandwidth—in other words, the 6MHz representing the available bandwidth is broken into time-slices, and each slice of time is referred to as a slot. Using this technique requires all cable modems to have the same notion of when a slot starts and finishes. Since all cable modems are at different distances from the CMTS, the modems somehow need to be synchronized. This is achieved by the CMTS *ranging* the modems before allowing them to transmit data packets. Ranging ensures that if any modem is told to transmit in Channel 1 (no matter where a modem is in the cable chain) all modem signals will arrive at the CMTS at the same time.

DOCSIS cable modems have a specific MAC protocol developed to run over the cable RF network. Addresses for this interface are assigned to the cable modem by the CMTS at network attachment time. All data over a cable network is framed inside these MAC messages, this includes management style messages as well as data messages. Data messages are generally sent in the form of Ethernet frames that are packaged inside the data component of a cable MAC message (see Figure 6.26).

When a cable modem is manufactured, it is assigned a unique IEEE 48-bit Ethernet MAC address by its manufacturer. A cable modem operating as a residential gateway takes data packets from the home network and reframes them with the cable modem's Ethernet address. This Ethernet frame is then encapsulated into a cable network MAC frame and sent to the CMTS. The MAC frame is removed at the CMTS and the resulting Ethernet packet is passed on to the ISP for the cable network.

Cable networks use cabling framing to convey Ethernet packets between the cable modem and the CMTS. The CMTS then conveys Ethernet frames to and from the ISP. The cable network can be thought of as a large distributed switched Ethernet network. Such an environment makes it less easy to support multiple ISPs, as is done in DSL environments, though not impossible. Most cable network operators therefore either run the ISP themselves or provide exclusive access to a dedicated ISP (see Figure 6.27).

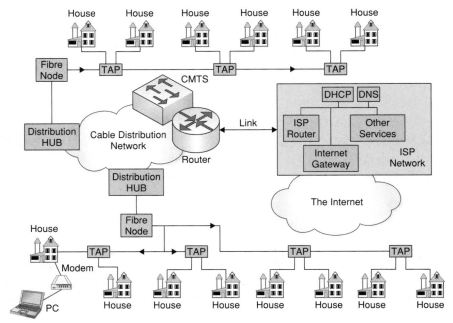

Figure 6.26   A cable network MAC frame.

Cable modems are not quite as plug-and-play as their DSL counterparts. A cable modem to some extent requires a degree of registration in the cable network in order to operate correctly. From a pure switching standpoint, the Ethernet address of the modem can generally be learned by the CMTS and other switching devices, but there is a need in cable networks to be able to associate the modem with a user's service to ensure that the correct services are made available. This registration often occurs online through special web pages and other registration mechanisms. Consequently, a direct association between the MAC address, the user, and the user's physical address is formed as part of the service provisioning and registration process.

Location in Cable Networks

The most common way to provide configuration information for the cable modems and hosts inside a cable network is through a combination of DHCP and TFTP. Given the close association between the cable network operator and the ISP, and the previously described modem registration process, an association between MAC address and physical address is possible. Unlike DSL networks that by and large use PPP, cable networks are in a serious position to consider DHCP as a location acquisition option. This choice comes not just because of the use of DHCP, but because of the strong coupling between the cable network operator and the ISP, and the tight control that many cable operators have over the configuration and firmware running in cable modems at customer sites.

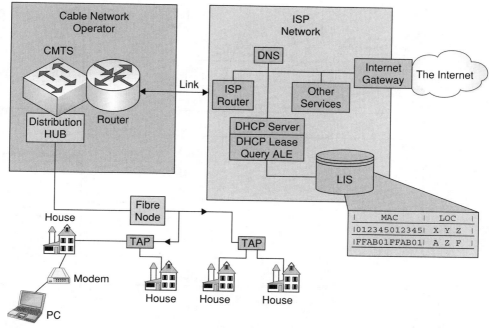

Figure 6.27 Cable Internet configuration.

This control allows the cable operator to automatically update many modems to support the DHCP location options. It does not, however, provide them with a unilateral ability to upgrade all systems, particularly those residing behind a residential firewall. These issues, combined with location dependability and compatibility with other network-based solutions, may cause cable Internet service providers to consider a HELD location acquisition solution in preference to a DHCP-based location acquisition solution.

Location determination in a cable network relies on the tie between the Ethernet MAC address and the physical address of the modem which are bound together at the time of service registration. The DHCP server in a cable network acts much the same as it would in an enterprise or DSL environment, and provides a binding between an IP address and an Ethernet MAC address. The DHCP lease query ALE described in Chapter 5 can be used to provide the binding between IP and Ethernet MAC address to the LIS. The LIS can then use this information to bind the IP address to the physical location of the end-point using the Ethernet MAC address to correlate the two. How this could be deployed in a cable network is shown in Figure 6.28.

There are a few things to note with this approach. If the DHCP server is not equipped with an ALE (such as the prototype ALE described in Chapter 5), then the LIS cannot determine location until the end-point makes a request for location. The reason for this is that the DHCP lease query ALE is a reactive element, not active as is the case with the

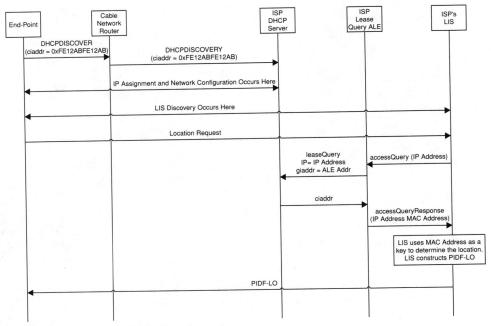

Figure 6.28 Cable Internet location configuration.

built-in ALE, which can send asynchronous notifications to the LIS. Tying the physical location of the user to the Ethernet MAC address of a cable modem presents problems if the cable modem moves within the same access network—that is, the LIS will associate the cable modem with its originally provided location unless a registration occurs.

The following steps through the diagram shown in Figure 6.29.

1. Cable modem initiates a DHCPDISCOVER that finds its way to the ISP DHCP server.

2. The ISP DHCP server allocates the cable modem an IP address and either provides additional configuration through DHCP options, or it provides the location of a TFTP server from which the cable modem can download configuration data.

3. The end-point learns the location of the LIS from the mechanism described in Chapter 4.

4. The end-point makes a HELD location request to the ISP LIS.

5. The ISP LIS uses the IP address to make a request to the DHCP lease query ALE.

6. The DHCP lease query ALE issues a DHCP lease query to the ISP DHCP server.

7. The DHCP server responds to the lease query with the MAC address of the cable modem to which the requesting end-point is connected.

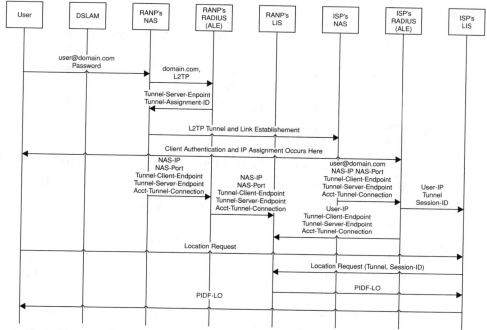

Figure 6.29   Cable network location acquisition.

8. The DHCP lease query ALE takes the response and sends a FLAP access query response message to the ISP LIS.

9. The ISP LIS uses the cable modem's MAC address to key into a database to retrieve the location of the cable modem.

10. The ISP LIS constructs a PIDF-LO and returns this to the end-point.

Summary

In conclusion, it is possible to provide IP location services in cable networks but owing to the architecture, physical termination points can only be associated with location based on a logical identifier such as an Ethernet MAC address. This requires each cable modem to be uniquely provisioned into the cable modem network, and for this information to be readily available to the ISP. Making this information available to the ISP is less challenging than in other network configurations since cable networks tend to provide service through a very small set of ISPs. The drawback of provisioning logical identifiers in this manner reveals itself in the guise of providing an incorrect location when a cable modem is moved from one residence to another without a re-registration occurring.

References

1. DSL Forum, *"Multi-Service Architecture & Framework Requirements,"* Technical Report 058.

2. DSL Forum, *"DSL Evolution—Architecture Requirements for the Support of QoS-Enabled IP Services,"* Technical Report 059.

3. DSL Forum, *"Migration to Ethernet-Based DSL Aggregation,"* Technical Report 101.

4. DSL Forum, *"Protocols at the U Interface for Accessing Data Networks using ATM / DSL,"* Technical Report 043.

5. Simpson, W., "The Point-to-Point Protocol (PPP)," STD 51, RFC 1661, July 1994.

6. Lloyd, B. and W. Simpson, "PPP Authentication Protocols," RFC 1334, October 1992.

7. Simpson, W., *"PPP Challenge Handshake Authentication Protocol (CHAP),"* RFC 1994, August 1996.

8. McGregor, G., *"The PPP Internet Protocol Control Protocol (IPCP),"* RFC 1332, May 1992.

9. Mamakos, L., Lidl, K., Evarts, J., Carrel, D., Simone, D., and R. Wheeler, *"A Method for Transmitting PPP Over Ethernet (PPPoE),"* RFC 2516, February 1999.

10. Rigney, C., Willens, S., Rubens, A., and W. Simpson, *"Remote Authentication Dial In User Service (RADIUS),"* RFC 2865, June 2000.

11. Rigney, C., Willats, W., and P. Calhoun, *"RADIUS Extensions,"* RFC 2869, June 2000.

12. Aboba, B. and M. Beadles, *"The Network Access Identifier,"* RFC 2486, January 1999.

13. Rigney, C., *"RADIUS Accounting,"* RFC 2866, June 2000.

14. Townsley, W., Valencia, A., Rubens, A., Pall, G., Zorn, G., and B. Palter, *"Layer Two Tunneling Protocol 'L2TP',"* RFC 2661, August 1999.

15. Zorn, G., Leifer, D., Rubens, A., Shriver, J., Holdrege, M., and I. Goyret, *"RADIUS Attributes for Tunnel Protocol Support,"* RFC 2868, June 2000.

16. Aboba, B. and G. Zorn, *"Implementation of L2TP Compulsory Tunneling via RADIUS,"* RFC 2809, April 2000.

17. Zorn, G., Aboba, B., and D. Mitton, *"RADIUS Accounting Modifications for Tunnel Protocol Support,"* RFC 2867, June 2000.

18. DSL Forum, *"Core Network Architecture Recommendations for Access to Legacy Data Networks over ADSL,"* Technical Report 025.

19. Patrick, M., *"DHCP Relay Agent Information Option,"* RFC 3046, January 2001.

20. Polk, J., Schnizlein, J., and M. Linsner, *"Dynamic Host Configuration Protocol Option for Coordinate-based Location Configuration Information,"* RFC 3825, July 2004.

WiFi and Ad Hoc Wireless Networks

Wireless technologies have advanced significantly in recent years, particularly those based on the IEEE 802.11 series of standards. Wireless technologies are a very attractive networking option in light of dramatic improvements in speed, usability, security, and mobility. The convenience of being able to deploy a network without the need to install cables is also a great advantage of wireless networking.

Location technologies in this area share some similarities with those used in cellular networks, the same basic primitives of location—location measurements—can be used for WiFi. However, WiFi presents a new set of challenges. In particular, ad hoc network architectures present difficult problems for location determination.

In this chapter, location determination in WiFi networks is examined. Basic technology options and how they can be applied in both infrastructure and ad hoc variants are discussed. These options are described with the LIS and ALE architecture in mind.

802.11 Wireless LANs

The 802.11 series of standards have made wireless network connectivity accessible for a great many people. Wireless LANs provide an alternative to wired Ethernet, and offer many advantages, particularly in terms of ease of use and ubiquity. Wireless LANs can be found in many workplaces and public areas—for instance, a great many airports make a WLAN available to people awaiting flights.

Wireless LANs fall into two categories: infrastructure-based and ad hoc. Infrastructure WLANs rely on access points (APs) to provide a connection to a wired LAN, as well as a central point for communication. Public wireless hotspots, such as those at coffee shops and airports, are typically infrastructure WLANs. Figure 7.1 shows a sample infrastructure-based WLAN.

An access point in this configuration performs functions that are similar to a wired Ethernet switch with a wireless link in place of a cable; both systems use hierarchical routing. Wired Ethernet and WLANs can be used together because they employ the

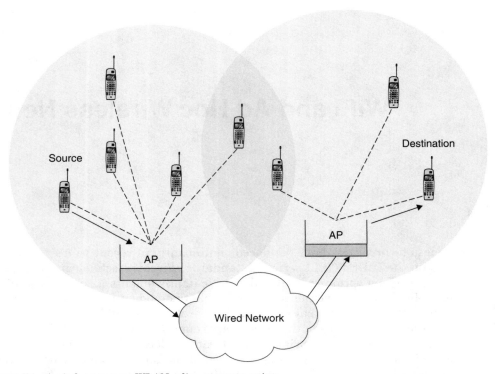

Figure 7.1   An infrastructure WLAN relies on access points.

same MAC address scheme. An access point can act as an IP router, which is necessary in places where Ethernet does not provide the wired link; many access points also act as network address translation (NAT) devices, which are common in home WLANs.

Ad hoc networks do not rely on the existence of infrastructure; each mobile station is able to communicate with peers directly, and messages can be forwarded to a destination that is not directly reachable. An ad hoc WLAN can route traffic to the Internet or any other network through the use of gateway nodes that are attached to both the wired and access point network.

Ad hoc networks rely on routing protocols to enable message forwarding (see Figure 7.2). Where a connection to the Internet is required, *gateway* nodes are able to route messages destined for the Internet. There are too many different routing protocols for ad hoc networks to summarize them all effectively here. This book simply assumes that they achieve their goal and that a packet can be routed using a path that minimizes the number of hops and the total distance in some fashion.

The multiple paths through an ad hoc network make it very robust in the presence of failures. This, combined with the fact that ad hoc networks do not rely on infrastructure, means they have a number of applications. Ad hoc networks can also provide good network coverage without the same infrastructure requirements as a network utilizing

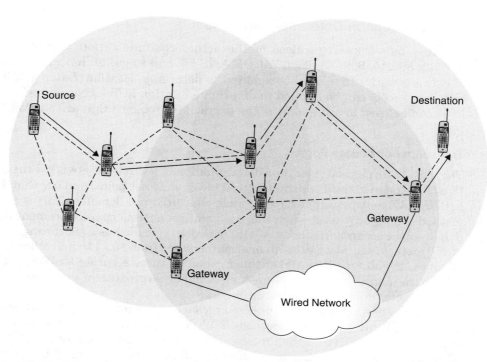

Figure 7.2 Participants in an ad hoc network are active in routing messages.

access points. Each access point can provide service to a limited number of stations in an area, whereas ad hoc networks can scale to relatively high densities.

The primary focus of this section is on the use of ad hoc networks for wireless mesh networks. Wireless mesh networks are often used to provide cost-effective Internet connectivity in residential areas, business precincts, and/or areas where people might congregate.

Wireless mesh networks that are used for residential Internet access have a number of properties that can be exploited to simplify or optimize location determination. The wireless nodes generally remain stationary and the access network provider often has some form of preexisting relationship with each of the network users. Network properties that affect location, like the network topology, remain static over time in these networks. Therefore, location in these networks is easier to manage over time and locations can usually be given by a residential civic address with relative reliability. Automatic location determination methods can, in some cases, be kept for secondary roles, such as to assist in network maintenance and troubleshooting, or to provide a check on a statically mapped location.

In a more dynamic mesh network, such as those that are used for public places, location determination is complicated by more mobile wireless nodes. Location determination in the more fluid mesh network is additionally challenging. Automatic location determination becomes imperative in these networks.

Basic Wireless Location Determination Toolset

Wireless networks, regardless of the actual communication technology employed (802.11, 802.15, 802.16, GSM, W-CDMA, IS-95, and so on) all have the same basic set of characteristics that can be exploited to determine location. Later it will be shown how these tools can be applied to determine location in WLANs, and what additional tools can be used to solve some of the particular problems that arise in WLANs.

Nearest Transmitter or Access Point

The most basic method of location determination in a wireless network is to take the location of the nearest fixed transmitter (cell tower or access point) and use that. For cellular and WiMAX networks that have a range measured in kilometers, this is a fairly crude method that is only used when there is insufficient time or measurement capability to employ more accurate methods. A WiFi network typically has a short range (on the order of 100 meters in most cases) with modest increases from 802.11n and other technological advances. A shorter range makes this method far more accurate for WiFi networks.

This method usually results in a reasonably large area of uncertainty, which can prove to be a problem for ad hoc networks.

A number of solutions have appeared recently using a method that is based on access point identification. In these methods, a WiFi-enabled computer reports all the service set identifiers (SSIDs) in the area to a location determination system. The SSID is a 32-character identifier that helps distinguish between different WLANs in any area. Based on these SSIDs and a database of known locations, the system provides a location estimate. These location determination systems operate independently of any access network and use a centrally maintained database, of which a copy may be kept locally. However, using the SSID of local access points is very dependent on having multiple wireless LANs in the area, and the accuracy of the databases that are used is critical. These systems are limited to more densely populated areas.

Ranging Measurements

The distance between two wireless antennae can be determined based on the round trip time for a simple message. Such information can be used, particularly in wireless systems with a longer range, to help reduce the probability of the contention that can occur when two transmissions are sent at the same time.

Ranging measurements, particularly in smaller networks, require precise timing, considering that a radio signal travels one meter in less than 3.4 nanoseconds. Ranging measurements also rely on being able to compensate for any delays that the other end of the link may add in receiving a message, processing it, and preparing a response for transmission.

A major weakness of ranging measurements is their susceptibility to signal reflection, or *multipath* signals. Multipath occurs when a signal reflects off a surface between the transmitter and receiver. If a signal does not take the most direct path from transmitter to receiver, the perceived distance can be inflated. For wireless transceivers that are designed for communication purposes, a stronger signal is likely to be preferred over a weaker signal that might be received earlier.

For 802.11 WLANs, ranging measurements rely on the requirement that an 802.11 receiver acknowledge frames that are addressed to it. This sort of message can be processed rapidly, and in a fashion that has a deterministic time. The processing time can be eliminated from the measurement if it is already known. (see Figure 7.3). Statistical methods can then be applied to multiple measurements to increase the confidence in the measurement.

A single range measurement for an omnidirectional transceiver reduces the overall area of uncertainty, or the *precision* of the estimate. The overall *accuracy*, whether or not the information is reliable, is not necessarily improved.

Trilateration The most common way to use ranging measurements is to take multiple-range measurements from fixed or known points. These ranges are combined to determine a location using a technique called *trilateration*. Trilateration is where range measurements become the most useful, particularly where no other measurements are available. This method is particularly applicable where omnidirectional antennae are used. Figure 7.4 shows how this can be applied in two dimensions.

Three circles are drawn from the fixed points with the given distances. The first two circles intersect at two points; the third circle is used to determine which of the two points the target location is. This principle can be applied in three dimensions using spheres instead of circles, but one additional range measurement is required.

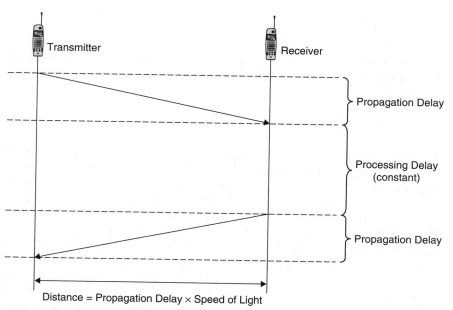

Distance = Propagation Delay × Speed of Light

Figure 7.3 Determining the distance between two transceivers.

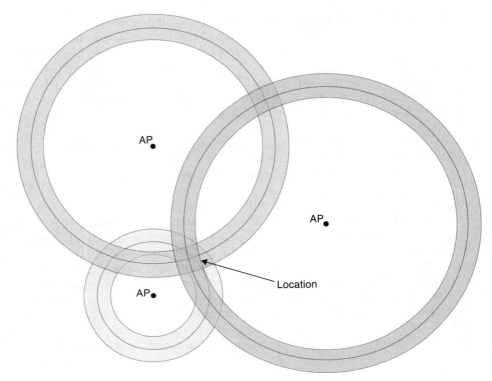

Figure 7.4 Using trilateration in two dimensions from three access points.

Sources of error in measurement mean that the circles do not always meet precisely. A region of uncertainty usually arises from trilateration methods. More measurements can be used to reduce this region in size.

Direction

Angle of arrival methods use shaped antennae or antenna arrays to determine which direction a signal was transmitted from. This permits a heading to be determined from an access point, or other transceiver. When combined with a range measurement, this can provide a reasonable location estimate from a single transceiver.

Directional antennae can be used to direct radio signals in a particular direction. The signal produced by some directional antennae can be controlled so that a narrow band can be transmitted. If the signal is rotated in a sweeping pattern in the same way that a radar system would be employed, then the location of another transceiver can be detected by determining which angles generate responses. The shaped signal isn't perfectly narrow, so several responses are likely to be generated, producing a range of angles. Figure 7.5 shows a possible scenario, where responses are generated for values of ω are 165, 170, and 175 degrees.

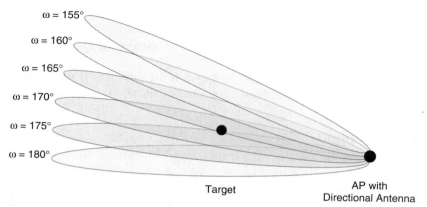

$\omega = 155°$
$\omega = 160°$
$\omega = 165°$
$\omega = 170°$
$\omega = 175°$
$\omega = 180°$

Target

AP with
Directional Antenna

Figure 7.5 A directional antenna can be used like a radar system to determine a direction.

Multiple direction measurements from different points in the network can be combined to refine a location estimate. This is known as *triangulation*.

This method is best suited to dedicated ALEs within the network since this sort of process interferes with the ability of a node to communicate on its usual radio channel and exchange data. Specialized antennae and radio control are also required for this process.

Signal Strength Measurements

The strength of a radio signal from nearby transmitters can usually be measured at each receiver in the network. Primarily, this information exists to assist in regulating transmission power levels, but this information can also be used to determine the location of a receiver.

The received signal strength must then be compared to the transmission power. From this, a rough range estimate can be derived using the inverse square principle for signal (signal power is inversely proportional to the square of the distance from the transmitter). Statistical methods are often used to compensate for variations that can occur.

Signal strength can be highly variable since radio signals are highly susceptible to environmental conditions. Weather conditions outdoors, such as wind and rain can make signal strength unreliable, unless additional data are collected to compensate for these variations. More sophisticated methods also take environmental conditions into consideration. Signal strength can be used in combination with other methods, which provide information that can refine the accuracy of results.

Radio camera is a term often used to describe location determination methods that use signal strength alone to determine location. Radio camera techniques use a survey of the area with signal strength measurements. They are more reliable than a straight estimate based on the inverse square principle, which provides a range estimate subject to all the error sources mentioned previously. This method is called radio camera because it takes a map, or image, of the network coverage area, arranging signal strength measurements in a grid format. The nearest access point is used as a starting point and maximum likelihood estimation techniques are employed to match the measured signal strength to the best fit within the signal strength map nearest to the initial estimate.

For WiFi, the received signal strength indicator (RSSI) and received channel power indicator (RCPI) are statistical measures of signal strength.

Time Difference of Arrival (TDOA)

If the target mobile station generates a well-known signal or training sequence, a number of measurement units can observe the precise time that the signal was received. In two dimensions, three time differences can be combined to determine the location of the mobile station. The method used to determine the location estimate is called *multilateration*. Figure 7.6 shows how multilateration is performed based on the time difference of arrival (TDOA). The intersection of hyperbolic curves is used in a similar method to that used when range measurements are known. Each hyperbolic curve describes a point where the difference between the distances a_{ij} and b_{ij} are constant.

TDOA relies on having time synchronization between measurement units. This is typically achieved in cellular networks by including GPS receivers in each unit to provide an accurate time base derived from GPS time. For WiFi, time synchronization is already available within the network; infrastructure networks only have one wireless

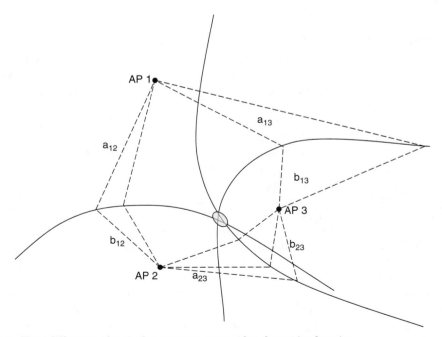

Figure 7.6   Time difference of arrival measurements used to determine location.

hop, which ensures good synchronization with little possibility of time skew. However, time synchronization across an ad hoc network can potentially take a short time to achieve; therefore, a time difference of one or two microseconds can be observed.

Like trilateration, more measurements can be used to refine location estimates that are produced by multilateration.

Two forms of time difference can be used for location estimation. In a network-based system, monitoring devices in the network capture an easily identifiable message that is transmitted by the device. Each monitoring device records the exact time that it receives the message. A device-based system is the exact inversion of network-based TDOA. The device measures the exact time that it receives signals from multiple points in the network. The device-based approach is complicated by the fact that the signals are transmitted at different times; these differences need to be known and accounted for. Both network- and device-based methods result in a similar multilateration calculation.

Ad Hoc Location Determination Methods

Ad hoc wireless networks present a number of challenges for location determination because few or none of the nodes involved in the network need to be fixed. Most location determination methods require that certain nodes in the network have well-known locations. One consequence of the flexibility of ad hoc networks is that nodes with known locations can be quite sparsely distributed throughout the network. If the known locations are sparse, then determining the location of other nodes can be difficult.

Known locations in a wireless ad hoc network can be determined by external means. If a gateway node is used, then its means of access to the Internet can provide other means of locating it, such as those previously described for DSL, Ethernet, or cellular networks. It is quite possible that the location of a gateway may be known to the LIS. GPS is also a realistic possibility. There could be a number of nodes within the network that are equipped with a GPS capability; the LIS can use asserted location information in determination calculations, providing the LIS trusted the information that it was provided.

The difficulty with having a sparse distribution of known locations is that uncertainty accumulates as the distance from those known locations increases. The uncertainty in the location of a node is increased for each hop from the known location. This is because the uncertainty in determining location is compounded with any uncertainty that exists in the reference locations used to determine that location. For instance, if a device is located using a method with an uncertainty radius of 10 meters, but the transceiver location that this estimate is based on also has an uncertainty radius of 8 meters; the actual uncertainty radius in the final device location is 18 meters. The total area of uncertainty increases in proportion to the square of the number of hops from the known location.

Figure 7.7 shows how precision degrades the further from an access point the target node is. This example assumes that the location of another node can be determined using a single reference point. In reality, location estimates depend on multiple known points, but the overall impact of imprecision in those known locations is similar.

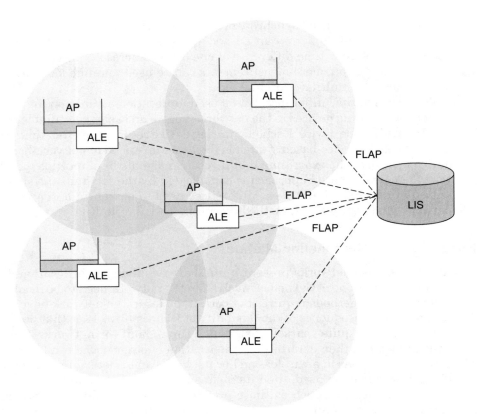

Figure 7.7 Degradation of precision caused by multiple hops in an ad hoc network.

The degradation of precision example demonstrates how improved location determination methods can contribute to the usability of location information. Even if the precision at one hop is far in excess of that which is required, the improvement can have a large impact in an ad hoc network. Figure 7.8 shows the effect that improving precision does to final accuracy over Figure 7.7; this demonstrates what an accuracy improvement can provide in the precision of the final location estimate.

Precision can be improved by a number of methods. The combination of multiple determination methods can often improve accuracy—for instance, combining angle and range measurements from one access point with a range measurement from another point can greatly improve precision. Another possibility is to combine network measurements with those from other sources; cellular networks, RFID beacons, and GPS are just some of the possible sources of other measurements. In particular, hybrid location determination methods have a greater yield, or probability of successfully determining a location.

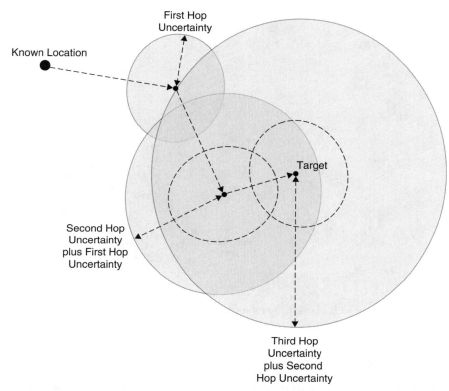

Figure 7.8   The final precision is greatly affected by the precision at each hop.

In the spirit of using multiple sources to derive location information, this information can also come from the network. If a particular node can be reached through a number of paths, then location determination along each of those paths can be used to refine the location estimate. Figure 7.9 shows how an estimate by one method can be refined when another estimate is available.

Network Topology in Location Determination

In the spirit of using multiple data points, there are a number of possibilities for ad hoc networks. The routing table that is maintained by each of the nodes in the network is a valuable location measurement. If it can be assumed that connectivity implies proximity, then routing information can be used to derive a possible network layout. The method proposed by Shang et al. (see Reference 1) minimizes each connection in the network to derive a network layout. This layout is not oriented and may be inverted, but if two or more nodes have known locations, it can be matched to the actual network with reasonable accuracy.

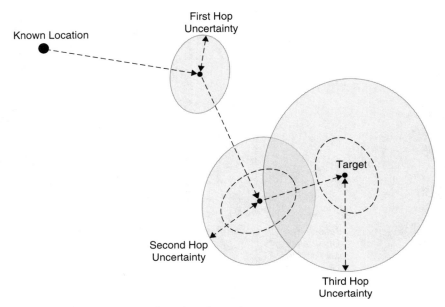

Figure 7.9 Using multiple paths to refine a location estimate.

Architectural Considerations

The primary problem that affects all these different scenarios is how measurement information is extracted and made available to the nodes that need it. Some of these methods require the collection of data from multiple nodes in the network, whereas some of the information is made available through MAC or routing layer messages.

Infrastructure Networks   In an infrastructure network, access points make a good choice for ALEs. The LIS can be provisioned with the location of each access point and can use range measurements from multiple access points effectively. Figure 7.10 shows this network architecture.

To achieve the most basic level of location determination, the ALE in the access point only needs to report the MAC addresses of the mobile stations that it is currently serving. This information can be used to provide a service that is adequate for most purposes. Additional information can be retrieved from the ALE to gain better accuracy and precision in the final location estimate.

Ad Hoc Networks

In ad hoc networks, ALEs can be employed in a number of ways, depending on the particular network configuration. In order to guarantee that all the necessary information was available, all nodes in the network could be configured with ALEs. However, it is

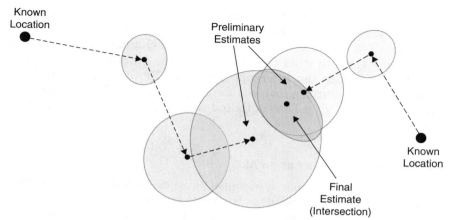

Figure 7.10   A LIS can use infrastructure (access points) to acquire location measurements.

neither likely nor practical to expect that the network provider is able to control all the nodes in the network.

A more practical configuration uses select nodes within the network to relay location measurements. This function can be provided by fixed gateways that also provide a connection from the WLAN to the Internet or larger network. These nodes are usually under the control of the network provider and can therefore be configured with ALEs.

In addition to configuring ALEs within the access network, the target node is an excellent source of location measurements in an ad hoc network. Chapter 9 discusses a number of ways that the LIS can extract location measurements from a device.

ALE Overlays

A possible alternative to using the inherent measurement capability of mobile nodes and access points in the WLAN is to add independent ALEs to the network. These ALEs are independent nodes with passive radio receivers that monitor the radio environment to acquire location measurements. These nodes are typically fixed, so that they have a known location, and they report signal strength and timing measurements. The ALEs report these measurements to the LIS, which combines the measurements to determine the location of devices.

This overlay technology follows the concepts employed for cellular networks. Each ALE is analogous to the GSM Location Measurement Unit (LMU) that is used for network-based Uplink Time Difference of Arrival (U-TDOA). However, for many indoor environments the GPS used in GSM LMUs would not be applicable to WLAN ALEs. GSM LMUs use GPS to provide time synchronization and sometimes location; WLAN ALEs would be able to use the inherent network synchronization and would be manually located.

Dedicated location measurement devices can also provide measurements without some of the inherent limitations of access points. Access points are often limited in their ability to measure signals outside of the channel that they operate in. In order to monitor signals in other channels, the access point has to temporarily switch to the new channel, which can interrupt service. ALEs that monitor radio signals over the network coverage area provide a means of receiving location measurements. These ALEs can provide signal strength and timing information without disrupting the network service.

The Wireless Network Controller as an ALE

For networks that employ a wireless network controller, the network controller can act as an ALE to provide measurements to the LIS. A number of wireless network controllers determine location as a part of their operation, in which case they can report location to the LIS. Having the network controller report location has advantages in terms of simplicity, but it limits the opportunity for hybrid location determination methods where measurements from the wireless network are combined with other measurements from other sources, such as devices themselves taking pseudorange measurements.

Location Support in 802.11v

The IEEE is currently working on the inclusion of support for location information in the 802.11 protocols. Draft changes in 802.11v would allow wireless nodes to exchange location measurements and information using 802.11. The goal of these changes is to grant each wireless node the ability to determine its own location.

The protocol additions enable wireless nodes to report location measurements that can be sent to wireless peers, or request measurements from neighboring peers. The supported location measurements include timing and signal strength measurements. The timing measurement that is reported can be used to eliminate the fixed processing time mentioned previously, it provides a value for the fixed delay between receipt of a message and when the acknowledgment is sent in response. This removes the dependencies on having manufacturer- and model-specific data available to make use of timing measurements. The signal strength measurements include the signal to noise and RCPI, along with information about the transmission system of the node: transmit power and antenna gain.

Wireless nodes can also include location information; the current form contains a range of encodings for location information, including the formats defined by the IETF in References 2 and 3. A number of other parameters are provided, including speed, direction, and precision indicators.

A wireless node can use this information, along with measurements that it is able to make, to determine its own location. If the location of adjacent nodes is known from these reports, the timing information in these reports can be used as input to a trilateration algorithm.

For a device to determine its own location requires that the device has the processing and battery capacity available to perform the necessary calculations. Devices with limited processing or battery capacity are able to use the proposed method to regularly report location measurements.

From the perspective of the location architecture, the location measurements provided by wireless peers are the most interesting. An ALE within this network can use these messages to request information from its peers, thus being able to provide location measurements with greater precision than a passive receiver would be able to provide. The measurements that are reported can also be centrally combined to improve overall precision and accuracy.

IP Mobility and Location Acquisition

IP mobility is a feature that is prevalent in networks that permit easy mobility, like wireless LANs. IP mobility provides a mobile device the option of retaining its original IP address. As the device moves, it acquires new IP addresses, but packets addressed to the original address are routed to the new address by a router in the original network. IP mobility presents similar problems to that generated by the Virtual Private Network (VPN) for the acquisition of location information. Figure 7.11 shows how a typical IP mobility solution might be used.

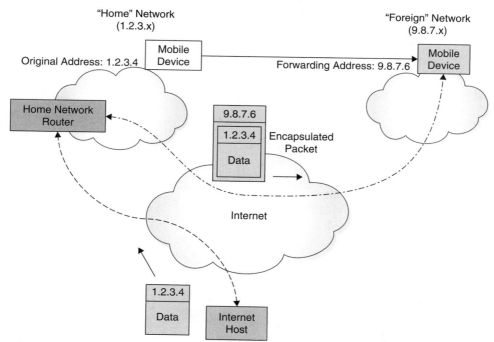

Figure 7.11   IP mobility allows changes in an IP address by tunneling messages.

In IP mobility, a router in the initial, or "Home," network forwards messages to the device at its new IP address. This means that sessions established using the original IP address can be maintained, even though the IP address of the device changes as it moves. A forwarding address is provided to the router in the Home network when it changes. The forwarding address can either point to the device or a similar router in the current, or "Visited," network. The host sending the mobile device data does not need to be aware that the device is moving.

The link between the original network and the mobile device is analogous to the tunnel that is established for a VPN. Just as with a VPN, the mobile device needs to be aware that it cannot contact the LIS in its home network. The device needs to be aware that it needs to contact the LIS in the network that provides physical network access and use the IP address that it has acquired from the same local access network.

References

1. Shang, Y., W. Ruml, Y. Zhang, and M. Fromherz. *"Localization from Mere Connectivity."* Proceedings of ACM MOBIHOC 2003, pg.: 201–212.

2. Polk, J., Schnizlein, J., Linsner, M., *"Dynamite Host Configuration Protocol Option for Coordinate-based Location Configuration Information,"* RFC 3825, July 2004.

3. Peterson, J., *"A Presence-based GEOPRIV Location Object Format,"* RFC 4199, December 2005.

IP Location in Wireless Public Carrier Networks

So far we have looked at how we can determine and provide location in enterprise and residential wireline environments. We have explored location determination techniques that can be employed in WiFi networks, both for fixed-WiFi and Wireless-Mesh networks. In this chapter, we will examine location determination and acquisition techniques that can be employed in wireless carrier networks that employ a range of IP-capable access technologies, including GPRS, 1xEVDO, and WiMAX. The chapter will conclude with a cursory examination of how IMS-based solutions can be employed to provide common services over a range of different access types.

Chapter 1 described the native location functionality that has been present in cellular networks for quite some time. Location capabilities that are built into the network infrastructure are referred to as "control-plane" location solutions. There are extensive control-plane location deployments in North America which have largely been driven by the need to support the FCC emergency service requirements for cellular networks. More recent events have seen the emergence of user-plane location protocols, such as the Open Mobile Alliance (OMA) Secure User Plane Location (SUPL) standard (see Reference 1 at the end of the chapter). SUPL seeks to use capabilities in IP-enabled handsets to reduce dependencies on roaming partners needing to support control-plane infrastructures. SUPL is described in Chapter 9, and Chapter 1 dealt with cellular control-plane location solutions. The remainder of this chapter will describe the basic wireless data access technologies and how the location determination and acquisition techniques we have described thus far in the book can be integrated to provide an optimal solution.

Cellular Data Networks

The general principle of cellular data systems is to separate the data stream bearer from the voice stream bearer and process it in a manner that is tailored specifically for data so that it can exit via a gateway into the wider Internet. How this separation of

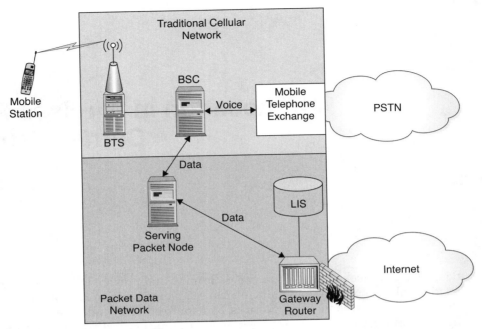

Figure 8.1 Packet data location architecture.

voice and data traffic is actually achieved is different depending on the access technology deployed; however, the concepts and principles of linking an IP location function into these environments are the same.

The IP address allocated to a mobile device in a cellular data network can come from a variety of sources, including private enterprises and ISPs, but more often than not, comes from the cellular operator. Regardless of where the IP address is allocated, the gateway router in the cellular network needs to be able to map the IP address to a physical cellular device to ensure data packets are delivered to and from the device correctly. If a device is to be able to request its location from a LIS based on the device's IP address, then the LIS will need to have an association with, or have access to, some of the same information as, the cellular operator's packet data gateway. This leads us to the general architecture shown in Figure 8.1.

Location in GPRS Networks

The General Packet Radio Service (GPRS) is the access technology used to provide packet data capabilities to 2G (GSM), and with some software upgrades provides support for 2.5G (EDGE) and 3G (UMTS) cellular devices. GPRS is specified under the 3GPP suite of protocols and integrates with the GSM and UMTS standards. The general architecture for a GPRS network is shown in Figure 8.2.

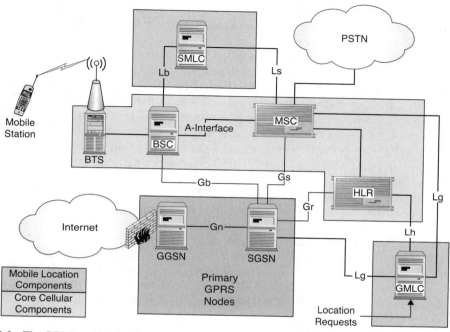

Figure 8.2   The GPRS architecture.

Figure 8.2 shows the core interfaces that are of interest to us in a GSM GPRS network. The general concepts are the same in a UMTS network, and we shall look at this a little later. While this is not a GPRS tutorial, it is necessary to understand some of the basics of a GPRS network before we can look at the options for location. First and foremost, GPRS is a way to provide packet data services to a GSM cellular network, consequently it is able to make use of some resources and information already available in the cellular network.

The heart of the GPRS network is controlled by two nodes: the Serving GPRS Support Node (SGSN) and the Gateway GPRS Support Node (GGSN). GPRS is viewed as being an always-on connection, and when a GPRS mobile first registers in a network, it is the SGSN that takes care of most of this. The SGSN is responsible for authentication, registration, and mobility management functions, very much like how the VLR is for cellular voice services. The SGSN is also responsible for the protocol conversions required between the mobile over the air interface, and core IP protocols used over the carrier's backbone network. All data sent by the mobile over the GPRS network, or to the mobile from the GPRS networks is transported by the SGSN.

The GGSN, on the other hand, connects from the carrier's GPRS network to other networks, such as the Internet, corporate LANs, or third-party ISPs. As a result, the GGSN may allocate IP addresses itself, solicit aid from a RADIUS or DHCP server, or it may broker the request to the enterprise or ISP to authenticate and assign

IP address information. The GGSN is a router and hides visibility of the GPRS network from external entities and networks. In order for the GGSN to be able to route packets between the GPRS network and the external network, it needs to have a context that allows it to associate the mobile in both networks. This context is called a Packet Data Protocol (PDP) context and it provides a binding between the mobile device using, amongst other things, the IMSI and MSISDN and the external network identifier. GPRS supports general packet protocol but, in practice, the PDP is IP, and this is the assumption that we shall use for the remainder of this chapter.

Figure 8.2 shows the GGSN connecting through a firewall to the Internet. In reality the GGSN can provide a connection to networks other than the Internet, including a corporate LAN, or a third-party ISP. The connecting node must inform the SGSN, and by association the GGSN, which network they wish connect to. To do this, the GRPS handset includes a specific Access Path Name (APN), which is used to identify the type of connection the handset requires. For each connection, a PDP context is created on the GGSN, and a new IP address is allocated. It is therefore possible that a terminal in a GPRS network may have more than one IP address assigned to it. We shall only consider the Internet PDP context type.

The control-plane location specification includes support for determining the location of a data device since the GMLC is able to use the Lg interface to request location information from the SGSN. The GMLC is able to determine which SGSN to query since this information is maintained in the HLR as part of the mobility management function. The SGSN is then able to send a BSSAP provide location request (PLR) to the BSC, which in turn sends a BSSAP-LE PLR to the SMLC. At the time of writing, not all the major suppliers of SGSN equipment support this functionality, consequently the GMLC may need to send the PLR to the MSC in the same way it would for a voice-based location request. This assumes that GPRS handsets also operate as voice terminals, which is generally true today.

Chapter 1 described the GMLC and its main query interface, the Le interface, which uses the OMA-defined Mobile Location Protocol (MLP) (see Reference 2). MLP provides an array of ways to identify a device, including IMSI, IMEI, MSISDN, and IP address. The problem is that the GMLC must be able to take the identifier provided in the MLP query, and map it to an SGSN or MSC, and to do this it must get information from the HLR. The GMLC obtains this information from the HLR by sending it a 3GPP MAP (see Reference 3) Send Routing Information (SRI) message, and this message must contain either the MSISDN or the IMSI so that the device can be identified. Hence the GMLC must be provided with either the IMSI or the MSISDN over the MLP interface.

In the networks we have described so far, the end-point has used a HELD request to a LIS to obtain location information, either as a reference location URI or a literal, PIDF-LO. Ideally, therefore, an IP-based handset can request location from a cellular IP network in the same way. If we want to do this in such a way as to leverage an existing control-plane infrastructure, then we need to introduce a LIS into the network, and we need to be able to obtain a binding between IP address and either MSISDN or IMSI. There are two ways to obtain this binding: either learn it from the network somehow, or have it provided by the end-point. The safest option is to learn it from the network but there is no standard defined on how to perform this. GGSN vendors may make this information available by providing a proprietary query interface, or indirect methods obtaining the data the DHCP server, RADIUS server, or charging records may be employed. The LIS may not be able to learn the IP-to-IMSI/MSISDN mapping from the network in all circumstances, however, and where it can't it will be dependent on the end-point providing the mapping. GPRS is a mobile network, and in most cases the end-point will create a HELD context and use a location URI to facilitate location retrieval. The end-point can therefore provide the IMSI/MSISDN-to–IP address binding when the HELD context is created using the HELD identity extensions schema defined in Appendix E. A HELD context creation message providing this mapping would look similar to the following code fragment.

```
<createContext xmlns="http://sitacs.uow.edu.au/ns/location/held">
    <lifetime>PT10M</lifetime>
    <profile>
        <presentity>pres:user@example.com</presentity>
        <retentionExpiry>2006-01-01T13:00:00</retentionExpiry>
        <retransmission>false</retransmission>
    </profile>
    <rules>
        <ruleset xmlns="urn:ietf:params:xml:ns:common-policy">
            <rule id="f3g44r1">
                <conditions>
                    <identity>
                        <one id="sip:mycallserver@goodcalls.com"/>
                    </identity>
                </conditions>
            </rule>
        </ruleset>
    </rules>
    <heldDevice
        xmlns="http://sitacs.uow.edu.au/ns/location/held:deviceIdentifiers">
        <msisdn>612448266004</msisdn>
        <imsi>50501997844001</imsi>
        <ipv4>47.181.192.205</ipv4>
    </heldDevice>
</createContext>
```

A LIS deployment in a GPRS network is shown in Figure 8.3. The DHCP protocol defined in Reference 4 allows a DHCP client to specify a particular Client-Identifier to the DHCP server that the server should use as a handle to the client-host's configuration data. This is DHCP option 61 and is defined in detail in Reference 5. The GGSN in a GPRS network acts as a client for a great many DHCP leases, one per PDP context, so the GGSN needs a way to associate a particular context with a DHCP lease and the easiest way to do this is to use the Client-Identifier DHCP option 61. One implementation option a GGSN vendor can use is to create the Client-Identifier for a PDP context in the IMSI or MSISDN concatenated with Network Service Access Point

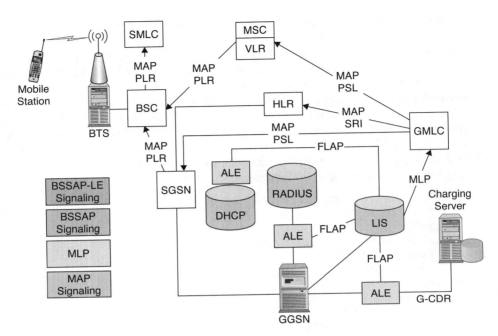

Figure 8.3 The LIS in a GPRS network.

Identifier (NSAPI), where NSAPI defines the type and possibly quality of service associated with the PDP context (this approach is used by at least one commercial GGSN vendor). Using this approach, a DHCP lease query ALE can be used to extract the Client-Identifier information from the DHCP server and subsequently provide the required IMSI/MSISDN-to-IP mapping.

Where RADIUS is used to provide the IP address, RADIUS accounting messages similar to those described in Chapter 6 can be used to obtain the necessary attribute associations. In Chapter 6, the RADIUS ALE was mapping IP address to circuit identifiers and correlators. In this case, the RADIUS ALE needs to map IP address to IMSI or MSISDN, which it can do using the `Framed-IP-Address` and `Callback-Number` `RADIUS` attributes defined in Reference 6. Essentially, this same method is used by a number of commercial WAP gateways that have to deal with a similar problem. In WAP gateway deployments, the RADIUS accounting messages are sent directly from the GGSN to the WAP gateway.

The 3GPP specification (see Reference 7) deals with the generation of charging records, referred to as call detail records (CDR) in GPRS networks. The node that is generating the CDR determines the prefix given to the CDR; G-CDRs, for example, are generated by the GGSN. G-CDRs are created and sent to a charging server based on various triggers that occur through the lifetime of an attachment; two such triggers are the creation and subsequent deletion of a PDP context. A G-CDR will generally contain the IMSI, MSISDN, and IP address assigned to the PDP context. These G-CDRs can be intercepted by an ALE and converted into FLAP correlation measurement messages and then subsequently used by the LIS to acquire the necessary client IMSI/MSISDN-to-IP binding.

Location in CDMA 1xEVDO

Evolution Data Optimized (1xEVDO) is a Code Division Multiple Access (CDMA) cellular-based technology used to provide a high-speed data service to mobile devices. The standards for this technology have been developed within 3GPP2 and are capable of supporting peak rates of 3072 kbps on the forward link (to a handset) and 1843.2 kbps on the reverse link (toward the network). It is a fully IP-based packet data architecture that is founded on the IETF mobile IP architecture. 1xEVDO is being deployed by a number of carriers in the United States and around the world to augment existing residential broadband service offerings with typical data download speeds of between 300 kbps and 700 kbps. Unlike existing residential broadband offerings such as DSL and cable, 1xEVDO supports fully mobile users, which adds to the complexity of systems that need to locate an end-device attached to the network.

Figure 8.4 shows the general mobile IP architecture, and the nodes perform similar functions to nodes in the GPRS network. The Access Network (AN) is made up of a base station controller and a set of base stations and is responsible for authenticating the mobile device and providing RF connectivity. The Packet Control Function (PCF) is responsible for managing data sessions seamlessly across ANs, this is equivalent to the SGSN in a GPRS environment. The Packet Data Serving Node (PDSN) is responsible for establishing a context, providing an IP address for the mobile device, and routing IP packets to and from the IP device and the network. The PDSN is equivalent to the GGSN in a GPRS network. The Home Agent (HA) is responsible for acting as a point of contact for the mobile device should a third party wish to reach the mobile; this provides the functionality that was added to the HLR to support GPRS in a 3GPP network. The HA is also required to support inter-PDSN/FA handovers. The resulting network will look something like Figure 8.5.

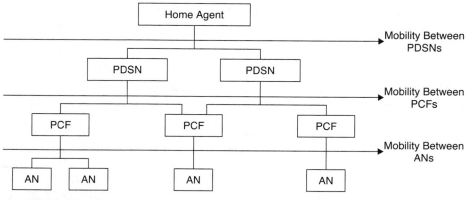

Figure 8.4   Mobile IP architecture.

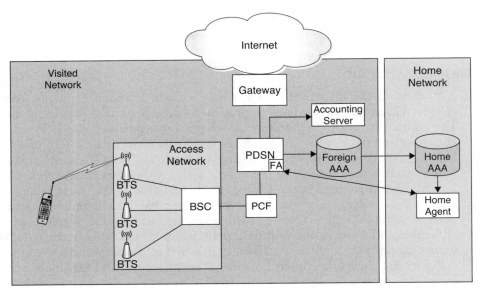

Figure 8.5   The 1xEVDO network.

In Figure 8.5, a mobile device connects to the network and proceeds to establish a PPP session with the PDSN. The PDSN proceeds to authenticate the mobile device using the foreign and home AAA servers, in 3GPP2 these are DIAMETER servers, which are viewed as a successor to RADIUS. The home AAA will authenticate the mobile device, based on CHAP and the device's Mobile Identification Number (MIN), which is a number associated with an actual mobile device. If the mobile device is authenticated, then a home agent is assigned and a Home-IP-Address for the device is provided. The result of the authentication, along with the identity of the home agent, if the authentication is successful, is returned to the PDSN. The PDSN foreign agent (FA) can then provide update information to the home agent, including the care-taker IP address allocated to the mobile device while it is in the visited network. The PDSN will also start generating accounting messages, which will include the care-taker IP address and the MIN of the mobile device.

The mobile device can learn the address of the LIS in this configuration using the DNS mechanism described in Chapter 4. The LIS is able to learn the IP address–to-MIN mapping through an ALE looking at accounting records, in much the same way as was described for GPRS (see Figure 8.6.). Unlike GPRS, no control plane location specification exists for the EVDO architecture; the only mechanism specified is to use the Secure User Plane Location (SUPL) standard, which is described in Chapter 9. In this environment, when a LIS needs to obtain the location of a mobile device, it will need to send an MLP request to a SUPL Location Platform (SLP). In reality, many mobile devices, particularly handheld devices, will also have CDMA voice capabilities. In this case, the LIS can query a Mobile Positioning Center (MPC) and IS-41 control-plane solutions can be used to determine the location of the mobile.

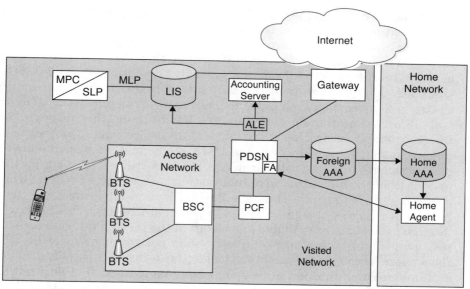

Figure 8.6   A LIS in the 1xEVDO network.

Unlicensed Mobile Access

A specific form of VoIP has been implemented in cellular networks in recent years called Unlicensed Mobile Access (UMA). UMA is generally provided in conjunction with cellular access so that the device, by policy or where cellular coverage is not available, may utilize Internet connectivity to perform mobile calling. Using a broadband access means not needing to provide voice service over the licensed radio frequency coverage used by the cellular operator—hence the "unlicensed" term in the label. This requires the operator to provide an IP-accessible UMA server to provide the VoIP functionality.

Rather than implement the call processing within the UMA server, the server acts as a BSC emulator interfacing into the core cellular network; thus, the call processing is done by the MSC in the cellular network and connectivity to other cellular and PSTN subscribers is provided transparently by the core network. For example, a UMA server in a GSM network emulates a traditional BSC and connects to the MSC over the A-interface.

Since the MSC expects to see mobility-related information, such as the current serving cell identifiers, the UMA server creates "virtual cell identifiers" to allocate to a given call in progress. If the user is on an access network that the UMA server is coupled with (for example, if the cellular operator is also the provider of the broadband IP access), the virtual cell identifiers may convey a specific significance as far as the location of the caller is concerned. However, if the user is connecting to the UMA server from an arbitrary Internet connection point—one which the UMA operator has no relationship with—then the virtual cell identifier needs to be relatively arbitrary, as long as it's unique and cannot imply any location information.

Looking once more at the GSM deployment scenario (see Figure 8.7), a typical mobile-terminated location request through the GMLC, or a network-initiated location request in response to an emergency call, will result in a location request being routed through to the UMA server. The MSC will do this since the UMA server appears to be a BSC and location requests are typically routed through the BSC to the SMLC. UMA server implementations typically integrate the SMLC functionality internally. Clearly measurements such as "timing advance" or "signal strength" as seen on a normal GSM base station do not apply to a device connecting through, for example, a DSL broadband service. Recalling that a UMA device is also generally a GSM cellular phone capable device, however, the UMA server may request the device to provide measurements from the cellular network if it is still visible, or from the latest time prior to losing contact with the cellular network. This request is made using UMA VoIP client-specific messaging. Thus, the SMLC function integrated into the UMA server may have a degree of sophistication in terms of making a "best guess" at a current location based on any available knowledge of the serving Internet access, or by an assessment of how current any cellular network measurements may be. Ultimately, this "best guess" becomes less useful the longer the device is only connected to an arbitrary and unassociated Internet access point and in a location that does not fall under the operator's cellular coverage. For example, if the user powers up their device in a WiFi hotspot in a foreign country, the UMA server will have no information which it can utilize in location determination.

UMA deployments, then, have already encountered the challenge of convergence and the service-provider access-provider separation associated with the Internet services model. Since the voice service provider—the UMA operator—does not necessarily control all access networks, a dependency on the access network provider to make location information available arises.

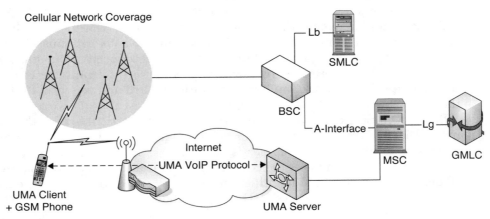

Figure 8.7   A UMA in a GSM network.

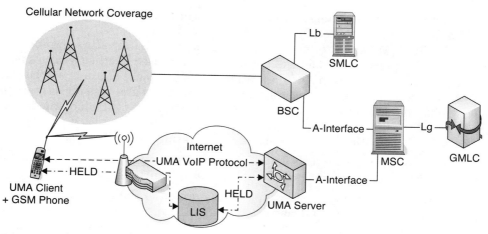

Figure 8.8 A UMA using LIS functionality.

Using the LIS architecture (see Figure 8.8), which assumes that location determination and acquisition is done by the access provider, the UMA client would be responsible for providing the UMA server with location information. A UMA client which is also a HELD client would consult with the access network LIS, obtain location, and convey that location information as part of the UMA VoIP–specific messaging. Location may be provided as a literal location value or it may be provided by reference. In the case of the latter, the UMA server would also act as a HELD client and be able to retrieve the location information directly from the LIS for as long as the location reference remained valid. From the cellular network perspective, in terms of the mobile-terminated requests through the GMLC or network-initiated requests from the MSC, normal location procedures would apply transparently. The UMA server and, in particular, the integrated SMLC function may then invoke HELD requests to the LIS in response to any location requests originating from the MSC. A complete UMA-SMLC implementation would utilize this mode while still supporting the "best guess" procedures as a fallback where the UMA client is not in an LIS-equipped access network.

WiMAX

Worldwide Interoperability for Microwave Access (WiMAX) is based on the IEEE 802.16 suite of specifications for wireless metropolitan area networks and seeks to provide very high bandwidth wireless access over significant distances. The earlier WiMAX specifications aimed to provide wireless broadband services to fixed and nomadic users, but the newer 802.16e specification also caters to the mobile broadband market. The expectation is that WiMAX will provide wireless broadband access to residential and commercial subscribers so as to offer competition to existing wireline DSL and cable providers since WiMAX currently provides specifications for operating in both the licensed and unlicensed frequency spectrums and can be deployed in point-to-point, point-to-multipoint, and fully mobile configurations.

While WiMAX will offer good coverage at high bandwidths to multiple users, the general deployment model will be similar to that used in other wireless networks, both cellular and WiFi. In this configuration, a series of base stations will be connected to a central hub, some kind of base station controller, and a series of base station controllers will be connected to some central infrastructure that will include the following:

- Authentication authorization and accounting (AAA) functions
- Local access configuration information such as IP address, DNS server address, access domain name, and default gateway address
- External routing functions providing access to the Internet, access to the PSTN, and other services infrastructure

A device end-point in WiMAX is referred to as a Subscriber Station (SS), and when it is manufactured it is provided with a 48-bit Ethernet MAC address, a manufacturer-issued and installed X.509 certificate and the X.509 certificate of the manufacturer. The SS uses these certificates and the 48-bit MAC address when registering with the network. Unlike an IMSI, MSISDN, or MIN, a manufacturer's X.509 certificate and device MAC address do not provide any indication as to the identity of a connecting device's home network. Without this identification, it is difficult to implement a network that will support user roaming while providing the access supplier with a mechanism for charging, and ensuring that the end-device has access to the services that they are paying for. WiMAX deployments today are largely point-to-point and point-to-multipoint installations designed to provide a competitive alternative to wired broadband offerings. Access providers provision authentication systems with the public key and MAC address of each end-point. These are then used to identify and authenticate a connecting end-point. Consequently, roaming support is not a significant factor at this point in time. With the advent of 802.16e and fully mobile WiMAX, higher-layer authentication schemes and network identifiers, such as those using NAI with fully qualified usernames, will become necessary.

The configuration shown in Figure 8.9 is similar to the Cable configuration described in Chapter 6. A central provider provides access to a group of subscriber installations, each of whom have to have their MAC address and physical location provisioned into the central office authentication system before a network connection can be established. In this model, a centralized LIS can be provisioned and accessed in very much the same way as the Cable or DSL network LIS can.

Where the SS can be nomadic or even mobile then other techniques for location determination beyond direct provisioning need to be employed. In previous sections, we have described some of the techniques available to other wireless technologies including timing and signal strength mechanisms and assisted GPS (A-GPS). Most of these will be applicable to WiMAX in some form though they may require modification to address the encoding schemes used in WiMAX communication. For example, the

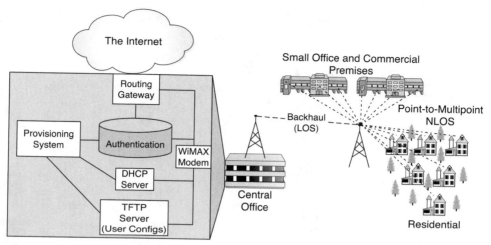

Figure 8.9   WiMAX as a wired broadband alternative.

symbol period for a digital encoding scheme is often used to provide timing advance information, where the distance between each subsequent timing advance increment is directly proportional to the symbol period. However, encoding schemes used in WiMAX have long symbol periods, so using conventional TA techniques will result in large errors. Adapting TA algorithms to operate with WiMAX OFDM encoding techniques may improve the accuracy of these location techniques. There is little doubt that a combination of network and device-based measurements will be required to provide accurate location information for mobile WiMAX subscriber stations the same as they are for cellular mobile devices today. The exchange of measurement information will require a negotiation of capabilities between the end-point and access network; the LIS and mechanisms to support this capabilities exchange are described in Chapter 9.

Location in an Open Services Network

In this section, we will look at the case of voice services being provided by an operator that is independent of the access network provider. This should be treated as an example only and may be equally applicable to a range of other services, such as those related to presence.

The need for a LIS in an IP access network is clear because without it there is no way to obtain location (see Figure 8.10), and without location, some services (emergency services amongst them) either won't work well, or won't work at all.

In a wireless network, even if the mobile device is able to obtain a location from the network, the location needs to be fresh, and this results in it having to be determined at the time of each call in order to ensure that the location the mobile has is still correct. While some devices can determine their own location, most cannot, and those that can, often require assistance in the form of data provided by the network—A-GPS,

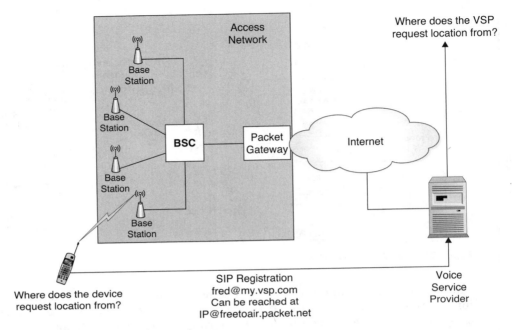

Figure 8.10 An access network conundrum.

for example. Providing a literal location at periodic intervals to the mobile is not a viable solution in most cases. First, to ensure a consistent level of precision, the rate at which data are pushed to the mobile needs to be directly associated with how fast a Target is moving, and for a large network with hundreds of users this is likely to be computationally impractical. Second, and perhaps more importantly, location data aren't required for all services, it is only necessary for the relatively small set of services that are tied to the physical location of a device at the time the service is requested. Since location information needs to be fresh, is relatively expensive to compute, and is not required for all services, it makes a lot of sense to compute it only when it is requested—that is, to use a location URI.

To use a location URI in wireless data networks, a LIS is needed. The LIS will determine the location of the device within the access network only when requested to do so and it may use any one of, or a mixture of, the following: ALEs, control-plane, user-plane, general network, and device-based measurement location techniques.

Figure 8.11 shows the IP Location architecture for a fully mobile data network. The LIS operates inside the access network, and the mobile device establishes a HELD context with the LIS, which includes an access rule that allows the mobile's voice service provider (VSP) access to the mobile's location information. The mobile device then registers with its VSP and includes the location URI in the registration message. Consequently, the mobile does not need to be aware of which services require location

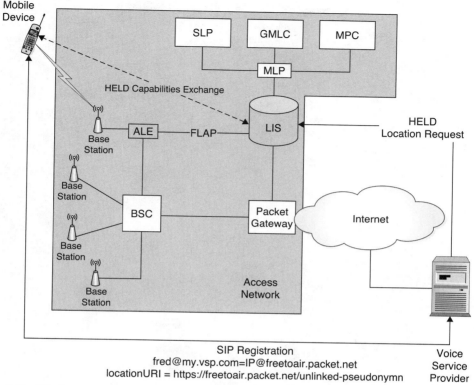

Figure 8.11 Wireless access location solution.

information and which do not; this decision is left to the VSP whose role it is to determine routing information for the requested service.

Location in an IMS Network

The IP Multimedia Subsystem (IMS) suite of standards is defined within 3GPP and is based around a services core network that operates over IP providing the benefits of a consistent set of services that are managed and offered in the same way over a range of different access technologies. The IMS suite of specifications offers little mention of location determination and acquisition beyond cursory commentary, such as stated assumptions that the UE will provide it and, more recently, in the IMS emergency sessions specification (see reference 8) where a Location Retrieval Function (LRF) and Route Determination Function (RDF) have been described.

The basic IMS architecture assumes that the core and the access network have an association which may be in the form of ownership, a roaming agreement, or some other kind of access arrangement (see Figure 8.12). The core network is made up of

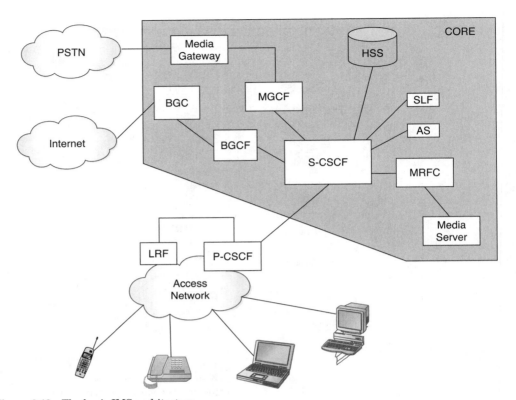

Figure 8.12   The basic IMS architecture.

a Call Session Control Function (CSCF) and a range of ancillary functions, such as: the Home Subscriber Server (HSS), which operates in a similar manner to the HLR in cellular mobile networks; the Media Gateway Control Function (MGCF) and media gateways that provide access to things such as the PSTN; the Border Gateway Control Function (BGCF) and border gateways that provide access to other IP-related services; Application Servers (ASs); and streaming media services.

When a host attaches to the network, it discovers the Proxy CSCF (P-CSCF) in the access network and establishes a session with it. The P-CSCF contacts the serving CSCF (S-CSCF) in the core network, which authenticates the user and determines the services that a user is entitled to use. The P-CSCF is then responsible for ensuring that the correct QoS is provided to the user's service as required. P-CSCF in this model therefore provides a bridge from the local access network to the core network services.

In the case of emergency calling, it is the responsibility of the P-CSCF to detect the condition and to direct the call to an emergency control function and subsequently route the call to the serving PSAP. The IMS emergency sessions specification (see Reference 8) indicates that the User Equipment (UE) should provide location information in-band with the signaling, or that P-CSCF should obtain location information and possibly routing information from a Location Retrieval Function (LRF) before passing the call on to an Emergency CSCF (E-CSCF), which is located in the same network as the P-CSCF. This all implies that the LRF also resides in the same network as the P-CSCF.

Since the LRF provides location information for IMS networks and the access network could be any one of a range of access types, it makes sense to support a common interface that can provide location information in the form most applicable to the access type; this may be a civic location for a residential DSL network or geodetic information for a wireless 3G network.

Figure 8.13 shows the advantage of using a LIS with a HELD interface as the Location Retrieval Function (LRF) in an access network that can accommodate IMS. The key advantage comes from the fact that all requests for location arrive in the same manner, regardless of whether they are from the core IMS network, the UE/UA/MS, a visited network LIS, or a third party. The LIS determines the access type most appropriate for calculating the location of the end-point. Whereas the LIS supports multiple access types—DSL, WiFi, and cellular—the end-point can be associated with more than one network. Because of this the LIS has the option of choosing the network technology best suited for providing location at that point in time. So while the IMS provides

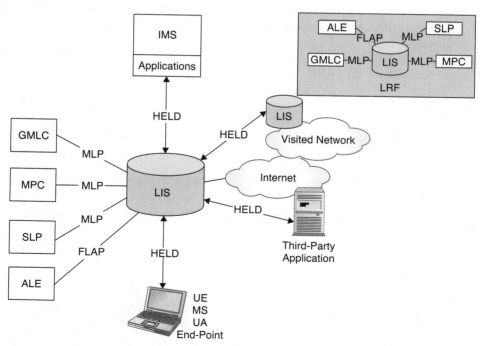

Figure 8.13 An integrated location solution.

integrated services across a range of access technologies, the LIS provides a common way to determine and acquire location across a range of access technologies.

Indeed, if IMS services are not to remain confined to a "walled garden" where subscribers can only use those services from a limited number of operator-provided access networks, then a LIS/HELD implementation becomes an imperative. Otherwise, the IMS applications will not know how to provide location-enhanced service to subscribers when they are on a third-party access network. Similarly, third-party applications will not be able to obtain location information from the operator network if the device cannot provide a location URI that refers back to a LIS in that network. A walled-garden model may be preferable to operators that want to maintain a full services model as seen in conventional cellular networks. However, it is counter to the Internet services model and it can be expected that users will consider it too inflexible in the long term.

Summary

Wireless carrier networks have evolved from providing voice-only services to being able to provide viable alternatives to wired residential and commercial broadband offerings. This new range of services can cater for fixed, nomadic, and mobile users, and can generally support network roaming. Where mature location infrastructure exists, this can be integrated with the packet data services, allowing an end-point to retrieve and use location information in the same manner as it would for any other data access network—that is, from a LIS using the HELD protocol. Where an intelligent core, such as IMS, is deployed, the network is able to request location from the LIS regardless of the access type. This leaves the arbitration of the best location determination technique to the LIS, which may, for a position, select more than one mechanism to determine the location of the end-point.

References

1. OMA, "*Secure User Plane Location (SUPL) 1.0*," SUPL Enabler 1.0, January 2006.

2. OMA, "*Mobile Location Protocol (MLP) 3.2*," MLS Enabler 1.0, November 2004.

3. 3GPP, "*Mobile Application Part (MAP) specification*," 3GPP TS 29.002. 6.14.0, June 2006.

4. Droms, R., "*Dynamic Host Configuration Protocol*," RFC 2131, March 1997.

5. Alexander, S. and R. Droms, "*DHCP Options and BOOTP Vendor Extensions*," RFC 2132, March 1997.

6. Rigney, C., Willens, S., Rubens, A., and W. Simpson, "*Remote Authentication Dial In User Service (RADIUS)*," RFC 2865, June 2000.

7. 3GPP, "*Telecommunications management; Charging management; 3G call and event data for the Packet Switched (PS) domain*," 3GPP TS 32.015 3.12.0, January 2004.

8. 3GPP, "*IP Multimedia Subsystem (IMS) emergency sessions*," 3GPP TS 23.167 7.0.0, March 2006.

9

Device Interactions in Location Determination

The HELD- and FLAP-based architecture discussed in previous chapters describes a structure whereby location measurement information is extracted from the access network, correlated with the device address information, and used to calculate the location of the device. This is the domain of the FLAP protocol. Device-LIS interaction occurs with the HELD protocol, but this is used for the conveyance of calculated location information, as opposed to the exchange of location measurements.

Any architecture that did not include the facility to utilize device-specific capabilities would be incomplete. Device measurements offer a greater range of options for location determination. Location determination techniques described thus far focus on the access network, where the final responsibility for location lies. This guarantees success to the extent that the network is in control of the available facilities, but device-based methods can improve the overall quality of the location information that is produced. This chapter will examine some of the options for using the device in location determination and investigate how this affects the location architecture.

The book has, until this point, concentrated on the way that the access network determines location. However, as introduced in Chapter 1, it must also be recognized that devices are capable of taking part in the location determination process. A device has a distinct advantage in this regard by virtue of the fact that it is actually at the location of interest. This fact can be exploited to improve the accuracy, precision, and reliability of location information.

A device may be able to take additional measurements that are not available to the access network. These measurements can be provided to the LIS in such a way that the device effectively acts as an ALE.

For example, devices may take measurements from nearby Radio Frequency Identifier (RFID) tags. RFID tags may only be readable to devices at a short range, and since RFID tags are passive, they cannot provide measurements to the LIS independently as an ALE.

Some devices are able to determine their own location. Devices with Global Navigation Satellite System (GNSS) capability, such as GPS devices, can take location measurements and calculate their position autonomously. This chapter describes how GNSS can be used by the LIS, including Assisted-GPS.

The Role of the Device in the Location Architecture

The device fills a specialized role in the location architecture. As previously described, it is both the subject of location data and a client for that data. In this chapter, the device can take on some of the roles of both an ALE and LIS. The advantages of device-based measurements and location are significant, but it is also important to consider how this affects the overall architecture. This section describes how the device can add value to the location architecture by working with an existing infrastructure.

Device Measurements

A device that provides location measurements effectively becomes an ALE. However, to characterize the device as an ALE is not sufficient—the device does not share a number of the key characteristics of the ALE. The LIS-ALE relationship is static. In comparison, the device is not a network element that is under the control of the access network provider. Devices come and go. A device is not tied to a particular access network. Therefore, no preexisting relationship between the device owner and access network provider can be assumed.

The static LIS-ALE relationship also has the aspect that, by design, the LIS should understand the measurements provided by the network ALEs. The LIS is directly coupled to the access network it is serving and, by definition, can be expected to understand the technology used to provide that access. On the other hand, a device visiting an access network may have some set of location measurement or determination capabilities that are not understood by the LIS or may not even be supportable in the specific access network serviced by that LIS. Thus, in order to properly recognize and take advantage of device measurement capabilities, some mechanism for the device and LIS to be able to exchange and match location determination capabilities is required.

The relationship between the LIS and a device differs from the LIS-ALE relationship. However, HELD already provides a means to establish a relationship between the LIS and the device, including the discovery procedure, which must occur before communications are established. It makes sense to use HELD, an already established means of communication, for device-based location measurements, or at the least, to bootstrap the process. The extension options for HELD are examined in more detail later in this chapter.

Autonomous Location Determination

Some devices will be able to determine their own location without access network assistance. If a device is able to determine its own location and fill the roles that the LIS would otherwise provide, it can operate completely autonomously. Location determination is the primary function, but the device can also provide an external subscription interface with a location URI and privacy management. That is, the device and the applications on it that use location information always have the option of working independently of the LIS.

For a range of devices, a location determination capacity is all that they can provide. The other features that are normally provided by the LIS may not be feasible. The full range of features that the LIS can provide could introduce unmanageable complexity in device implementation; these features could also stretch limited network and computing resources available to the device. The decision on whether or not to use the LIS depends on the requirements of the application or the user of location information. In particular, providing a verifiable signature for location information that identifies a recognized provider is generally out of the scope of an individual device's capabilities.

Later in this chapter, several configurations are shown where a device is able to delegate responsibility for certain functions to the LIS.

Preventing Location Fraud

Location fraud, or providing incorrect location information for personal gain, turns into a real problem when devices become part of the location determination process. This is of special interest to the LIS since the LIS becomes the nominal source of the information and may represent the party responsible for the veracity of the information. This is true even when the LIS does not digitally sign location information.

The LIS should not use information provided by the device unless it can have some way of ensuring that it is correct. When location is provided by a device using autonomous location determination, the LIS must verify that this information is correct.

A basic way of verifying location information is to perform a simple containment check. The LIS determines a location estimate using trusted sources of measurements, which it then compares to the estimate provided by the device. If the device-provided location falls within the region of uncertainty determined by the trusted method, or it lies close enough, the LIS can use the device-provided information. The precise method of validation of asserted location information is a matter of specific policy at the LIS—the validation decision needs to balance the needs of applications for precision against the imperative that the LIS remain a trustable source of accurate data.

Location measurements from the device provide a means for a device to improve the quality of a location estimate. This presents another opportunity for providing fraudulent information to the LIS. Measurements can be dynamic or hard to obtain outside of a particular network; therefore, tricking the LIS into providing an incorrect location is more difficult to manage using measurements. However, it is equally difficult for the LIS to ensure that measurements received from a device are valid. Therefore, if the LIS cannot check the measurements, it should check any location estimate derived from those measurements. This check occurs in the same way that it would check location information that is sourced entirely from the device.

These checks ensure that a LIS can be trusted to provide accurate location information, while benefiting from the improved precision that can be gained by including the device in the calculation process. Location information that is provided by the LIS can be used with fewer concerns about fraud as long as the validation policies implemented in the LIS correctly balance the application's security, accuracy, and reliability needs against their precision and utility requirements.

Architectural Goals

It is important that the protocols and architecture facilitate choice. Devices that support any set of features should be able to operate independently where possible and then call on the LIS to provide those functions they do not support, or they cannot support, natively. If a device is capable of providing measurements, then the LIS should be able to use that information. But if a device can determine its own location, the LIS needs to provide supporting functions, like digital signatures, location URIs, or even GPS assistance data, as appropriate.

Autonomous Location Determination

A device can determine its own location in a number of ways. One of the simplest, and sometimes overlooked, possibilities is to ask the user of the device where they are. A manually provided location can sometimes be more accurate and precise than other options—in fact, it is particularly useful for civic addresses. A number of the technologies described in this book can also be used by a device to determine its location without assistance from the LIS.

There is also the question of why a device would need to establish a LIS relationship at all. Of course, it does not have to—it is the user of, or using application on, the device which determines what will make the decision to utilize a LIS. Application and users may require features that only the LIS is able to provide. This section describes autonomous location determination and explores instances where a LIS can still add value. Using the LIS in this way also decouples application requirements from device capability such that per-application semantics are not required to take advantage of device self-location capability. The LIS is able to ensure that a consistent set of features is always available for all applications, and common location reference semantics are used regardless of whether the device is involved or not.

Device Independence

It is possible that a device could provide all of the features necessary for location so that it did not need any assistance from a LIS. A fully independent device is capable of determining its own location from measurements that it can obtain. This device is also responsible for providing location information to location users, which could include serving a location URI and subscriptions for location information. Figure 9.1 shows the logical roles in this configuration.

The device in this scenario can either push location information to recipients (by-value) or it can serve subscriptions by providing a location URI (by-reference). The device can publish a location reference by using some application-specific protocol, or by emulating a LIS by supporting the server side of HELD.

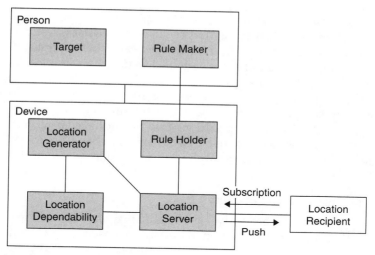

Figure 9.1 Device roles in completely independent operation.

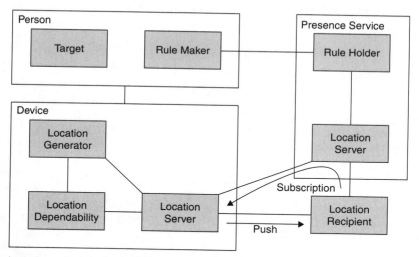

Figure 9.2 An independent device is able to use a presence service to simplify its role.

A presence service can be employed by the device, providing that the device is able to generate sufficient notifications, or serve a subscription. The presence service can provide a layer of protection for the device by compositing all subscriptions into a single session and by authenticating all location recipients. Figure 9.2 shows that the location server role is taken by both the device and presence service.

This configuration allows the device to push location directly to the location recipient (location by-value), or to service subscriptions that are directed through the presence server (location by-reference). The presence server enforces the authorization policy for location subscriptions, ensuring that the device does not have to manage this complexity.

These configurations require that the device is able to digitally sign location information if an application requires dependable location. This implies that the digital signature has to be adequately trusted by the users of the location information. This may not be feasible for location users since the complexity of managing trust relationships with individuals is greater than managing trust with a smaller group of access network providers. This is especially true for applications that do not have prearranged arrangements with their users. For instance, emergency services care about the integrity of location information but will not undertake to establish a trust relationship with every potential user.

The LIS Provides Credentialed Location

The LIS, due to its authoritative position in an access network, is well suited to providing credentialed location information. By using the assertion mechanism provided in HELD, the device can generate location information and provide this in a message to the LIS that requests a signed PIDF-LO. The device is then able to operate independently for most functions, only using the LIS when credentialed location information is required for a particular application. Figure 9.3 shows the allocation of roles in this arrangement.

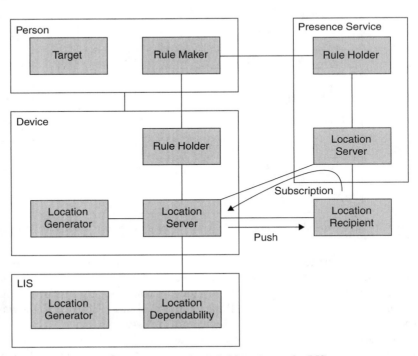

Figure 9.3 Delegating the responsibility for credentialed location to the LIS.

The LIS needs to be able to check location information before it can certify that it is accurate. A second location generator at the LIS is included so that the LIS can check the location information provided by the device against a location that is generated by a trusted source.

A LIS-Provided Location URI

Access network configurations sometimes prevent network users from creating their own services. This is often because a firewall or Network Address Translation (NAT) device is deployed to improve network security or for address management. This prevents a device from creating a publicly accessible location URI.

The LIS within that network is able to provide a publicly accessible location URI. The device requests that the LIS provide a location URI by creating a context on the LIS. The device then ensures that all requests are forwarded to it by indicating a capability to determine its own location. The LIS will then forward all requests through to the device. Figure 9.4 shows how this might be achieved.

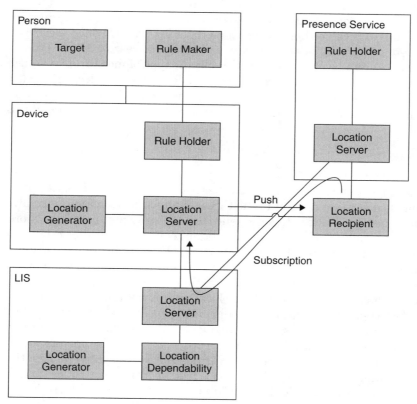

Figure 9.4   The LIS can be used to provide publicly accessible location URIs.

This is, to a large extent, the same method that is used by SIP proxies to ensure that SIP URIs are reachable. In comparison, this configuration is more complex than a direct proxy arrangement. The LIS is now directly in the request path, therefore it assumes some responsibility for the accuracy of the location information. The LIS validates location information against the location that comes from its own location generator to protect against fraud.

The LIS is also able to use its location determination capacity to serve requests where appropriate, only contacting the device when necessary.

Location Measurements in HELD

The extensibility options provided in HELD permit the inclusion of arbitrary content. This flexibility means that devices are able to provide the LIS with location measurements. The LIS is able to then use these measurements to determine the location of the device. In some cases, like ad hoc wireless LANs, the LIS might even be able to use these measurements to determine the location of other devices in the network.

The capabilities indication extension to HELD can be used by the device to indicate that it is capable of providing different sets of measurements. This information is carried in the context creation response and includes enough information for the LIS to be able to receive these measurements. The way in which location measurements are given to the LIS is dependent on the type of access network. This means that suitable protocols can be developed for the specific type of measurement; each measurement access protocol needs to have appropriate features to address the nature of the measurements, from relatively static information from LLDP, to the complex Assisted-GNSS data exchanges provided in SUPL (see Reference 1 at the end of this chapter).

Location Assertion

The easiest way that a device can participate in location determination is through the use of location assertion, which is described in more detail in Chapter 4. When the device makes a location request to the LIS, it can include location information in the request. If the request is made with a reference to a LIS context, the LIS can store the device-created location and use it in response to later requests instead of relying on the location generation capability in the LIS. This means that applications are able to receive the more precise device-determined location information. If a device pushes this information to the LIS regularly, then this information is always available. Figure 9.5 shows how an assertion could be made and the location information could be cached for later use.

Asserted location information is only kept for a short time at the LIS to prevent the information from being invalidated as the device moves beyond the ability of the LIS to detect. Location assertion provides a crude, but effective, means of including the device as a part of location determination. The more precise location information from the device is only available to the LIS if the device has recently asserted location. This means that the device needs to push location information to the LIS regularly. It is more effective if the LIS is able to request location information directly from the device as it is needed. Having a way for the LIS to query the device for information is desirable.

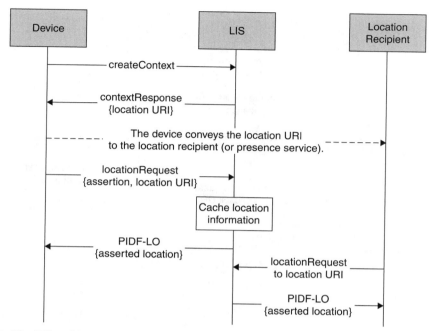

Figure 9.5 The LIS could cache location information for later use.

Device Callback

HELD and HTTP requests are single operations; a persistent session between the LIS and device is not established. The communications are established in one direction only—the device contacts the LIS for information. However, a location URI causes requests to be directed to the LIS. Therefore, if the device is to provide location information or measurements for the LIS to use in serving a request, the LIS needs to be able to contact the device when the request arrives. To do this, the device either provides the LIS with a means for contact, or establishes a more permanent communications channel.

The concept of a callback URI provides a simple means for the LIS to retrieve location information from the device. The device includes a URI in a context creation request or context update request. Additional information is included in the request that assists the LIS in deciding when to use the URI, such as the expected amount of time that the device could take to create a response. The LIS can then use this callback URI to contact the device when it receives a request from an external location recipient. Figure 9.6 shows how a callback can be used to request location information when triggered by an external location recipient.

Using a URI for callback purposes has some limitations that could cause it to fail in a range of network configurations. For instance, a NAT device or firewall between the device and LIS can ensure that any contact information provided by the device is

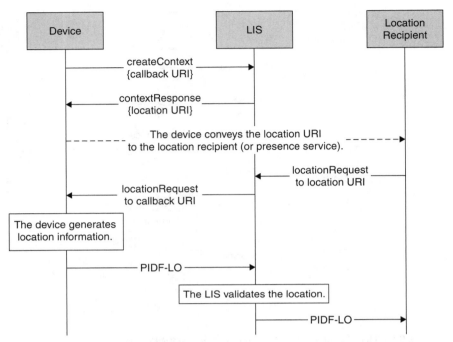

Figure 9.6 The LIS uses a callback to access device-based information on demand.

not usable by the LIS. In some networks, particularly residential broadband, a home router with NAT and a firewall is extremely common. In these situations, callback fails unless steps are taken to ensure that the LIS can contact the device. For current deployments, UPnP is a common feature of home NAT devices, which can be used by the device to enable a callback. Alternatively, a LIS "proxy" feature can be implemented in the NAT/firewall device that enables LIS communications and facilitates the creation of callback details.

In larger networks, the LIS needs to be able to access the network. That is, the LIS is required on the same network segment as the device, behind the same NAT/firewall device. These types of LIS can act autonomously, or they can use another LIS outside the network to provide services, in much the same way a device requests certain services of a LIS.

Capability Negotiation

If location measurements from the device are to be used, the LIS has to be aware that they exist. For an unknown device that enters the access network, the LIS cannot assume that it is able to provide measurements. Therefore, the device must first advertise its capabilities to the LIS. The device includes a capabilities indication parameter in the HELD context creation request. The LIS can then indicate which of these capabilities it is able to use in the response to this message. The LIS stores this additional information in the context that it creates; the device can update this information using the update context request if conditions change.

Figure 9.7 shows how capabilities are indicated at context creation, and how they can change using the context update procedure. In this scenario, the initial context is created when the device is able to provide LLDP and WiFi measurements; the LIS indicates that it will only be able to use the LLDP measurements. The context is updated when the device moves off the wired connection and LLDP is no longer available.

Along with a general indication of capabilities, both the LIS and device include enough additional information for the actual exchange to take place. Each capability indication can include additional information that expands on the basic capability, such as network addresses and ports that can be used, protocol requirements, any constraints on the information, and how long measurements will take to acquire. This additional information ensures that both the LIS and the device have adequate information to successfully communicate.

Once this capability indication phase has been completed, the location measurements are exchanged in a manner that is most suited to the type of measurement. This flexibility permits the use of more advanced protocols where those protocols are most appropriate. For instance, A-GNSS is a cooperative location determination technology that requires a specialized protocol for the exchange of assistance data and associated information. Using capability negotiation, the LIS and the device can agree to use SUPL, which defines advanced procedures specific to A-GNSS, and the LIS can provide the SUPL Location Platform (SLP) address for a SET-initiated SUPL session.

Capability indications make it possible for the LIS and device to cooperate in location determination. A few examples of this process are included later in this chapter.

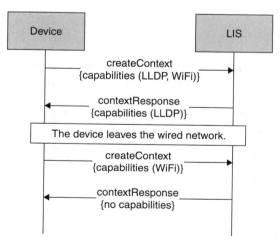

Figure 9.7 A capabilities indication is made so the device can be updated as circumstances change.

Device-Based Technologies

This section looks at how a number of location determination methods can be used. This includes information on the measurements that can be taken and some scenarios where those technologies are useful. A few examples are included to demonstrate how the LIS and the device communicate this information.

A User-Entered Location

While user-entered location information is not exactly a "technology," it cannot be disregarded as a way of providing accurate and precise location information. A user may be more readily able to provide precise information about their location than a network-based method with its potential inaccuracies. This method involves the user manually entering location information into a form, which the device is then able to provide to the LIS or location recipients. This information is usually in the form of civic address information because that form is most readily available to users. Geodetic information can still be entered by this method, particularly if the user has a means of measuring coordinates—for instance, they could source latitude and longitude measurements from a handheld GPS unit.

User-entered location information can be dynamic, but since this requires constant interaction from a user, it is more useful when location doesn't change over time. Therefore, fixed and nomadic devices are best suited to this approach. With HELD, this means that location assertion is used and the callback methods are rarely applicable. The assertion and validation process also provides a valuable "safety net" for when a user moves the location without updating the user-entered location information.

It is important to note that user-entered location is especially subject to location fraud unless basic checks are put in place. This means that the ability of a LIS to validate location information is particularly useful in protecting against fraud for manually entered data.

LLDP Measurements

The base LLDP specification (see Reference 1) includes mandatory parameters that are provided from any compliant device within a network. These values are not explicit indications of location, but identify the network attachment point for a device. This means the LIS is able to use a database to determine location based on the attachment information. The mandatory fields of interest in LLDP are:

- **Chassis ID**   This can be used to uniquely identify a switch or LAN entity. A range of identifiers are possible, including MAC and IP addresses or a locally defined identifier.
- **Port ID**   This unambiguously identifies a port on the switch.
- **Time To Live**   This value is useful in determining when this information becomes stale and should be refreshed.

LLDP is a one-way protocol in that messages are triggered by a state change or the passage of time; LLDP messages cannot be solicited. If LLDP is used for location measurements, the device must provide an LLDP receive module. Other nodes on the LAN segment also need to implement an LLDP transmit module that transmits LLDP frames. The device uses the information in these frames to build a remote system MIB (Management Information Base) that contains this information. This information can then be provided to the LIS as location measurements. In this case, the information can often be retrieved using the Simple Network Management Protocol (SNMP) as direct SNMP queries, or possibly traps.

In the example shown in Figure 9.8, the device receives an LLDPDU (LLDP Data Unit) from a switch when it attaches to the network. The device then stores this information in its remote system MIB. It then creates a context on the LIS and indicates that it is capable of providing measurements from LLDP using SNMP, including the community string so that the LIS is able to access the information. The LIS indicates that LLDP is supported in the context response message. After this, when a request is made to the location URI at the LIS, the LIS is able to query the device using SNMP for the Chassis and Port IDs of the switch. The LIS uses these measurements and a database to determine location.

Note that this usage of LLDP demonstrates another possible way of using the LLDP primitives that differs from the descriptions of LLDP-MED in Chapter 5.

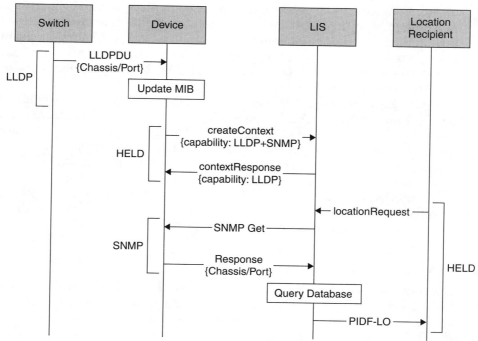

Figure 9.8   An LLDP-capable device can provide measurements using SNMP.

Wireless LAN Measurements

Chapter 7 described a number of measurements that could be acquired from a wireless LAN. The LIS can use these measurements to determine the location of a wireless terminal within a wireless network. One important observation about location measurements in WLANs is that they can be acquired by any participant in that network. For infrastructure networks, it makes sense for the LIS to rely on access points, whereas in an ad hoc network more information is required.

The device is a good source of location measurements in a WLAN. Many of the measurements described in Chapter 7 are available to all WLAN devices. The device is able to provide the LIS with information that is directly useful in determining its location. This area remains the subject of research.

RFID Beacons

Passive RFID tags in fixed locations can be used in location determination. If a device is able to read an identifier from an RFID tag that is in its proximity, then it can transmit this identifier to the LIS. The LIS can then use a database of known RFID tag locations to determine where the device is located. Alternatively, an RFID tag could include an encoded location value, which the device could use to determine location autonomously.

As an example, RFID tags can be used to provide desk-level precision in the absence of wired connections. Wireless LANs are used in place of wired Ethernet in enterprise networks due to their cost and deployment benefits. However, wireless location determination may not be able to resolve location with sufficient precision to identify a single desk. An RFID tag placed at each desk with either a unique identifier or an encoded location value can be read by a device. With a range of only a few meters, RFID provides a good desk-level resolution of location.

Figure 9.9 shows a possible request sequence where the device provides the LIS with a code from nearby RFID tags. The device indicates that it is capable of reading RFID tags when it creates the context at the LIS. The LIS then requests that the device take a measurement when a request is made. The protocol mechanisms used for this request are not yet specified, but may be indicated in the capability indication. The LIS uses its database to produce a location estimate based on the RFID codes.

Alternatively, the RFID tags could encode location information, which would make it possible for the LIS to provide location without a database. Either the LIS or the device can decode the location information from the RFID code.

GNSS and Assisted-GNSS

The term Global Navigation Satellite System (GNSS) is a generic term that is applied to location systems that use satellites to determine location. The prime example of this is the Global Positioning System, GPS, a system of satellites that are operated by the United States military (see References 2 and 3). There are a number of satellite constellations in space that provide navigation signals, including the European Union's

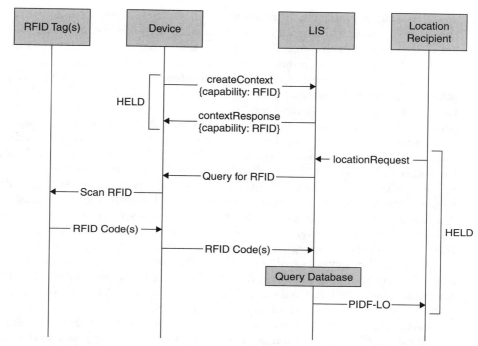

Figure 9.9   A device that can read RFID tags can provide those codes as measurements.

Galileo, Russia's GLONASS, and a range of other constellations including those of Japan and China. This section deals with GPS and Galileo, which are very similar in function and features.

A device that is equipped with the appropriate antenna and circuitry can make measurements from GNSS satellites. The device measurements consist of a set of *pseudorange* measurements, which are determined by calculating how long the signal took to travel from the satellite. This is done by taking the known sequence transmitted by the satellite and comparing it against a local copy at various offsets and finding the offset where the two signals match. For GPS, each satellite uses a different 1023-bit pseudorandom sequence that repeats continuously. The observed Doppler shift in the signal is also included in measurements (the Doppler shift is used to calculate the velocity of the device).

GNSS signals are transmitted at low power to preserve the energy storage on the satellite and prolong its life. Satellites are also a significant distance from the Earth's surface. Therefore, signals are very weak when they reach the ground and they can be easily blocked by buildings or foliage. Receivers have to search for this weak signal in two dimensions: the offset of the pseudorandom sequence; and a range of Doppler shifts that arise because the satellites are moving. Finding this signal can be difficult, therefore sophisticated hardware has been developed that can search a larger area of space in a short time. The effectiveness of a GNSS receiver depends on how much of this sophistication is incorporated into its circuitry—for instance, one cost of improved speed is the greater amount of power that more complex circuitry consumes.

Once the signal is acquired, a device that is operating autonomously uses data that are overlaid on the signal at very low data rates to extract additional information. This information includes satellite *ephemeris*, the current position and speed of each satellite, time data, and other data that can be used in calculating the location of the device. This process can take a while because the information is transmitted at a very low data rate.

Both the search time and the time required to receive data can be reduced by using *assistance data*. Assistance data include the data that the device would otherwise have to receive from the satellites and this can also be used to reduce the size of the search window. Based on a rough estimate of where the device is, a server calculates a likely range of values for the sequence offset and Doppler shift and sends that to the device. The device can use assistance data to speed up the signal acquisition time. If the device is indoors, or the signal is weak for any other reason, assistance data can allow the device to more thoroughly search for the signal, meaning that weaker signals can be received. The server can also send satellite information using the higher bandwidth available in the access network, further reducing the time required for location determination. Using assistance data with GNSS is known as Assisted-GNSS (A-GNSS); due to the popularity of GPS, the term A-GPS is often used.

Devices that operate autonomously can use these measurements to determine their own location. This calculation provides the device with the precise time that the measurements were taken. However, the calculation phase can require significant processing resources be devoted to the measurements, which can be relayed to a server for the processing phase. This can avoid draining device resources and also allows the server to use network measurements in the calculation phase. Where a server performs the final calculation phase is known as device-assisted A-GNSS; if the device calculates its own location, it is termed device-based A-GNSS. In device-assisted A-GNSS, the device does not require as much satellite data, which can save network bandwidth, assistance data delivery time, and handset battery life.

Secure User Plane Location   Version 1.0 of the Secure User Plane Location (SUPL) Specification (see Reference 3) provides an architecture and protocol specification for cellular networks for GPS. Version 2.0, which is under development, includes support for Galileo. SUPL supports autonomous device-based GNSS, as well as device-assisted and server-assisted A-GNSS. SUPL can be invoked by either the device to determine its own location, or the network at the request of an external application, another device, or as needed for network operation.

From the network architecture perspective, SUPL is based on a closed model where roaming agreements must exist between access networks before the service can operate. This works for cellular access networks because those arrangements need to exist before network access can be provided, but these same agreements are contrary to the open architecture upon which the Internet is based. However, the assistance data exchanges and other core messages in SUPL are useful for either assisting the device in determining its own location or for acquiring A-GNSS measurements from the device. Reusing the protocol aspects of SUPL with some modifications is advantageous because specifications and implementations can be developed more rapidly.

The example SUPL flow in Figure 9.10 shows how the LIS can use SUPL messaging to deliver messaging information. This is a device-assisted scenario where it is assumed that the LIS also acts as a SUPL Location Platform (SLP).

If a device indicates that it is a SUPL Enabled Terminal, or SET in SUPL terminology, the LIS can then initiate SUPL procedures to retrieve location measurements or location information from the device. The LIS indicates its intentions with a SUPL INIT, to which the device responds with a SUPL POS INIT. The LIS then needs to determine a coarse location estimate so that it can provide appropriate assistance data. Following this, the device uses the assistance data to acquire the satellite signals. In this scenario, the device returns the raw measurements to the LIS, but it is also possible for the device to calculate location and return this information to the LIS instead.

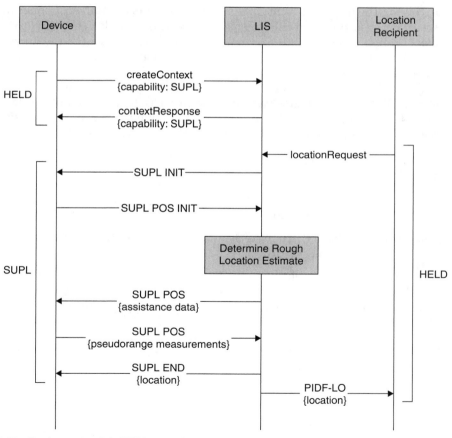

Figure 9.10   Device-assisted A-GNSS using SUPL messaging that directly involves the LIS.

The advantage of using this configuration is that the LIS is given the pseudorange measurements determined by the device. These measurements can be combined with other forms of measurement to form hybrid location determination methods, which are likely to produce more accurate results with a lower chance of failure. The alternatives to this method involve the device calculating the final location, or a separate SLP could manage the SUPL messaging, assistance data, and calculation.

Utilizing SUPL in a LIS in this fashion calls for very minor modifications to the current specifications and SET implementations. In particular, it requires that the SET is able to communicate with an SLP in the access network rather than assuming it only uses its service provider's SLP. Interestingly, at the time of writing, this exact function was under discussion in the OMA with a view to supporting emergency service using SUPL-determined location in cellular networks.

Summary

Involving the device in location determination has a number of benefits for the overall accuracy, precision, and reliability of the results. The device is able to provide location measurements or calculated results to the LIS. The impact to the location architecture has been discussed, including how the device can interact with the LIS to access features it cannot provide on its own.

Examples of location determination technologies that use the device have been shown. These technologies were examined for their applicability in location measurements, autonomous location determination, or both. Sample methods for a range of technologies that could be used by the LIS were also covered.

References

1. IEEE Computer Society, "Station and Media Access Control Connectivity Discovery," IEEE Std 802.1AB, 2005.

2. Dana, P., "Global Positioning System Overview", <http://www.colorado.edu/geography/gcraft/notes/gps/gps.html>.

3. US Department of Defence, "Global Positioning System Standard Positioning Service Signal Specification," 2d ed., June 1995.

4. OMA, "Secure User Plane Location (SUPL) 1.0," SUPL Enabler 1.0, January 2006.

Privacy Considerations for Internet Location

The word "privacy" has at least two common meanings. One refers to the situation of being free from interruption, harassment, or general interference, including being observed. The other has to do with having information related to an individual that is kept in confidence—just to themselves or between them and others.

In discussing privacy with particular reference to location information, the second meaning of these definitions is the most pertinent. Of course, loss of confidentiality with respect to the location of a person may lead to their peace and chosen solitude (in the first sense of the word *privacy*) being invaded. However, the focus of the discussion in this chapter is about how and when location information with respect to an individual can be made available to others and how this should be prevented when privacy constraints require that it be maintained in confidence.

Generally speaking, privacy control means having a set of rules controlling the relationship between the two following quantities.

- **Identity**   A set of data that uniquely distinguish a person
- **Personal information**   A set of data from which others could be said to learn about, or gain insight into, that person

It is not as straightforward as might be thought to codify identity. Names are a useful start; they were largely invented for the purpose, but they are not necessarily unique and they can be changed. From a philosophical perspective, it could be argued that identity is, in fact, the sum-total of the personal information. We do not need to wrestle with that, however. Suffice it to say that, in a system where "location" can be regarded as a piece of personal information, privacy is about ensuring that location is only associated with identity in the appropriate situation.

Privacy Legislation

While privacy as a subjective viewpoint or as a topic of ethical study may be understood in various ways, it must be rendered in quite hard and fast terms when it comes to legislation. Privacy legislation, explicitly labeled as such, is primarily about protecting privacy as opposed to outlawing privacy. When a type of personal information falls outside the scope of legislation, privacy can be said to be unprotected.

Once an aspect of privacy is unprotected, then it should not be assumed that there is any mechanism in place that provides privacy control with respect to that aspect. For example, there may be no law against an individual—when in a public place and regardless of the nature of the observer—being visually observed in terms of how they look, and what they are wearing, what they are doing, and who they are with. In this case, it should not be assumed by the individual that there is protection against this loss of privacy—whether they feel it is natural law or not.

Much of the technical discussion in this book has pointed out that an access network operator is able to put physical mechanisms in place to determine the location of a device using that network. Where the operator has the means to associate a person's identity with that device, then they are in a position of control with respect to this piece of privacy information. Note that the existence (or otherwise) of a protocol such as HELD does not change this situation; the mechanisms for determining location and associating it with a person's identity exist independently of the protocol. Using a network where location and identity can be associated means trusting the operator of the network with respect to maintaining the privacy of that information. Legislation is the only basis for assuming that this privacy is protected whether it is legislation directly addressing location information or legislation preventing a network operator from making false or misleading assurances with respect to that privacy.

On the specific topic of protecting the privacy of information associating instantaneous or historical location with identity, legislation is not necessarily clear. Examining the Australian Privacy Act of 1988 (see Reference 1) as an example, the focus is on records of information kept about a person, the manner in which information is solicited, notification to the person with respect to the existence of the records, and details of any access to those records, ensuring the person themselves have access and, of course, the circumstances under which third parties should be able to access the records. Typical records identified in the act are credit details, medical history, and similar forms of data. Indeed, the act defines a record as meaning

- A document
- A database (however kept)
- A photograph or other pictorial representation of a person

It is a matter of interpretation as to whether the instantaneous location of a person as determined by a network constitutes a "record" as far as the intent of this act goes. A historical record of their location may more readily fit the definition. Similarly, any legislation based on the OECD privacy guidelines [OECD-Privacy-1980] may leave the inclusion of instantaneous location information within its scope open to interpretation.

Where legislation is considered to cover location, the rules governing it are likely to be similar to those relating to more conventional forms of personal records. Going back to Reference 1, the act defines 11 information privacy principles (see Figure 10.1). Most deal with the manner of collection, storage, and management of the records, and the access rights of the person being the subject of the records. Principles 10 and 11, however, detail the limits on the use and disclosure of personal information.

Australian laws are chosen because they are considered a model application of the OECD guidelines. Similar laws have been adopted by other OECD nations, although in the United States, each state administers its own privacy laws. The U.S. situation means that large organizations might operate under different laws. As of 2006, uniform federal laws were being sought by a number of large technology companies.

Such rules are typical in the sense that the information is to be kept confidential unless the user has given consent, the information is used for the (agreed) purpose for which it was created, or disclosure is required for safety or law enforcement authority purposes. In accordance with such constraints, network technology governing the control of location information should be able to support corresponding controls. Regardless of the fact that such controls may be latent in network technology, as mentioned previously, the activation of the controls can only be safely assumed where a legislative imperative to do so exists.

Principle 10
Limits on use of personal information

1. A record-keeper who has possession or control of a record that contains personal information that was obtained for a particular purpose shall not use the information for any other purpose unless:
(a) the individual concerned has consented to use of the information for that other purpose;
(b) the record-keeper believes on reasonable grounds that use of the information for that other purpose is necessary to prevent or lessen a serious and imminent threat to the life or health of the individual concerned or another person;
(c) use of the information for that other purpose is required or authorised by or under law;
(d) use of the information for that other purpose is reasonably necessary for enforcement of the criminal law or of a law imposing a pecuniary penalty, or for the protection of the public revenue; or
(e) the purpose for which the information is used is directly related to the purpose for which the information was obtained.
2. Where personal information is used for enforcement of the criminal law or of a law imposing a pecuniary penalty, or for the protection of the public revenue, the record-keeper shall include in the record containing that information a note of that use.

Extract from the Australian Privacy Act of 1988

Principle 11
Limits on disclosure of personal information

1. A record-keeper who has possession or control of a record that contains personal information shall not disclose the information to a person, body or agency (other than the individual concerned) unless:
(a) the individual concerned is reasonably likely to have been aware, or made aware under Principle 2, that information of that kind is usually passed to that person, body or agency;
(b) the individual concerned has consented to the disclosure;
(c) the record-keeper believes on reasonable grounds that the disclosure is necessary to prevent or lessen a serious and imminent threat to the life or health of the individual concerned or of another person;
(d) the disclosure is required or authorised by or under law; or
(e) the disclosure is reasonably necessary for the enforcement of the criminal law or of a law imposing a pecuniary penalty, or for the protection of the public revenue.
2. Where personal information is disclosed for the purposes of enforcement of the criminal law or of a law imposing a pecuniary penalty, or for the purpose of the protection of the public revenue, the record-keeper shall include in the record containing that information a note of the disclosure.
3. A person, body or agency to whom personal information is disclosed under clause 1 of this Principle shall not use or disclose the information for a purpose other than the purpose for which the information was given to the person, body or agency.

Figure 10.1   Two privacy principles from the Australian Privacy Act of 1988.

Location Privacy Mechanisms in 3GPP

As previously noted in this book, cellular network specifications are a useful starting point when LCS concepts are being discussed. This is because LCS functionality is relatively mature in this category of networks. Using the 3GPP specification as a point of reference, the functionality in place in support of privacy can be studied and some general principles can be derived.

The discussion of privacy legislation highlighted that four types of location requesters are pertinent.

- Those with implicit permission
- Those with explicit permission
- Emergency services
- Law enforcement

Implicit permission exists where access to, and use of, the location information is associated with an existing service arrangement. A clear example of this is the cellular telephony service itself. In order to route a call to a subscriber, the cellular network needs to locate that subscriber, at least to the precision of the current serving cell. That is, locating the person and using the location information is part and parcel of the service arrangement, is understood in principle as being required to provide that service, and implicit permission to do so therefore exists.

Emergency services are well understood as a service in which permission to provide location is offered implicitly in the act of dialing the service. This is essentially an example of implicit permission. The principles of legislation, however, indicate that location may also be disclosed where there are reasonable grounds to believe that the person's or other persons' safety may be in danger. In this case, the requester of location effectively assumes that the person would give their permission if they could. If any network privacy constraints exist, a mechanism by which they can be overridden is required in this kind of scenario.

Explicit permission is more obvious. This can occur at the time of a location request—when a notification is sent to the person's handset indicating that a particular person would like the location of the handset. A positive response is explicit permission to provide that location in this particular instance. Alternatively, permission may be provided in advance. For instance, the handset location may be provided to any predefined group of "friends" who may be authenticated by a PIN or other mechanism.

Law enforcement agencies are typically provided with privileged access to information which would otherwise be held in confidence when it is necessary to proceed with investigations relating to crime and/or national security. These privileges are generally defined in some separate legislation relating to these activities. Due process incorporating the desired checks and balances will normally require the application and granting of a warrant or other formal permission before the information can be accessed and used.

As for emergency services, a network mechanism is required that permits properly controlled requests for location in a valid lawful requirement scenario.

To see how 3GPP supports these different requester types, reference is made to the Stage 2 LCS specifications (see Reference 2). The "portal" through which applications may request location in a 3GPP network is called the gateway mobile location center (GMLC). Section 10.3 of Reference 2 documents the characteristics that may be attributed to applications—or "LCS clients" as they are referred to in the terminology of that specification. To begin with, LCS clients can be placed in one of four categories:

- Emergency Services
- Value Added Services
- PLMN Operator Services
- Lawful Intercept Services

Once an application is authenticated as being of type Emergency Services or PLMN (Public Land Mobile Network) Operator, then permission is considered to be implicit and/or any preference for denial is legitimately overridden. Similarly, an authenticated Lawful Intercept–type service will override privacy restrictions without any notification to the user of the device.

Value Added Services are those that require some form of conscious user permission and this may be required to be explicit. From the perspective of the GMLC, the permission may be considered implicit, particularly where the exchange of permission occurred at the application layer. This may have been permission granted as part of the process of subscribing to the application, or it may be granted as part of execution of the application. For example, the user may select a checkbox on their web browser if the restaurant-finder application they are using asks for permission to automatically locate them at the time of each use of the service. In this case, by the time the application requests location via the GMLC, permission is considered to have been already granted.

Other value-added services, particularly those where the user of the target device is not also the user of the service, may require that the user be notified via the device before location is provided. Continuing with providing location may also require the subsequent granting of permission via the device. With this model in mind, section 10.1.1 of Reference 2 describes the information that each subscriber can define with respect to their LCS privacy preferences. For example, each user can specify the default privacy preference, and/or for a list of specific LCS clients they can specify precise preferences just for those services. The following options are defined preferences that a subscriber can assign to a given LCS client:

- Location not allowed
- Location allowed without notification
- Location allowed with notification

- Location with notification and privacy verification; location allowed if no response
- Location with notification and privacy verification; location restricted if no response

There are more aspects than those just described, which govern the application of LCS privacy in a 3GPP network, including privacy being determined based on whether the user is currently on a call to the application requesting the location. This is known as a call-related–type request.

Thus, in the 3GPP model, privacy is controlled at two separate points. First of all, the LCS client (the application) is authenticated at the GMLC. The GMLC associates the correct characteristics with the application such as whether it is an emergency service or a value-added service and it includes this information in the location request sent to the serving network. Final permission approval is determined in the visitor location register (VLR) just before location determination procedures are invoked. The VLR contains a copy of the subscriber's privacy preferences as stored in the HLR. If the application information doesn't indicate that privacy preferences should be overridden, the VLR consults the list of specific LCS clients identified for the subscriber. If found, the preferences are observed. For example, the request is denied, permitted, or some combination of notification and permission granting occurs. If the service is not specifically listed, then the subscriber's default privacy preference prevails. This gating of location at the GMLC and VLR is shown in Figure 10.2.

The preceding description of LCS privacy controls for a 3GPP network is as documented up to Release 5 of those standards. In recent times, an additional network element has been added called the Privacy Profile Register (PPR). This can be found in Release 6 onwards of the 3GPP specifications. This modification moves the hosting of the subscriber privacy preferences from the HLR and VLR into the PPR. This was done to provide a mechanism whereby privacy preference checking could be constrained to the home network. Privacy checking done in the VLR requires this to be done in the visited network. The protocol for interacting with the PPR, the Privacy Checking Protocol (PCP), is still to be defined. While some additional functionality is available, such as actually restricting location information based on the location itself, the effective capability is much as previously described. The identification of the PPR as a standalone function, however, is a significant move as, with its associated query protocol, it establishes a mechanism whereby any appropriately authorized network element can perform privacy checks on behalf of a given user. Doing the privacy checking in the VLR tightly coupled this operation with the services control of the 3GPP network. Placing the privacy rule evaluation in an external element means that this evaluation may be requested by another network element which is independent of the service provider. For example, an LIS may be informed of the identity of the PPR and given permission by a device to evaluate requests for location by referring to that PPR.

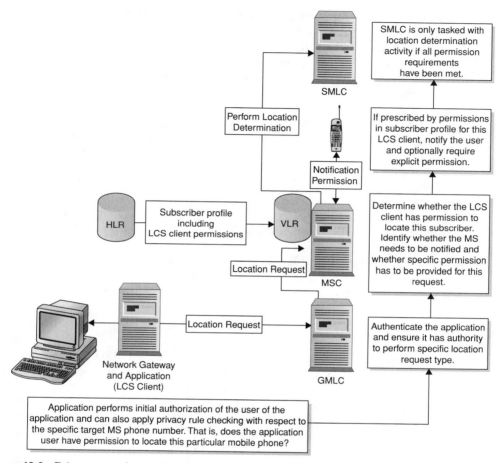

Figure 10.2 Privacy control in a 3GPP GSM network.

Gaining Consent

Before looking at a generic architecture for supporting location privacy controls, it is worthwhile looking at some of the general principles concerning "consent." Some of these principles have already been observed in terms of the 3GPP implementation of privacy control, but they have been thought about in the IP domain as well.

The GEOPRIV model described in this book assumes that prior consent has been established. The published authorization policy document is the result of a consent decision that has to be made before location is requested.

If no prior arrangement has been determined, the location service can actively seek consent from the user. Such active consent requires a decision from the user at the time that location is sought.

Active consent is employed in cellular networks as one of a number of privacy options. The user is shown a message that includes the name of the service requesting location. The user is then able to choose whether to grant or deny access.

Another form of active consent is made when location information is provided directly (by-value). The decision to make location available in this manner is usually preceded by a question.

Active consent is particularly useful where location is required for unplanned, temporary or transitory use; however, active consent requires user interaction, which makes it unsuitable for presence applications, long-term use, or any situation where location needs to be updated frequently. Constant requests for authorization in these circumstances would be intrusive.

Emergency services are a special instance where consent is implicit. An emergency call by nature requires location information to succeed; therefore, by initiating an emergency call, the caller implicitly relinquishes any privacy rights. Emergency calls are usually treated as if prior consent has been established; this behavior can be mandated by legislation.

For cases of prior (or implicit) consent, the user can also request notification about who is using location information. This does not allow for gaining consent, but ensures that the user is aware of when their location information is being used.

Generalized Consent

Another concept highlighted by 3GPP that wasn't described previously is that of giving consent to a class of requesters, rather than individuals. For instance, a user might want to provide all pizza restaurants or roadside assistance services access to their location. If such a decision can be made without making the decision specific to a single service, that greatly simplifies the management of an authorization policy.

This concept relies on being able to ensure that the requester does indeed belong to one of these classes of services, or that they have certain traits. In a cellular network, a decision can be made based on a trust or business relationship; the user can trust this assertion because their cellular provider is making it.

On the Internet, due to the decoupling between the access provider and the service provider, there is no easy way to ensure that a trusted relationship exists. However, the benefit of such general consent is undeniable. A solution for this is the Security Assertion Markup Language (SAML) (see Reference 3), which supports trait-based authentication. This remains as future work for authorization policy standardization.

Simplifying Privacy

The privacy considerations detailed so far provide a wide range of options for managing how location information is disseminated. There is little doubt that many users when presented with this information would not know what to do with it. However, those same users would be very definite about what privacy they expect.

Expressing user expectations as simple statements helps in understanding what the privacy rules need to contain. For instance, the following statements can lead to definite authorization policy rules:

- *"Joanne wants her mother to be able to locate her at all times."* The resulting rule simply includes the identity of Joanne's mother.

- *"Helen wants all her business contacts to be able to locate her only when she is at work."* Aside from a list identifying each of Helen's business contacts, this "want" can be interpreted in several ways. However, the most robust solution checks if Helen's location is the same as the location of her workplace. A presence service might also be able to identify work in other ways, such as with the Rich Presence extensions (see Reference 4).

- *"Philip wants the Pizza Delivery Co. to be able to locate him only when he has ordered a pizza."* The rule matches the identity of Pizza Delivery Co. with an extra condition that Ted has ordered a pizza. How this last is determined may be as simple as checking if Ted has made a recent phone call to Pizza Delivery Co.

Thus, this is just a matter of reducing the requirements down to a small set of use cases.

It is also helpful to understand how similar existing systems provide privacy protections and to evaluate their merits. For instance, instant messaging services provide a simple authorization policy: if a requester is on a "friends" list, permit; if they are on a "blocked" list, deny; otherwise, ask the user. To a certain extent this model is provided by the GEOPRIV common-policy and will likely dictate how it is used in the short term.

Simplifying privacy rules to the point where they can be easily understood makes the service more accessible. Complicated authorization rules are likely to be beyond all but the most enthusiastic of "power" users. Developers of user interfaces that capture privacy preferences need to ensure that these simple desires can be communicated easily.

Protecting the privacy of a user while still providing a viable location-based service remains a large and complex task. Providing users with reassurances about the protection of their privacy is important. Therefore, providing a simple means for a user to express their privacy preferences is likely to increase the adoption of these services.

Privacy considerations in the area of location services will remain an important component that determines its success. It is likely that a better understanding of the area through research will help provide technological solutions that improve user experience or data protection. Similarly, legislative protections that enhance privacy will continue to develop as location services for the Internet become more prevalent.

Architectures for Privacy Protection

Once user preferences are understood and codified, the network architectures for enforcing these preferences need to be understood. How privacy is stored and enforced both affect the overall privacy architecture. This section will discuss several architectural permutations and their respective advantages and disadvantages.

Each one of these architectures has the same four logical entities:

- The *Rule Maker* is the entity responsible for making the rules. Typically, the subject of the location information—the Target—also makes the decisions necessary to create the rules. The Rule Maker codifies the rules, possibly as a common-policy document, and makes them available to the Rule Holder.

- The *Rule Holder* stores rules. Usually, the Rule Holder provides an interface that allows the Rule Maker to modify the rules over time. The Rule Holder also makes rules available to the Rule Evaluator. In addition, Rule Holder is responsible for ensuring that rules are protected. Rules include information that could reveal private information about an individual; therefore, they are also subject to restrictions that ensure that only authorized entities can retrieve the information.

- The *Rule Evaluator* checks whether a specific request for location information is permitted. The Rule Evaluator acquires rules from a Rule Holder and evaluates those rules against a set of information about the request. The Rule Evaluator produces an authorization decision.

- The *Rule Enforcer* takes an authorization decision and either permits or blocks a request for location information. This role is usually assumed by an entity on the request path that can block requests that are not permitted.

A number of options exist to determine where each of these functions is implemented and how each is connected.

Architectural Choices

The architectures discussed so far in this book concentrate on the delivery part of location. Architectural choices relating to the way that privacy rules are communicated, stored, and enforced are critical to providing a general and viable location service.

This section outlines a number of options based on the four roles already identified. It can be seen that these options can coexist, which provides users with a choice about how their location information is used.

Minimal Architecture   The simplest architectural configuration that protects user privacy is shown in Figure 10.3. The LIS in this architecture assumes the responsibility of the Rule Evaluator and Enforcer. The device user, or some legal authority, is assumed to be the Rule Maker. The device is the Rule Holder.

The advantage of this architecture lies in its simplicity. The only protocol interface that needs to carry privacy-related information exists in the access network between the LIS and the device. This simplicity ensures a greater chance of success, both in terms of achieving deployment and in protecting privacy.

Centralized Rule Management   One drawback of the minimal approach is that an individual must maintain a privacy profile for every device that they use in this fashion.

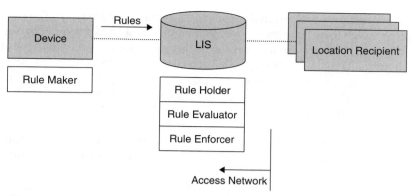

Figure 10.3 The LIS assumes many of the privacy roles in this architecture.

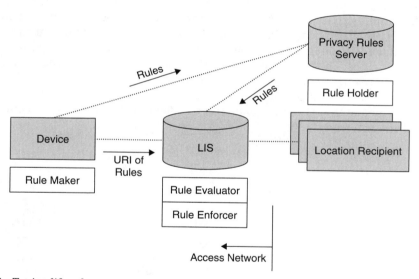

Figure 10.4 To simplify rule management, an external service can host privacy preferences.

Centralized management of a privacy profile gives a user the ability to employ the same profile with each device they use to access the Internet.

The first variation on the minimal architecture moves the role of Rule Holder to a centralized service, as shown in Figure 10.4.

Privacy rules can be made accessible to the LIS over secure HTTP. The Device provides a URL to the LIS when it requests a Location URI and establishes a context. The LIS retains the role of Rule Evaluator and Rule Enforcer and, indeed, from the LIS's perspective the device appears to continue in the role of rule holder while, in fact, it is actually just a proxy for the centralized privacy profile manager.

The interface provided to the user to apply updates to the profile can be as simple as an FTP or a web form. In some cases, proprietary tools are provided to assist in the management of rules. There are also protocols designed for the management of rules documents, such as XCAP (see Reference 5), which can be used to more efficiently update rules.

This architecture can be supported concurrently with the minimal architecture in Figure 10.3. The LIS only needs to be able to de-reference a URI to retrieve rules in addition to being able to accept rules directly from the device.

Delegating Rule Evaluation   3GPP defines a node, the Privacy Profile Register (PPR) that not only stores privacy rules, but also evaluates them. This delegation model can also be used by the LIS, as shown in Figure 10.5.

The PPR in this scenario requires sufficient information about the context of a request to be able to make a decision. When the LIS sends a request to the PPR, it includes enough context information in that request to allow the PPR to evaluate the rules. This context information includes the identity of the requester and the determined location. This implies that the PPR is authorized to receive location information.

This architecture provides some additional protection to a user's privacy preferences. Because the Rule Evaluator role is delegated, the LIS does not gain access to the user's privacy rules. This additional protection may be desirable if the user does not trust the access network enough to provide this information.

A benefit of this option is that the PPR already exists in the 3GPP architecture, which means that the same node can be used to make decisions for the cellular network and the Internet.

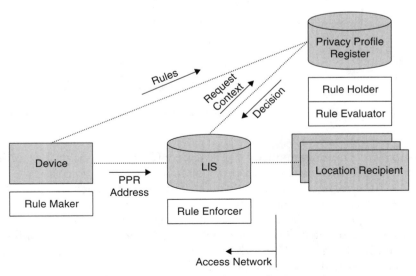

Figure 10.5 The LIS can use a PPR to delegate the evaluation of privacy rules.

This option can be provided to a user through the use of a PPR URI within the framework already described for HELD. This URI type is not yet defined, but it could be used in place of a ruleset URI to request that the LIS use the PPR. Note that this logical architecture also supports an implementation where the device itself adopts the role of rule evaluator. It can do this by hosting the delegate URI itself. This allows a kind of hybrid implementation where the privacy holder role may be as per either of the first two models.

Privacy with a Presence Service   A presence server can provide the advantages of the centralized service by assuming the roles of Rule Holder and Rule Evaluator. In addition, because it is also in the request path, a presence service can act as a Rule Enforcer. Figure 10.6 shows the simplest arrangement of this architecture.

This architecture permits the same variations as have already been seen with either an external Rule Holder or PPR. User expectations will likely mean that this separation will only exist for operational reasons, load balancing, and better functional separation rather than the case where a user employs a completely separate privacy service. Without a certain depth of understanding of the issues involved, a user is likely to view privacy as either part of a presence service (as it is today in the cellular domain) or merely as prerequisite for the service. Separate privacy services may not develop but will depend on factors such as legislative regimes which could require the storage of user information with state-approved operatives.

The additional presence information available to a presence service can provide more flexibility in evaluating rules. Some of the rules that were discussed in previous sections rely on information that is not normally available to the LIS.

This architecture moves much of the responsibility for privacy that was present in the LIS to the presence service. On the other hand, this does not preclude the LIS from

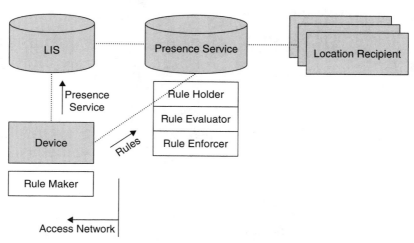

Figure 10.6   A presence service assumes much of the responsibility for controlling privacy.

providing a service directly. The LIS still requires a reduced capacity to process privacy rules—it must be able to authenticate and authorize the presence service.

The presence service option is a special case of those architectures that rely on the LIS directly. In order to use the presence service in this manner, the user must provide rules to the LIS that authorize the presence service. This is an effective means of delegating the privacy roles to the presence service; the presence service now protects privacy before the request reaches the LIS.

Architecture Combinations   A combination of the different configurations is also possible if the privacy rules provided to the LIS include clients other than the presence service. A combination of the two is likely for special cases like i2 emergency, where the Rule Maker role is filled by legislation. Legislation is not always going to affect the presence service, only the LIS is guaranteed to fall within its jurisdiction. Figure 10.7 shows how these different choices can be integrated.

Both the LIS and presence service provide some level of rule evaluation and enforcement, depending on the rules that they receive. For emergency services, the LIS receives rules from a Rule Maker other than the user: the emergency services legislation.

Choice of Architecture   The choice of architecture is left to a user of the service, the provider of their device, the operator of the service, or all of these in concert. How the choice is made depends on the requirements of user, and how they use location services. If a user employs a presence service for other purposes, protecting privacy at that point may not

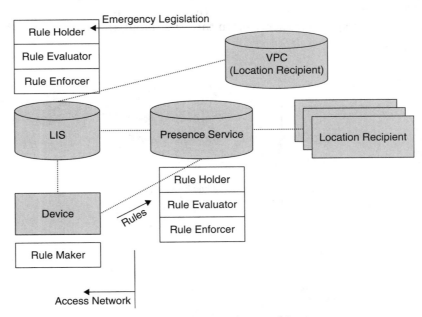

Figure 10.7   The i2 emergency impact on the presence privacy architecture.

require too large an increment to their use of that service. If the user does not already use a presence service, having the LIS protect their privacy could be a better option. Service providers can choose whether or not to provide these options to users.

The Internet service model, unlike the full services model applicable to the cellular domain, means that much more variability will exist in terms of prevailing architectures. Whether this settles down over time still remains to be seen. Currently, users habitually access services in the Internet independently of each other. A streaming video service, an e-mail service, a VoIP service, and a number of instant messaging services may all be subscribed to without any connection existing between them. A number of these services include presence functionality in some form or other. Generally, instant messaging and VoIP services aren't able to direct a message or phone call to a user unless their presence, including network location, is registered with the service.

The advantages of centralized privacy management are clear, but the relatively random service adoption patterns at present militate against the effectiveness of these approaches. To a certain extent, the way that an LIS makes privacy decisions is dependent on how a user chooses to structure their services. A user who opts to use a range of services will consequently need to make a decision about how their policy is communicated to the LIS, potentially making that decision for each service involved.

Related to this is the fact that some users maintain multiple identities—sometimes simply as a consequence of subscribing to multiple presence–type services. This is sometimes a deliberate choice; a user can use this as a way of partitioning aspects of their life. For example, they may have an instant messaging identity for work and another for personal communications. There are also services that users will access directly and independently of any presence function. For example, accessing a free web-based navigation service, which may make periodic location requests, does not imply any prior need for a presence function to exist, nor for the service to know the identity of the user.

The form in which location is provided (by-value versus by-reference), the rules applied (or otherwise) to the acquisition of that location information by applications, and the need to associate any user identity with the location information are very dependent on circumstances. For this reason, and because the population and needs of users come and go arbitrarily within a given public Internet access network, the LIS function associated with those networks will need to be able to support all of the models described. Disparate services are able to concurrently interact with the LIS in different ways, each of which is best suited to that particular application. To support maximum flexibility, the mixture of models used at any given time must be made at the discretion of the user, with regard to any prevailing legal obligations for that operator.

Focus on Law Enforcement

The ready accessibility of location information not only opens up new service opportunities; it provides new options for law enforcement, public safety, and security. The example of emergency calling has already been covered in quite some detail. For law enforcement and public safety uses, the privacy implications are not as well defined.

When and how location information can be given to the police and similar agencies is important to consider. One critical consideration in this area is how legislation provides for privacy overrides, that is, the agency can acquire location regardless of the wishes of the individual being located, and the individual is not even aware that they are being located.

HELD, with the additional identity parameters (as described in Appendix E), can be used by a law enforcement or public safety agency to request location information of an LIS based on a public identifier, such as an IP address. This form of request permits an instant response from an LIS, without the knowledge of the user.

Obviously, location can be a powerful tool for law enforcement, and it opens a number of possibilities for locating or tracking criminals. Controlling when this is permitted becomes an important question, a question that must be resolved in legislation. Legislation constrains law enforcement agencies by stating under what circumstances location information can be acquired. These constraints specify what conditions must be satisfied, whether permission needs to be sought, and whether the attempt must be publicly recorded. For instance, a court order might be required, which could, in turn, require evidence suggesting criminal activity or an imminent threat to public safety.

The use of information for public security and law enforcement is also subject to different legislative constraints than for standard social and commercial use. Local legislation varies greatly in this area, and some aspects relating to location are untested. Location can be covered under different laws depending on whether it is considered real-time information or recorded data (tracked by mobile phone).

Regardless of what local laws dictate, the availability of location information will guarantee its desirability for law enforcement. The implications for privacy depend on local legislation.

Location Acquisition Challenges for Law Enforcement

Assuming that a Law Enforcement Agency (LEA) is able to acquire appropriate permission as mandated by local legislation, determining location without knowledge of the target presents a number of challenges.

Initially, the target is usually only identified by a transitory identifier. An IP address or a TCP connection rarely remains static for any considerable period of time. Therefore, where these are the only identifiers available, they need to be acted upon quickly.

An IP address can be traced to its end-point; however, there are a number of measures that can be used to obscure the true source of messages. Internet traffic can be forwarded through a proxy, which masks the true source address. Many services like this exist, or the proxy might be run by a friend, or on a compromised machine. Virtual Private Networks (VPNs), which are commonly used by corporations for remote access, also provide a similar problem.

Assuming that the actual address of a target can be determined, the LIS that serves that address needs to be identified. This can be possible using DNS in the same fashion that a device would be used to determine the location of the LIS. Again, this step can be thwarted if the access network only makes their LIS and the associated DNS records available to users within the access network.

Once the LIS has been identified, assuming that the LIS is subject to the jurisdiction of the LEA, a request can be made using the IP address as a key. The LIS can then use whatever network-based methods it has to determine the location of the target.

An alternative method for acquiring location relies on knowing the presentity of the target. Knowing a presentity means that the LEA can request location information, along with other presence information, directly from the presence service. This assumes that location information is available to the presence service—that is, the target has provided the presence service with location information or a location URI.

One reason that a presence service is less useful in this situation is that a presence service is not necessarily located in the same physical region as the target. Where the access network requires physical presence in order to provide access, the presence service does not have this constraint. This can mean that the presence service is not within the jurisdiction of the LEA, so a request for location by the LEA may not be honored.

As has been a general theme in this book, the challenges before the LEA essentially arise from the service-provider access-provider decoupling. When an LEA asked for a conventional wireline phone tap, they applied the warrant against the telephone company. The telephone company provided the voice service to be monitored; the target identity was well understood as the telephone number to be tapped, and the telephone company owned the access network which physically needed to be tapped. Further, since the access network was in the jurisdiction of the LEA and, because the service provider was also the operator of the access network, the provider of the service to be tapped was also guaranteed to be in the same jurisdiction. This didn't change completely with mobile telephony. The network provider and the voice service provider remained one and the same; placing a tap on the service was still a matter of applying the warrant to the same operator against a given phone number. However, a flavor of what was to come with Internet services was provided with mobile telephony. GSM networks and other modern cellular standards support global roaming. It became possible, for example, to purchase a prepaid service from a foreign network operator. The user could operate their phone on that subscription while on a local cellular network. For the LEA, placing a warrant on the foreign service provider was not necessarily practical, not least because none of the voice data of interest would actually be visible to that operator. Similarly, placing a warrant on the local cellular network operators meant dealing with a user identity that was not under their control; their network equipment may not have even been able to intercept the necessary data.

At least in the preceding cellular scenario, user identity is still transferred from the home to the visited network in the form of subscriber profiles being read from the HLR into the VLR. This is done for authentication purposes primarily related to the need to ensure that billing charges are appropriately transferred. In the Internet, even this tenuous link is finally lost. Internet access is a purchasable service in itself. The user acquires it independently of the services that can be reached on the Internet. User identity from the access provider perspective is limited to that which may need to be authenticated for the purposes of billing the access alone. The only access identity that the remote Internet-based services see is the relatively anonymous IP address and, as described earlier, even this may have been obfuscated by the time the service sees it.

In the final analysis, the challenge for the LEA comes down to this: A choice has to be made to monitor the broadband access that the target is using and to acknowledge that obtaining content directly from a service provider is not always feasible. The warrant goes against the access provider who is in the jurisdiction of the LEA. The identity of the user is the login and authentication information that the network provider allocates to them. The service content becomes the equivalent of the voice content that was monitored and recorded in the traditional telephone tap. Untangling the many streams of application data, and decoding them is the difficult part. If the user moves to a different access network—such as a free public hotspot—their identity is lost; it is the analog of moving to a public phone box.

Location in this perspective is mostly of interest in mobile broadband access networks. As long as the target's authentication identity is known and a warrant can be placed on the operator of that network, then the IP location infrastructure described in this text, together with the necessary privacy controls described in this chapter, will permit lawful intercept of the location information.

References

1. Australian Government, "Privacy Act 1988," Act No. 119, 1988, December 2005.

2. 3GPP, *"Functional stage 2 description of Location Services (LCS),"* 3GPP TS 23.271 5.13.0, January 2005.

3. Cantor, S., Kemp, J., Philpott, R., and E. Maler, *"Assertions and Protocol for the OASIS Security Assertion Markup Language (SAML) V2.0,"* OASIS Standard saml-core-2.0-os, March 2005.

4. Schulzrinne, H., Gurbani, V., Kyzivat, P. & J. Rosenberg, *"RPID: Rich Presence Extensions to the Presence Information Data Format (PIDF),"* RFC 4480, July 2006.

5. Rosenberg, J., *"The Extensible Markup Language (XML) Configuration Access Protocol (XCAP),"* (work in progress), May 2006.

Abridged FLAP Specification

This appendix includes an extract from version 2.2 of the FLAP specification. This documents the FLAP messages and includes the FLAP XML schema.

BEEP Protocol Binding

FLAP uses the Block Extensible Exchange Protocol (BEEP) (see Reference 1) for the session-layer protocol. BEEP provides a secure, asynchronous communication layer that allows for two-way communication between client and server. It also manages message framing and message-response correlation.

The FLAP profile is identified by the URN:

```
http://sitacs.uow.edu.au/ns/location/flap/beep
```

Following the guidelines of Reference 1, Table A.1 summarizes the FLAP profile.

Table A.1 BEEP Profile Summary

Registration Item	Value
Profile Identification	http://sitacs.uow.edu.au/ns/location/flap/beep
Messages exchanged during channel creation	ns-prefix
Messages starting one-to-one exchanges	ns-prefix, ntfy, aq
Messages in positive replies	syncr, aqr
Messages in negative replies	error
Messages in one-to-many exchanges	sync
Message syntax	This appendix
Message semantics	Chapter 3 of this book
Contact information	The authors of this book

BEEP Transport

The TCP [binding for BEEP] is *required*(see References 1 and 2). In addition, it is *recommended* that the TLS profile for BEEP be used for FLAP. TLS provides a reliable connection with authentication and protection from replay, intercept, and eavesdropping. However, where performance requirements demand it, unsecured TCP may be used, providing that link security is ensured through other means (dedicated media, VPN, and so on).

No specific TLS ciphersuite is required for this protocol, although due to the nature of the relationship between the LIS and ALE, those defined in Reference 3 are recommended. Pre-shared keys provide a degree of security over unsecured TCP without significantly affecting ALE performance or increasing the management overhead of maintaining the ALE. The pure Pre-Shared Key (PSK) ciphersuites described in Section 2 of Reference 3 do not protect against dictionary attacks, other ciphersuites may be selected if this is considered insufficient.

No TCP port is reserved for FLAP communications.

Connection Management   Connection establishment is the responsibility of the LIS. This ensures that the LIS is able to regulate the rate at which it establishes connections. The LIS is also responsible for starting the FLAP channel.

The ALE MAY support the establishment of multiple connections from a LIS for link redundancy. Where multiple connections exist, response messages and error indications *must* be transmitted on the same connection as the original request or detected error condition. If multiple connections to an ALE have been established, the ALE must send notification messages on all connections; the ALE *should not* assume that the connections have been established by the same LIS.

A single BEEP connection may have any number of FLAP channels, although it is recommended that only one channel be established. Where multiple channels are employed, the ALE *must not* send duplicate notification messages; one channel should be selected for notifications.

Note that in certain situations, particularly where NAT is employed, inactive connections may go "stale," preventing further use of the connection. The LIS should either close unused connections or use the resynchronization message as a "keep-alive" request. The TCP "keep-alive" method is *not recommended* because the minimum interval is too short to be practical.

BEEP and XML

FLAP uses XML messages to convey data. The character encoding for XML documents should be UTF-8 or UTF-16.

Implementations also should validate each message against the schema. The Post Schema Validation Infoset (PSVI) can contain more information that is explicitly expressed in the message, because default and fixed values are included in schema. Errors in well formedness and schema validation *must* be reported.

Note that each message is an XML fragment only. Fragments can be validated by insertion. The fragment is inserted into the last `ns-prefix` message received, which then forms a complete XML document.

FLAP Versions

The FLAP namespace is identified by the http://sitacs.uow.edu.au/ns/location/flap/beep URN. New versions of this protocol will be identified by a different URN.

Error Handling

If a LIS or ALE notices an error in the received stream, they should generate an error message to notify the sender of the error. Errors include badly formed XML, unsupported protocol versions, and errors relating to the state of either LIS or ALE.

Error messages typically arise from the receipt of a message that displays an error (or errors) in processing a request. In these cases, the error indication is included in a standard BEEP ERR response. If an error is detected in any response message (RPY, ANS, NUL), the MSG frame is used to send the error indication. An error that is raised in this manner *must* be acknowledged with an empty RPY frame. Error messages, however, *must not* be generated in response to errors in an error (ERR) message.

If a particular error renders the connection unusable for any reason, the connection *must* be closed. Likewise, the channel should be stopped if an unrecoverable error occurs in the channel.

A LIS or ALE should respond to requests within a short amount of time. BEEP uses an acknowledged transport; the sender can be sure that the message was received. From this, it can be assumed that an unanswered request indicates an application error. If the other end does not respond within a certain amount of time, two possibilities are recommended:

- Further to the recommendations in the earlier section titled "Connection Management," if no messages are received on the FLAP channel over a similar period, the channel should be terminated and restarted. Similarly, if there is no activity on the connection, the connection can be terminated and restarted.

- If it is only a single message that has not been answered within a certain period and other messages have been received, the message may be re-sent. An upper limit should be set on the number of times retransmission is attempted. Alternatively, the request can be considered as having failed with the error code 500 (see the later section titled "Result Codes").

FLAP Messages

This section describes the format and contents of FLAP messages. FLAP messages are XML fragments that use namespaces in XML (see Reference 4) to provide extensibility for both technologies and vendors.

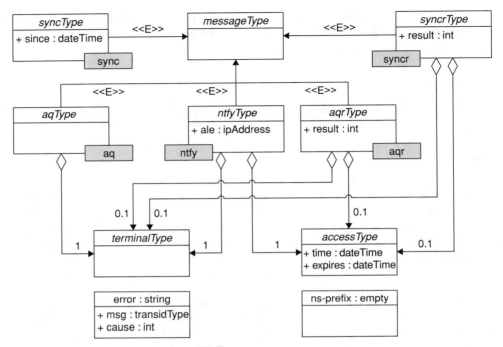

Figure A.1   A high-level message schema UML.

Schema UML

The UML notation for the base schema is shown in Figure A.1. This diagram displays the relationships between the types used in this section.

Core Message Definitions

The core FLAP message types are the Notification, Resynchronization, Resynchronization Response, Access Query, and Access Query Response messages. The core message types are composed into a substitution group named _message.

The Notification Message   The LIS or ALE sends a Notification message to inform the other that the access conditions of a particular terminal have changed. Table A.2 shows the components of the Notification message.

The Resynchronization Message   The Resynchronization message is sent by the LIS to request that the ALE provide information on all terminals that have changed access conditions in a given time period. The time period is specified as the time from the given time to the present.

Table A.2   Components of the Notification Message

Name	Type	#	Description
ale	Attribute (ipAddress)	0..1	This attribute identifies the ALE that has provided this information to the LIS. This attribute should be provided by the LIS where it is notifying an ALE that another ALE has provided the access information.
terminal	Element (terminalType)	1	This element identifies the terminal.
access	Element (accessType)	1	This element provides information about the terminal's physical network access.

Table A.3   Components of the Resynchronization Message

Name	Type	#	**Description**
since	Attribute (dateTime)	0..1	This attribute specifies the start time for the period. The period ends at the time the request is received. The ALE must be able to deal with a value in the future, as this message may be used for a connection "keep-alive" mechanism.

The ALE *must* respond to the Resynchronization message in a timely manner. Table A.3 shows the components of the Resynchronization message.

The Resynchronization Response Message   The Resynchronization Response message is sent by the ALE in response to a Resynchronization message. The contents of the Resynchronization Response are similar to the Notification, except that an empty Resynchronization Response is sent if no changes have occurred during the requested interval.

If the since attribute is specified, the ALE must provide information on terminals that have left the network, including an empty access element. If the since attribute is omitted from the Resynchronization message, the Resynchronization Response messages sent in reply may omit information for terminals that are not currently within the network monitored by the ALE.

The Resynchronization Response must include terminal and access information when there have been changes in the monitored network. If no changes have occurred, the response shall be a BEEP NUL message with no content.

Table A.4 shows the components of the Resynchronization Response message.

The Access Query Message   The Access Query message is used by the LIS to request information from the ALE.

The ALE *must* respond to the Access Query in a timely manner. Table A.5 shows the components of an Access Query message.

Table A.4   Components of the Resynchronization Response Message

Name	Type	#	Description
result	Attribute (`resultCodeType`)	1	This attribute contains a code indicating the result type for this message.
terminal	Element (`terminalType`)	1	This element identifies the terminal.
access	Element (`accessType`)	1	This element provides information about the terminal's physical network access.

Table A.5   Components of an Access Query Message

Name	Type	#	Description
exact	Attribute (`boolean`)	0..1	If present and set to true, the ALE must send only one response. If set to true, the terminal identification, optionally excluding vendor extensions, at the ALE must be identical to that specified by the LIS, that is, no partial matches are allowed.
terminal	Element (`terminalType`)	1	This element identifies the terminal.
access	Element (`accessType`)	1	This element provides information about the terminal's physical network access.

Table A.6   Components of an Access Query Response Message

Name	Type	#	Description
result	Attribute (`resultCodeType`)	1	This attribute contains a code indicating the result type for this message.
terminal	Element (`terminalType`)	0..1	This element optionally identifies the terminal. This should be used where the identification information provided by the LIS in the Access Query was incomplete or inaccurate.
access	Element (`accessType`)	0..1	This element provides information about the terminal's physical network access. This element is omitted if a failure result is indicated.

The Access Query Response Message   The Access Query Response message is sent by the ALE in response to an Access Query message from the LIS. Table A.6 shows the components of the Access Query Response message.

Management Message Definitions

Management messages can be used by either LIS or ALE outside of core FLAP messaging. These messages establish namespace prefix bindings, indicate error conditions, and provide feedback.

Table A.7   Components of an Error Indication

Name	Type	#	Description
cause	Attribute (resultCodeType)	1	This attribute indicates the reason for the error.
xml:lang	Attribute (language)	0..1	This attribute specifies the language (and character set) of the content text.
{content}	Text (0..256 characters)	0..1	The error element may contain human-readable text describing the error condition in more detail.

Namespace Declaration Type Definition   To avoid having to include a number of namespace prefix attributes in every request (using the xmlns attribute), FLAP includes the ns-prefix message. The ns-prefix message establishes a context for all messages that follow it in the channel. Namespace prefixes declared by the ns-prefix message must be considered in scope when evaluating all subsequent messages.

The ns-prefix message may be sent in the start message.

The ns-prefix message must always include the FLAP namespace. It is recommended that either the FLAP namespace or the namespace of a technology extension be the default namespace.

The ns-prefix message permits any content in order to enable schema validation by insertion. In this method, the ns-prefix element is taken as the document element for all messages; each message is inserted into the ns-prefix element before validation. This ensures that the namespace prefixes defined on the ns-prefix are in scope for each message.

Error Indication   An error indication is sent when the converse stream contains an error or there is a failure in the node that is not related to any specific message. Error indications may be used for XML parsing errors, administrative actions, congestion, or as necessary.

The error indication is not a part of the _message substitution group, so it does not contain the common elements described in the later section "Result Codes." Table A.7 shows the components that form the error indication.

Common Type Definitions

Terminal Identification Type   Terminal identification is dependent on the type of access technology used. Therefore, the terminal type defined does not require any specific content.

Access Information Type   Information about the access characteristics of a terminal is also dependent on the specific access technology employed.

The access element is defined to include two attributes that specify the time period over which this information is valid.

For a Notification or Resynchronization Response message, the access information may be left empty to indicate that a terminal has left the domain managed by the ALE. In this case, the time attribute should be set to the time at which the ALE detects the change; the `expires` attribute should *not* be set, unless it contains an identical value to time.

Table A.8 describes the time attributes associated with access information.

IP Address   The only element definition defined for FLAP is the IP Address element, `ip`. This type is included for use in technology extensions either directly, or through use of the `ipAddress` type.

Result Codes

Result codes are defined to use the same three-digit scheme as applied by FTP, HTTP, and SIP (among others) (see Reference 5). In this scheme, the first digit indicates the general type of the message, while the second and third digits are specific. Table A.9 enumerates the meaning of common result codes.

Table A.8   Access Information Attributes

Name	Type	#	Description
time	Attribute (dateTime)	1	The time at which the access information was determined.
expires	Attribute (dateTime)	0..1	The time beyond which the information must not be used. This attribute may be omitted where this information cannot be determined. Note also that this is the latest time only; access information might become incorrect before this time.

Table A.9   Meanings of Common Result Codes

Code	Short Description	Usage Notes
200	Success	Indicates success.
201	Terminal left	Used for a notification or resynchronization response that indicates that the terminal has left the domain monitored by the ALE.
400	Badly formed XML	The stream or message, if one can be reliably determined, contained badly formed XML. This includes illegal characters, unbalanced elements, and any errors. Note that while validation is not performed on the contents of the vendor element, badly formed XML may result in an unrecoverable parsing error. Parsers should attempt to ignore errors within vendor elements.

Code	Short Description	Usage Notes
401	XML validation failure	The stream or message, if one can be reliably determined, contained validation errors against the schema. Note that validation is not required for the contents of the vendor element by definition. Therefore, although implementations may choose validate vendor extensions, validation errors must not be generated for such errors.
402	Unsupported encoding	The encoding used by the end stream is not supported.
403	Unknown namespace prefix	A namespace prefix was used, but the namespace binding was not established with the last `ns-prefix` message.
404	Unknown message type	The request type is not known.
405	Technology not supported	The access technology indicated in the request is not supported by the ALE.
406	Insufficient identification	This result code indicates that the terminal identification provided did not include sufficient information to uniquely identify a single terminal.
407	Conflicting identification	This result code indicates that the terminal identification resulted in a possible match for more than one terminal. This code is used where the terminal identification provided was not sufficient to uniquely identify a single terminal. For example, this result code applies if the request provided mismatched IP and hardware addresses for an Ethernet host.
408	Terminal not found	This result code indicates that the terminal indicated in a request could not be found.
409	Inadequate history for resynchronization	This result code indicates that the ALE was unable to provide resynchronization information for the entire period requested. This error is provided in response to a Resynchronization request with the `since` parameter.
410	Unsupported operation	The request type is not supported.
500	Unknown error	The type of error could not be determined.
501	Unspecified error	The type of error is known, but no code exists to describe it.
502	Administrative action in progress	A request could not be processed due to an administrative action.
503	Processing overload	A request could not be processed due to congestion. This code may also be sent to indicate a general level of congestion.
504	Network error	A request could not be completed due to network connectivity failure, or lack of response to a network request. This message may be sent to indicate that requests may fail due to a network outage.

Extensions

Extensions to FLAP are classified into two groups. Different access technologies may require an extension to the protocol in order to transport either terminal or access information. In addition, specific vendors may have proprietary information that may add to the quality or efficiency of location determination methods. A new access technology warrants more detailed specification than the proprietary extension, so both of these cases are accommodated by this section.

Extensions are differentiated by the use of XML namespaces (see Reference 4).

Access Technology Extensions

This protocol is designed to be extended for use in different access technologies, which necessitates different sets of both access and terminal data. Definitions for DHCP and Ethernet technologies are included in the base specification, but this is by no means exhaustive. Extensions for additional access technologies may be made by defining an XML schema in a new namespace.

Technologies are identified by a short identifier, like "ethernet," that is included in each message. This enables the management of multiple technologies from a single LIS, or even from a single ALE, although that is not encouraged.

The most basic extension defines a set of XML elements that are to be used for access and terminal data. Since both the terminal and access elements permit any content, these can be included as necessary. This minimal form of technology extension is very similar to what an individual vendor might do to include their extension.

A more complete extension also provides new type definitions for access and terminal elements so that their cardinality can be controlled. Extensions in this fashion are optional, but offer greater control over the encoding of messages. By using the restriction rules of XML schema, the extension can ensure that the correct information is provided in a predictable format.

Terminal and Access Definitions   The most primitive extension method derives schema for the terminal and access elements by restriction from the base types. The `terminalType` and `accessType` type definitions are derived by restriction into type definitions for the access technology.

For example, the Ethernet extension defines the following types for terminal and access elements.

```
<xsd:element name="terminal" type="terminalType"
             substitutionGroup="flap:terminal"/>
<xsd:complexType name="terminalType">
  <xsd:complexContent>
    <xsd:restriction base="flap:terminalType">
      <xsd:sequence>
        <xsd:choice>
          <xsd:sequence>
            <xsd:element ref="flap:ip"/>
            <xsd:element ref="mac" minOccurs="0"/>
          </xsd:sequence>
          <xsd:element ref="mac"/>
        </xsd:choice>
        <xsd:element ref="flap:_vendor"
                    minOccurs="0" maxOccurs="unbounded"/>
      </xsd:sequence>
    </xsd:restriction>
  </xsd:complexContent>
</xsd:complexType>
```

```
<xsd:element name="access" type="accessType"
            substitutionGroup="flap:access"/>
<xsd:complexType name="accessType">
  <xsd:complexContent>
    <xsd:restriction base="flap:accessType">
      <xsd:sequence minOccurs="0">
        <xsd:element ref="switch"/>
        <xsd:element ref="port"/>
        <xsd:element ref="vlan" minOccurs="0"/>
        <xsd:element ref="flap:_vendor"
                    minOccurs="0" maxOccurs="unbounded"/>
      </xsd:sequence>
    </xsd:restriction>
  </xsd:complexContent>
</xsd:complexType>
```

This schema defines the types that make up terminal identification and access data. This schema also defines a new element type for both terminal and access, which are substitutable for the base elements. Both of these definitions permit vendor-specific content through the flap:_vendor element, as described in the later section titled "Vendor-Specific Content."

This results in a message that uses these elements. The following example shows an intermediate form of a Notification:

```
<ntfy tech="ethernet">
  <enet:terminal>
    <ip>192.168.0.1</ip>
    <enet:mac>12:34:56:78:90:ab</enet:mac>
  </enet:terminal>
  <enet:access time="2005-04-14T10:51:23.000+10:00">
    <enet:switch><ip>192.168.0.1</ip></enet:switch>
    <enet:port>4</enet:port>
  </enet:access>
</ntfy>
```

Message Definitions   Restricting the types for terminal and access is sufficient to ensure that validation is applied correctly to the new elements. However, this does not ensure consistency across the entire message. In other words, validation of a message using individual types does not ensure that a terminal element is associated with the same technology as its matched access element. This section describes how to both simplify message instances and to guarantee consistency of technology application within each type.

A derived message type may be defined by restricting the core message type definitions. The new message type restricts the terminal and access elements to use the types defined for that access technology. Because this new type is applied to the message as a whole, the terminal and access elements implicitly receive the correct type definition.

The new Notification message definition for Ethernet is

```
<xsd:attributeGroup name="techAttr">
  <xsd:attribute name="tech" type="xsd:anyURI" fixed="ethernet"/>
</xsd:attributeGroup>

<xsd:complexType name="ntfy">
  <xsd:complexContent>
    <xsd:restriction base="flap:ntfyType">
      <xsd:sequence>
        <xsd:element ref="terminal"/>
        <xsd:element ref="access"/>
      </xsd:sequence>
      <xsd:attributeGroup ref="techAttr"/>
    </xsd:restriction>
  </xsd:complexContent>
</xsd:complexType>
```

The extension definition also sets the `tech` attribute to a fixed value of "ethernet".

One notable feature of this method is that the code for restricting message types is almost identical for all types of technology extension. The technology extensions in this document only differ in the fixed value assigned to the `tech` attribute.

An instance of a Notification message using the newly defined type looks like:

```
<ntfy xsi:type="enet:ntfy">
  <enet:terminal>
    <ip>192.168.0.1</ip>
    <enet:mac>12:34:56:78:90:ab</enet:mac>
  </enet:terminal>
  <enet:access time="2005-04-14T10:51:23.000+10:00">
    <enet:switch><ip>192.168.0.1</ip></enet:switch>
    <enet:port>4</enet:port>
  </enet:access>
</ntfy>
```

Note that other access technology extensions will use a different namespace for their new elements, as well as the `xsi:type` attribute.

Additional Message Types

Message elements all belong to a substitution group, the head of which is an abstract element named _message. New message types are defined by extending the type definition, `messageType`, and creating a new element of this type that belongs to the _message substitution group. The following definition describes an example message that contains a new `"host"` element:

```
<xsd:element name="example" substitutionGroup="_message">
  <xsd:complexType>
    <xsd:complexContent>
      <xsd:extension base="flap:messageType">
```

```
        <xsd:element name="host" type="flap:ipAddress"/>
      </xsd:extension>
    </xsd:complexContent>
  </xsd:complexType>
</xsd:element>
```

Given that the preceding example is defined in the `"urn:example"` namespace, this leads to the following new message:

```
<example xmlns:ex="urn:example">
  <host>47.153.203.21</host>
</example>
```

Vendor-Specific Content

Vendor-specific content should be permitted by technology extensions through the `_vendor` element. Vendor extensions are made by defining a new element in the substitution group headed by the `_vendor` element. These elements are defined in a new namespace and schema. The optional attribute on this element should include a URI that uniquely identifies a vendor, which may be the same as the namespace URI.

A receiver should ignore the contents of messages that it does not understand. Errors in XML well formedness always result in errors.

The namespace prefix for the vendor extension can either be declared with the `ns-prefix` element, or declared when used. The following example assumes that the `exco:` prefix has been declared previously.

```
<ntfy xsi:type="enet:ntfy">
  <enet:terminal>
    <ip>192.168.0.1</ip>
    <enet:hwaddr>12:34:56:78:90:ab</enet:hwaddr>
    <exco:hw serial="167332" revision="1.2"/>
  </enet:terminal>
  <enet:access time="2005-04-14T10:51:23.000+10:00">
    <enet:switch><ip>192.168.0.1</ip></enet:switch>
    <enet:port>4</enet:port>
  </enet:access>
</ntfy>
```

The `exco:hw` element in the preceding example sets a fixed value for the `flap:vendor` attribute in its XML schema definition. The following XML schema fragment defines this vendor extension:

```
<xsd:element name="hw" type="hwType"
             substitutionGroup="flap:_vendor"/>
<xsd:complexType name="hwType">
  <xsd:complexContent>
    <xsd:restriction base="flap:vendorExtensionType">
      <xsd:attribute ref="flap:vendor"
                     fixed="http://exampleco.com/"/>
```

```
            <xsd:attribute name="serial" type="xsd:token"/>
            <xsd:attribute name="revision" use="required">
              <xsd:simpleType>
                <xsd:restriction base="xsd:normalizedString">
                  <xsd:pattern value="\w+(\.\w+)*"/>
                </xsd:restriction>
              </xsd:simpleType>
            </xsd:attribute>
          </xsd:restriction>
        </xsd:complexContent>
    </xsd:complexType>
```

FLAP Base XML Schema

The base schema document does not directly include any definitions for access technology elements.

```
<?xml version="1.0"?>
<xsd:schema xmlns:xsd="http://www.w3.org/2001/XMLSchema"
            targetNamespace="http://sitacs.uow.edu.au/ns/location/flap/beep"
            xmlns="http://sitacs.uow.edu.au/ns/location/flap/beep"
            elementFormDefault="qualified"
            attributeFormDefault="unqualified"
            finalDefault="extension">

  <xsd:annotation>
    <xsd:documentation>
      This schema describes the format of messages exchanged between a
      LIS and ALE.
    </xsd:documentation>
  </xsd:annotation>

  <xsd:import namespace="http://www.w3.org/XML/1998/namespace"
              schemaLocation="http://www.w3.org/2001/xml.xsd"/>

  <!-- ============= Miscellaneous Messages ================ -->
  <xsd:element name="ns-prefix" type="ns-prefixType">
    <xsd:annotation>
      <xsd:documentation>
        The error element indicates an error with a particular message,
        the stream or the session as a whole.
      </xsd:documentation>
    </xsd:annotation>
  </xsd:element>
  <xsd:complexType name="ns-prefixType" final="#all">
    <xsd:complexContent>
      <xsd:restriction base="xsd:anyType">
        <xsd:sequence>
        <xsd:any namespace="##any" processContents="strict"
                 minOccurs="0" maxOccurs="unbounded"/>
```

```xsd
        </xsd:sequence>
      </xsd:restriction>
    </xsd:complexContent>
  </xsd:complexType>

  <xsd:element name="error" type="errorType">
    <xsd:annotation>
      <xsd:documentation>
        The error element indicates an error with a particular message,
        the stream or the session as a whole.
      </xsd:documentation>
    </xsd:annotation>
  </xsd:element>
  <xsd:simpleType name="errorText" final="restriction">
    <xsd:restriction base="xsd:normalizedString">
      <xsd:maxLength value="256"/>
    </xsd:restriction>
  </xsd:simpleType>
  <xsd:complexType name="errorType" final="#all">
    <xsd:simpleContent>
      <xsd:extension base="errorText">
        <xsd:attribute name="cause" type="resultCodeType"
                       use="required"/>
        <xsd:attribute ref="xml:lang" use="optional"/>
      </xsd:extension>
    </xsd:simpleContent>
  </xsd:complexType>

  <!-- ============== Core Message Types =================== -->
  <xsd:complexType name="messageType" abstract="true" final="restriction">
    <xsd:complexContent>
      <xsd:restriction base="xsd:anyType">
        <xsd:attribute name="tech" type="xsd:anyURI"/>
      </xsd:restriction>
    </xsd:complexContent>
  </xsd:complexType>

  <xsd:complexType name="responseType">
    <xsd:complexContent>
      <xsd:extension base="messageType">
        <xsd:sequence minOccurs="0">
          <xsd:element ref="terminal" minOccurs="0"/>
          <xsd:element ref="access" minOccurs="0"/>
        </xsd:sequence>
        <xsd:attribute name="result" type="resultCodeType"
                       use="required"/>
      </xsd:extension>
    </xsd:complexContent>
  </xsd:complexType>

  <xsd:complexType name="ntfyType" final="extension">
```

```
      <xsd:complexContent>
        <xsd:extension base="messageType">
          <xsd:sequence>
            <xsd:element ref="terminal"/>
            <xsd:element ref="access"/>
          </xsd:sequence>
          <xsd:attribute name="ale" type="ipAddress"/>
        </xsd:extension>
      </xsd:complexContent>
    </xsd:complexType>

    <xsd:complexType name="syncType" final="extension">
      <xsd:complexContent>
        <xsd:extension base="messageType">
          <xsd:attribute name="since" type="xsd:dateTime" use="optional"/>
        </xsd:extension>
      </xsd:complexContent>
    </xsd:complexType>

    <xsd:complexType name="syncrType" final="extension">
      <xsd:complexContent>
        <xsd:restriction base="responseType">
          <xsd:sequence>
            <xsd:element ref="terminal"/>
            <xsd:element ref="access"/>
          </xsd:sequence>
        </xsd:restriction>
      </xsd:complexContent>
    </xsd:complexType>

    <xsd:complexType name="aqType" final="extension">
      <xsd:complexContent>
        <xsd:extension base="messageType">
          <xsd:sequence>
            <xsd:element ref="terminal"/>
          </xsd:sequence>
        </xsd:extension>
      </xsd:complexContent>
    </xsd:complexType>

    <xsd:complexType name="aqrType" final="extension">
      <xsd:complexContent>
        <xsd:restriction base="responseType">
          <xsd:sequence minOccurs="0">
            <xsd:element ref="terminal" minOccurs="0"/>
            <xsd:element ref="access"/>
          </xsd:sequence>
        </xsd:restriction>
      </xsd:complexContent>
    </xsd:complexType>
```

```
<!-- ============== Message Elements ==================== -->
<xsd:element name="_message" type="messageType"
             final="" abstract="true"/>

<xsd:element name="aq" type="aqType"
             substitutionGroup="_message" block="extension"/>
<xsd:element name="aqr" type="aqrType"
             substitutionGroup="_message" block="extension"/>
<xsd:element name="ntfy" type="ntfyType"
             substitutionGroup="_message" block="extension"/>
<xsd:element name="sync" type="syncType"
             substitutionGroup="_message" block="extension"/>
<xsd:element name="syncr" type="syncrType"
             substitutionGroup="_message" block="extension"/>

<!-- ================= Base Types ===================== -->
<xsd:simpleType name="resultCodeType">
  <xsd:restriction base="xsd:token">
    <xsd:pattern value="\d{3}"/>
  </xsd:restriction>
</xsd:simpleType>

<xsd:simpleType name="ipAddress">
  <xsd:annotation>
    <xsd:documentation>
      This represents any IP address, IPv4 or IPv6.
    </xsd:documentation>
  </xsd:annotation>
  <xsd:union memberTypes="ipv4 ipv6"/>
</xsd:simpleType>

<xsd:simpleType name="ipv4">
  <xsd:annotation>
    <xsd:documentation>
      An IP version 4 address.
    </xsd:documentation>
  </xsd:annotation>
  <xsd:restriction base="xsd:token">
    <xsd:pattern value="(25[0-5]|2[0-4][0-9]|[0-1]?[0-9]?[0-9])\.(25[0-
5]|2[0-4][0-9]|[0-1]?[0-9]?[0-9])\.(25[0-5]|2[0-4][0-9]|[0-1]?[0-9]?[0-
9])\.(25[0-5]|2[0-4][0-9]|[0-1]?[0-9]?[0-9])"/>
    <xsd:pattern value="[0-9A-Fa-f]{8}"/>
  </xsd:restriction>
</xsd:simpleType>

<xsd:simpleType name="ipv6">
  <xsd:annotation>
    <xsd:documentation>
      An IP version 6 address, based on RFC 2373.
    </xsd:documentation>
```

```
      </xsd:annotation>
      <xsd:restriction base="xsd:token">
        <xsd:pattern value="[0-9A-Fa-f]{1,4}(:[0-9A-Fa-f]{1,4}){7}"/>
        <xsd:pattern value=":(:[0-9A-Fa-f]{1,4}){1,7}"/>
        <xsd:pattern value="([0-9A-Fa-f]{1,4}:){1,6}(:[0-9A-Fa-f]{1,4}){1}"/>
        <xsd:pattern value="([0-9A-Fa-f]{1,4}:){1,5}(:[0-9A-Fa-f]{1,4}){1,2}"/>
        <xsd:pattern value="([0-9A-Fa-f]{1,4}:){1,4}(:[0-9A-Fa-f]{1,4}){1,3}"/>
        <xsd:pattern value="([0-9A-Fa-f]{1,4}:){1,3}(:[0-9A-Fa-f]{1,4}){1,4}"/>
        <xsd:pattern value="([0-9A-Fa-f]{1,4}:){1,2}(:[0-9A-Fa-f]{1,4}){1,5}"/>
        <xsd:pattern value="([0-9A-Fa-f]{1,4}:){1}(:[0-9A-Fa-f]{1,4}){1,6}"/>
        <xsd:pattern value="([0-9A-Fa-f]{1,4}:){1,7}:"/>
        <xsd:pattern value="((:(:0{1,4}){0,3}(:(0{1,4}|[fF]{4}))?)|(0{1,4}:(:0{
1,4}){0,2}(:(0{1,4}|[fF]{4}))?)|((0{1,4}:){2}(:0{1,4})?(:(0{1,4}|[fF]{4}))?)|
((0{1,4}:){3}(:(0{1,4}|[fF]{4}))?)|((0{1,4}:){4}(0{1,4}|[fF]{4})?)):(25[0-
5]|2[0-4][0-9]|[0-1]?[0-9]?[0-9])\.(25[0-5]|2[0-4][0-9]|[0-1]?[0-9]?[0-
9])\.(25[0-5]|2[0-4][0-9]|[0-1]?[0-9]?[0-9])\.(25[0-5]|2[0-4][0-9]|[0-1]?[0-
9]?[0-9]))"/>
        <xsd:pattern value="::"/>
      </xsd:restriction>
    </xsd:simpleType>

    <!-- ============== Element Definitions =================== -->
    <xsd:element name="terminal" type="terminalType"/>
    <xsd:complexType name="terminalType" abstract="true"
                     final="extension">
      <xsd:complexContent>
        <xsd:restriction base="xsd:anyType">
          <xsd:sequence>
           <xsd:any namespace="##any" processContents="lax"
                    minOccurs="0" maxOccurs="unbounded"/>
          </xsd:sequence>
        </xsd:restriction>
      </xsd:complexContent>
    </xsd:complexType>

    <xsd:element name="access" type="accessType"/>
    <xsd:complexType name="accessType" abstract="true"
                     final="extension">
      <xsd:complexContent>
        <xsd:restriction base="xsd:anyType">
          <xsd:sequence minOccurs="0">
            <xsd:any namespace="##any" processContents="lax"
                     minOccurs="0" maxOccurs="unbounded"/>
          </xsd:sequence>
          <xsd:attribute name="time" type="xsd:dateTime"
                         use="required"/>
          <xsd:attribute name="expires" type="xsd:dateTime"
                         use="optional"/>
        </xsd:restriction>
      </xsd:complexContent>
    </xsd:complexType>
```

```
    <xsd:element name="ip" type="ipAddress"/>

    <xsd:element name="_vendor" type="vendorExtensionType"
                 abstract="true"/>
    <xsd:complexType name="vendorExtensionType" abstract="true"
                     final="extension">
      <xsd:complexContent>
        <xsd:restriction base="xsd:anyType">
          <xsd:sequence>
            <xsd:any namespace="##any" processContents="strict"
                     minOccurs="0" maxOccurs="unbounded"/>
          </xsd:sequence>
          <xsd:attribute ref="vendor" use="optional"/>
          <xsd:anyAttribute namespace="##any" processContents="strict"/>
        </xsd:restriction>
      </xsd:complexContent>
    </xsd:complexType>
    <xsd:attribute name="vendor" type="xsd:anyURI"/>
  </xsd:schema>
```

Access Technology Extensions

DHCP Technology Extension

This extension includes support for ALE technology as part of a DHCP server that has BOOTP relays capable of including information from Reference 5, DHCP option 82.

DHCP Terminal Identification   A terminal in the DHCP context uses the information listed in Table A.10.

DHCP Access Information   For DHCP, the time and expires attributes, as described in the earlier section titled "Access Information Type," correspond to the DHCP lease grant and expiry times, respectively. In addition to the time values, the DHCP access uses the values listed in Table A.11.

Table A.10   Terminal Identification for DHCP

Name	Type	#	Description
ip	Element (ipAddress)	1	The IP address of the terminal, which is the value included in the ciaddr parameter of the DHCP header.
hwaddr	Element (chaddrType)	1	The hardware address, which is the value included in the chaddr parameter of the DHCP header.
remote-id	Element (hexBinary)	0..1	This value may contain the information included in sub-option 2 of Reference 6 option, the remote identifier of the terminal.

Table A.11   Access Information Extension Values for DHCP

Name	Type	#	Description
server	Element (token)	0..1	This is an identifier that is unique from the context of the ALE for the DHCP server that provided this information. This element is not necessary unless multiple DHCP servers are managed by a single ALE.
relay	Element (ipv4)	1	This is the IPv4 address of the DHCP relay. This value is extracted from the giaddr parameter in the DHCP header.
circuit-id	Element (hexBinary)	1	This element contains the value of sub-option 1 as described by Reference 6, the circuit identifier.

DHCP Technology Extension Schema

```
<?xml version="1.0"?>
<xsd:schema xmlns:xsd="http://www.w3.org/2001/XMLSchema"
            targetNamespace="http://www.andrew.com/ns/flap/dhcp"
            xmlns="http://sitacs.uow.edu.au/ns/location/flap/beep/dhcp"
            xmlns:flap="http://sitacs.uow.edu.au/ns/location/flap/beep"
            elementFormDefault="qualified"
            attributeFormDefault="unqualified">

  <xsd:annotation>
    <xsd:documentation>
      This is the DHCP extension for LIS-ALE communications.
    </xsd:documentation>
  </xsd:annotation>

  <xsd:import namespace="http://sitacs.uow.edu.au/ns/location/flap/beep"
              schemaLocation="flap.xsd"/>

  <!-- ==== Define type for 'terminal' ==== -->
  <xsd:element name="hwaddr" type="chaddrType"/>
  <xsd:simpleType name="chaddrType">
    <xsd:restriction base="xsd:hexBinary">
      <xsd:minLength value="2"/>
      <xsd:maxLength value="32"/>
      <xsd:pattern value="([0-9a-fA-F]{2}){1,16}"/>
    </xsd:restriction>
  </xsd:simpleType>

  <xsd:element name="remote-id" type="xsd:hexBinary"/>

  <xsd:element name="terminal" type="terminalType"
               substitutionGroup="flap:terminal"/>
```

```
<xsd:complexType name="terminalType">
  <xsd:complexContent>
    <xsd:restriction base="flap:terminalType">
      <xsd:sequence>
        <xsd:element ref="hwaddr" />
        <xsd:element ref="remote-id" minOccurs="0"/>
        <xsd:element ref="flap:_vendor"
                    minOccurs="0" maxOccurs="unbounded"/>
      </xsd:sequence>
    </xsd:restriction>
  </xsd:complexContent>
</xsd:complexType>

<!-- ==== Define type for 'access' ==== -->
<xsd:element name="server" type="xsd:token"/>
<xsd:element name="relay" type="ipv4"/>
<xsd:element name="circuit-id" type="xsd:hexBinary"/>

<xsd:element name="access" type="accessType"
             substitutionGroup="flap:access"/>
<xsd:complexType name="accessType">
  <xsd:complexContent>
    <xsd:restriction base="flap:accessType">
      <xsd:sequence minOccurs="0">
        <xsd:element ref="server" minOccurs="0"/>
        <xsd:element ref="relay"/>
        <xsd:element ref="circuit-id"/>
        <xsd:element ref="flap:_vendor"
                    minOccurs="0" maxOccurs="unbounded"/>
      </xsd:sequence>
    </xsd:restriction>
  </xsd:complexContent>
</xsd:complexType>

<!-- ==== Restrict core messages  ==== -->
<xsd:attributeGroup name="techAttr">
  <xsd:attribute name="tech" type="xsd:anyURI" fixed="dhcp"/>
</xsd:attributeGroup>

<xsd:complexType name="ntfy">
  <xsd:complexContent>
    <xsd:restriction base="flap:ntfyType">
      <xsd:sequence>
        <xsd:element ref="terminal"/>
        <xsd:element ref="access"/>
      </xsd:sequence>
      <xsd:attributeGroup ref="techAttr"/>
    </xsd:restriction>
```

```
      </xsd:complexContent>
    </xsd:complexType>

    <xsd:complexType name="sync">
      <xsd:complexContent>
        <xsd:restriction base="flap:syncType">
          <xsd:attributeGroup ref="techAttr"/>
        </xsd:restriction>
      </xsd:complexContent>
    </xsd:complexType>

    <xsd:complexType name="syncr">
      <xsd:complexContent>
        <xsd:restriction base="flap:syncrType">
          <xsd:sequence>
            <xsd:element ref="terminal"/>
            <xsd:element ref="access"/>
          </xsd:sequence>
          <xsd:attributeGroup ref="techAttr"/>
        </xsd:restriction>
      </xsd:complexContent>
    </xsd:complexType>

    <xsd:complexType name="aq">
      <xsd:complexContent>
        <xsd:restriction base="flap:aqType">
          <xsd:sequence>
            <xsd:element ref="terminal"/>
          </xsd:sequence>
          <xsd:attributeGroup ref="techAttr"/>
        </xsd:restriction>
      </xsd:complexContent>
    </xsd:complexType>

    <xsd:complexType name="aqr">
      <xsd:complexContent>
        <xsd:restriction base="flap:aqrType">
          <xsd:sequence minOccurs="0">
            <xsd:element ref="terminal" minOccurs="0"/>
            <xsd:element ref="access"/>
          </xsd:sequence>
          <xsd:attributeGroup ref="techAttr"/>
        </xsd:restriction>
      </xsd:complexContent>
    </xsd:complexType>

</xsd:schema>
```

Table A.12 **Terminal Identification for Ethernet Switches**

Name	Type	#	Description
ip	Element (ipAddress)	0..1	The IP address of the terminal
mac	Element (chaddrType)	0..1	The MAC address of the terminal

Table A.13 **Ethernet Switch Access Information**

Name	Type	#	Description
switch	Complex element (ip and name)	1	The switch may be identified by name, IP address, or both. Enough information must be included to uniquely identify a switch.
name	Element (token)	0..1	The name of the switch.
ip	Element (ipAddress)	0..1	This is the IP address of the switch that the terminal is connected to. This datum should be included if the switch has been assigned an IP address.
port	Element (nonNegativeInteger)	1	This is the physical port on the switch that the terminal is connected to.
vlan	Element (nonNegativeInteger)	0..1	The VLAN element optionally identifies the VLAN number that the port is assigned.

Ethernet Switch Technology Extension

This extension includes support for ALE technology embedded in a managed Ethernet switch.

Ethernet Switch Terminal Identification
Terminal identification for the Ethernet switch ALE is similar to the DHCP extension, except that the hwaddr element is replaced by a MAC address. One or both IP and MAC addresses *must* be specified.

An Ethernet terminal is identified by IP and MAC addresses, as shown in Table A.12.

Ethernet Switch Access Information
In addition to the time values described in the earlier section titled "Access Information Type," the Ethernet switch access uses the values listed in Table A.13.

Ethernet Switch Technology Extension Schema

```
<?xml version="1.0"?>
<xsd:schema xmlns:xsd="http://www.w3.org/2001/XMLSchema"
    targetNamespace="http://sitacs.uow.edu.au/ns/location/flap/beep/ethernet"
    xmlns="http://sitacs.uow.edu.au/ns/location/flap/beep/ethernet"
    xmlns:flap="http://sitacs.uow.edu.au/ns/location/flap/beep"
    elementFormDefault="qualified"
    attributeFormDefault="unqualified">
```

```
<xsd:annotation>
  <xsd:documentation>
    This is the wired Ethernet part for the LIS-ALE protocol schema.
  </xsd:documentation>
</xsd:annotation>

<xsd:import namespace="http://sitacs.uow.edu.au/ns/location/flap/beep"
            schemaLocation="flap.xsd"/>

<!-- ==== Define type for 'terminal' ==== -->
<xsd:element name="mac" type="macAddress"/>
<xsd:simpleType name="macAddress">
  <xsd:restriction base="xsd:token">
    <xsd:pattern value="([0-9A-Fa-f]{2}[\-:]?){5}[0-9A-Fa-f]{2}"/>
  </xsd:restriction>
</xsd:simpleType>

<xsd:element name="terminal" type="terminalType"
            substitutionGroup="flap:terminal"/>
<xsd:complexType name="terminalType">
  <xsd:complexContent>
    <xsd:restriction base="flap:terminalType">
      <xsd:sequence>
        <xsd:choice>
          <xsd:sequence>
            <xsd:element ref="flap:ip"/>
            <xsd:element ref="mac" minOccurs="0"/>
          </xsd:sequence>
          <xsd:element ref="mac"/>
        </xsd:choice>
        <xsd:element ref="flap:_vendor"
                    minOccurs="0" maxOccurs="unbounded"/>
      </xsd:sequence>
    </xsd:restriction>
  </xsd:complexContent>
</xsd:complexType>

<!-- ==== Define type for 'access' ==== -->
<xsd:complexType name="switch">
  <xsd:complexContent>
    <xsd:restriction base="xsd:anyType">
      <xsd:choice>
        <xsd:sequence>
          <xsd:element name="name" type="xsd:token"/>
          <xsd:element ref="flap:ip" minOccurs="0"/>
        </xsd:sequence>
        <xsd:element ref="flap:ip"/>
      </xsd:choice>
    </xsd:restriction>
  </xsd:complexContent>
</xsd:complexType>
```

```
<xsd:element name="switch" type="switch"/>
<xsd:element name="port" type="xsd:nonNegativeInteger"/>
<xsd:element name="vlan" type="xsd:nonNegativeInteger"/>

<xsd:element name="access" type="accessType"
             substitutionGroup="flap:access"/>
<xsd:complexType name="accessType">
  <xsd:complexContent>
    <xsd:restriction base="flap:accessType">
      <xsd:sequence minOccurs="0">
        <xsd:element ref="switch"/>
        <xsd:element ref="port"/>
        <xsd:element ref="vlan" minOccurs="0"/>
        <xsd:element ref="flap:_vendor"
                    minOccurs="0" maxOccurs="unbounded"/>
      </xsd:sequence>
    </xsd:restriction>
  </xsd:complexContent>
</xsd:complexType>

<!-- ==== Restrict core messages  ==== -->
<xsd:attributeGroup name="techAttr">
  <xsd:attribute name="tech" type="xsd:anyURI" fixed="ethernet"/>
</xsd:attributeGroup>

<xsd:complexType name="ntfy">
  <xsd:complexContent>
    <xsd:restriction base="flap:ntfyType">
      <xsd:sequence>
        <xsd:element ref="terminal"/>
        <xsd:element ref="access"/>
      </xsd:sequence>
      <xsd:attributeGroup ref="techAttr"/>
    </xsd:restriction>
  </xsd:complexContent>
</xsd:complexType>

<xsd:complexType name="sync">
  <xsd:complexContent>
    <xsd:restriction base="flap:syncType">
      <xsd:attributeGroup ref="techAttr"/>
    </xsd:restriction>
  </xsd:complexContent>
</xsd:complexType>

<xsd:complexType name="syncr">
  <xsd:complexContent>
    <xsd:restriction base="flap:syncrType">
      <xsd:sequence>
        <xsd:element ref="terminal"/>
        <xsd:element ref="access"/>
```

```
            </xsd:sequence>
            <xsd:attributeGroup ref="techAttr"/>
          </xsd:restriction>
        </xsd:complexContent>
    </xsd:complexType>

    <xsd:complexType name="aq">
      <xsd:complexContent>
        <xsd:restriction base="flap:aqType">
          <xsd:sequence>
            <xsd:element ref="terminal"/>
          </xsd:sequence>
          <xsd:attributeGroup ref="techAttr"/>
        </xsd:restriction>
      </xsd:complexContent>
    </xsd:complexType>

    <xsd:complexType name="aqr">
      <xsd:complexContent>
        <xsd:restriction base="flap:aqrType">
          <xsd:sequence minOccurs="0">
            <xsd:element ref="terminal" minOccurs="0"/>
            <xsd:element ref="access"/>
          </xsd:sequence>
          <xsd:attributeGroup ref="techAttr"/>
        </xsd:restriction>
      </xsd:complexContent>
    </xsd:complexType>

</xsd:schema>
```

DHCP Lease Query Technology Extension

The DHCP Lease Query Technology extension includes support for ALE technology that can support a DHCP Lease Query, as defined in Reference 6.

DHCP Lease Query Terminal Identification   Terminal identification for the DHCP Lease Query ALE is similar to the DHCP extension except that DHCP Option 61 (client identifier) is also supported. Only one IP, hwaddr address, or client-identifier must be specified.

DHCP Lease Query terminal identifiers are shown in Table A.14.

DHCP Lease Query Access Information   In addition to the time values described in the earlier section titled "Access Information Type," the DHCP Lease Query access uses the values listed in Table A.15.

Table A.14   Terminal Identification for DHCP Lease Query

Name	Type	#	Description
ip	Element (ipAddress)	0..1	The IP address of the terminal
hwaddr	Element (chaddrType)	0..1	The hardware address, which is the value included in the chaddr parameter of the DHCP header
client-id	Element (token)	0..1	The unique value used by the DHCP client to identify itself to the DHCP server

Table A.15   DHCP Lease Query Access Values

Name	Type	#	Description
server	Element (token)	0..1	This is an identifier that is unique from the context of the ALE for the DHCP server that provided this information. This element is not necessary unless multiple DHCP servers are managed by a single ALE.
relay	Element (ipv4)	1	This is the IPv4 address of the DHCP relay. This value is extracted from the giaddr parameter in the DHCP header.
circuit-id	Element (hexBinary)	1	This element contains the value of sub-option 1 as described by Reference 6, the circuit identifier.
ip	Element (ipAddress)	0..1	The IP address of the terminal.
hwaddr	Element (chaddrType)	0..1	The hardware address, which is the value included in the chaddr parameter of the DHCP header.
client-id	Element (token)	0..1	The unique value used by the DHCP client to identify itself to the DHCP server.

DHCP Lease Query Technology Extension Schema

```xml
<?xml version="1.0"?>
  <xsd:schema xmlns:xsd="http://www.w3.org/2001/XMLSchema"
        targetNamespace="http://sitacs.uow.edu.au/ns/location/flap/dhcp-lq"
        xmlns="http://sitacs.uow.edu.au/ns/location/flap/dhcp-lq"
        xmlns:flap="http://sitacs.uow.edu.au/ns/location/flap"
        elementFormDefault="qualified"
        attributeFormDefault="unqualified">

  <xsd:annotation>
    <xsd:documentation>
        This is the DHCP Lease Query extension for LIS-ALE communications.
    </xsd:documentation>
  </xsd:annotation>

  <xsd:import namespace="http://sitacs.uow.edu.au/ns/location/flap"
            schemaLocation="flap.xsd"/>

  <!-- ==== Define type for 'terminal' ==== -->

  <xsd:element name="hwaddr" type="chaddrType"/>
```

```
<xsd:simpleType name="chaddrType">
   <xsd:restriction base="xsd:hexBinary">
      <xsd:minLength value="2"/>
      <xsd:maxLength value="32"/>
      <xsd:pattern value="([0-9a-fA-F]{2}){1,16}"/>
   </xsd:restriction>
</xsd:simpleType>

<xsd:element name="remote-id" type="xsd:hexBinary"/>

<xsd:element name="client-id" type="xsd:token"/>

<xsd:element name="terminal" type="terminalType"
            substitutionGroup="flap:terminal"/>

<xsd:complexType name="terminalType">
   <xsd:complexContent>
      <xsd:restriction base="flap:terminalType">
         <xsd:sequence>
            <xsd:choice>
               <xsd:element ref="flap:ip"/>
               <xsd:element ref="hwaddr" />
               <xsd:element ref="client-id"/>
            </xsd:choice>
            <xsd:element ref="flap:_vendor"
                 minOccurs="0" maxOccurs="unbounded"/>
         </xsd:sequence>
      </xsd:restriction>
   </xsd:complexContent>
 </xsd:complexType>

<!-- ==== Define type for 'access' ==== -->

<xsd:element name="server" type="xsd:token"/>

<xsd:element name="relay" type="flap:ipv4"/>

<xsd:element name="circuit-id" type="xsd:hexBinary"/>

<xsd:element name="access" type="accessType"
            substitutionGroup="flap:access"/>

<xsd:complexType name="accessType">
   <xsd:complexContent>
      <xsd:restriction base="flap:accessType">
         <xsd:sequence minOccurs="0">
            <xsd:element ref="server" minOccurs="0"/>
            <xsd:element ref="relay"  minOccurs="0"/>
            <xsd:element ref="circuit-id" minOccurs="0"/>
            <xsd:element ref="flap:ip" minOccurs="0"/>
            <xsd:element ref="hwaddr" minOccurs="0"/>
            <xsd:element ref="client-id" minOccurs="0"/>
            <xsd:element ref="flap:_vendor"
```

```
                    minOccurs="0" maxOccurs="unbounded"/>
          </xsd:sequence>
        </xsd:restriction>
      </xsd:complexContent>
    </xsd:complexType>

    <!-- ==== Restrict core messages  ==== -->

    <xsd:attributeGroup name="techAttr">
        <xsd:attribute name="tech" type="xsd:anyURI" fixed="dhcp-lq"/>
    </xsd:attributeGroup>

    <xsd:complexType name="aq">
      <xsd:complexContent>
        <xsd:restriction base="flap:aqType">
          <xsd:sequence>
            <xsd:element ref="terminal"/>
          </xsd:sequence>
          <xsd:attributeGroup ref="techAttr"/>
        </xsd:restriction>
      </xsd:complexContent>
    </xsd:complexType>

    <xsd:complexType name="aqr">
      <xsd:complexContent>
        <xsd:restriction base="flap:aqrType">
          <xsd:sequence minOccurs="0">
            <xsd:element ref="terminal" minOccurs="0"/>
            <xsd:element ref="access"/>
          </xsd:sequence>
          <xsd:attributeGroup ref="techAttr"/>
        </xsd:restriction>
      </xsd:complexContent>
    </xsd:complexType>

  </xsd:schema>
```

RADIUS Technology Extension

This extension provides support for the RADIUS ALE that is able to provide information relating to RADIUS sessions to the LIS.

RADIUS Terminal Identification   Terminal identification for the RADIUS ALE is quite different compared to those described thus far. How these identifiers are used in DSL deployments are described in detail in Chapter 6, and the list of terminal identifiers is shown in Table A.16.

RADIUS Access Information   In addition to the time values described in the earlier section titled "Access Information Type," the RADIUS access uses the values listed in Table A.17.

Table A.16   Terminal Identification for a RADIUS ALE

Name	Type	#	Description
user-name	Element (token)	0..1	The NAI for the user establishing the session
framed-ip-address	Element (ipAddress)	1	The IP address of the terminal

Table A.17   Access Values for a RADIUS ALE

Name	Type	#	Description
nas-ip-address	Element (ipAddress)	0..1	This is the IP address of the Network Access Server (NAS) originating the RADIUS request.
nas-identifier	Element (token)	0..1	A name that can be used to identify the NAS originating the RADIUS request. This can be used instead of, or as well as, nas-ip-address.
nas-port	Element (token max length = 12)	0..1	The physical port on the NAS on which the session origination was received. Normally this will be a number.
nas-port-id	Element (token min length = 3)	0..1	The port on the NAS on which the session origination was received. This is generally more descriptive than nas-port and is often formatted.
callback-number	Element (callback-number-type)	0..1	Used to represent the number on which the user originating the session can be called back. This is formatted as an E.164 number.
l2tp	Element (complexType)	0..1	Contains information relating to L2TP tunnel accounting session identification. It identifies the IP addresses for either end of the tunnel, plus acct-session-id.

RADIUS ALE Technology Extension Schema

```
<?xml version="1.0"?>

<xsd:schema xmlns:xsd="http://www.w3.org/2001/XMLSchema"
            targetNamespace="http://sitacs.uow.edu.au/ns/location/flap/radius"
            xmlns="http://sitacs.uow.edu.au/ns/location/flap/radius"
            xmlns:flap="http://sitacs.uow.edu.au/ns/location/flap"
            elementFormDefault="qualified"
            attributeFormDefault="unqualified">

  <xsd:annotation>
    <xsd:documentation>
       This is the RADIUS extension for LIS-ALE communications.
    </xsd:documentation>
  </xsd:annotation>

  <xsd:import namespace=http://sitacs.uow.edu.au/ns/location/flap
          schemaLocation="flap.xsd"/>
```

```
<!-- ==== Define type for 'terminal' ==== -->

<xsd:element name="user-name" type="xsd:token"/>

<xsd:element name="framed-ip-address" type="flap:ipAddress"/>

<xsd:element name="terminal" type="terminalType"
              substitutionGroup="flap:terminal"/>
<xsd:complexType name="terminalType">
  <xsd:complexContent>
    <xsd:restriction base="flap:terminalType">
      <xsd:sequence>
        <xsd:element ref="user-name" minOccurs="0"/>
        <xsd:element ref="framed-ip-address"/>
        <xsd:element ref="flap:_vendor"
                     minOccurs="0" maxOccurs="unbounded"/>
      </xsd:sequence>
    </xsd:restriction>
  </xsd:complexContent>
</xsd:complexType>

<!-- ==== Define type for 'access' ==== -->

<!-- Layer 2 Tunneling Protocol attributes -->

<xsd:complexType name="l2tp-type">
  <xsd:sequence>
    <xsd:element name="tunnel-client-endpoint" type="flap:ipAddress"/>
    <xsd:element name="tunnel-server-endpoint" type="flap:ipAddress"/>
    <xsd:element name="acct-session-id" type="xsd:nonNegativeInteger"/>
  </xsd:sequence>
</xsd:complexType>


<xsd:simpleType name="nas-port-type">
  <xsd:restriction base="xsd:token">
    <xsd:maxLength value="12"/>
  </xsd:restriction>
</xsd:simpleType>


<xsd:simpleType name="nas-port-id-type">
  <xsd:restriction base="xsd:token">
    <xsd:minLength value="3"/>
  </xsd:restriction>
</xsd:simpleType>


<xsd:simpleType name="callback-number-type">
  <xsd:restriction base="xsd:token">
    <xsd:pattern value="[0-9]{1,15}"/>
  </xsd:restriction>
</xsd:simpleType>

<xsd:element name="nas-ip-address" type="flap:ipAddress"/>
```

```xml
<xsd:element name="nas-identifier" type="nas-port-id-type"/>

<xsd:element name="nas-port" type="nas-port-type"/>

<xsd:element name="callback-number" type="callback-number-type"/>

<xsd:element name="nas-port-id" type="nas-port-id-type"/>

<xsd:element name="l2tp" type="l2tp-type"/>


<xsd:element name="access" type="accessType"
             substitutionGroup="flap:access"/>
<xsd:complexType name="accessType">
  <xsd:complexContent>
    <xsd:restriction base="flap:accessType">
      <xsd:sequence minOccurs="0">
        <xsd:element ref="nas-ip-address" minOccurs="0"/>
        <xsd:element ref="nas-identifier" minOccurs="0"/>
        <xsd:element ref="nas-port" minOccurs="0"/>
        <xsd:element ref="nas-port-id" minOccurs="0"/>
        <xsd:element ref="callback-number" minOccurs="0"/>
        <xsd:element ref="l2tp" minOccurs="0"/>
        <xsd:element ref="flap:_vendor"
                    minOccurs="0" maxOccurs="unbounded"/>
      </xsd:sequence>
    </xsd:restriction>
  </xsd:complexContent>
</xsd:complexType>

<!-- ==== Restrict core messages  ==== -->

<xsd:attributeGroup name="techAttr">
  <xsd:attribute name="tech" type="xsd:anyURI" fixed="radius"/>
</xsd:attributeGroup>


<xsd:complexType name="ntfy">
  <xsd:complexContent>
    <xsd:restriction base="flap:ntfyType">
      <xsd:sequence>
        <xsd:element ref="terminal"/>
        <xsd:element ref="access"/>
      </xsd:sequence>
      <xsd:attributeGroup ref="techAttr"/>
    </xsd:restriction>
  </xsd:complexContent>
</xsd:complexType>

<xsd:complexType name="sync">
  <xsd:complexContent>
    <xsd:restriction base="flap:syncType">
      <xsd:attributeGroup ref="techAttr"/>
```

```
      </xsd:restriction>
    </xsd:complexContent>
  </xsd:complexType>

  <xsd:complexType name="syncr">
    <xsd:complexContent>
      <xsd:restriction base="flap:syncrType">
        <xsd:sequence>
          <xsd:element ref="terminal"/>
          <xsd:element ref="access"/>
        </xsd:sequence>
        <xsd:attributeGroup ref="techAttr"/>
      </xsd:restriction>
    </xsd:complexContent>
  </xsd:complexType>

  <xsd:complexType name="aq">
    <xsd:complexContent>
      <xsd:restriction base="flap:aqType">
        <xsd:sequence>
          <xsd:element ref="terminal"/>
        </xsd:sequence>
        <xsd:attributeGroup ref="techAttr"/>
      </xsd:restriction>
    </xsd:complexContent>
  </xsd:complexType>


  <xsd:complexType name="aqr">
    <xsd:complexContent>
      <xsd:restriction base="flap:aqrType">
        <xsd:sequence minOccurs="0">
          <xsd:element ref="terminal" minOccurs="0"/>
          <xsd:element ref="access"/>
        </xsd:sequence>
        <xsd:attributeGroup ref="techAttr"/>
      </xsd:restriction>
    </xsd:complexContent>
  </xsd:complexType>

</xsd:schema>
```

References

1. Rose, M., *"The Blocks Extensible Exchange Protocol Core,"* RFC 3080, March 2001.

2. Rose, M., *"Mapping the BEEP Core onto TCP,"* RFC 3081, March 2001.

3. Eronen, P. and H. Tschofenig, *"Pre-Shared Key Ciphersuites for Transport Layer Security (TLS),"* RFC 4279, December 2005.

4. Bray, T., Hollander, D., and A. Layman, *"Namespaces in XML,"* W3C REC-xml-names, January 1999.

5. Fielding, R., Gettys, J., Mogul, J., Frystyk, H., Masinter, L., Leach, P., and T. Berners-Lee, *"Hypertext Transfer Protocol—HTTP/1.1,"* RFC 2616, June 1999.

6. Patrick, M., *"DHCP Relay Agent Information Option,"* RFC 3046, January 2001.

7. Woundy, R. and K. Kinnear, *"Dynamic Host Configuration Protocol (DHCP) Leasequery,"* RFC 4388, February 2006.

HELD Base Schema

This appendix provides a base HELD schema. Examples on message construction are not provided in this section. If required, they can be obtained from Chapter 4 and Appendix E.

HELD Schema

```xml
<?xml version="1.0"?>
<xs:schema
    targetNamespace="http://sitacs.uow.edu.au/ns/location/held"
    xmlns:xs="http://www.w3.org/2001/XMLSchema"
    xmlns:held="http://sitacs.uow.edu.au/ns/location/held"
    xmlns:gp="urn:ietf:params:xml:ns:pidf:geopriv10"
    xmlns:ca="urn:ietf:params:xml:ns:pidf:geopriv10:civicAddr"
    xmlns:cp="urn:ietf:params:xml:ns:common-policy"
    xmlns:gml="http://www.opengis.net/gml"
    xmlns:xml="http://www.w3.org/XML/1998/namespace"
    xmlns:saml="urn:oasis:names:tc:SAML:2.0:assertion"
    elementFormDefault="qualified"
    attributeFormDefault="unqualified">
    <xs:annotation>
        <xs:documentation>
            This document defines HELD messages.
        </xs:documentation>
    </xs:annotation>
    <xs:import namespace="http://www.w3.org/XML/1998/namespace"
            schemaLocation="xml.xsd"/>
    <xs:import namespace="urn:ietf:params:xml:ns:pidf:geopriv10"
            schemaLocation="geopriv10.xsd"/>
    <xs:import
            namespace="urn:ietf:params:xml:ns:pidf:geopriv10:civicAddr"
            schemaLocation="civicAddress.xsd"/>
    <xs:import namespace="urn:ietf:params:xml:ns:common-policy"
            schemaLocation="common-policy.xsd"/>
```

```
<xs:import namespace="http://www.opengis.net/gml"
           schemaLocation="GML-3.1.1/base/geometryBasic2d.xsd"/>
<xs:import namespace="urn:oasis:names:tc:SAML:2.0:assertion"
           schemaLocation="saml-schema-assertion-2.0.xsd"/>

<!-- Context Information Element Definitions -->

<xs:complexType name="returnContextType">
   <xs:complexContent>
      <xs:restriction base="xs:anyType">
         <xs:sequence>
            <xs:element name="locationURI" type="xs:anyURI"
                        maxOccurs="unbounded"/>
            <xs:element name="password" type="xs:token"/>
         </xs:sequence>
         <xs:attribute name="expires" type="xs:dateTime"
                        use="required"/>
      </xs:restriction>
   </xs:complexContent>
</xs:complexType>


<xs:complexType name="usesContextType">
   <xs:complexContent>
      <xs:restriction base="xs:anyType">
         <xs:sequence>
            <xs:element name="locationURI" type="xs:anyURI"/>
            <xs:element name="password" type="xs:token"/>
         </xs:sequence>
      </xs:restriction>
   </xs:complexContent>
</xs:complexType>


<!-- HELD Duration Type Definition -->

<xs:simpleType name="durationType">
    <xs:union>
      <xs:simpleType>
         <xs:restriction base="xs:decimal">
            <xs:minInclusive value="0.0"/>
         </xs:restriction>
      </xs:simpleType>
      <xs:simpleType>
         <xs:restriction base="xs:duration">
            <xs:minInclusive value="PT0S"/>
         </xs:restriction>
      </xs:simpleType>
    </xs:union>
  </xs:simpleType>


<!-- HELD Profile Element Definitions -->

<xs:complexType name="pidfloProfileType">
```

```xml
        <xs:complexContent>
          <xs:restriction base="xs:anyType">
            <xs:sequence>
              <xs:choice minOccurs="0">
                  <xs:element name="presentity" type="xs:anyURI" nillable="true"/>
                  <xs:element ref="saml:Assertion"/>
                  <xs:element ref="saml:EncryptedAssertion"/>
              </xs:choice>
              <xs:choice minOccurs="0">
                  <xs:element name="retentionExpiry" type="xs:dateTime"
                          nillable="true"/>
                  <xs:element name="retentionInterval" type="held:durationType"
                          nillable="true"/>
              </xs:choice>
              <xs:element name="retransmission" type="xs:boolean"
                      minOccurs="0" nillable="true"/>
              <xs:element name="rulesetURI" type="xs:anyURI"
                      minOccurs="0" nillable="true"/>
            </xs:sequence>
          </xs:restriction>
        </xs:complexContent>
</xs:complexType>


<!--Rules Element Definition -->

<xs:complexType name="rulesType">
   <xs:choice minOccurs="0">
      <xs:element name="rulesetURI" type="xs:anyURI"/>
      <xs:element ref="cp:ruleset"/>
   </xs:choice>
</xs:complexType>


<!-- Location Type Element Definitions -->

<xs:simpleType name="locationTypeBase">
   <xs:union>
      <xs:simpleType>
         <xs:restriction base="xs:token">
            <xs:enumeration value="any"/>
         </xs:restriction>
      </xs:simpleType>
      <xs:simpleType>
         <xs:list>
            <xs:simpleType>
               <xs:restriction base="xs:token">
                  <xs:enumeration value="civic"/>
                  <xs:enumeration value="geodetic"/>
                  <xs:enumeration value="postalCivic"/>
                  <xs:enumeration value="jurisdictionalCivic"/>
               </xs:restriction>
            </xs:simpleType>
         </xs:list>
      </xs:simpleType>
```

```
            </xs:union>
        </xs:simpleType>


        <xs:complexType name="locationTypeType">
            <xs:simpleContent>
                <xs:extension base="held:locationTypeBase">
                    <xs:attribute name="exact" type="xs:boolean"
                                  use="optional" default="false"/>
                </xs:extension>
            </xs:simpleContent>
        </xs:complexType>


        <!-- Location Assertion -->

        <xs:complexType name="locationAssertionType">
            <xs:complexContent>
                <xs:restriction base="xs:anyType">
                    <xs:choice>
                        <xs:element ref="ca:civicAddress"/>
                        <xs:sequence>
                            <xs:element ref="gml:_Geometry"/>
                            <xs:element ref="ca:civicAddress" minOccurs="0"/>
                        </xs:sequence>
                    </xs:choice>
                    <xs:attribute name="method" type="xs:token"/>
                    <xs:attribute name="timestamp" type="xs:dateTime"/>
                    <xs:attribute name="expires" type="xs:dateTime"/>
                    <xs:attribute name="exact" type="xs:boolean"
                                  use="optional" default="false"/>
                </xs:restriction>
            </xs:complexContent>
        </xs:complexType>


        <!-- Response code -->

        <xs:simpleType name="codeType">
            <xs:restriction base="xs:nonNegativeInteger">
                <xs:pattern value="[0-5][0-9][0-9]"/>
            </xs:restriction>
        </xs:simpleType>


        <!-- Base response Message Definitions -->
        <xs:complexType name="baseRequestType">
            <xs:complexContent>
                <xs:restriction base="xs:anyType">
                    <xs:sequence/>
                    <xs:attribute name="responseTime" type="held:durationType"
                                  use="optional"/>
                </xs:restriction>
            </xs:complexContent>
        </xs:complexType>
```

```xml
<xs:complexType name="baseResponseType">
   <xs:complexContent>
      <xs:restriction base="xs:anyType">
         <xs:sequence/>
         <xs:attribute name="code" type="held:codeType" use="required"/>
         <xs:attribute name="message" type="xs:token" use="optional"/>
         <xs:attribute ref="xml:lang" use="optional"/>
      </xs:restriction>
   </xs:complexContent>
</xs:complexType>


<!-- ERROR MESSAGE DEFINITION -->

<xs:element name="error" type="held:baseResponseType"/>


<!-- Create Context -->
<xs:complexType name="createContextType">
   <xs:complexContent>
      <xs:extension base="held:baseRequestType">
         <xs:sequence>
            <xs:element name="lifetime" type="held:durationType"/>
            <xs:element name="profile" type="held:pidfloProfileType"
                     minOccurs="0"/>
            <xs:element name="rules" type="held:rulesType" minOccurs="0"/>
            <xs:any namespace="##other" processContents="lax"
                  minOccurs="0" maxOccurs="unbounded"/>
         </xs:sequence>
      </xs:extension>
   </xs:complexContent>
</xs:complexType>


<!-- CREATE CONTEXT MESSAGE DEFINITION -->

<xs:element name="createContext" type="held:createContextType"/>


<!-- Context Response -->

<xs:complexType name="contextResponseType">
   <xs:complexContent>
      <xs:extension base="held:baseResponseType">
         <xs:sequence>
            <xs:element name="context" type="held:returnContextType"/>
         </xs:sequence>
      </xs:extension>
   </xs:complexContent>
</xs:complexType>


<!-- CONTEXT RESPONSE MESSAGE DEFINITION -->

<xs:element name="contextResponse" type="held:contextResponseType"/>


<!-- Update Context -->
```

```xml
<xs:complexType name="updateContextType">
    <xs:complexContent>
        <xs:extension base="held:baseRequestType">
            <xs:sequence>
                <xs:element name="context" type="held:usesContextType"/>
                <xs:element name="lifetime" type="held:durationType"
                            minOccurs="0"/>
                <xs:element name="profile" type="held:pidfloProfileType"
                            minOccurs="0"/>
                <xs:element name="rules" type="held:rulesType" minOccurs="0"/>
                <xs:any namespace="##other" processContents="lax"
                        minOccurs="0" maxOccurs="unbounded"/>
            </xs:sequence>
        </xs:extension>
    </xs:complexContent>
</xs:complexType>


<!-- UPDATE CONTEXT MESSAGE DEFINITION -->

<xs:element name="updateContext" type="held:updateContextType"/>

<!-- ... response to updateContext is contextResponse -->


<!-- Location Request -->

<xs:complexType name="locationRequestType">
    <xs:complexContent>
        <xs:extension base="held:baseRequestType">
            <xs:sequence>
                <xs:choice minOccurs="0">
                    <xs:element name="locationType" type="held:locationTypeType"/>
                    <xs:element name="assert" type="held:locationAssertionType"/>
                </xs:choice>
                <xs:choice minOccurs="0">
                    <xs:element name="context" type="held:usesContextType"/>
                    <xs:element name="profile" type="held:pidfloProfileType"/>
                </xs:choice>
                <xs:any namespace="##other" processContents="lax"
                        minOccurs="0" maxOccurs="unbounded"/>
            </xs:sequence>
            <xs:attribute name="signed" type="xs:boolean"
                          use="optional" default="false"/>
        </xs:extension>
    </xs:complexContent>
</xs:complexType>


<!-- LOCATION REQUEST MESSAGE DEFINITION -->

<xs:element name="locationRequest" type="held:locationRequestType"/>

</xs:schema>
```

Digital Signature for PIDF-LO

Users of location information may require some assurances about its veracity before they will use the information. The most convenient way to provide such an assurance is to identify the source of the information, then ensure that the information is not modified between the source and destination. A digital signature provides a way to provide this assurance.

Digital signatures can be applied in two ways to a PIDF-LO: the Secure MIME (S/MIME) method in Reference 1 or an XML digital signature (see Reference 2). S/MIME offers features that are not useful in this context, like encryption; whereas an XML digital signature offers some flexibility. This flexibility is what makes the XML digital signature useful in signing PIDF-LO.

This appendix describes how a PIDF-LO document can be digitally signed. In particular, a transform is described that can be used to selectively sign parts of the PIDF-LO document.

What Needs to Be Signed

A digital signature is useful for linking different data together, but not all of the information in a PIDF-LO needs to be protected by the digital signature. If a PIDF-LO is generated by an LIS, certain information must be signed for the signature to be effective, but other elements can be unsigned so that it can be changed.

The following pieces of information must be signed for a digital signature to have any effect:

- **Location information** The location information is the primary piece of interesting data.

- **The presentity identifier** This field identifies the subject of location information; a link between location and identity is the most important factor in protecting against theft of location information.

■ **Time limits** A timestamp indicates the time that the location information was generated, and an expiry time ensures that the information cannot be used beyond the time when it is deemed valid.

All of this information is already present in the PIDF-LO document, except that an explicit expiry time is not provided for. A new element, the `domain-auth` element, is added to provide this information, and to house the digital signature elements. The name is derived from the fact that the information is authorized by the operator of the access network, or network domain.

The Digital Signature

The XML signature specification (see Reference 2) describes a means to sign XML documents. The `Signature` element consists of three major parts:

■ A description of the signed elements, which may be an entire document, or selected parts of a document
■ A digital signature
■ Information on the key used to sign the document

PIDF-LO Transformation

Since the content of XML documents is indeterminate based on similar data sets, Reference 3 describes a set of transforms that may be applied to a document before applying a digital signature.

The input PIDF-LO document must be canonicalized using either Canonical XML, identified by the URI *http://www.w3.org/TR/2001/REC-xml-c14n-20010315* or Exclusive Canonical XML, identified by the URI *http://www.w3.org/TR/2002/REC-xml-exc-c14n-20020718/*. Note that both of these canonicalization methods remove comments from the source document (see References 3 and 4).

The signature form selected for this document is an enveloped signature. Therefore, the enveloped signature transform (identified by the URI *http://www.w3.org/2000/09/xmldsig#enveloped-signature*) must be applied to the document.

To limit the coverage of the signature to the necessary elements only, a filter is applied to the input document in order to select the correct elements for signing. It is desirable that the transformed document is also a valid PIDF-LO. In addition, the transform also excludes tuple elements other than the element that is directly signed. This ensures that other content may be included in other tuple elements, including other digital signatures.

The following elements are selected:

■ The `presence` element, which includes the `entity` attribute
■ The `location-info` element and all of its contents
■ The `timestamp` element associated with the signed `tuple` element
■ The `domain-auth` element

The minimum set of elements required to ensure that the signed document is a valid PIDF-LO are also to be included.

The XML Path Language (XPath) filter defined later in this section meets the preceding criteria. For convenience, and to reduce the size of a signed PIDF-LO document, this transform may be identified by the URN *http://sitacs.uow.edu.au/ns/location/held/domain-auth#PIDF-LO*.

Note that any elements from other namespaces included within the `domain-auth` element are selected by this XPath filter. This ensures that additions to this element are covered by the digital signature.

Algorithms

As recommended in Reference 2, implementations of this specification must provide the following algorithms:

- **Digest algorithm**   The SHA1 digest, as identified by the URN *http://www.w3.org/2000/09/xmldsig#sha1*.

- **Signature algorithm**   DSA with SHA1, as identified by the URN *http://www.w3.org/2000/09/xmldsig#dsa-sha1*.

- **Canonicalization method**   Canonical XML (Reference 3), as identified by the URN *http://www.w3.org/TR/2001/REC-xml-c14n-20010315*.

- **Transforms**   The enveloped signature transform, as identified by the URN *http://www.w3.org/2000/09/xmldsig#enveloped-signature*; and the transform defined in this note, as identified by the URN *http://sitacs.uow.edu.au/ns/location/held/domain-auth#PIDF-LO*.

It is also *recommended* that the following also be supported:

- **Signature algorithm**   The PKCS1 (RSA-SHA1) signature algorithm, as identified by *http://www.w3.org/2000/09/xmldsig#rsa-sha1*.

- **Canonicalization method**   Exclusive Canonical XML, as identified by the URN *http://www.w3.org/TR/2002/REC-xml-exc-c14n-20020718/* (see Reference 4).

Signature Key Data

Reference 2 describes a number of methods for describing the key used to sign the document. For this specification, the `KeyInfo` element must be provided in the `Signature` element.

The domain authority must also describe a means to retrieve an X.509 certificate that includes the key used to sign the document. This can be done either by including an `X509Certificate` element, or by referencing another certificate.

A reference to a certificate within the same document may be made using the `X509SubjectName` element or a fragment identifier URI. A fragment identifier

URI might be applicable where multiple signatures are applied to different parts of the document. External certificate sources should be described by URI only in the `RetrievalMethod` element. It is recommended that the scheme for the `RetrievalMethod` URI indicates a secure protocol, such as secure HTTP, as an *https:* URI.

The LIST may also include additional information in the `KeyInfo` element that could assist the location user in validating the certificate. For example, a certificate chain and certificate revocation list may be added. However, this specification does not specify how the location user validates the certificate.

XML Definitions

This section includes XML that supports the text in previous sections.

XML Schema

The following XML schema describes the `domain-auth` element. This schema defines a new namespace: *http://sitacs.uow.edu.au/ns/location/held/domain-auth*.

```
<?xml version="1.0"?>
<xsd:schema xmlns:xsd="http://www.w3.org/2001/XMLSchema"
  targetNamespace="http://sitacs.uow.edu.au/ns/location/held/domain-auth"
  xmlns="http://sitacs.uow.edu.au/ns/location/held/domain-auth"
  xmlns:dsig="http://www.w3.org/2000/09/xmldsig#"
  elementFormDefault="unqualified" attributeFormDefault="unqualified">

  <xsd:import namespace="http://www.w3.org/2000/09/xmldsig#"/>

  <xsd:element name="domain-auth">
    <xsd:annotation>
      <xsd:documentation>
        The domain authorization that is applied to the PIDF-LO.
        This element should be included within the scope of a
        &lt;tuple&gt; element.
      </xsd:documentation>
    </xsd:annotation>
    <xsd:complexType>
      <xsd:complexContent>
        <xsd:restriction base="xsd:anyType">
          <xsd:sequence>
            <xsd:element ref="dsig:Signature"/>
            <xsd:any namespace="##other" processContents="lax"
                    minOccurs="0" maxOccurs="unbounded"/>
          </xsd:sequence>

          <xsd:attribute name="expires" use="required"
                    type="xsd:dateTime">
            <xsd:annotation>
              <xsd:documentation>
```

```
                      The expiry time associated with the authorization.
                  </xsd:documentation>
              </xsd:annotation>
          </xsd:attribute>

        </xsd:restriction>
      </xsd:complexContent>
    </xsd:complexType>
  </xsd:element>

</xsd:schema>
```

XPath Filter

The following XPath transform follows the recommendations in Reference 2 to select the elements for signing. This specification defines a new URN for this transform: *http://sitacs.uow.edu.au/ns/location/held/domain-auth#PIDF-LO*.

```
<?xml version="1.0"?>
<dsig:Transform id="PIDF-LO"
   Algorithm="http://www.w3.org/TR/1999/REC-xpath-19991116"
   xmlns:dsig="http://www.w3.org/2000/09/xmldsig#">
  <dsig:XPath
   xmlns:pidf="urn:ietf:params:xml:ns:pidf"
   xmlns:gp="urn:ietf:params:xml:ns:pidf:geopriv10"
   xmlns:da="urn:urn:ietf:params:xml:ns:pidf:geopriv10:domain-auth">
<!-- Select elements -->
(
<!-- The enclosing presence element -->
((count(self::pidf:presence | here()/ancestor::pidf:presence[1]) = 1)
<!-- The enclosing pidf:tuple element -->
 or (count(self::pidf:tuple | here()/ancestor::pidf:tuple[1]) = 1)
<!-- enclosing()/pidf:tuple with the following portions ... -->
 or ((count(ancestor::pidf:tuple[1]
      | here()/ancestor::pidf:tuple[1]) = 1)
<!-- ... pidf:status, pidf:status/pidf:timestamp[/text()] -->
    and (self::pidf:status or ancestor-or-self::pidf:timestamp
<!-- ... gp:geopriv, gp:usage-rules -->
        or self::gp:geopriv or self::gp:usage-rules
<!-- ... gp:location-info and descendants -->
        or ancestor-or-self::gp:location-info))
<!-- the enclosing da:domain-auth element -->
 or (count(self::da:domain-auth
      | here()/ancestor::da:domain-auth[1]) = 1)
) or (
<!-- Select attributes and xmlns for those elements -->
  (count(self::node() | parent::*/attribute::*
        | parent::*/namespace::*)
    &lt; (count(self::node()) + count(parent::*/attribute::*)
      + count(parent::*/namespace::*)))
```

```
and parent::*[
<!-- Repeat of element selection -->
((self::pidf:presence and (count(ancestor::pidf:presence) = 0))
 or (count(self::pidf:tuple | here()/ancestor::pidf:tuple[1]) = 1)
 or ((count(ancestor::pidf:tuple[1]
        | here()/ancestor::pidf:tuple[1]) = 1)
      and (self::pidf:status
            or self::gp:geopriv or self::gp:usage-rules))
 or (count(self::da:domain-auth
      | here()/ancestor::da:domain-auth[1]) = 1))
])
  </dsig:XPath>
</dsig:Transform>
```

Example

The following PIDF-LO document has been signed using the filter.

```
<presence xmlns="urn:ietf:params:xml:ns:pidf"
          xmlns:gml="http://opengis.net/gml"
          xmlns:gp="urn:ietf:params:xml:ns:pidf:geopriv10"
          entity="pres:user@example.com">
  <tuple id="pidfloc832d2">
    <status>
      <gp:geopriv>
        <gp:location-info>
          <gml:Point srsName="urn:ogc:def:crs:EPSG::4326">
            <gml:pos>-43.5723 153.21760</gml:pos>
          </gml:Point>
        </gp:location-info>
        <gp:usage-rules>
          <gp:retransmission-allowed>no</gp:retransmission-allowed>
          <gp:retention-expiry>
            2006-06-16T10:06:46.387+10:00
          </gp:retention-expiry>
        </gp:usage-rules>
      </gp:geopriv>
    </status>
    <da:domain-auth
        xmlns:da="http://sitacs.uow.edu.au/ns/location/held/domain-auth"
        expires="2006-06-15T01:18:14.235Z">
<ds:Signature xmlns:ds="http://www.w3.org/2000/09/xmldsig#">
<ds:SignedInfo>
<ds:CanonicalizationMethod
  Algorithm="http://www.w3.org/TR/2001/REC-xml-c14n-20010315"/>
<ds:SignatureMethod Algorithm="http://www.w3.org/2000/09/xmldsig#rsa-sha1"/>
<ds:Reference URI="">
<ds:Transforms>
<ds:Transform
  Algorithm="http://www.w3.org/2000/09/xmldsig#enveloped-signature"/>
<ds:Transform
```

```
    Algorithm="http://sitacs.uow.edu.au/ns/location/held/domain-auth#PIDF-LO"/>
</ds:Transforms>
<ds:DigestMethod Algorithm="http://www.w3.org/2000/09/xmldsig#sha1"/>
<ds:DigestValue>fadt8IZIlnHZzUX50L3v5JCF/tY=</ds:DigestValue>
</ds:Reference>
</ds:SignedInfo>
<ds:SignatureValue>
ESnPq7L4GwFFXwYox0+QlvsNsu+4afu0mGmd45N7jhBwx8i3NGZpphepDeUjEIG07Ub0GkkjN5X/
X2nXeCCv5w==
</ds:SignatureValue>
<ds:KeyInfo>
<ds:X509Data>
<ds:X509Certificate>
MIICHjCCAcgCBESQpzcwDQYJKoZIhvcNAQEEBQAwgZgxCzAJBgNVBAYTAkFVMQwwCgYDVQQIEwNO
U1cxEzARBgNVBAcTCldvbGxvbmdvbmcxDzANBgNVBAoTBkFuZHJ1dzEuMCwGA1UECxMlQW5kcmV3
IE5ldHdvcmsgU29sdXRpb25zIEFzaWEtUGFjaWZpYzElMCMGA1UEAxMcRG9tYWluIEF1dGhvcml6
YXRpb24gRXhhbXBsZTAeFw0wNjA2MTUwMDE3NTlaFw0wNjA5MTMwMDE3NTlaMIGYMQswCQYDVQQG
EwJBVTEMMAoGA1UECBMDTlNXMRMwEQYDVQQHEwpXb2xsb25nb25nMQ8wDQYDVQQKEwZBbmRyZXcx
LjAsBgNVBAsTJUFuZHJldyBOZXR3b3JrIFNvbHV0aW9ucyBBc2lhLLVBhY2lmaWMxJTAjBgNVBAMT
HERvbWFpbiBBdXRob3JpemF0aW9uIEV4YW1wbGUwWzANBgkqhkiG9w0BAQEFAANKADBHAkB1nljj
c0ctJbuqRe9SZf4jXcdmD7lzBeS15fBIysEqYQYUvXdvZvNvdhcwu2yiixzruIEad3DyBfaQATI4
TAGRAgMBAAEwDQYJKoZIhvcNAQEEBQADQQBbbBAIKD8qlR+hK8POk3p6WBLjTHBT5GlJAg1XIyaS
1hziF6T5hSWmE+GYgWnmUYUQ5PCUkn29Zsg+b1K3SSmq
</ds:X509Certificate>
</ds:X509Data>
</ds:KeyInfo>
</ds:Signature>
        </da:domain-auth>
        <note>
           This note may be changed without affecting the signature.
        </note>
        <timestamp>2006-06-15T10:06:46.387+10:00</timestamp>
     </tuple>
</presence>
```

Several elements are included in the preceding example that are not covered by the signature because of the transform, in particular usage-rules and note-well elements. The transform removes these supplementary elements, resulting in the following PIDF-LO, which only includes the signed elements (whitespace has been added for readability).

```
<presence xmlns="urn:ietf:params:xml:ns:pidf"
          xmlns:gml="http://opengis.net/gml"
          xmlns:gp="urn:ietf:params:xml:ns:pidf:geopriv10"
          entity="pres:user@example.com">
  <tuple id="pidfloc832d2">
    <status>
      <gp:geopriv>
        <gp:location-info>

          <gml:Point srsName="urn:ogc:def:crs:EPSG::4326">
```

```
            <gml:pos>-43.5723  153.21760</gml:pos>

        </gml:Point>

      </gp:location-info>
      <gp:usage-rules></gp:usage-rules>
    </gp:geopriv>
  </status>
  <da:domain-auth
    xmlns:da="http://sitacs.uow.edu.au/ns/location/held/domain-auth"
    expires="2006-06-15T01:18:14.235Z">
  </da:domain-auth>
  <timestamp>2006-06-15T10:06:46.387+10:00</timestamp>
  </tuple>
</presence>
```

Security Considerations

The security limitations of this specification are no more significant than those already identified in Reference 2. In particular, the rules *Only What Is Signed Is Secure*, *Only What Is "Seen" Should Be Signed*, and *"See" What Is Signed* should be applied.

It is recommended that, where certitude of information is important, only the signed information is transmitted or stored—in other words, the PIDF-LO document formed by performing the transform. This ensures that no additional information may be misconstrued as being verifiable. This is particularly applicable if the contents of the PIDF-LO document are displayed on screen.

A degree of trust must exist between the domain authority and the location user. It is the responsibility of the location user to verify the identity of the domain authority and assert the appropriate level of trust. If the location user is unable to validate the identity of the domain authority for any reason, then the PIDF-LO document must be considered unsigned.

References

1. Peterson, J. "A Presence-based GEOPRIV Location Object Format." RFC 4119, December 2005.

2. Eastlake, D., J. Reagle, and D. Solo. "(Extensible Markup Language) XML-Signature Syntax and Processing." RFC 3275, March 2002.

3. Boyer, J. "Canonical XML Version 1.0." W3C REC REC-xml-c14n-20010315, March 2001.

4. Boyer, J., and J. Reagle. "Exclusive XML Canonicalization Version 1.0." 3d, ed., W3C REC REC-xml-exc-c14n-20020718, July 2002.

HELD Protocol Bindings

This appendix describes the protocol bindings for HELD. Two bindings are included: an HTTP binding that uses a web services form, and a BEEP binding that can be used for more permanent client/server connections.

HELD HTTP Protocol Binding

This section defines an HTTP (see Reference 1) binding for the HELD protocol, which all conforming implementations *must* support. This binding takes the form of a Web Service (WS) that can be described by the Web Services Description Language (WSDL) document that is included in this section.

The three request messages are carried in this binding as the body of an HTTP POST request. The MIME type of both request and response bodies should be *application / xml*, except that a PIDF-LO document should have the MIME type *application / pidf+xml*.

The LIS should populate the HTTP headers so that they are consistent with the contents of the message. In particular, the Expires and cache control headers should be used to control the caching of any PIDF-LO document. The HTTP status code should have the same first digit as any `contextResponse` or error body included, and it should indicate a *2xx* series response when a PIDF-LO document is included.

This binding also includes a default behavior, which is triggered by a GET request, or a POST with no request body. If either of these queries is received, the LIS must attempt to provide a PIDF-LO document, as if the request was a location request.

This binding must use TLS as described in Reference 2. TLS provides message integrity and privacy between the device and the LIS. It is recommended that the LIS also use the server authentication method described in Reference 2.

The HELD HTTP Binding WSDL Document

The following [WSDL 2.0 (see Reference 3)] document describes the HTTP binding for this protocol. Actual service instances must provide a service with at least one endpoint that implements the `heldHTTP` binding. A service description document may include this schema directly or by using the import or include directives.

```xml
<?xml version="1.0"?>
<wsdl:definitions
    xmlns:wsdl="http://www.w3.org/2005/05/wsdl"
    xmlns:whttp="http://www.w3.org/2005/05/wsdl/http"
    xmlns:held="urn:ietf:params:xml:ns:geopriv:held"
    xmlns:pidf="urn:ietf:params:xml:ns:pidf"
    xmlns:heldhttp="urn:ietf:params:xml:ns:geopriv:held:http"
    targetNamespace="urn:ietf:params:xml:ns:geopriv:held:http"
    type="http://www.w3.org/2005/05/wsdl/http">

  <wsdl:types>
    <xsd:schema xmlns:xsd="http://www.w3.org/2001/XMLSchema">
      <xsd:import namespace="urn:ietf:params:xml:ns:geopriv:held"
                  schemaLocation="held.xsd"/>
      <xsd:import namespace="urn:ietf:params:xml:ns:pidf"/>
    </xsd:schema>
  </wsdl:types>

  <wsdl:interface name="held">

    <wsdl:operation name="createContext" method="POST">
      <wsdl:input message="held:createContext"/>
      <wsdl:output message="held:contextResponse"/>
      <wsdl:fault message="held:error"/>
    </wsdl:operation>

    <wsdl:operation name="updateContext" method="POST">
      <wsdl:input message="held:updateContext"/>
      <wsdl:output message="held:contextResponse"/>
      <wsdl:fault message="held:error"/>
    </wsdl:operation>

    <wsdl:operation name="locationRequest" method="POST">
      <wsdl:input message="held:locationRequest"/>
      <wsdl:output ref="pidf:presence"/>
      <wsdl:fault message="held:error"/>
    </wsdl:operation>

    <wsdl:operation
        name="getLocation" method="GET"
        pattern="http://www.w3.org/2004/08/wsdl/out-only">
```

```
            <wsdl:output ref="pidf:presence"/>
            <wsdl:fault message="held:error"/>
        </wsdl:operation>

    </wsdl:interface>

    <wsdl:binding name="heldHTTP" whttp:defaultMethod="POST">
        <wsdl:operation ref="heldhttp:createContext"/>
        <wsdl:operation ref="heldhttp:updateContext"/>
        <wsdl:operation
            ref="heldhttp:locationRequest"
            whttp:outputSerialization="application/pidf+xml"/>
        <wsdl:operation
            ref="heldhttp:getLocation"
            whttp:method="GET"
            whttp:outputSerialization="application/pidf+xml"/>
    </wsdl:binding>

</wsdl:definitions>
```

The HELD BEEP Protocol Binding

The HTTP binding for HELD is constrained to a single request-response exchange. If a particular location recipient requires location information over time, or for multiple targets, a more permanent association could provide benefits. HTTP pipelining permits the queuing of requests on a single connection, but this suffers from head-of-queue blocking and is limited in its flexibility. BEEP provides a protocol framework that is based on an established TCP (or TLS) connection between two hosts that can be reused. BEEP also includes message identifiers, which means that multiple requests can be interleaved and processed independently.

The HELD BEEP binding is limited to trusted party queries from nodes such as proxy servers and call routing functions. This is because it does not support queries to location URIs; there is no generic BEEP URI type, and no HELD-BEEP-specific URI type has been defined.

To ensure confidentiality, connections should be established using TLS with mutual authentication. The following cipher suites are recommended: **TLS_RSA_WITH_AES_256_CBC_SHA**, **TLS_RSA_WITH_AES_128_CBC_SHA**.

The MIME types of requests and responses are the same as for the HTTP binding. The function served by the HTTP **Expires** header is replicated by an identical entity-header that is included with a BEEP frame.

The HELD BEEP binding does not include a default request. All requests must include XML content.

The HELD profile is identified by the URN:

```
http://sitacs.uow.edu.au/ns/location/held/beep
```

Following the guidelines of Reference 4, Table D.1 summarizes the HELD profile.

TABLE D.1 The Held Beep Profile Summary

Registration Item	Value
Profile Identification	http://sitacs.uow.edu.au/ns/location/held/beep
Messages exchanged during Channel Creation	(None)
Messages starting one-to-one exchanges	held:locationRequest, held:createContext, held: updateContext
Messages in positive replies	pidf:presence, held:contextResponse
Messages in negative replies	held:error
Messages in one-to-many exchanges	(None)
Message syntax	See Reference 5 and Appendix B.
Message semantics	See Reference 5.
Contact information	The authors of this book.

References

1. Fielding, R., Gettys, J., Mogul, J., Frystyk, H., Masinter, L., Leach, P., and T. Berners-Lee, *"Hypertext Transfer Protocol—HTTP/1.1,"* RFC 3081, June 1999.

2. Rescorla, E., *"HTTP Over TLS,"* RFC 2818, May 2000.

3. Chinnici, R., Moreau, J., Ryman, A., and S. Weerawarana, *"Web Services Description Language (WSDL) Version 2.0 Part 1: Core Language,"* W3C CR CR-wsdl20-20060106, January 2006.

4. Rose, M., *"The Blocks Extensible Exchange Protocol Core,"* RFC 3080, March 2001.

5. Winterbottom, J., Thomson, M., and B. Stark, *"HTTP Enabled Location Delivery (HELD),"* draft-winterbottom-http-location-delivery-03 (work in progress), May 2006.

HELD Identity Extensions

This appendix provides a schema permitting Target identity information to be included in a HELD location request. The HELD identity extensions should be used where the source IP address of a location request message is inadequate to identify the Target being sort. Some circumstances where this may arise are described in Chapters 4, 5, 6, and 8; however, the scenarios explored in these chapters are not exhaustive and the HELD identity extensions may be used in scenarios not discussed. Furthermore, the HELD identity schema described here provides identity information for scenarios that have been considered by the authors and industry experts. New scenarios may well lead to new identity information being required, and thus a revision to this schema.

HELD Identity Extensions Schema

```
<?xml version="1.0"?>

<xs:schema
    targetNamespace="http://sitacs.uow.edu.au/ns/location/held:deviceIdentifiers"
    xmlns:xs="http://www.w3.org/2001/XMLSchema"
    xmlns:heldDI="http://sitacs.uow.edu.au/ns/location/held:deviceIdentifiers"
    xmlns:xml="http://www.w3.org/XML/1998/namespace"
    elementFormDefault="qualified" attributeFormDefault="unqualified">


    <!-- Directory Number Definition -->
    <xs:simpleType name="dn">
       <xs:restriction base="xs:token">
          <xs:pattern value="[0-9]{1,15}"/>
       </xs:restriction>
    </xs:simpleType>

    <!-- International Mobile Subscriber Identity -->
    <xs:simpleType name="imsi">
       <xs:restriction base="xs:token">
```

```xml
            <xs:pattern value="[0-9]{6,15}"/>
        </xs:restriction>
</xs:simpleType>

<!-- Hostname definition -->
<xs:simpleType name="host">
    <xs:restriction base="xs:token">
        <xs:pattern value="([a-zA-Z0-9]([\-a-zA-Z0-9]*[a-zA-Z0-9])?\.)*
                            [a-zA-Z0-9]([\-a-zA-Z0-9]*[a-zA-Z0-9])?\.?"/>
    </xs:restriction>
</xs:simpleType>

<!-- Octet definition -->
<xs:simpleType name="heldOctet">
    <xs:restriction base="xs:integer">
        <xs:minInclusive value="0"/>
        <xs:maxInclusive value="255"/>
    </xs:restriction>
</xs:simpleType>

<!-- IPv6 format definition -->
<xs:simpleType name="ipV6">
    <xs:annotation>
        <xs:documentation>
            An IP version 6 address, based on RFC 1884.
        </xs:documentation>
    </xs:annotation>
    <xs:restriction base="xs:token">
        <!-- Fully specified address -->
        <xs:pattern value="[0-9A-Fa-f]{1,4}(:[0-9A-Fa-f]{1,4}){7}"/>
        <!-- Double colon start -->
        <xs:pattern value=":(:[0-9A-Fa-f]{1,4}){1,7}"/>
        <!-- Double colon middle -->
        <xs:pattern value="([0-9A-Fa-f]{1,4}:){1,6}(:[0-9A-Fa-f]{1,4}){1}"/>
        <xs:pattern value="([0-9A-Fa-f]{1,4}:){1,5}(:[0-9A-Fa-f]{1,4}){1,2}"/>
        <xs:pattern value="([0-9A-Fa-f]{1,4}:){1,4}(:[0-9A-Fa-f]{1,4}){1,3}"/>
        <xs:pattern value="([0-9A-Fa-f]{1,4}:){1,3}(:[0-9A-Fa-f]{1,4}){1,4}"/>
        <xs:pattern value="([0-9A-Fa-f]{1,4}:){1,2}(:[0-9A-Fa-f]{1,4}){1,5}"/>
        <xs:pattern value="([0-9A-Fa-f]{1,4}:){1}(:[0-9A-Fa-f]{1,4}){1,6}"/>
        <!-- Double colon end -->
        <xs:pattern value="([0-9A-Fa-f]{1,4}:){1,7}:"/>
        <!-- Embedded IPv4 addresses -->
        <xs:pattern value="((:(:0{1,4}){0,3}(:(0{1,4}|[fF]{4}))?)|(0{1,4}:
                            (:0{1,4}){0,2}(:(0{1,4}|[fF]{4}))?)|((0{1,4}:)
                            {2}(:0{1,4})?:(:(0{1,4}|[fF]{4}))?)|((0{1,4}:){3}
                            (:(0{1,4}|[fF]{4}))?)|((0{1,4}:)
                            {4}(0{1,4}|[fF]{4})?)):(25[0-5]|2[0-4][0-9]
                            |[0-1]?[0-9]?[0-9])\.(25[0-5]|2[0-4][0-9]
                            |[0-1]?[0-9]?[0-9])\.(25[0-5]|2[0-4][0-9]
                            |[0-1]?[0-9]?[0-9])\.(25[0-5]|2[0-4][0-9]
                            |[0-1]?[0-9]?[0-9]))"/>
        <!-- The unspecified address -->
        <xs:pattern value="::"/>
```

```xml
        </xs:restriction>
    </xs:simpleType>

    <!-- IPv4 format definition -->
    <xs:simpleType name="ipV4">
        <xs:restriction base="xs:token">
            <xs:pattern value="(25[0-5]|2[0-4][0-9]|[0-1]?[0-9]?[0-9])\.
                               (25[0-5]|2[0-4][0-9]|[0-1]?[0-9]?[0-9])\.
                               (25[0-5]|2[0-4][0-9]|[0-1]?[0-9]?[0-9])\.
                               (25[0-5]|2[0-4][0-9]|[0-1]?[0-9]?[0-9])"/>
        </xs:restriction>
    </xs:simpleType>

    <!-- Ethernet MAC address -->
    <xs:simpleType name="ethernetMAC">
        <xs:restriction base="xs:hexBinary">
            <xs:minLength value="12"/>
            <xs:maxLength value="12"/>
        </xs:restriction>
    </xs:simpleType>

    <!-- General IP address definition -->
    <xs:simpleType name="anyIP">
        <xs:union memberTypes="heldDI:ipV4 heldDI:ipV6"/>
    </xs:simpleType>

    <!-- Layer 2 Tunneling Protocol attributes -->
    <xs:complexType name="l2tp">
        <xs:sequence>
            <!-- Tunnel Originator -->
            <xs:element name="sourceIP" type="heldDI:anyIP"/>
            <!-- Tunnel Destination -->
            <xs:element name="destinationIP" type="heldDI:anyIP"/>
            <xs:element name="sessionID" type="xs:nonNegativeInteger"/>
        </xs:sequence>
    </xs:complexType>

    <!-- VLAN tagging definitions -->
    <xs:complexType name="vlanTags">
        <xs:sequence>
            <xs:element name="slot" type="xs:token" minOccurs="0"/>
            <xs:element name="port" type="xs:token" minOccurs="0"/>
            <xs:element name="ctag" type="xs:token"/>
            <xs:element name="stag" type="xs:token" minOccurs="0"/>
        </xs:sequence>
    </xs:complexType>

    <!-- ATM Permanent Virtual Circuit (PVC) definitions -->
    <xs:complexType name="atmTags">
        <xs:sequence>
            <xs:element name="slot" type="xs:token" minOccurs="0"/>
            <xs:element name="port" type="xs:token" minOccurs="0"/>
            <xs:element name="vpi" type="xs:token"/>
            <xs:element name="vci" type="xs:token"/>
```

```
        </xs:sequence>
    </xs:complexType>

    <!-- DHCP definitions -->
    <xs:complexType name="dhcpTags">
        <xs:sequence>
            <xs:element name="giaddr" type="heldDI:anyIP"/>
            <xs:element name="agentID" type="xs:token" minOccurs="0"/>
            <xs:element name="circuitID" type="xs:token" minOccurs="0"/>
        </xs:sequence>
    </xs:complexType>

    <!-- LLDP definitions -->
    <xs:complexType name="lldpTags">
        <xs:sequence>
            <xs:element name="chassisType" type="heldDI:heldOctet"/>
            <xs:element name="chassisID" type="xs:token"/>
            <xs:element name="portType" type="heldDI:heldOctet"/>
            <xs:element name="portID" type="xs:token"/>
        </xs:sequence>
    </xs:complexType>

    <!-- RADIUS Identification attributes -->

    <xs:simpleType name="nas-port-id">
        <xs:restriction base="xsd:token">
            <xs:minLength value="3"/>
        </xs:restriction>
    </xs:simpleType>

    <xs:element name="nas-ip-address" type="heldDI:anyIP"/>
    <xs:element name="nas-identifier" type="heldDI:nas-port-id"/>
    <xs:element name="access-node-id" type="heldDI:nas-port-id"/>

    <!--Identity construct -->
    <xs:complexType name="idParameters">
        <xs:sequence>
            <xs:element name="msisdn" type="heldDI:dn" minOccurs="0"/>
            <xs:element name="imsi" type="heldDI:imsi" minOccurs="0"/>
            <xs:element name="directoryNumber" type="heldDI:dn" minOccurs="0"/>
            <xs:element name="imei" type="heldDI:dn" minOccurs="0"/>
            <xs:element name="ipV4" type="heldDI:ipV4" minOccurs="0"/>
            <xs:element name="ipV6" type="heldDI:ipV6" minOccurs="0"/>
            <xs:element ref="nas-ip-address" minOccurs="0"/>
            <xs:element ref="nas-identifier" minOccurs="0"/>
            <xs:element ref="access-node-id" minOccurs="0"/>
            <xs:element name="mdn" type="heldDI:dn" minOccurs="0"/>
            <xs:element name="min" type="heldDI:dn" minOccurs="0"/>
            <xs:element name="extension" type="heldDI:dn" minOccurs="0"/>
            <xs:element name="mac" type="heldDI:ethernetMAC" minOccurs="0"/>
            <xs:element name="lldp" type="heldDI:lldpTags" minOccurs="0"/>
            <xs:element name="hostname" type="heldDI:host" minOccurs="0"/>
            <xs:element name="l2tp" type="heldDI:l2tp" minOccurs="0"/>
            <xs:element name="vlan" type="heldDI:vlanTags" minOccurs="0"/>
```

```
            <xs:element name="atm" type="heldDI:atmTags" minOccurs="0"/>
            <xs:element name="dhcp" type="heldDI:dhcpTags" minOccurs="0"/>
            <xs:element name="link" type="xs:anyURI" minOccurs="0"/>
            <xs:element name="ssid" type="xs:token" minOccurs="0"/>
        </xs:sequence>
    </xs:complexType>

    <xs:element name="heldDevice" type="heldDI:idParameters"/>

</xs:schema>
```

Identity Extension Examples

The following sections provide examples of how HELD identity extensions may be used to assist with location determination for the correct end-point.

DHCP Example

```
<heldDevice xmlns="http://sitacs.uow.edu.au/ns/location/held:deviceIdentifiers">
    <dhcp>
        <giaddr>192.168.5.9</giaddr>
        <agentID>Netgear-1</agentID>
        <circuitID>010/50</circuitID>
    </dhcp>
</heldDevice>
```

The preceding sample describes DHCP-related information that may assist in identifying a Target. This may be employed in a DSL network where an ISP uses DHCP to allocate IP addresses but needs to send the circuit information to an RANP LIS in order to obtain the actual location. A HELD request containing this additional information would look similar to the following code fragment.

```
<locationRequest
    xmlns="http://sitacs.uow.edu.au/ns/location/held">
    <heldDevice
        xmlns="http://sitacs.uow.edu.au/ns/location/held:deviceIdentifiers">
        <dhcp>
            <giaddr>192.168.5.9</giaddr>
            <agentID>Netgear-1</agentID>
            <circuitID>010/50</circuitID>
        </dhcp>
    </heldDevice>
</locationRequest>
```

L2TP Example

```
<heldDevice xmlns="http://sitacs.uow.edu.au/ns/location/held:deviceIdentifiers">
    <l2tp>
        <sourceIP>192.168.4.10</sourceIP>
```

```
        <destinationIP>10.1.0.60</destinationIP>
        <sessionID>528</sessionID>
    </l2tp>
</heldDevice>
```

The preceding sample describes L2TP session information that may assist in identifying a Target. This may be used in a DSL network where an ISP is connected to an RANP BRAS over an L2TP link. A HELD request containing this additional information would look similar to the code fragment that follows.

```
<locationRequest xmlns="http://sitacs.uow.edu.au/ns/location/held">
    <heldDevice
        xmlns="http://sitacs.uow.edu.au/ns/location/held:deviceIdentifiers">
        <l2tp>
            <sourceIP>192.168.4.10</sourceIP>
            <destinationIP>10.1.0.60</destinationIP>
            <sessionID>528</sessionID>
        </l2tp>
    </heldDevice>
</locationRequest>
```

LLDP Example

```
<heldDevice xmlns="http://sitacs.uow.edu.au/ns/location/held:deviceIdentifiers">
    <lldp>
        <chassisType>211</chassisType>
        <chassisID>10.1.0.60</chassisID>
        <portType>10</portType>
        <portID>192.168.55.7</portID>
    </lldp>
</heldDevice>
```

The preceding sample describes switch and port information provided to an endpoint using LLDP. A Target may provide this information to an LIS in an enterprise environment to assist in Target identification and location determination. A HELD request containing this additional information would look similar to the following code fragment.

```
<locationRequest xmlns="http://sitacs.uow.edu.au/ns/location/held">
    <heldDevice
        xmlns="http://sitacs.uow.edu.au/ns/location/held:deviceIdentifiers">
        <lldp>
            <chassisType>211</chassisType>
            <chassisID>10.1.0.60</chassisID>
            <portType>10</portType>
            <portID>192.168.55.7</portID>
        </lldp>
    </heldDevice>
</locationRequest>
```

Glossary

1x Evolution Data Optimized (EVDO)
EVDO is a revision of CDMA that adds high-speed data capabilities. Originally, this stood for Evolution Data Only, because the channels only carry data, not voice, traffic.

3rd Generation Partnership Project (3GPP)
The 3GPP is a standards development organization that covers the definition of the GSM and UMTS cellular network standards. They also define standards for the IMS.

access location entity (ALE)
The ALE is responsible for the provision of location measurements to a LIS.

access network (AN)
In EVDO networks, the AN acronym refers to the radio segment and the elements that support the radio segment.

access point (AP)
In 802.11, an access point is a term used to refer to an infrastructure node. *See* WiFi.

Address of Record (AOR)
See Session Initiation Protocol.

Address Resolution Protocol (ARP)
ARP provides a protocol for discovering the binding between network and hardware addresses, most often between IP and Ethernet addressing.

application service provider (ASP)
The provider of higher-level network services as e-mail, web servers, and voice services.

Assisted GNSS (A-GNSS)

A-GNSS is a means of using GNSS systems where the target host receives assistance data to help with signal acquisition and calculations.

Assisted GPS (A-GPS)

See Assisted-GNSS.

Asymmetric Digital Subscriber Line (ADSL)

See Digital Subscriber Line.

Asynchronous Transfer Mode (ATM)

ATM is a link layer protocol that uses very small frames (53 bytes) and predetermined routes, which allow for efficient switching.

Authentication Authorization Accounting (AAA)

AAA is a service that manages access control and billing for network access. Typically, this service is centralized and accessed using a standardized protocol, such as RADIUS or DIAMETER.

automatic location identification (ALI)

A database system used in North American emergency services that provides location information to a PSAP based on.

automatic number identification (ANI)

The number used to query an ALI system in order to obtain location information.

Base Station Controller (BSC)

In both CDMA and GSM networks, the BSC manages the radio resources of a number of BTSs.

Base Station Subsystem Application Part (BSSAP)

BSSAP is a protocol layer in the GSM RAN. A location protocol, BSSAP with Location Extensions (BSSAP-LE) uses this protocol.

Base Transceiver Station (BTS)

A BTS is the name given to the radio transceiver in many cellular networks. UMTS uses the name Node B.

Blocks Extensible Exchange Protocol (BEEP)

BEEP is a protocol framework that provides a common framing and streaming mechanism for the use of other protocols.

Border Gateway Control Function (BGCF)

See IP Multimedia Subsystem.

Bootstrap Protocol (BOOTP)
See Dynamic Host Configuration Protocol.

Broadband Remote Access Server (BRAS)
A BRAS is the name given to the aggregating node in some DSL configurations.

Cable Modem Termination System (CMTS)
The node used to control cable modems in a cable network system.

Call Detail Records (CDR)
Call Detail Records include information that is retained in response to a number of events within 3GPP networks. They have a common format, but can include data related to a range of network events, in particular call establishment and termination. These are used for charging purposes, and they are known as a Charging Data Record in other contexts.

Call Session Control Function (CSCF)
In IMS, the CSCF is a SIP proxy that manages call flow. There are three forms of CSCF: the Proxy CSCF (P-CSCF), which exists in the access network; the Serving CSCF (S-CSCF), which exists in the core network; and the Interrogating CSCF (I-CSCF), which acts as a gateway server for external access purposes. The S-CSCF has the most important role; it acts as registrar and is on the signaling path for all calls.

challenge handshake authentication protocol (CHAP)
CHAP is one possible PPP authentication protocol.

Code Division Multiple Access (CDMA)
CDMA is a radio transmission technology that uses spreading codes to layer multiple signals in the same frequency spectrum.
   Also, CDMA is used to refer to a 3GPP2 cellular network technology that uses CDMA for radio access.

confidence
Confidence is a measure of the likelihood of a target being at a specified location or within a given region of uncertainty, which is usually expressed as a percentage. *See* uncertainty.

coordinate reference system (CRS)
A coordinate system is a means of assigning a tuple of numbers to a point in space. A coordinate reference system links this to real space by defining the origin, orientation, and scale of the coordinate system.

Data Over Cable Service Interface Specifications (DOCSIS)
DOCSIS is the name given to the specifications for residential cable Internet access.

Diameter
Diameter is an AAA protocol that is designed to improve on RADIUS. The major differences are that it uses a secured streaming protocol rather than a datagram protocol, and has changes that reduce the management overhead of deployment (discovery, capability negotiation).

Digital Subscriber Line (DSL)
DSL is a "last mile" solution that uses existing telephony infrastructure to deliver high-speed Internet access. DSL standards are administered by the DSL Forum (http://dslforum.org/).

Digital Subscriber Line Access Module (DSLAM)
A DSLAM terminates DSL signals at the local exchange.

Domain Name System (DNS)
DNS is a globally distributed database for the resolution of names to addresses.

Dynamic Host Configuration Protocol (DHCP)
DHCP is a widely used configuration protocol that allows a host to acquire configuration information from a visited network and, in particular, an IP address. DHCP is based on BOOTP with which it retains backward compatibility with.

Enhanced 911 (E911)
E911 is a series of enhancements to the U.S. emergency telephony system that ensures a PSAP is able to acquire location information about a caller.

Enhanced Data rates for Global Evolution (EDGE)
EDGE is an enhancement to GSM and GPRS that increases data transmission rates.

European Telecommunications Standards Institute (ETSI)
ETSI is the organization responsible for setting ICT standards within Europe.

eXtensible Markup Language (XML)
XML is a data format that permits the expression of human-readable data in structured form.

Federal Communications Commission (FCC)
The FCC is the U.S. regulatory body responsible for telecommunications policy.

Flexible LIS-ALE Protocol (FLAP)
The FLAP protocol represents a protocol framework for the acquisition of location measurements.

Foreign Agent (FA)
In Mobile IP, the FA is the agent in the visited network responsible for ensuring that packets arrive at the device.

gateway mobile location center (GMLC)

The GMLC provides location information from a UMTS or GSM network. The GMLC has a number of clients, including LCS applications, emergency services, and network services.

General Packet Radio Service (GPRS)

GPRS is a "2.5G" enhancement to GSM that adds a packet data service.

Geographic Information System (GIS)

A GIS is a computer system that uses, creates, edits, or stores geographic or spatial data. Usually this involves visualization of features as maps with overlaid detail.

Geographic Location/Privacy (GEOPRIV)

The IETF GEOPRIV working group is looking at aspects of location, in particular privacy issues relating to the use of location information in respect to a person.

geoid

A mathematical representation of the Earth, usually described as an oblate spheroid.

Global Navigation Satellite System (GNSS)

A GNSS is a navigation system that uses satellites to provide navigational and time data to ground-based systems.

Global Positioning System (GPS)

GPS is a GNSS developed by the U.S. military, now in wide civilian use. *See* Global Navigation Satellite System.

Global System for Mobile Communications (GSM)

GSM is a "2G" cellular network technology that uses a time division for signal separation. The acronym was originally used for Groupe Spécial Mobile, which started standards development. GSM standards cover all aspects of network architecture from modulation schemes to roaming models.

Home Agent (Mobile IP) (HA)

In Mobile IP, the Home Agent provides a way for a roaming IP device to be contacted through a well-known identifier. The HA also provides a mechanism to support seamless handovers for a device roaming between two remote networks.

Home Subscriber Server (HSS)

The HSS (or, previously, the Home Location Register) houses subscriber records in 3GPP network architectures. The HSS can be thought of as a presence server.

HTTP Enabled Location Delivery (HELD)

HELD is a location acquisition protocol. See Chapter 4.

HyperText Transfer Protocol (HTTP)
HTTP is the widely used protocol for the retrieval of documents over the Internet.

i2
i2 is the common name of the NENA interim VoIP architecture for providing enhanced 911 services. This standard provides a migration towards IP-based telephony by allowing VoIP callers to access existing emergency infrastructure.

i3
i3 is the name given to the NENA architecture under development which will support a fully IP-enabled emergency infrastructure.

instant message (IM)
An instant message is a small unit of data that is sent for immediate display to others. IM services rely on presence for addressing information amongst other data.

Institute of Electrical and Electronics Engineers (IEEE)
The IEEE is a professional group and standards development organization (SDO) that is responsible for administering the 802.x series of standards, which include Ethernet (802.3), WiFi (802.11), and WiMAX (802.16).

Internet Engineering Task Force (IETF)
The IETF is a standards development organization (SDO) responsible for Internet protocols.

International Mobile Station Identifier (IMSI)
The IMSI is a unique identifier for a GSM or UMTS terminal that is stored in the subscriber identity module (SIM).

Internet Protocol (IP)
IP is the network protocol used on the Internet. Two versions of IP are used, 4 and 6, with version 4 being the most widely used.

Internet Protocol Control Protocol (IPCP)
IPCP is the control protocol for PPP. *See* Point-to-Point Protocol.

Internet service provider (ISP)
The ISP is a provider of Internet access; most importantly, the provider of an IP address.

IP Multimedia Subsystem (IMS)
IMS is the 3GPP architecture that supports VoIP protocols like SIP for IP networks.

L2TP Access Concentrator (LAC)
For L2TP, the LAC is an aggregation node that instantiates tunnels.

L2TP Network Server (LNS)
For L2TP, the LNS terminates tunnels.

Layer 2 Tunneling Protocol (L2TP)
L2TP allows PPP sessions to be tunneled over IP and ATM networks.

Lightweight Directory Access Protocol (LDAP)
LDAP is a protocol that provides directory listings, such as a listing of e-mail addresses or contact information.

Link Configuration Protocol (LCP)
LCP is the link management part of PPP. *See* Point-to-Point Protocol.

Link Layer Discovery Protocol (LLDP)
LLDP is a link layer protocol built on the 802.x series of protocols whereby devices can provide information about themselves to other devices on the same network segment.

Link Layer Discovery Protocol for Media Endpoint Devices (LLDP-MED)
LLDP-MED is an extension of LLDP that includes support for media-related information.

local area network (LAN)
A LAN is a network that operates over a small area.

location acquisition
Location acquisition is the retrieval of location information in an understood and consistent form by a location recipient.

location conveyance
Location conveyance is the provision of location information to a location recipient.

location determination
Location determination is the combining of a set of measured parameters, contextual data, and algorithms to calculate a position.

Location Generator (LG)
The source of location information; performs location determination.

location information server (LIS)
The LIS is responsible for determining the location of devices within an access network and making that information available.

location measurement
Location measurement (v) is the obtaining of specific key and transient parameters associated with a target device which will be useful in determining location. A location measurement (n) is the actual unit of data that relates to location.

Location Measurement Unit (LMU)
In 3GPP networks, an LMU provides location measurements to the network. *See* access location entity.

Location Recipient (LR)
A Location Recipient is a consumer of location information.

Location Server (LS)
A Location Server is a provider of location information. An LS is not necessarily the source or generator.

location services (LCS)
LCS (derived from LoCation Services) is a service that relies on location information and is used by 3GPP.

Management Information Base (MIB)
An MIB is a structured repository of information that is maintained by managed devices.

Master Street and Address Guide (MSAG)
The MSAG is a database of U.S. addresses.

Media Access Control (MAC)
MAC refers to the second OSI layer and applies to shared media protocols where access to a common media needs to be managed. A MAC address is the address used to uniquely identify a device at this layer. For 802.x protocols, this address has been standardized and is a 48-bit sequence that is managed by the IEEE.

Media Gateway Control Function (MGCF)
In IMS, the MGCF performs call signaling conversion between SIP and ISUP.

meridian
A meridian is a line of equal longitude that runs in a north-south direction.

Mobile Identification Number (MIN)
The MIN is a unique identifier assigned to CDMA handsets.

mobile station (MS)
A mobile station in GSM is the term used to refer to the mobile telephone, or other GSM device. *See* User Equipment (UE).

Mobile Station International Subscriber Dial Number (MSISDN)
The MSISDN is a 15-digit E.164 number used for a mobile telephone. The MSISDN is the real "phone number" of a device.

Mobile Switching Center (MSC)
In cellular networks, the MSC is the external interface of the circuit-switched (voice) part of the RAN. The MSC manages signaling for voice.

Multipurpose Internet Mail Extensions (MIME)
MIME provides metadata, in particular a file type, or MIME-type, for mail contents. MIME has become a standard for the transmission of files on the Internet and is used in HTTP, SIP, and other protocols as well as SMTP (e-mail).

National Emergency Network Association (NENA)
NENA is an organization that is responsible for the implementation, availability, and improvement of the 911 system in the U.S. and Canada.

Network Access Identifier (NAI)
An identifier commonly used to tie a user to a specific realm.

Network Access Server (NAS)
The Network Access Server aggregates layer 2 connections to an access network. The NAS performs access control functions.

Network Address Translation (NAT)
NAT is a means of providing Internet access to a group of hosts without using multiple IP addresses. A NAT device translates addresses from an internal range into a publicly routable IP address by modifying the TCP or UDP port on sessions.

Network Control Protocol (NCP)
See Point-to-Point Protocol.

Open Mobile Alliance (OMA)
OMA is a standards body that develops standards for cellular networks.

Open System Interconnection (OSI)
The OSI model was developed by ISO as a framework for network protocols. It is most useful as a reference model. The OSI model consists of seven layers: physical, link, network, transport, session, presentation, and application.

Operations Support Systems (OSS)
OSS are used to assist in the management of systems that are made of a number of different components.

Organization for Economic Cooperation and Development (OECD)
The OECD is an international organization formed of affluent member nations that develops social and economic policy.

Orthogonal Frequency Division Multiplex (OFDM)

OFDM is a radio frequency modulation scheme that uses spread spectrum over a number of carriers that are designed to avoid cross-carrier interference.

Packet Control Function (PCF)

Analogous to the SGSN in 3GPP, the PCF manages data sessions within an EVDO network segment that consists of several ANs.

Packet Data Protocol (PDP)

In GPRS and UMTS, PDP is the protocol used between the SGSN and GGSN to transport data traffic.

Packet Data Serving Node (PDSN)

In EVDO, the PDSN provides IP network access and control functions, including the allocation of addresses and routing.

parallel

A parallel in geodesy is a line of equal latitude that runs east-west.

password authentication protocol (PAP)

PAP is an authentication protocol component of PPP. *See* challenge handshake authentication protocol.

Permanent Virtual Circuit (PVC)

PVCs are permanent, or semi-permanent, links that are configured in an ATM network. A PVC follows a fixed path through a network.

Plain Old Telephone Service (POTS)

POTS is an acronym sometimes used to refer to a legacy telephony network (the public switched telephone network, or PSTN) to distinguish it from VoIP.

Point-to-Point Protocol (PPP)

PPP is a protocol that is used to establish a network link over a dedicated channel. It is widely used for Internet access. PPP is modular in design and can support different authentication protocols, such as PAP, CHAP, and EAP.

PPP over ATM (PPPoA)

PPPoA is a specific binding that allows PPP to be used for ATM links. PPPoA is used for DSL networks.

PPP over Ethernet (PPPoE)

PPPoE is a specific binding that allows PPP to be used for Ethernet networks links. PPPoE is used for DSL networks.

Position Determination Entity (PDE)
In CDMA networks, the PDE is the node responsible for location determination.

Presence Information Data Format (PIDF)
The PIDF document is a generic container for presence information, defined by the IETF.

Presence Information Data Format - Location Object (PIDF-LO)
The PIDF-LO is a specific use of PIDF for the purposes of location information.

Private Automatic Branch eXchange (PABX)
A PABX is a privately owned telephone switch that is often used by organizations to consolidate their telephony services.

Privacy Checking Protocol (PCP)
PCP is an OMA protocol that enables the delegation of authorization decisions to a Privacy Profile Register.

Privacy Profile Register (PPR)
The PPR is a node in the 3GPP network architecture responsible for the evaluation of a user privacy policy.

presence
Presence is information about a person, in particular their "online" status and how they can be reached. Presence is currently expanding to include a range of additional information. A presence service provides a way for a user to make presence information about them available to others.

presentity
A presentity is the subject of presence information. A presentity identifier, which is codified as a URI, is used to identify the subject of presence information.

Public Safety Answering Point (PSAP)
The PSAP is where an emergency call is terminated—in other words, where an operator answers a call.

Quality of Service (QoS)
In networking, Quality of Service relates to the performance characteristics of a network connection: bandwidth, delay, jitter, and packet loss. For location services, QoS refers to the performance characteristics of a location provider: accuracy, precision, and time to locate. Sometimes for location, this is termed Quality of Position (QoP).

Radio Access Network (RAN)
RAN refers to the part of the cellular access network that includes the air interface, or the wireless portion of the network, and the associated control functions. The RAN includes everything up to the MSC.

Radio Frequency Identifier (RFID)
RFID is a technology using electronic tags that are similar in function to bar codes. RFID tags can be read wirelessly by a reader that is in close proximity.

received channel power indicator (RCPI)
RCPI is one method for codifying signal strength in WiFi networks.

received signal strength indicator (RSSI)
RSSI is one method for codifying signal strength in WiFi networks.

Regional Access Network Provider (RANP)
A RANP is the entity that provides wide area DSL coverage. The RANP provides logical links to an ISP in the form of ATM PVCs, L2TP tunnels, or IP routed traffic.

Remote Authentication Dial-In User Service (RADIUS)
RADIUS is an Authentication, Authorization, and Accounting protocol.

Secure User Plane Location (SUPL)
SUPL is an architecture for cellular networks that enables the acquisition of location information from mobile devices without relying on network-specific, or "control plane," signaling. SUPL primarily uses IP protocols for its signaling.

Security Assertion Markup Language (SAML)
SAML is a language for making security assertions. It is used for identity federation, or Single Sign-On (SSO), and where identity information is held by one party and required by another.

Service Set Identifier (SSID)
In WiFi, the SSID is used to allow overlapping WiFi networks to operate by distinguishing messages for different networks.

Serving Mobile Location Center (SMLC)
The node used to determine location in a GSM network.

Session Initiation Protocol (SIP)
Session Initiation Protocol is the IETF signaling protocol for VoIP, instant messaging, presence, and world domination.

Simple Authentication and Security Layer (SASL)
SASL is a protocol layer that provides a framework for authentication and data security in IP protocols.

Simple Network Management Protocol (SNMP)
SNMP is the standard protocol used to monitor and manage IP-based devices.

Simple Traversal of UDP NATs (STUN)
STUN is a simple protocol that enables a device to detect the presence of a NAT device and provide a sure method for ensuring bidirectional UDP message exchanges past the NAT device.

Stand-Alone SMLC (SAS)
The SAS is the node used to determine location in a UMTS network.

Subscriber Station (SS)
Subscriber Station is the name given to an end-point in a WiMAX network.

SUPL Enabled Terminal (SET)
In SUPL, a mobile device that supports SUPL messaging is called a SET.

SUPL Location Platform (SLP)
The SUPL Location Platform provides the network side of SUPL signaling: an interface to applications, assistance data for A-GNSS, and network-specific knowledge to provide reference locations.

time difference of arrival (TDOA)
TDOA is a wireless location determination technology that relies on measuring difference in the time between when a signal is received.

Time Division Multiple Access (TDMA)
TDMA is an older form of cellular access technology. Telephone conversations are kept orthogonal by dividing access to a common frequency channel into timeslots and allocating each conversation its own timeslot. Each timeslot provides exclusive access to the channel frequency but only for a very short period of time.

Timing Advance (TA)
In GSM networks, TA is a measure of the timing difference between MS and BTS; a location measurement.

Transmission Control Protocol (TCP)
TCP is a reliable, connection-oriented, streaming protocol that is widely used on the Internet.

Transport Layer Security (TLS)
TLS is a protocol based on TCP that provides security through a range of cryptographic methods. It offers features that allow for authentication, data privacy, protection against forgery, and data integrity. TLS is the successor to Secure Sockets Layer (SSL).

Trusted-Party Query (TPQ)
A trusted-party query is made against an LIS by a privileged node inside the access network and is used to retrieve location information about Targets that are unable to provide location for themselves.

uncertainty
Uncertainty is an area or volume where a particular target could be found that reflects the inherent variation in the location determination method. *See* confidence.

Uniform Resource Identifier (URI)
A URI is an addressing scheme that can be used to refer to resources, either a document or network location (for a URL); or a concept or other identifier (for a URN).

Uniform Resource Location (URL)
See Uniform Resource Identifier.

Uniform Resource Name (URN)
See Uniform Resource Identifier.

Universal Mobile Telecommunications System (UMTS)
UMTS is the 3GPP third-generation wireless standard.

Universal Plug and Play (UPnP)
UPnP is a suite of standards that enable discovery, configuration, and control of IP devices. These are typically devices used in the home, including routers and other appliances.

Uplink TDOA (U-TDOA)
U-TDOA is a TDOA technology that observes the time difference in a signal sent from a target device at several fixed points in the network.

User Agent (UA)
In SIP, the UA refers to an end-point in a transaction or dialog.

User Datagram Protocol (UDP)
UDP is the datagram, best-effort protocol in the IP suite.

User Equipment (UE)
In 3GPP, the UE is the mobile device—a generic name that covers the wide array of devices that can be connected to these networks.

Virtual Circuit (VC)
Because ATM frames are too small to include unique node addresses, ATM relies on the establishment of a virtual circuit for the routing of messages.

Virtual Circuit Identifier (VCI)
The VCI is part of the addressing information used in an ATM frame that identifies a particular virtual circuit.

Virtual LAN (VLAN)
In Ethernet, a virtual LAN can be established on a switch to effectively split the switch into two or more logical devices.

Virtual Path Identifier (VPI)
The VPI is part of the addressing information used in an ATM frame that identifies a particular virtual path.

virtual private network (VPN)
A VPN is a network extension that uses security and tunneling protocols to, in effect, establish a separate network that operates on top of another network. This is frequently used to provide remote access to enterprise networks.

Voice over Internet Protocol (VoIP)
VoIP is a generic term used to refer to technologies that carry voice traffic over the Internet.

Voice Service Provider (VSP)
A VSP is a provider of a voice service. This includes a registrar, call server, and possibly a PSTN gateway service.

VoIP Position Center (VPC)
The VPC is the node responsible for providing routing information based on location information in the NENA i2 standard. The VPC is also responsible for making location information available to the PSAP over VE2 interface.

watcher
A watcher is an entity that subscribes to, or views, presence information.

Wideband CDMA (W-CDMA)
W-CDMA is a spread spectrum wireless technology used in some 3G cellular access.

wireless access point (WAP)
A wireless access point is an infrastructure node in a wireless network.

Wireless Application Protocol (WAP)
WAP is a standard for providing lightweight devices with information services, like web pages and e-mail.

Wireless Broadband (WiBro)
WiBro is a wireless broadband technology similar to WiMAX.

Wireless Fidelity (WiFi)
WiFi is a common name for 802.11 wireless networks.

wireless network controller (WNC)
In a wireless network, a WNC is an operational node that manages aspects of the wireless network, including access control, radio resource management, routing, and location.

World Geodetic System 1984 (WGS84)
A coordinate reference system, or model, for the surface of the earth that is used in GPS.

Worldwide Interoperability for Microwave Access (WiMAX)
WiMAX is a brand name and a certification mark for IEEE 802.16–compliant products.

X.509
X.509 is an ITU-T standard format for the publication of digital credentials, usually a signed X.500 directory fragment that contains a public key.

Index

E

O

P